MW01254071

CULTURAL AND CONTEXTUAL PERSPECTIVES ON DEVELOPMENTAL RISK AND WELL-BEING

Developmental risk refers to conditions, characteristics, experiences, or situations with potentially deleterious effects that lead to outcomes later in life that do not meet societal expectations. While risk is typically framed as the statistical probability of a problematic outcome in relation to the general population, the converse notion of well-being is considered in relation to the level of functioning at a given developmental stage. The contributors to this volume provide insight into developmental well-being by examining cultural and contextual perspectives and influences on development and developmental outcomes associated with various types of risk, such as those related to oppression, academic failure, problematic family and life experiences, and psychiatric conditions. Although certain outcomes may seem inevitable in cases involving harmful environments, diseases, and disorders, they are virtually all influenced by complex transactions among individuals, their families, communities, and societies.

Jacob A. (Jake) Burack is Professor of School/Applied Child Psychology and Human Development in the Department of Educational and Counselling Psychology at McGill University, a researcher at Hôpital Rivières-des-Prairies, and the founder and Director of the McGill Youth Study Team. Along with his students and colleagues, he studies and works with a variety of populations, including First Nations adolescents, persons with autism spectrum disorders, and persons with Down syndrome.

Louis A. Schmidt is Professor of Psychology in the Department of Psychology, Neuroscience, and Behavior and Director of the Child Emotion Laboratory at McMaster University in Hamilton, Canada. He is also a core member of the Offord Centre for Child Studies at McMaster Children's Hospital and a Fellow of the Association for Psychological Science. His research interests include the origins and development of individual differences in temperament and the impact of early-life events on the human brain and socioemotional development.

INTERDISCIPLINARY APPROACHES TO KNOWLEDGE AND
DEVELOPMENT: THE JEAN PIAGET SYMPOSIUM SERIES

Series Editor

Nancy Budwig

Clark University

Current Titles: Published by Cambridge University Press

40 *Self-Regulation and Autonomy: Social and Developmental Dimensions of Human Conduct*, edited by Bryan W. Sokol, Frederick M. E. Grouzet, and Ulrich Müller, 2013.

39 *Cultural and Contextual Perspectives on Developmental Risk and Well-Being*, edited by Jacob A. Burack and Louis A. Schmidt, 2014.

38 *Adolescent Vulnerabilities and Opportunities: Developmental and Constructivist Perspectives*, edited by Eric Amsel and Judith G. Smetana, 2011.

Prior Editors: Lynn S. Liben and Ellin Kofsky Scholnick

Published by Lawrence Erlbaum Associates/ Taylor and Francis/ Psychology Press

37 *Art and Human Development*, edited by Constance Milbrath and Cynthia Lightfoot, 2009.

36 *Developmental Social Cognitive Neuroscience*, edited by Philip David Zelazo, Michael Chandler, and Eveline Crone, 2009.

35 *Social Life and Social Knowledge: Toward a Process Account of Development*, edited by Ulrich Müller, Jeremy I. M. Carpendale, Nancy Budwig, and Bryan W. Sokol, 2009.

34 *Social Development, Social Inequalities, and Social Justice*, edited by Cecilia Wainryb, Judith G. Smetana, and Elliot Turiel, 2007.

33 *Developmental Perspectives on Embodiment and Consciousness*, edited by Willis F. Overton, Ulrich Müller, and Judith Newman, 2007.

32 *Play and Development: Evolutionary, Sociocultural, and Functional Perspectives*, edited by Artin Goncu and Suzanne Gaskins, 2007.

31 *Biology and Knowledge Revisited: From Neurogenesis to Psychogenesis*, edited by Sue Taylor Parker, Jonas Langer, and Constance Milbrath, 2004.

30 *Changing Conceptions of Psychological Life*, edited by Cynthia Lightfoot, Michael Chandler, and Chris Lalonde, 2004.

29 *Reductionism and the Development of Knowledge*, edited by Terrance Brown and Leslie Smith, 2002.

(continued after the index)

Cultural and Contextual Perspectives on Developmental Risk and Well-Being

Edited by

Jacob A. Burack
McGill University

Louis A. Schmidt
McMaster University

CAMBRIDGE
UNIVERSITY PRESS

32 Avenue of the Americas, New York, NY 10013-2473, USA

Cambridge University Press is part of the University of Cambridge.

It furthers the University's mission by disseminating knowledge in the pursuit of education, learning, and research at the highest international levels of excellence.

www.cambridge.org
Information on this title: www.cambridge.org/9781107008854

© Cambridge University Press 2014

First published 2014

Printed in the United States of America

A catalog record for this publication is available from the British Library.

Library of Congress Cataloging in Publication data
Cultural and contextual perspectives on developmental risk and well-being / [edited by] Jacob A. Burack, McGill University, Louis A. Schmidt, McMaster University.
pages   cm. – (Interdisciplinary approaches to knowledge and development)
Includes bibliographical references and index.
ISBN 978-1-107-00885-4 (hardback)
1. Developmental psychology.   2. Well-being.   3. Developmental psychology – Social aspects.
4. Well-being – Social aspects.   I. Burack, Jacob A.   II. Schmidt, Louis A.
BF713.C847   2014
155–dc23   2014001776

ISBN 978-1-107-00885-4 Hardback

Contents

Figures

Tables

Contributors

THOMAS M. ACHENBACH, University of Vermont
STEVEN ARNOCKY, Nipissing University
CHRISTINE BLAIN-ARCARO, University of Ottawa
AMY BOMBAY, University of Ottawa
NANCY BRADY, University of Kansas
JACOB A. BURACK, McGill University
TONY CHARMAN, King's College London
XINYIN CHEN, University of Pennsylvania
LAUREN DRVARIC, McMaster University
HEIDI FLORES, McGill University
STEPHANIE A. FRYBERG, University of Arizona
JAN S. GREENBERG, University of Wisconsin–Madison
JENNIFER HEPDITCH, University of Ottawa
JINKUK HONG, University of Wisconsin–Madison
JENNIFER M. KNACK, Clarkson University
AMANDA KRYGSMAN, University of Ottawa
CHRISTINE L. LACKNER, Brock University
PETER A. LEAVITT, University of Arizona
MARSHA MAILICK, University of Wisconsin–Madison
MATILDA E. NOWAKOWSKI, Ryerson University
VLADIMIR PONIZOVSKY, McGill University
LOUIS A. SCHMIDT, McMaster University
SIDNEY J. SEGALOWITZ, Brock University
LEANN E. SMITH, University of Wisconsin–Madison
AUDRA STERLING, University of Wisconsin–Madison
JILLIAN STEWART, McGill University
WENDY TROOP-GORDON, North Dakota State University
TRACY VAILLANCOURT, University of Ottawa

RYAN J. VAN LIESHOUT, McMaster University
IRENE VITOROULIS, University of Ottawa
STEVEN F. WARREN, University of Kansas
JORDANA WAXMAN, McMaster University
FAN YANG, University of Pennsylvania
SIMAN ZHAO, University of Pennsylvania

Series Editor's Preface

In 1970, Jean Piaget participated in a workshop that instigated vigorous discussion in higher education circles about the importance of traversing the boundaries across the disciplines. The workshop, entitled "L'interdisciplinarité – Problèmes d'enseignement et de recherche dans les universities," was held in Nice, France, in September, and the proceedings were published by the Organisation for Economic Cooperation and Development (OECD) in 1972 as a monograph entitled *Interdisciplinarity: Problems of Teaching and Research in Universities*. This workshop and the book that resulted from it set the stage for ongoing debates about how best to view work going on at the intersection of disciplinary boundaries. Piaget's remarks made clear that new conceptual frameworks were needed, frameworks that underscored the importance of augmenting disciplinary knowledge in order to address enduring challenges of our times. Whether to do so from multi-, trans-, or interdisciplinary bases and what precisely each of these constructs adds to disciplinary discussions has been hotly debated for the ensuing four decades. What Piaget was wrestling with in 1970 and many others have been pursuing since then are two enduring issues: the complexity of knowledge and the importance of viewing knowledge construction as a process embedded in real time. Piaget understood early on what has become more obvious now, namely the importance of going beyond disciplinary limitations both theoretically and methodologically. This insight has shaped modern thinking on knowledge and development in significant ways.

Around the same time Piaget spoke at the OECD workshop, a new society was formed. In 1970, the Jean Piaget Society (JPS) was founded and has since provided an internationally recognized forum for inquiry and advances about significant problems in the developmental sciences. The Society has had a long-standing commitment to developmental perspectives and has been deeply concerned with theories and conceptualizations of development and the ways developmental perspectives connect to and influence research. Since renamed The Jean Piaget Society for Knowledge and Development, the Society has organized and sponsored a book series, an annual meeting of plenary addresses and scholarly presentations, a scholarly journal (*Cognitive Development*), and a website (http://www.piaget.org). Across venues, participating scholars come from a range of disciplines, including departments of psychology, anthropology, linguistics, sociology, biology, philosophy, and education.

The Society has had a long-standing dedication to the publication of a book series that addresses core problems in the developmental sciences. For more than 30 years, Lawrence Erlbaum Press (currently Psychology Press/Taylor and Francis) published the series. Each of the volumes in the Jean Piaget Symposium Series engages well-recognized scholars on a set of themes that bring together divergent disciplinary perspectives. The series, which has included nearly 40 published volumes, has dealt with topics such as human understanding, developmental psychopathology, concept formation, and relations between learning and development.

In a time when there appears to be a proliferation of edited volumes, one can ask what makes this series thrive. The high regard for these volumes has been due to the careful way interdisciplinary thinking has shed light on enduring issues with which scholars interested in human development are grappling. To a large measure, the rigorous system of cultivation and review plays a significant role in arriving at cutting-edge thinking that goes beyond juxtaposition of new ideas. Careful attention is given to taking a theme at the center of developmental science (e.g., epigenesis of mind; culture, thought, and development; social development and social justice; developmental social cognitive neuroscience) and weaving scholarship from neighboring disciplines into discussions in ways that hold the potential to significantly shape ongoing scientific discourse.

Each of the JPS series volumes emanates from the Society's themed annual meeting that includes plenary addresses and invited symposia, a meeting structure that itself is the outcome of a long and rigorous academic review process. Typically, several revisions are made in the proposal before it obtains approval from the full board of directors. The annual meeting organizers also serve as editors of the volume. To supplement chapters by the five or six plenary speakers, the volume editors typically invite other contributors to the volume. The editors also inform contributors about the requirements with regard to the volume's theme and scope. Finally, the editors engage in a thorough evaluation of each contribution, providing extensive feedback and soliciting revisions until it is of the required quality. This process ensures that extraordinary scholars will contribute to the volumes. In summary, we believe the book series has provided a distinctive intellectual contribution to the study of knowledge and development by focusing on developmental inquiry from an interdisciplinary perspective. Further information about the series can be found at http://www.piaget.org/Series/series.html.

This volume is the third in our new book series – Interdisciplinary Perspectives on Knowledge and Development: The Jean Piaget Symposium Series with Cambridge University Press. This volume continues to exemplify the strong interdisciplinary approach that has been central to all of our prior volumes. Edited by Jacob A. Burack and Louis A. Schmidt, *Cultural and Contextual Perspectives on Developmental Risk and Well-Being* continues the JPS series' tradition of providing a recognized forum for advancing inquiry about both enduring and emergent problems in the developmental sciences. The focus on both adaptive development and a holistic perspective on development as part of the study of development at risk provides an extremely important lens on human development. The authors in this volume also raise important questions by adopting a nuanced view of culture and context as they consider normative development. The volume not only stretches our thinking about what typical development and psychopathology look like when considered in tandem, but also provides insights into how the integration of theory and research about these important themes can translate into usable knowledge. As such, this newest volume continues to represent the goals of the series in important ways by paving the way for further interdisciplinary scholarship at the frontiers of new knowledge about human development.

Nancy Budwig
Clark University
Worcester, MA
April 2013

Acknowledgments

We would like to thank the invited keynote and symposia speakers along with the many attendees at the Jean Piaget Society meeting in Park City, Utah, in June 2009. We thank the Jean Piaget Society, and especially Eric Amsel, for inviting us and helping us organize the meeting. We thank Nancy Budwig, also from the Jean Piaget Society, and Adina Berk, Bhavani Ganesh Kumar, Eve Mayer, Alexandra Poreda, David Repetto, and Robert Swanson from Cambridge University Press and affiliate companies for their assistance in the preparation and publication of this volume. We thank Rhoda Inukpuk and her family for allowing us to use the artwork on the cover, Mark London from Galerie Elca London (Montreal) for providing the photograph, and Richard Murdoch from Art Nunavik, La Fédération des Coopératives du Nouveau-Québec for contacting the artist's family and obtaining the copyright. We thank all the authors for their wonderfully compelling and innovative contributions to the volume. We hope that this volume helps at least in some small way in promoting well-being among different groups of young people and their families.

Introductory Remarks: Cultural and Contextual Perspectives on Developmental Risk and Well-Being

JACOB A. BURACK AND LOUIS A. SCHMIDT

This volume is based on the 39th Annual Meeting of the Jean Piaget Society (JPS), with a theme of "Development at Risk: Typical and Atypical Developmental Pathways," which was held on June 4–6, 2009, in Park City, Utah. The primary goal of the meeting, and therefore of this volume, was to provide insights into essential ways to understand development at risk. Developmental risk simply refers to an increased likelihood for a deleterious outcome, and does not imply inevitability in any way. Thus, adaptive development in the face of risk is as, and probably more, interesting and important to study than maladaptive pathways. Both adaptive development and development in the face of risk must be considered with regard to the "whole person." This includes every aspect of the physical, psychological, social, and emotional being of the individual in an ongoing transactional relationships with all the people and aspects of the environment that have some, even minimal, impact on the individual. These issues are central to this volume, with a specific focus on ways that culture and context can lead to both developmental risk and to well-being, maladaptation and adaptation, as part of these complex ongoing transactional relationships that affect the developing individual in every aspect of their lives throughout the lifespan.

RISK AND WELL-BEING WITHIN THE DISCIPLINE OF DEVELOPMENTAL PSYCHOPATHOLOGY

The discipline of developmental psychopathology emerged from the integration of two "parent" fields of developmental psychology and psychopathology, and is based on the premise that the study of typical and atypical development is mutually informative. Accordingly, the knowledge of the typical course of development provides an essential metric for assessing the extent to which any individual pattern of development might be considered pathological or atypical in some way. Conversely, examples of atypical development are essential to understanding fundamental developmental notions of universality and the inherent intactness and organization of the developing systems. In this context, atypicality is considered within its broadest context to include any situation in which development may be at risk for less than optimal attainment in relation to societal or communal expectations at the relevant developmental stages. Risk is typically discussed within the context of some statistical likelihood of outcome that is of some concern, especially when it is meaningfully greater than that of the general population or of some other relevant comparison group. However, the notion of risk is clouded by the rather amorphous concepts associated with problematic or deleterious outcomes. Although certain types of outcome may be virtually universal, such as in the case of certain disorders, diseases, and environments, most are largely determined by complex transactions among the individuals, families, physical and social environments, communities, and larger societies. Conversely, resilience is considered to be the attainment of well-being or a positive outcome, as indicated by the successful attainment of stage-salient developmental abilities and accomplishments despite heightened levels of risk. The definitions of well-being and positive outcome in this case are certainly relative as they are largely dependent on the severity and nature of the risk. In this volume, the contributors address various types and aspects of risk and different perspectives of well-being within diverse contexts and cultures.

OVERVIEW OF THE VOLUME

Each chapter, in its own way, contributes to our understanding of risk and well-being within the frameworks of development and psychopathology across different levels and conceptualizations of context. These contributions have been organized into three parts.

The focus of Part I is on cultural perspectives on developmental risk and well-being. The four chapters comprising it range from studies of cultures in the East and West to those of the Aboriginal peoples of North America with regard to their influences on understanding socioemotional development. In Chapter 2, Thomas Achenbach provides both historical and current state-of-the-art perspectives on the use of multicultural research to expand the scope of developmental psychopathology. In Chapter 3, Xinyin Chen, Siman Zhao, and Fan Yang describe cultural influences on children's temperament and socioemotional development, with a particular emphasis on shyness and behavioral inhibition in Eastern cultures. In Chapter 4, Stephanie Fryberg and Peter Leavitt provide a sociocultural analysis of high-risk Native American children in the school environment. In Chapter 5, Jacob Burack, Amy Bombay, Heidi Flores, Jillian Stewart, and Vladimir Ponizovsky address the role of cultural identity in ameliorating risk and promoting well-being among Aboriginal youth in Canada.

In Part II of the volume, the chapters are organized around contextual perspectives on developmental risk and well-being. These three chapters are related to contextual influences related to peers, academics, and school settings and range from behavioral to physiological levels of analysis. In Chapter 6, Jennifer Knack, Tracy Vaillancourt, Amanda Krygsman, Steven Arnocky, Irene Vitoroulis, Jennifer Hepditch, and Christine Blain-Arcaro address issues of how peers and peer victimization place children and youth at risk for socioemotional, physical, and academic problems. In Chapter 7, Wendy Troop-Gordon discusses the risks and adaptive correlates of elite social status and how these impact youth development. In Chapter 8, Christine Lackner and Sidney Segalowitz describe how culture and context influence certain aspects of brain physiology, which then increase adolescent risk-taking behavior.

In Part III, the chapters are organized around the theme of contextual perspectives in the lives of persons whose development might be described as atypical in some way. These chapters deal with multiple meanings of context and familial influences on the study of risk and well-being in a range of special populations from prematurity to genetic disorders. In Chapter 9, Lauren Drvaric, Jordana Waxman, Ryan Van Lieshout, and Louis Schmidt suggest that context has a broader meaning than do influences that are traditionally thought of as being outside of the individual, by arguing that prematurity and low birthweight can be conceptualized as a context that influences developmental risk and well-being. In Chapter 10, Matilda Nowakowski, Louis Schmidt, and Tracy Vaillancourt, using evidence from depressed mothers, discuss how perturbations in mother–children interactions may place the child at risk for concurrent and future socioemotional problems. In Chapter 11, Marsha Mailick, Jan Greenberg, Leann Smith, Audra Sterling, Nancy Brady, Steven Warren, and Jinkuk Hong use evidence from children with Fragile X disorder to highlight ways the family environment interacts with genotype to confer socioemotional outcomes. In Chapter 12, Tony Charman imposes the context of development on the understanding and treatment of children with autism spectrum disorders.

These chapters are illustrative of the multiple meanings of culture and context, the many diverse set of perspectives, multiple measures, and populations that researchers consider in the study of the development of risk and well-being. We hope that the collection of chapters represented in this volume will provide the reader with an appreciation of the historical and contemporary views in the field.

PART I

CULTURAL PERSPECTIVES ON DEVELOPMENTAL
RISK AND WELL-BEING

Using Multicultural Research to Expand the Scope of Developmental Psychopathology

THOMAS M. ACHENBACH

When Jean Piaget was appointed Professor of Philosophy at the Sorbonne, he said that this was

> one of the greatest surprises of my life. I do not refer to the delightful welcome of the students, some of whom asked if this Swiss would know French (nor do I refer to my first correction of the examination answers, for some candidates, not noticing that the professor had changed, explained that Piaget had understood nothing whatever, "as M. Merleau-Ponty has demonstrated": I, nevertheless, raised their marks). I refer to the reasons for this appointment, for I have never known whether they rested on a misunderstanding. (Piaget, 1971, pp. 23–24)

The "misunderstanding" concerned the Sorbonne's apparent ignorance of Piaget's rejection of philosophical approaches to knowledge.

After an early interest in philosophical approaches to epistemology, Piaget sought to learn more about how human minds actually develop knowledge. He initially did this by interviewing young children in order to probe their thinking about various natural phenomena, relations between words and their referents, and so forth. Although Piaget expected to need only about 5 years to learn how knowledge develops, he ultimately spent the rest of his life on this little project.

After decades of research on cognitive development, Piaget (1965) wrote a book about his experiences as "a former future ex-philosopher" (p. 28) and the philosophical questions that initially prompted him to begin interviewing children. The English-language version of the book was called *Insights and Illusions of Philosophy* (Piaget, 1971). In this book,

Author Note: I am grateful to Drs. Masha Ivanova and Leslie Rescorla for their helpful comments on a draft of this chapter.

Piaget critiqued the epistemological views of Descartes, Leibniz, Locke, Kant, Hegel, Bergson, Sartre, and other philosophers. Although he had great interest in philosophical issues, Piaget concluded that "Philosophers have long believed that they have the right to speak of every question without making use of methods of verification .... It is a much more serious matter if they take the results of their reflections as a form of knowledge" (Piaget, 1971, p. 215). In other words, philosophers' wisdom (*sagesse*) cannot be equated with knowledge (*connaissance*), which requires empirical evidence.

Piaget's characterization of philosophers' wisdom also applied to the clinical wisdom that then dominated views of psychopathology. The dominance of clinical wisdom over empirically based knowledge was especially apparent in views of child psychopathology, which were based largely on downward extrapolations from adult psychopathology. Children's problems were often interpreted in terms of theories of adult disorders, which implied that children's problems constituted diminutive precursors of adult disorders. The paucity of programmatic research on child psychopathology was reflected in the first edition of the American Psychiatric Association's *Diagnostic and Statistical Manual* (DSM-I; American Psychiatric Association, 1952), which was the official American nosology for psychopathology until 1968. The DSM-I provided only two diagnostic categories for children's problems: *Adjustment Reaction of Childhood*, which was the diagnosis applied to most children seen in outpatient settings; and *Schizophrenic Reaction, Childhood Type*, which was applied to children manifesting diverse kinds of very deviant behavior, thoughts, and emotions. Reflecting their subordinate status, child mental health services were known as "kiddie psychiatry."

EMPIRICALLY BASED EFFORTS TO IDENTIFY SYNDROMES

As recognition of the need for more direct study of children's problems began to dawn, an initial challenge was to identify actual patterns of children's problems and to determine whether more patterns could be identified than were implied by the two DSM-I diagnostic categories. Based primarily on factor analyses of problems reported for various samples of children, several studies identified considerably more patterns of problems than were implied by the DSM-I (e.g., Achenbach, 1966; Borgatta & Fanshel, 1965; Dreger et al., 1964; Miller, 1967; Quay, Morse, & Cutler, 1966; Spivack & Spotts, 1967). These finding, plus studies of behavioral treatments for children's problems, helped promote systematic empirical research on child psychopathology per se, rather than merely on kiddie versions of adult disorders.

DEVELOPMENTAL PSYCHOPATHOLOGY

The need for direct study of children's problems prompted me to propose *developmental psychopathology* as a conceptual framework for researching and understanding behavioral, emotional, and social problems in relation to developmental levels, processes, tasks, sequences, and norms. After beginning work on a book titled *Developmental Psychopathology* (Achenbach, 1974; 2nd edition 1982), I had the good fortune to meet Piaget, who invited me to be a Fellow at his Centre d'Épistémologie Génétique at the University of Geneva. I learned that Piaget himself had used the term "developmental psychopathology," reflecting his conviction that abnormal as well as normal aspects of human functioning must be understood on the basis of developmental research. However, Piaget was much more interested in normal development than in its aberrations.

I had the additional good fortune to participate in a Yale seminar with Anna Freud, who used her clinical wisdom to illustrate the psychoanalytic view of relations between development and psychopathology. She later published this view in a paper titled "A Psychoanalytic View of Developmental Psychopathology" (Freud, 1974). However, her work did not extend to the empirically based knowledge advocated by Piaget.

In *Developmental Psychopathology*, I sought to show that "psychopathology in children is best understood in relation to the changes – progressions, regressions, deviations, successes, and failures – that occur in the course of children's attempts to master the developmental tasks they face" (Achenbach, 1974, p. iii). I also argued that developmental approaches can shed light on all phases of the life cycle but that the dramatic changes from birth to maturity make an especially compelling case for a developmental view of problems during that period. By the time my second edition appeared in 1982, the conceptual framework of developmental psychopathology was becoming more popular (e.g., Rutter & Garmezy, 1983). By 1995, the framework had generated enough research to warrant a 1,659-page compendium of chapters by many authors (Cicchetti & Cohen, 1995). And by 2006, the second edition of this compendium had grown to nearly 3,000 pages (Cicchetti & Cohen, 2006). As would be expected from a 3,000-page work comprising 67 chapters by 175 authors, developmental psychopathology had by then grown to span many different concepts, topics, and approaches.

EMPIRICALLY BASED ASSESSMENT AND TAXONOMY
OF PSYCHOPATHOLOGY

The early multivariate studies of various samples of children revealed much more differentiation among patterns of child psychopathology than implied by the two DSM-I diagnostic categories. Systematic reviews of the multivariate studies indicated that, despite differences in methods and samples, the findings showed considerable convergence on a few broad-band groupings of problems and a larger number of narrow-band syndromes (Achenbach & Edelbrock, 1978; Quay, 1979). An essential next step was to extend the empirical methodology to assessment of individuals' problems in ways that could yield empirically derived syndrome scales. In other words, links needed to be forged between data on the kind and degree of problems reported for each child and the taxonomic patterns derived statistically from data on many children. To meet needs for assessing a great variety of children under a great variety of conditions, it was necessary to construct instruments for obtaining assessment data directly from informants familiar with the children's functioning in their typical environments, including parents, teachers, and children themselves.

Cross-Informant Challenges

When mothers, fathers, teachers, and children completed parallel assessment instruments, differences were often found between the problems reported by different informants. The limited levels of cross-informant agreement were systematically documented in meta-analyses of many different assessment instruments used in many different studies. The meta-analyses yielded mean correlations of .60 between pairs of informants who played similar roles vis-à-vis the children (pairs of parents, teachers, mental health workers, observers), .28 between informants who played different roles vis-à-vis the children (e.g., parents vs. teachers), and .22 between children's self-reports and reports by adults (Achenbach, McConaughy, & Howell, 1987). Subsequently cited in more than 4000 publications (Google Scholar, 2014), the meta-analytic findings of modest cross-informant correlations are regarded as being among "the most robust findings in child clinical research" (De Los Reyes & Kazdin, 2005, p. 483). Modest cross-informant correlations are not limited to children, however, as meta-analyses have shown that correlations between self-reports and collateral reports of adult psychopathology are not materially larger than the cross-informant correlations found for children (Achenbach, Krukowski, Dumenci, & Ivanova,

2005). The challenges of obtaining and synthesizing data thus span many kinds of psychopathology, assessment procedures, and assessment targets (Achenbach, 2011; De Los Reyes, 2011).

Meeting the Challenges of Empirically Based Assessment

When views of child psychopathology depended primarily on clinical wisdom, assessment consisted mainly of clinicians' interviews and observations of patients in clinical contexts. Although clinicians often interviewed parents as well as children, the clinicians would idiosyncratically elicit, mentally process, and combine information into judgments about the problems to be treated, their causes, and the treatment to be provided. As empirically based approaches advanced, the use of standardized instruments to obtain assessment data from multiple informants posed challenges such as the following:

1. What reliable, valid, and useful data can be quickly and economically obtained from multiple informants?
2. How can data from each informant be linked to taxonomic constructs for psychopathology?
3. How can data from each informant regarding a particular child be compared to what is reported for typical children?
4. How can data from each informant be efficiently displayed for clinicians' use?
5. How can specific cross-informant agreements and discrepancies be documented for each child?

Just as Piaget found that supplanting philosophical *sagesse* with empirically based *connaissance* regarding the development of knowledge raised more challenges than could be mastered in 5 years, the goal of supplanting clinical *sagesse* with empirically based *connaissance* regarding psychopathology raised many challenges such as those just listed. In this chapter, I outline ways in which my international colleagues and I are meeting the challenges and are conducting multicultural research to expand the scope of developmental psychopathology.

How we obtain reliable, valid, and useful data from multiple informants. Building on efforts to empirically identify syndromes of co-occurring problems, my colleagues and I have developed standardized instruments for obtaining parent (Child Behavior Checklist; CBCL), teacher (Teacher's Report Form; TRF), and self-reports (Youth Self-Report; YSR) of behavioral, emotional, and social problems and competencies (Achenbach

& Edelbrock, 1983, 1986, 1987; Achenbach & Lewis, 1971). The items to be rated were assembled from previous research, examination of clinical case records, and input from clinicians, parents, teachers, and youths. The instruments were iteratively tested by having large samples of parents, teachers, and youths complete them, comment on their content, and suggest additional candidate items. Items that were endorsed by hardly any respondents or by nearly all respondents were revised or deleted, as were items that respondents found unclear. Items suggested by respondents were tested in subsequent iterations. Items were retained if they discriminated significantly between children referred for mental health or special education services and demographically matched nonreferred children.

The problem items are scored on factor-analytically derived syndrome scales. The competence items are scored on scales for assessing children's adaptive functioning, activities, social relations, and school performance. The instruments have high test-retest reliability, and hundreds of studies support their content, criterion-related, and construct validity (Achenbach & Rescorla, 2000, 2001; Bérubé & Achenbach, 2014). Thousands of published studies have demonstrated the utility of the instruments in more than 80 societies and cultural groups (Bérubé & Achenbach, 2014).

Linking informant data to taxonomic constructs. Taxonomic constructs consisting of empirically based syndromes are operationally defined as the sum of the ratings of the items comprising each syndrome. For example, a syndrome designated as Aggressive Behavior comprises items such as *Gets in many fights*, *Physically attacks people*, and *Threatens people*. Because each problem item on the instruments is rated *0 = not true, 1 = somewhat or sometimes true*, and *2 = very true or often true*, a youth's standing on Aggressive Behavior – according to his mother's ratings – is operationally defined by summing his mother's *0, 1*, and *2* ratings of the items of the Aggressive Behavior syndrome that are on the CBCL his mother completed to describe the youth. Likewise, the youth's standing on the Aggressive Behavior syndrome – according to ratings by his father, his teachers, and himself – is operationalized by summing each of their ratings on the relevant items of the instruments that they completed.

Comparing each informant's data with data for peers of the individual being assessed. Most psychopathology must be evaluated in relation to developmental norms. For example, certain behaviors may be typical for one developmental period but quite deviant if they occur at earlier or later developmental periods. To enable users to evaluate syndrome scores in relation to developmental norms and also in relation to norms for each gender and for parent, teacher, and self-ratings, the CBCL, TRF, and YSR have been completed for nationally representative samples of children and youth living in the United States (Achenbach & Rescorla, 2000, 2001). To base the norms on what epidemiologists call healthy samples, data were used only for children and youth who had not received mental health, substance abuse, or major special educational services in the preceding 12 months. *T* scores and percentiles for each syndrome are based on the distributions of syndrome scores obtained by the national normative sample, separately by developmental period, gender, and type of informant. To provide guidelines for identifying syndrome scores that are sufficiently deviant to warrant professional help, cut points are provided for scores in the normal range, borderline clinical range, and clinical range.

Displaying assessment data for clinicians' use. To make it easy to see an individual's standing on each syndrome, the syndromes are displayed on profiles in relation to norms for the individual's age, gender, and parent, teacher, and self-ratings. As illustrated in Figure 2.1, broken lines printed on the profiles indicate cut points between the normal and borderline clinical range (lower broken line) and between the borderline and clinical range (upper broken line). (Names in the figures are fictitious.) Users can thus see at a glance whether any syndrome scores are high enough to indicate possible (borderline range) or probable (clinical range) needs for professional help. As shown in Figure 2.1, raw scores, *T* scores, and percentiles are printed beneath the profile for each syndrome. To enable users to see the informant's ratings of each item, all the items are displayed with the 0, 1, or 2 ratings given them by the informant. A separate profile is printed for ratings by each informant, including parents, teachers, and youths.

Comparing ratings by different informants. To enable users to compare ratings by different informants, the computer software for scoring the forms prints out three kinds of comparisons. Figure 2.2 illustrates side-by-side comparisons of ratings of each item by different informants. Users can thus identify problems that were endorsed by all informants (i.e., rated 1 or 2), endorsed by no informants (i.e., rated 0), or endorsed by some but not all informants. Discrepancies between informants' endorsements versus non-endorsements of particular problem items may reveal patterns suggesting that certain problems are limited to particular contexts. For example, if several teachers endorse a problem that is not endorsed by either parent, this suggests that the problem may be specific to the school setting.

Figure 2.3 illustrates bar graph comparisons of syndrome scores obtained from each informant's ratings of a particular individual. These comparisons enable users to see whether scores on certain syndromes are deviant according to all informants, some informants, or no informants. For example, in Figure 2.3, all six bars for the Withdrawn/Depressed syndrome are above the upper broken line. Both parents, the youth, and all three teachers

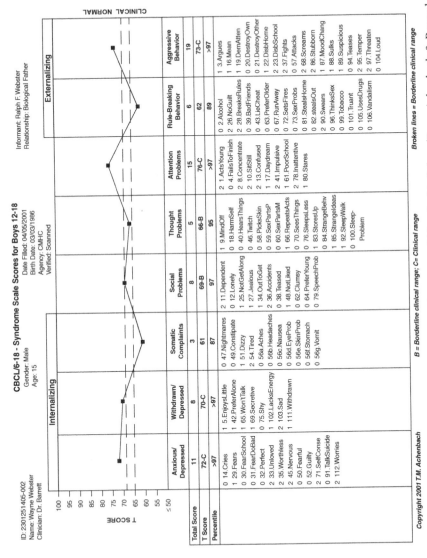

CBCL/6-18 - Syndrome Scale Scores for Boys 12-18

ID: 2301251405-002
Name: Wayne Webster
Clinician: Dr. Barrett

Gender: Male
Age: 15

Date Filled: 04/05/2001
Birth Date: 03/03/1986
Agency: CMHC
Verified: Scanned

Informant: Ralph F. Webster
Relationship: Biological Father

	Anxious/ Depressed	Withdrawn/ Depressed	Somatic Complaints	Social Problems	Thought Problems	Attention Problems	Rule-Breaking Behavior	Aggressive Behavior
Total Score	11	8	3	8	5	15	6	19
T Score	72-C	70-C	61	69-B	66-B	76-C	62	73-C
Percentile	>97	>97	87	97	95	>97	89	>97

Copyright 2001 T.M. Achenbach

B = Borderline clinical range; C= Clinical range

Broken lines = Borderline clinical range

FIGURE 2.1. Profile of syndrome scores from ratings of a 15-year-old boy by his father. (From Achenbach & Rescorla, 2001. Used by permission.)

14

thus endorsed enough problems of this syndrome to place the youth in the clinical range for boys of his age. On the other hand, all six bars for the Rule-Breaking Behavior syndrome are below the lower broken line, that is, in the normal range. For the Anxious/Depressed syndrome, the bars for both parents' ratings and the youth's self-ratings are in the clinical range. However, the bar for one teacher's ratings is in the borderline clinical range, whereas the bars for two teachers' ratings are in the normal range. These differences indicate that problems of the Anxious/Depressed syndrome were less salient to the teachers than to the parents and youth.

To enable users to see the overall level of agreement between each pair of informants, the software displays Q correlations between ratings by each pair of informants, as illustrated in Figure 2.4. (The Q correlations are computed by applying the formula for Pearson r to two informants' 0–1–2 ratings of all problem items.) In addition to displaying the actual Q correlations – which can range from –1.00 to +1.00 – the software displays the 25th percentile, mean, and 75th percentile Q correlations obtained from large reference samples of each kind of informant pair. If the Q correlation for a particular informant pair is between the 25th and 75th percentile, it is designated as *average*, as exemplified by the Q correlation between the mother's and father's CBCL ratings in Figure 2.4. Q correlations below the 25th percentile are designated as *below average*, whereas Q correlations above the 75th percentile are designated as *above average*, as shown in Figure 2.4.

DSM-Oriented Scales

The selection of items, the data obtained by having informants rate the items, and the syndromes derived by factor-analyzing the items embody a "bottom-up" approach whereby assessment and taxonomic procedures are based on statistical analyses of data for large samples of individuals. The DSM nosology, by contrast, embodies a "top-down" approach whereby panels of experts formulate diagnostic categories, decide how to define the categories, and select criteria for classifying individuals' problems in terms of the categories. Although the experts consider research findings and the results of field trials that have been used to evaluate criteria for some diagnostic categories, neither the diagnostic categories nor their criteria have been directly derived from research data on large samples of individuals.

Because DSM diagnostic categories are widely used in clinical practice, research, training, and reimbursement for services, it is important to link empirically based assessment with DSM categories. Consequently, we have asked expert psychiatrists and psychologists from many cultures to

DSM-Oriented Cross-Informant Comparison – Problem Items Common to the CBCL/TRF/YSR (2001 version)

| ID: 230125405 | | Name: Wayne Webster | | Gender: Male | | Birth Date: 03/03/1986 | | Comparison Date: 04/13/2001 |

Form	Eval ID	Age	Informant Name	Relationship	Date
CBC1	001	15	Alice N. Webster	Biological Mother	04/04/2001
CBC2	002	15	Ralph F. Webster	Biological Father	04/05/2001
YSR3	003	15	Self	Self	04/08/2001
TRF4	004	15	George Jackson	Classroom Teacher {M}	04/10/2001

Form	Eval ID	Age	Informant Name	Relationship	Date
TRF5	005	15	Carmen Hernandez	Classroom Teacher {F}	04/11/2001
TRF6	006	15	Charles Dwyer	Classroom Teacher {M}	04/12/2001

Anxious/Depressed

	CBC 1	CBC 2	YSR 3	TRF 4	TRF 5	TRF 6	TRF 7	TRF 8
14. Cries	0	0	1	0	0	0		
29. Fears	0	1	0	0	0	0		
30. FearSchool	1	0	0	0	0	0		
31. FearDoBad	0	0	0	0	0	0		
32. Perfect	0	0	0	0	0	1		
33. Unloved	2	2	2	0	0	0		
35. Worthless	2	2	2	1	0	0		
45. Nervous	2	2	2	0	0	0		
50. Fearful	0	0	0	0	0	0		
52. Guilty	0	0	0	0	0	0		
71. SelfConc	2	2	1	1	2	0		
91. Suicide	0	0	2	0	0	0		

Social Problems

	CBC 1	CBC 2	YSR 3	TRF 4	TRF 5	TRF 6	TRF 7	TRF 8
11. Dependent	0	2	2	0	1	2		
12. Lonely	2	0	2	1	0	0		
25. NotGetAlong	2	1	1	2	1	2		
27. Jealous	2	1	0	0	0	0		
34. OutToGet	2	1	2	2	1	1		
36. GetsHurt	0	2	2	0	1	0		
38. Teased	0	0	1	1	0	0		
48. NotLiked	0	1	2	2	1	2		
62. Clumsy	0	0	1	0	0	1		
64. PreferYoung	0	0	1	1	0	0		
79. SpeechProb	0	0	0	0	0	0		

Rule-Breaking Behavior

	CBC 1	CBC 2	YSR 3	TRF 4	TRF 5	TRF 6	TRF 7	TRF 8
26. NoGuilt	1	2	0	1	0	0		
28. BreaksRules	1	2	0	2	1	1		
39. BadFriends	0	0	0	0	0	0		
43. LieCheat	0	0	0	0	0	0		
63. Preferolder	0	0	0	0	0	0		
82. StealsOther	0	0	0	0	0	0		
90. Swears	1	2	1	2	0	0		
96. ThinkSex	0	0	1	0	0	0		
99. Tobacco	0	0	0	0	0	0		
101. Truant	0	0	0	0	0	0		
105. UsesDrugs	0	0	1	0	0	0		

16

FIGURE 2.2 data table (rotated). Item ratings for a 15-year-old boy.

Withdrawn/Depressed							
112.Worries	2	2	2	2	0	0	
5.EnjoysLittle	2	1	1	2	2	2	0
42.PreferAlone	1	1	1	2	2	0	1
65.Won'tTalk	2	1	2	2	1	1	2
69.Secretive	2	2	2	2	1	2	
75.Shy	0	0	0	0	0	1	
102.LacksEnergy	0	1	0	0	1	0	
103.Sad	2	2	2	2	2	2	
111.Withdrawn	2	1	2	2	2	2	

Somatic Complaints						
51.Dizzy	0	1	1	0	0	0
54.Tired	0	2	1	0	1	2
56a.Aches	0	0	0	0	0	0
56b.Headaches	2	0	1	0	0	0
56c.Nausea	0	0	0	0	0	0
56d.EyeProb	0	0	0	0	0	0
56e.SkinProb	0	0	0	1	0	0
56f.Stomach	0	0	0	0	0	0
56g.Vomit	0	0	0	0	0	0

Thought Problems						
9.MindOff	2	1	2	2	1	1
18.HarmSelf	0	0	0	0	0	0
40.HearsThings	0	0	1	0	0	0
46.Twitch	0	0	2	0	0	0
58.PicksSkin	0	0	0	0	0	0
66. RepeatsActs	0	1	2	1	1	0
70.SeesThings	0	0	0	0	0	0
83.StoresUp	0	0	1	0	0	2
84.StrangeBehav	0	0	2	1	0	0
85.StrangeIdeas	1	1	0	2	2	1

Attention Problems						
1.ActsYoung	0	1	0	0	2	2
4.FailsToFinish	2	2	2	2	0	
8.Concentrate	2	2	2	2	2	1
10.SitStill	0	2	0	0	0	1
13.Confused	2	2	2	2	2	2
17.Daydream	2	1	1	1	2	2
41.impulsive	1	2	2	2	2	2
61.PoorSchool	1	1	1	0	0	0
78.Inattentive	2	2	2	2	2	1

Aggressive Behavior						
3.Argues	2	1	2	2	2	1	2
16.Mean	2	1	1	1	2	0	0
19.DemAtten	0	1	0	0	0	1	2
20.DestroyOwn	0	0	0	1	1	1	1
21.DestroyOther	0	0	0	0	0	0	1
23.DisobeySchl	0	2	1	2	1	0	0
37.Fights	1	2	1	1	1	0	0
57.Attacks	0	0	0	0	1	0	0
68.Screams	1	2	2	1	0	0	0
86.Stubbom	2	1	1	2	2	2	2
87.MoodChang	1	1	1	2	2	2	1
89.Suspicious	2	2	2	2	0	1	
94.Teases	0	0	0	0	0	0	
95.Temper	2	2	2	2	2	1	
97.Threaten	1	2	2	2	0	0	
104.Loud	1	0	0	1	0	0	

Other Problems						
44.BiteNail	0	0	0	1	0	0
55.Overweight	0	0	0	0	1	0
56h.OtherPhys	0	2	0	0	0	0

FIGURE 2.2. Cross-informant comparisons of item ratings for a 15-year-old boy. (From Achenbach & Rescorla, 2001. Used by permission.) {F}=Female; {M}=Male.

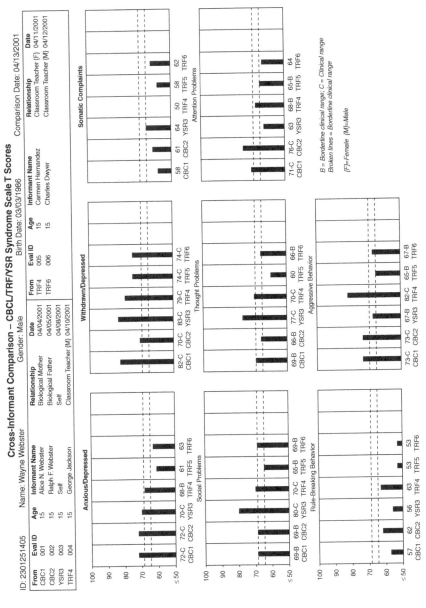

FIGURE 2.3. Cross-informant comparisons of syndrome scores for a 15-year-old boy. (From Achenbach & Rescorla, 2001. Used by permission.)

18

Cross-informant Comparison – CBCL/TRF/YSR Cross-Informant Correlations (2001 version)

ID: 2301251405   Name: Wayne Webster   Gender: Male   Birth Date: 03/03/1986   Comparison Date: 04/13/2001

Form	Eval ID	Age	Informant Name	Relationship	Date	Form	Eval ID	Age	Informant Name	Relationship	Date
CBC1	001	15	Alice N. Webster	Biological Mother	04/04/2001	TRF5	005	15	Carmen Hernandez	Classroom Teacher	04/11/2001
CBC2	002	15	Ralph F. Webster	Biological Father	04/05/2001	TRF6	006	15	Charles Dwyer	Classroom Teacher	04/12/2001
YSR3	003	15	Self	Self	04/08/2001						
TRF4	004	15	George Jackson	Classroom Teacher {M}	04/10/2001						

Q Correlations Between Item Scores

Forms	Informants	Cross-Informant Agreement	Q Corr	Reference Group 25th %ile	Reference Group Mean	Reference Group 75th %ile
CBC1 x CBC2	Biological Mother x Biological Father	Average	.51	.51	.59	.69
CBC1 x YSR3	Biological Mother x Self	Above average	.41	.17	.29	.40
CBC1 X TRF4	Biological Mother x Classroom Teacher {M}	Above average	.54	.09	.23	.37
CBC1 x TRF5	Biological Mother x Classroom Teacher {F}	Above average	.49	.09	.23	.37
CBC1 x TRF6	Biological Mother x Classroom Teacher {M}	Above average	.42	.09	.23	.37
CBC2 x YSR3	Biological Father x Self	Above average	.56	.17	.29	.40
CBC2 x TRF4	Biological Father x Classroom Teacher {M}	Above average	.76	.09	.23	.37
CBC2 x TRF5	Biological Father x Classroom Teacher {F}	Above average	.40	.09	.23	.37
CBC2 X TRF6	Biological Father x Classroom Teacher {M}	Average	.30	.09	.23	.37
YSR3 X TRF4	Self x Classroom Teacher {M}	Above average	.60	.07	.19	.30
YSR3 X TRF5	Self x Classroom Teacher {F}	Above average	.36	.07	.19	.30
YSR3 x TRF6	Self x Classroom Teacher {M}	Above average	.35	.07	.19	.30
TRF4 x TRF5	Classroom Teacher {M} x Classroom Teacher {F}	Average	.43	.40	.51	.63
TRF4 x TRF6	Classroom Teacher {M} x Classroom Teacher {M}	Below average	.39	.40	.51	.63
TFF5 x TRF6	Classroom Teacher {F} x Classroom Teacher {M}	Above average	.67	.40	.51	.63

FIGURE 2.4. Cross-informant Q correlations for a 15-year-old boy. (From Achenbach & Rescorla, 2001. Used by permission.) nc = not calculated due to insufficient data.

19

select items from our assessment instruments that they judged to be very consistent with DSM diagnostic categories, initially using DSM-IV criteria and subsequently DSM-5 criteria (Achenbach, 2013; Achenbach & Rescorla, 2000, 2001). We used items selected by a large majority of experts as being very consistent with particular DSM diagnostic categories to construct DSM-oriented scales for those categories. The DSM-oriented scales are scored by summing 0–1–2 ratings of items that are on the same assessment forms as are used to score the empirically based syndromes. Like the profile of empirically based syndromes shown in Figure 2.1, the DSM-oriented scales are displayed on normed profiles. Consequently, users can view ratings of an individual's problems in terms of the top-down DSM-oriented scales in the same format as the bottom-up empirically based syndromes. Cross-informant comparisons of DSM-oriented scale scores are also provided, like those for empirically based syndromes.

MULTICULTURAL RESEARCH

Much of the literature on development – both normal and abnormal – has originated in a handful of rather similar societies. This literature contains numerous generalizations implying developmental uniformity across the human species. However, the degree of uniformity with respect to particular human characteristics needs to be tested empirically. One approach has been to conduct cross-cultural studies in which people from two cultural groups are compared on certain variables. When significant differences are found between Group A and Group B, it has been tempting to conclude that Group A people are categorically different from Group B people. On the other hand, when significant differences are not found, it has been tempting to conclude that Group A people and Group B people are alike.

Comparing Many Populations

A multicultural approach to research enlarges on traditional cross-cultural comparisons in several ways (Achenbach & Rescorla, 2007b; Achenbach, Rescorla, & Ivanova, 2012). First, a multicultural approach applies the same standardized assessment procedures (in translation when necessary) to large representative samples from many populations. By comparing samples from many populations, we can evaluate similarities and differences found between particular populations in relation to the broad spectrum of populations that are assessed. For example, if we find a statistically significant difference between mean scores for samples from Population A versus

Population B, we can determine whether the difference is smaller than the differences between most of the populations or whether the difference is larger than most of the differences. Data from many populations thus enable us to determine whether scores that differ significantly are nevertheless close together or far apart in the spectrum of scores for all the populations that were assessed. This is much more informative than cross-cultural comparisons between just two populations where a statistically significant difference between Population A and Population B might be erroneously interpreted as indicating a major difference when the difference is actually smaller than the differences that might be found between many other populations, had they been assessed.

Comparing Distributions of Scores

A second way in which a multicultural approach enlarges on cross-cultural comparisons is by taking account of the distributions of scores in every sample from all the populations that are compared. Thus, even though populations' mean scores may differ significantly, the distributions of the populations' scores may overlap considerably. This would indicate that, despite a difference between mean scores, many members of Population A and Population B obtain similar scores. For example, the mean height of 10-year-olds in Population A may be greater than in Population B. However, many 10-year-olds in both populations may be the same height, and some 10-year-olds in Population B may be taller than some or even all 10-year-olds in Population A. By examining the *distributions* of scores, we can counteract erroneous tendencies to think that all members of one population differ from all members of other populations.

Meta-Analytic Framework

A third way in which a multicultural approach enlarges on cross-cultural comparisons is by providing a meta-analytic framework for statistically testing the consistencies and differences among societies. When we statistically test data from many societies in the same analyses, we are creating a framework like that of a meta-analysis for identifying findings that are robust across multiple societies. Like meta-analyses of many studies, analyses of data from many societies also expand our opportunities to detect interactions between variables, as well as to detect exceptions to general findings. Findings that are robust across many societies thus deserve much more confidence than findings from one or even two or three societies, just as meta-analytic findings that are robust across many studies deserve more confidence than findings from one, two, or three studies.

Emic and Etic Research

When standardized procedures yield similar results in most but not all populations, research to determine the reasons for the exceptions can be tailored to the particular populations for which the exceptions are found. Research that is thus designed to illuminate the meaning of particular phenomena within a particular population is called *emic*, which is a shortening of *phonemic*, a term used by linguists for speech sounds that speakers of a particular language recognize as meaningful (Pike, 1967). Emic research is often contrasted with *etic* research, which applies the same standardized methods to multiple populations (*etic* is a shortening of *phonetic*, i.e., linguists' term for all the sounds used in human languages; Pike, 1967).

USING MULTICULTURAL RESEARCH TO EXPAND THE SCOPE OF DEVELOPMENTAL PSYCHOPATHOLOGY

Empirically based assessment and taxonomy take account of variance related to development, gender, and informant. These sources of variance may be associated with differences in the nature, patterning, and prevalence of maladaptive functioning. Rather than assuming that official diagnostic categories truly pinpoint types of psychopathology that are each intrinsically different from other types, my colleagues and I have sought to identify actual syndromes of problems that can then be used for research on the etiology, developmental course, outcome, treatment, and prevention of maladaptive functioning. In addition to research on variance associated with development, gender, and informant, we have used multicultural research methods to take account of variance that may be associated with different populations. We have done this by using etic procedures to assess and compare population samples from many societies. We define a society as a population of people living in a geographically demarcated area having a particular government and being conversant in a particular language. Most of the societies are countries, although some are not, such as the Flemish-speaking region of Belgium, the German-speaking region of Switzerland, Hong Kong, and Puerto Rico. Developmentally appropriate instruments have been used to assess children's problems in population samples from the 54 societies listed in Table 2.1.

TABLE 2.1 *Societies that have provided data for multicultural norms*

Albania	Greece	Poland
Algeria	Hong Kong	Portugal
Argentina	Iceland	Puerto Rico
Australia	India (Telegu)	Romania
Austria	Iran	Russia
Bangladesh	Israel	Serbia
Belgium (Flanders)	Italy	Singapore
Brazil	Jamaica	Spain
Chile	Japan	Sweden
China	Korea (South)	Switzerland (German)
Colombia	Kosovo	Taiwan
Croatia	Latvia	Thailand
Czech Republic	Lebanon	Tunisia
Denmark	Lithuania	Turkey
Ethiopia	Netherlands	United Arab Emirates
Finland	Norway	United States
France	Pakistan	Uruguay
Germany	Peru	Vietnam

Note: Details of samples and procedures are provided by Achenbach and Rescorla (2007a, 2010, 2014).

Patterning of Problem Scores in Different Societies

We have obtained parent and preschool teacher/daycare provider ratings for ages 1½ through 5 years, parent and teacher ratings for ages 6 through 18 years, and self-ratings for ages 11 through 18 years. In data from all the societies assessed to date, confirmatory factor analyses (CFAs) have supported syndromes that we derived from ratings of Anglophone samples (Ivanova et al., 2007a, 2007b, 2007c, 2010, 2011). The syndromal patterns of problems that tend to co-occur are thus similar in dozens of societies.

To determine whether particular problems tend to receive similarly high, medium, or low ratings in different societies, we computed correlations between the mean of the 0–1–2 ratings of each problem item in each society and the mean of the 0–1–2 ratings of each problem item in every other society. As an example, for the German sample, we computed the mean of the 0–1–2 ratings of each of the 112 CBCL/6–18 items included in the multicultural analysis of the CBCL/6–18 (Rescorla et al, 2007b). For the Swiss sample, we also computed the mean of the 0–1–2 ratings of each of the 112 CBCL/6–18 items. Using the formula for Pearson r, we then computed the correlation between the 112 mean item scores for the German sample and the Swiss sample. (In effect, this was a Q correlation – i.e., a correlation between two sets of scores for 112 items.) We obtained a correlation of .94 between the German and Swiss mean item ratings. This meant that CBCL items that received the highest mean ratings for German children also received the highest mean ratings for Swiss children. Similarly, items that received medium mean ratings for German children also received medium mean ratings for Swiss children, and items that received the lowest mean ratings for German children also received the lowest mean ratings for Swiss children.

After we computed the correlations between the mean CBCL item scores for every pair of societies, we computed the mean of all the bi-society correlations. For the CBCL/1½–5, CBCL/6–18, and TRF, the mean of the bi-society correlations was .78. For the YSR, the mean of the bi-society correlations was .69 (Rescorla et al., 2007a, 2007b, 2007c, 2011). All large according to Cohen's (1988) criteria, these correlations indicated substantial similarity in the rank ordering of the ratings of problem items across many societies. Coupled with the CFA support for the syndromes, the large correlations between the mean item ratings indicated that the performance of the items was similar in many societies.

Societal Differences in Mean Scale Scores

Comparisons of scale scores across societies have yielded effect sizes (ESs) that ranged from small to medium according to Cohen's (1988) criteria for the percentage of variance accounted for by societal differences in ANOVAs (Rescorla et al., 2007a, 2007b, 2007c, 2011, 2012). Scores for the DSM-oriented Conduct Problems scale and for the Aggressive Behavior syndrome have shown especially small differences across societies, with small ESs of 3% for Conduct Problems and 4%–5% for Aggressive Behavior in parent, teacher, and self-ratings of school-age children (Rescorla et al., 2007a, 2007b, 2007c).

Despite tendencies for some societies to be stereotyped as more violent or aggressive than others, these findings indicate that the mean level of conduct problems and aggressive behavior reported for school-age children do not differ much across a broad spectrum of societies. The mean scores on other problem scales showed bigger differences between societies, with ESs for the Anxious/Depressed syndrome ranging up to 12% for parents' ratings of preschool children and 13% for teachers' ratings of school-age children (Rescorla et al., 2007a, 2011). However, in ratings by all the kinds of informants, the differences between mean scale scores from different societies were much smaller than the differences between scale scores obtained by individual children within each society. For example, the standard deviation (*SD*) of the means of the CBCL Total Problems scores obtained from parent ratings in 31 societies was 5.7. However, when the *SD*s were computed separately within the samples for each of the 31 societies, the mean of these 31 *SD*s was 16.9 (Rescorla et al., 2007b). In other words, there was much greater variance among Total Problems scores obtained by individual children *within* each of the 31 societies than there was *among* the 31 *mean* Total Problems scores across all the societies.

Distributions of Scale Scores in Different Societies

Figure 2.5 graphically illustrates the finding that the distribution of CBCL Total Problems scores in every society greatly overlapped with the distributions of Total Problems scores in every other society. The bars in Figure 2.5 represent the CBCL Total Problems scores from the 5th to the 95th percentiles in the samples from each society. The star in the middle of the bar for each society reflects the mean Total Problems score for that society. By looking at the stars in Figure 2.5, you can see that Japan (leftmost bar) had the lowest mean Total Problems score, whereas Puerto Rico (rightmost bar) had the highest mean Total Problems score. However, by looking at the bars for Japan and Puerto Rico, you can see that many Japanese Total Problems scores spanned the same range as many Puerto Rican Total Problems scores. Thus, despite societal differences in mean Total Problems scores, no society was categorically different from any other society. In other words, no distributions of individuals' Total Problems scores failed to overlap with all the other distributions. The narrower-spectrum problem scale scores (i.e., scales other than Total Problems) similarly yielded larger *SD*s within each society than among the mean scores for all societies. That is, for each narrow-spectrum scale score, the mean of the 31 *SD*s calculated within each of the 31 societies ranged from 2.5 to 4.8 times larger than the *SD* of the distribution of 31 mean scale scores. The much greater variance among individual children's scores within each society than among the mean scores of the 31 different societies indicates that individual differences in problems account for more of the variation among scale scores than do effects associated with societies.

Gender Effects Across Societies

For each type of informant, gender effects were quite consistent across societies. In parent and self-ratings, ESs for gender were very small, with few reaching even 2% of the variance (Rescorla et al., 2007a, 2007c; 2011, 2012).

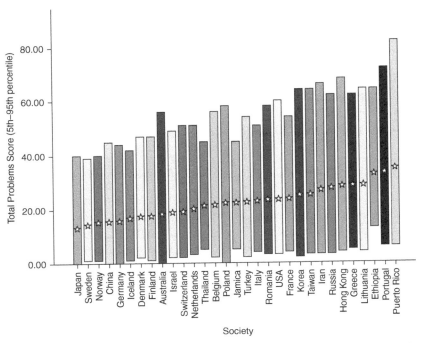

FIGURE 2.5. Range of CBCL/6–18 Total Problems scores from the 5th to the 95th percentile for each society. The star on a society's bar indicates the mean Total Problems score for that society. (Copyright © T. M. Achenbach. Used by permission.)

Although not reaching Cohen's (1988) criterion for medium ESs, teachers' ratings of 6- to 18-year-old students showed larger ESs for gender, with ESs of 4% to 5% reflecting higher scores for boys than girls on the Attention Problems syndrome and the DSM-oriented Attention Deficit/Hyperactivity Problems and Conduct Problems scales (Rescorla et al., 2007b).

Within-society comparisons showed that teachers rated boys higher than girls on the Attention Problems syndrome in all societies except Iran, where teachers rated girls slightly, though not significantly, higher than boys. As Iran was the only society in which all participants attended single-gender schools (90 boys' schools and 90 girls' schools), we might infer that – because Iranian teachers' classroom observations included only one gender – the teachers were not affected by differences between boy and girl students that could have affected teachers in other societies. However, unlike parents in most other societies, Iranian parents also rated girls higher

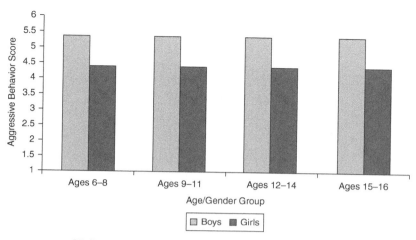

FIGURE 2.6. CBCL Aggressive Behavior syndrome scores by gender and age for 24 cultures (*N* = 47,987). (From Achenbach & Rescorla 2007b, p. 75. Reproduced by permission.)

than boys on the Attention Problems syndrome. The etic findings of higher Attention Problems scores for girls than boys in Iranian teacher and parent ratings, but the opposite gender difference in other societies, suggest a need for emic research on reasons for the difference in the Iranian ratings. In self-ratings on the YSR, boys' and girls' Attention Problems scores did not differ significantly across societies.

Age-by-Gender Interactions Across Societies

Standardized data for tens of thousands of boys and girls of many ages from many societies make it possible to test interactions between variables such as age and gender in meta-analytic ways that deserve more confidence than findings from single societies. For example, Figure 2.6 shows mean CBCL Aggressive Behavior syndrome scores for 47,987 6- to 16-year-old boys and girls from 24 societies. Although boys are often reported to be more aggressive than girls, Figure 2.6 shows that this gender difference declined progressively between ages 6 to 8 and 15 to 16, when the gender difference became negligible. By contrast, although girls are often reported to exceed boys in Internalizing problems (anxiety, depression, withdrawal, somatic complaints), Figure 2.7 shows negligible gender differences in Internalizing scores at ages 6 to 8 but increasing differences through ages 15 to 16 for the same sample of 47,987 boys and girls. Figure 2.8 shows a similar gender-by-age interaction for DSM-oriented Affective Problems scale scores from ages

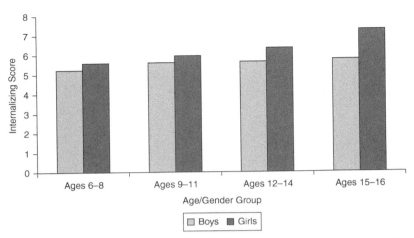

FIGURE 2.7. CBCL Internalizing scores by gender and age for 24 cultures ($N = 47,987$). (From Achenbach & Rescorla, 2007b, p. 74. Reproduced by permission.)

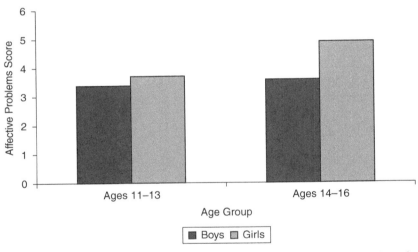

FIGURE 2.8. YSR DSM-Oriented Affective Problems scores by gender and age for 24 cultures ($N = 27,206$). (From Achenbach & Rescorla, 2007b, p. 85. Reproduced by permission.)

11 to 13 to 14 to 16 in YSR self-ratings by 27,206 youths from 24 societies. Data from many societies thus enable us to test effects of variables such as age, gender, and their interactions with much greater confidence than data from one or a few societies.

Cross-Informant Findings in Different Societies

Meta-analyses of many studies have yielded cross-informant correlations that have subsequently proven to be very robust in other studies (Achenbach et al., 1987; De Los Reyes & Kazdin, 2005). The studies in the meta-analyses included many kinds of assessment instruments but only a few societies. Multi-informant data obtained with parallel instruments in many societies make it possible to greatly advance our understanding of multi-informant issues by testing the degree to which various permutations of data from different informants yield similar or different findings in different societies. As an example, Rescorla et al. (2013) compared differences between Total Problems scores for YSR ratings by youths in 24 societies versus CBCL ratings of parallel items by their parents. In every society, the YSR Total Problems scores were significantly higher than the CBCL Total Problems scores. Across great variations in ethnicity, language, religion, political system, socioeconomic level, and geographic region, youths thus tended to report more problems than their parents reported for them. Nevertheless, there was also much variation in the magnitudes of the YSR versus CBCL differences and in factors associated with the differences. For example, the greatest difference was found between YSR and CBCL scores for Japanese youths. In fact, the mean Japanese CBCL (and also the TRF) Total Problems score was the lowest among the societies that were compared, whereas the mean Japanese YSR Total Problems score was in the middle of the societies that were compared. As a consequence, Japanese CBCL (and TRF) scores qualify for the multicultural low-problem normative group, whereas Japanese YSR scores qualify for the multicultural middle-problem normative group, as detailed in the following section.

MULTICULTURAL NORMS

In addition to contributing scientific knowledge, multicultural research yields practical benefits for conceptualizing, assessing, and treating psychopathology, as well as for international training of mental health workers. Multicultural etic research has supported similar syndromes in reports by multiple informants in many societies. Multicultural etic research has also revealed substantial similarity in the rank ordering of item ratings by similar informants across many societies. Furthermore, multicultural research has revealed broad distributions of problem scores that overlap among all societies, albeit with statistically significant differences between the mean scale scores from some societies.

To apply the results of multicultural research to assessment of individual children for research and clinical purposes, we have constructed multicultural norms as follows (Achenbach & Rescorla, 2007a, 2010):

1. For each instrument, such as the CBCL/6–18, we divided societies into those whose mean Total Problems scores were more than 1 *SD* below the *omnicultural mean* (the mean Total Problems score obtained by averaging the mean Total Problems scores for all available societies; Ellis & Kimmel, 1992); societies whose mean Total Problems scores were between –1 and +1 *SD* from the omnicultural mean; and societies whose mean Total Problems scores were more than 1 *SD* above the omnicultural mean.

2. We designated societies in the low group as Group 1, the middle group as Group 2, and the high group as Group 3.

3. We averaged the cumulative frequency distributions of scores for each scale from all the Group 1 societies to form a Group 1 cumulative frequency distribution for each scale. Likewise, we formed a Group 3 cumulative frequency distribution for each scale by averaging the cumulative frequency distributions for all the Group 3 societies. For Group 2, we used the cumulative frequency distribution for the U.S. national normative sample because the U.S. mean Total Problems score approximated the omnicultural mean and because the U.S. distribution had already been used in many published studies.

4. To construct Group 1 norms for each scale, we based normalized *T* scores on the cumulative frequency distribution that we had constructed by averaging the cumulative frequency distributions from all the Group 1 societies. We followed the same procedure to assign Group 3 *T* scores on the basis of the cumulative frequency distributions averaged from all the Group 3 societies. The Group 2 *T* scores were those previously assigned on the basis of the U.S. cumulative frequency distribution for each scale.

5. The Group 1, Group 2, and Group 3 norms were then incorporated into software for scoring all the problem scales from each form. Users can choose the Group 1, Group 2, or Group 3 norms for computing *T* scores and percentiles and for the profiles to be displayed for each form that is completed for a child, as explained in the following sections.

Applying Multicultural Norms for Natives of a Society

For children who live in the society where they were raised and where their parents were raised, scale scores from each kind of form can be displayed on a profile in relation to norms for that society. For example, scores from CBCLs and TRFs completed for a Japanese 13-year-old would be displayed on profiles in relation to Group 1 norms, because the mean CBCL and TRF Total Problems scores for the Japanese normative samples met criteria for Group 1, that is, they were more than 1 *SD* below the omnicultural mean for the CBCL and TRF. However, the scale scores obtained from the Japanese youth's YSR would be displayed on a profile in relation to Group 2 norms, because the mean YSR Total Problems score for the Japanese normative sample met criteria for Group 2, that is, it was between –1 and +1 *SD* from the omnicultural mean for the YSR. The elevation of scores on each problem scale would thus be standardized in relation to Japanese norms appropriate for each kind of informant, that is, Group 1 norms for the CBCL and TRF but Group 2 norms for the YSR.

Applying Multicultural Norms for Immigrants

For an immigrant parent who is not well acculturated to a host society, CBCL norms would typically be chosen on the basis of the parent's home society norm group. Suppose, for example, that a child's father came from a Group 3 society but the child's mother came from a Group 2 society. The user would typically elect to display the father's CBCL scale scores in relation to Group 3 norms and the mother's CBCL scale scores in relation to Group 2 norms. If the child attended school in a society where the TRF norms qualified for Group 1, the user would elect the Group 1 TRF norms. And if the child was moderately acculturated to the host society and completed the YSR, the user might elect to display the YSR scale scores in relation to the host society norms and also in relation to the parents' home societies' norms to see whether the YSR scores would reach clinical cutpoints according to any of the relevant norms. In this example, the relevant norms would include Group 3 for the father's CBCL, Group 2 for the mother's CBCL, and Group 1 for the TRF, plus the norms for whichever societies the user deemed appropriate for evaluating the YSR scores.

The options for displaying scale scores from each informant in relation to one or more sets of norms thus enable users to see whether decisions about needs for help would differ according to the different sets of norms. To make it easy for users to view scale scores from ratings by different informants in relation to norms appropriate for each informant, as well as in relation to norms for the child's age and gender, each of the side-by-side bar graphs of scale scores printed by the software is standardized in relation to the user's choice of Group 1, 2, or 3 norms. As an illustration, Figure 2.9

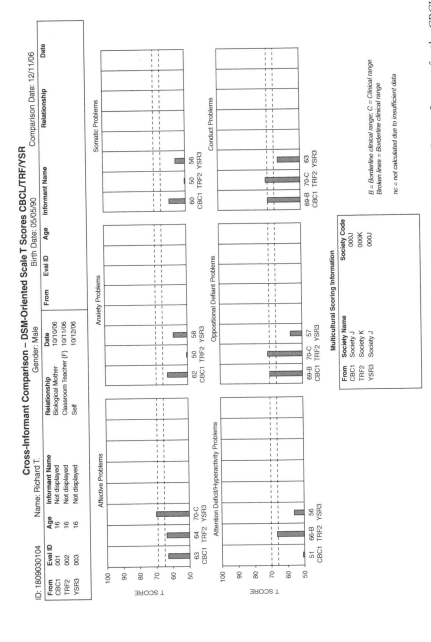

FIGURE 2.9. Cross-informant comparisons of Richard's scores on DSM-oriented scales in relation to Society J norms for the CBCL, Society K norms for the TRF, and Society J norms for the YSR. (From Achenbach & Rescorla, 2007a, p. 16. Reproduced by permission.)

displays bar graphs for DSM-oriented scale scores obtained by 16-year-old Richard in relation to CBCL and YSR norms for Richard's home society (Society J) and in relation to TRF norms for the host society (Society K), to which Richard's family had immigrated. The bars show that all three informants rated Richard in the normal range (below the bottom broken line) on the Anxiety Problems and Somatic Problems scales. However, only Richard's YSR yielded a score in the clinical range for Affective Problems and in the normal range for Oppositional Defiant Problems and Conduct Problems. Only the TRF yielded a score as high as the borderline clinical range for Attention Deficit/Hyperactivity Problems, suggesting that these problems were evident only in school. In relation to CBCL and YSR norms for Richard's home society and TRF norms for the host society, the user could thus see that Richard probably needed help with affective problems that were less salient to Richard's mother and teacher than to Richard. On the other hand, Richard probably also needed help with oppositional and conduct problems that were less salient to Richard than to his mother and teacher. According to the TRF, Richard might also need help with attention deficit hyperactivity problems in school.

Assessment of Parents and Other Adults

Although developmental research on psychopathology has focused mainly on the period from infancy through adolescence, it is important to extend such research to adulthood. Consequently, we have constructed empirically based collateral and self-report assessment instruments for ages 18 to 59 and 60 to 90+ (Achenbach, Newhouse, & Rescorla, 2004; Achenbach & Rescorla, 2003). Developmentally appropriate syndrome scales, DSM-oriented scales, and adaptive functioning scales have been constructed according to procedures analogous to those for ages 1.5 to 18. Representative U.S. national samples of adults have been used to obtain norms that are age, gender, and informant specific. Multicultural norms for ages 18 to 59 are also available for dozens of other societies (Achenbach & Rescorla, 2014).

The adult instruments are especially useful for evaluating relations between children's and parents' problems. Because the adult instruments have developmentally appropriate versions of many of the same items and scales as the child instruments, correlations and multivariate statistics can be used to test the correspondence between children and their parents on parallel item and scale scores, as well as the correspondence between their profile patterns. For clinical purposes, the adult instruments are used to assess parents of clinically referred children who are assessed with the

CBCL, TRF, and YSR. If deemed appropriate by the practitioner and if both parents consent, the practitioner can show the parents the profiles scored from the adult self-report instrument (Adult Self-Report; ASR) and from the adult collateral-report instrument completed by each parent to describe the other parent (the Adult Behavior Checklist; ABCL). Discrepancies between parents' ASR and ABCL profiles can be discussed to help the parents understand differences between informants' perspectives and how such differences might apply to differences between reports of their child's functioning.

With both parents' consent, the practitioner can also show them the profiles scored from the CBCL that each completed for their child. The CBCL profiles can be compared with the ASR and ABCL profiles to further illuminate the importance of informant perspectives and to identify similarities and differences between problems reported for the parents and for their child. For example, elevated scores on the Attention Problems syndrome might be found for one or both parents, as well as for their child. This would argue for interventions to ameliorate attention problems in the parent(s), as well as the child. On the other hand, differences between the kinds of problems reported for one or both parents and the child might be illuminating in other ways. For example, if the Aggressive Behavior syndrome score is elevated for one or both parents but the Anxious/Depressed syndrome score is elevated for the child, this would suggest that the child's problems might be responses to the aggressive behavior of the parent(s). The parental aggressive behavior may need to be ameliorated to help the child. After interventions for the child and/or parent(s) are implemented, the child and adult assessment instruments can be re-administered to assess the progress and outcomes of the interventions. Parallel assessment of parents and children can thus promote more effective family-based approaches to mental health services.

SUMMARY AND CONCLUSIONS

In his work on cognitive development, Piaget contrasted the *sagesse* (wisdom) sought by philosophers with *connaissance* (knowledge) based on empirical research. At the time when Piaget wrote of this distinction, views of psychopathology were dominated by clinical wisdom rather than empirically based knowledge. Since then, developmental psychopathology has emerged as a conceptual framework for integrating empirical research on development and its aberrations. An important component of this research has been the empirical identification of syndromes of co-occurring problems at various developmental levels, based on multiple sources of data. The empirically identified syndromes provide foundations for taxonomy of psychopathology and for the assessment of individuals in terms of that taxonomy. Empirically based assessment instruments make it possible to efficiently obtain multiple informants' ratings of children's problems in everyday contexts and to systematically compare different informants' ratings with respect to specific problem items, scale scores, and Q correlations between pairs of informants. Scale scores obtained from ratings by each informant are displayed on profiles in relation to age-, gender-, and informant-specific norms.

To expand the study and assessment of psychopathology beyond a handful of similar societies, standardized data from dozens of societies have been used to test syndromes, differences between scale scores, similarities in item ratings, and age and gender effects in meta-analytic ways. The findings reveal important similarities among very different societies but also differences that provide the basis for several sets of multicultural norms. The multicultural norms are incorporated into software that enables users to display children's scale scores in relation to norms for different societies as well as for different types of informants and the children's age and gender. This work enables researchers and clinicians in many societies to collaborate in advancing the developmental understanding of psychopathology beyond what might be found in one or a few societies.

REFERENCES

Achenbach, T. M. (1966). The classification of children's psychiatric symptoms: A factor-analytic study. *Psychological Monographs*, 80 (615).

(1974; 1982). *Developmental psychopathology*. New York, The Ronald Press; (2nd ed.) Wiley.

(2011). Commentary: Definitely more than measurement error: But how should we understand and deal with informant discrepancies? *Journal of Clinical Child and Adolescent Psychology*, 40, 80–86.

(2013). *DSM-oriented guide for the ASEBA*. Burlington: University of Vermont, Research Center for Children, Youth, & Families.

Achenbach, T. M., & Edelbrock, C. (1978). The classification of child psychopathology: A review and analysis of empirical efforts. *Psychological Bulletin*, 85, 1275–1301.

(1983). *Manual for the Child Behavior Checklist and Revised Child Behavior Profile*. Burlington: University of Vermont, Department of Psychiatry.

(1986). *Manual for the Teacher's Report Form and Teacher Version of the Child Behavior Profile*. Burlington: University of Vermont, Department of Psychiatry.

(1987). *Manual for the Youth Self-Report and Profile*. Burlington: University of Vermont, Department of Psychiatry.

Achenbach, T. M., Krukowski, R. A., Dumenci, L., & Ivanova, M. Y. (2005). Assessment of adult psychopathology: Meta-analyses and implications of cross-informant correlations. *Psychological Bulletin*, 131, 361–382.

Achenbach, T. M., & Lewis, M. (1971). A proposed model for clinical research and its application to encopresis and enuresis. *Journal of the American Academy of Child Psychiatry*, 10, 535–554.

Achenbach, T. M., McConaughy, S. H., & Howell, C. T. (1987). Child/adolescent behavioral and emotional problems: Implications of cross-informant correlations for situational specificity. *Psychological Bulletin*, 101, 213–232.

Achenbach, T. M., Newhouse, P. A., & Rescorla, L. A. (2004). *Manual for the ASEBA Older Adult Forms & Profiles*. Burlington: University of Vermont, Research Center for Children, Youth, and Families.

Achenbach, T. M., & Rescorla, L. A. (2000). *Manual for the ASEBA Preschool Forms & Profiles*. Burlington: University of Vermont, Research Center for Children, Youth, and Families.

(2001). *Manual for the ASEBA School-Age Forms & Profiles*. Burlington: University of Vermont, Research Center for Children, Youth, and Families.

(2003). *Manual for the ASEBA Adult Forms & Profiles*. Burlington: University of Vermont, Research Center for Children, Youth, and Families.

(2007a). *Multicultural supplement to the manual for the ASEBA School-Age Forms & Profiles*. Burlington: University of Vermont Research Center for Children, Youth, and Families.

(2007b). *Multicultural understanding of child and adolescent psychopathology: Implications for mental health assessment*. New York: Guilford Press.

(2010). *Multicultural supplement to the manual for the ASEBA Preschool Forms & Profiles*. Burlington: University of Vermont Research Center for Children, Youth, and Families.

(2014). *Multicultural supplement to the manual for the ASEBA Adult Forms & Profiles*. Burlington: University of Vermont Research Center for Children, Youth, and Families.

Achenbach, T. M., Rescorla, L. A., & Ivanova, M. Y. (2012). International epidemiology of child and adolescent psychopathology: 1. Diagnoses, dimensions, and conceptual issues. *Journal of the American Academy of Child and Adolescent Psychiatry*, 51, 1261–1272.

American Psychiatric Association. (1952). *Diagnostic and statistical manual of mental disorders* (1st ed.). Washington, DC: APA.

Bérubé, R. L., & Achenbach, T. M. (2014). *Bibliography of published studies using the Achenbach System of Empirically Based Assessment (ASEBA)*. Burlington: University of Vermont, Research Center for Children, Youth, and Families.

Borgatta, E. F., & Fanshel, D. (1965). *Behavioral characteristics of children known to psychiatric outpatient clinics*. New York: Child Welfare League of America.

Cicchetti, D., & Cohen, D. J. (Eds.). (1995, 2006). *Developmental psychopathology*. New York: Wiley.

Cohen, J. (1988). *Statistical power analysis for the behavioral sciences* (2nd ed.). New York: Academic Press.

De Los Reyes, A. (2011). Introduction to the special section. More than measurement error: Discovering meaning behind informant discrepancies in clinical assessments of children and adolescents. *Journal of Clinical Child and Adolescent Psychology*, 40, 1–9.

De Los Reyes, A., & Kazdin, A. E. (2005). Informant discrepancies in the assessment of childhood psychopathology: A critical review, theoretical framework, and recommendations for further study. *Psychological Bulletin*, 131, 483–509.

Dreger, R. M., Lewis, P. M., Rich, T. A., Miller, K. S., Reid, M. P., Overlade, D. C., et al. (1964). Behavioral classification project. *Journal of Consulting Psychology*, 28, 1–13.

Ellis, B. B., & Kimmel, H. D. (1992). Identification of unique cultural response patterns by means of item response theory. *Journal of Applied Psychology*, 77, 177–184.

Freud, A. (1974). A psychoanalytic view of developmental psychopathology. *Journal of the Philadelphia Association for Psychoanalysis*, 1, 7–17.

Google Scholar. (2014). Retrieved February 4.

Ivanova, M. Y., Achenbach, T. M., Dumenci, L., Rescorla, L. A., Almqvist, F., Weintraub, S., et al. (2007a). Testing the 8-syndrome structure of the CBCL in 30 societies. *Journal of Clinical Child and Adolescent Psychology*, 36, 405–417.

Ivanova, M. Y., Achenbach, T. M., Rescorla, L. A., Dumenci, L. Almqvist, F., Bathiche, M., et al. (2007b). Testing the Teacher's Report Form syndromes in 20 societies. *School Psychology Review*, 36, 468–483.

Ivanova, M. Y., Achenbach, T. M., Rescorla, L. A., Dumenci, L., Almqvist, F., Bilenberg, N., et al. (2007c). The generalizability of the Youth Self-Report syndrome structure in 23 societies. *Journal of Consulting and Clinical Psychology*, 75, 729–738.

Ivanova, M. Y., Achenbach, T. M., Rescorla, L. A., Harder, V. S., Ang, R. P., Bilenberg, N., et al. (2010). Preschool psychopathology reported by parents in 23 societies: Testing the seven-syndrome model of the Child Behavior Checklist for Ages 1.5–5. *Journal of the American Academy of Child & Adolescent Psychiatry*, 49, 1215–1224.

Ivanova, M. Y., Achenbach, T. M., Rescorla, L. A., Bilenberg, N., Dias, P., Dobrean, A., et al. (2011). Syndromes of preschool psychopathology reported by teachers and caregivers in 14 societies. *Journal of Early Childhood and Infant Psychology*, 7, 87–103.

Miller, L. C. (1967). Louisville Behavior Checklist for males, 6–12 years of age. *Psychological Reports*, 21, 885–896.

Piaget, J. (1965). *Sagesse et connaissance*. Paris: Presses Universitaires de France.
   (1971). *Insights and illusions of philosophy*. New York: World Publishing.

Pike, K. L. (1967). *Language in relation to a unified theory of the structure of human behavior*. The Hague: Mouton.

Quay, H. C. (1979). Classification. In H. C. Quay & J. S. Werry (Eds.), *Psychopathological disorders of childhood* (2nd ed., pp. 1–34). New York: Wiley.

Quay, H. C., Morse, W. C., & Cutler, R. L. (1966). Personality patterns of pupils in special classes for the emotionally disturbed. *Exceptional Children*, 32, 297–301.

Rescorla, L. A., Achenbach, T. M., Ginzburg, S., Ivanova, M. Y., Dumenci, L., Almqvist, F., et al. (2007a). Consistency of teacher-reported problems for students in 21 countries. *School Psychology Review*, 36, 91–110.

(2007b). Behavioral and emotional problems reported by parents of children ages 6 to 16 in 31 societies. *Journal of Emotional and Behavioral Disorders*, 15, 130–142.

(2007c). Epidemiological comparisons of problems and positive qualities reported by adolescents in 24 countries. *Journal of Consulting and Clinical Psychology*, 75, 351–358.

Rescorla, L. A., Achenbach, T. M., Ivanova, M. Y., Harder, V. S., Otten, L., Bilenberg, N., et al. (2011). International comparisons of behavioral and emotional problems in preschool children: Parents' reports from 24 societies. *Journal of Clinical Child and Adolescent Psychology*, 40, 456–467.

Rescorla, L. A., Achenbach, T. M., Ivanova, M. Y., Bilenberg, N., Bjarnadottir, G., Denner, S., et al. (2012). Behavioral/emotional problems of preschoolers: Caregiver/teacher reports from 15 societies. *Journal of Emotional and Behavioral Disorders*, 20, 68–81.

Rescorla, L. A., Ginzburg, S., Achenbach, T. M., Ivanova, M. Y., Almqvist, F., Bilenberg, N., et al. (2013). Cross-informant agreement between parent-reported and adolescent self-reported problems in 25 societies. *Journal of Clinical Child & Adolescent Psychology*, 42, 262–273.

Rutter, M., & Garmezy, N. (1983). Developmental psychopathology. In P. Mussen (Ed.), *Handbook of child psychology* (4th ed., Vol. 4, pp. 775–911). New York: Wiley.

Spivack, G., & Spotts, J. (1967). Adolescent symptomatology. *American Journal of Mental Deficiency*, 72, 74–95.

3

Cultural Perspectives on Shyness-Inhibition

XINYIN CHEN, SIMAN ZHAO, AND FAN YANG

Cultural context may be involved in human development through various processes such as facilitation and suppression of specific behaviors (Weisz, Weiss, Suwanlert, & Chaiyasit, 2006). Moreover, cultural norms and values provide guidance for social judgments and evaluations of behaviors and thus impart "meaning" to the behaviors (Chen & French, 2008). Whether and to what extent a behavior is considered a risk factor in development depend largely on cultural context (e.g., Benedict, 1934; Kleinman, 1980).

The arguments about the role of culture in normal and at-risk development, especially in socioemotional areas, are supported by findings from a number of cross-cultural projects that our research team and other researchers have conducted over the past decades. In this chapter, we focus on how culture is involved in shaping the development of one of the fundamental dimensions or aspects of socioemotional functioning: shyness-inhibition. We first discuss some conceptual issues in the study of culture and children's shyness-inhibition. Then we review research on the prevalence, functional meanings, and developmental patterns of shyness-inhibition among children in different cultures. In our discussion, we pay particular attention to how the macro-level social, economic, and cultural changes that are occurring in most countries in the world influence children's shyness-inhibition. The chapter concludes with a discussion of future directions in the field.

SHYNESS-INHIBITION: CONCEPTUAL ISSUES

Researchers have observed substantial individual differences in reactions to challenging social situations in childhood and adolescence (e.g., Asendorpf, 1991; Fox, Henderson, Marshall, Nichols, & Ghera, 2005; Kagan, 1997; Stevenson-Hinde, Shouldice, & Chicot, 2011). Some children are relaxed and display relatively little distress, but others tend to be vigilant, anxious, and wary. The term "behavioral inhibition" has been used to characterize individual differences in children's reactions to novel social and nonsocial situations (Garcia Coll, Kagan, & Reznick, 1984; Rubin, Hastings, Stewart, Henderson, & Chen, 1997; Schmidt & Buss, 2010). Whereas inhibition in infants is reflected mainly by their latency to approach novel objects or non-social stimuli, research on inhibition in older children is often focused on their reluctance to spontaneously interact with unfamiliar adults or peers in laboratory play sessions (e.g., Asendorpf, 1991). Inhibition of approach to unfamiliar peer situations represents an important form of inhibition from preschool ages to adolescence and is typically indicated by onlooker, unoc-cupied, and other anxious behaviors (e.g., watching others playing with-out joining in, whining, nail biting; e.g., Asendorpf, 1991; Rubin, Coplan, Fox, & Calkins, 1995). From a different perspective, researchers who study shyness as a personality trait, especially in adults, focus on the feelings of self-consciousness and anxiety in social interactions (e.g., Cheek & Buss, 1981; Eysenck & Eysenck, 1969). Asendorpf (1991) conceptualizes shyness as deriving from an internal conflict of approach and avoidance motiva-tions in social settings. According to Asendorpf (1991), shy children are interested in social interactions, but this approach motivation is hindered by vigilance, fear, and anxiety. Taken together, inhibition and shyness both seem to tap individual reactivity to stressful or challenging situations, with the former focusing on the dispositional characteristic in early childhood to be fearful when encountering unfamiliar social or nonsocial situations and the latter focusing on the anxious response to social novelty or per-ceived social evaluation (Coplan & Armer, 2007; Rubin, Coplan, & Bowker, 2009; Schmidt & Buss, 2010).

Based on the converging evidence for the conceptual and empirical overlap between inhibition and shyness and their similar behavioral mani-festations, Chen and colleagues (e.g., Chen & French, 2008; Chen, Rubin, & Li, 1995) use the term "shyness-inhibition" to refer to children's wary and anxious reactivity in stressful or challenging social situations. The integra-tive conceptualization allows for an understanding of the phenomenon at temperamental, behavioral, and social-judgmental levels and provides a framework for investigation of its developmental origins, processes, and outcomes using multiple methods (e.g., observation, self-report, and physi-ological assessment). Shyness-inhibition is related to reticence, anxious sol-itude, shyness-sensitivity, and some other constructs that researchers use to describe behaviors that indicate internal anxiety and fearfulness in social settings (e.g., Coplan & Armer, 2007; Gazelle & Ladd, 2003).

Nevertheless, the construct of shyness-inhibition is different from those representing social withdrawal such as unsociability or social disinterest (e.g., "would rather be alone"; Coplan & Armer, 2007). Unsociability is concerned with solitary behavior due to the lack of desire to interact with others. Unsociable children may possess object-oriented as opposed to people-oriented personalities and appear to be satisfied with playing alone without social interaction (Coplan, Prakash, O'Neil, & Armer, 2004). Distinction between shyness-inhibition and unsociability is important in cross-cultural research because they may be valued differently in different cultures. For example, in Western individualistic societies, unsociability or preference for solitude may be viewed as more normal than shyness-inhibition because the former is sometimes considered an expression of autonomous action and personal choice and beneficial to emotional health and performance on constructive tasks (e.g., Burger, 1995; Coplan et al., 2004; Leary, Herbst, & McCrary, 2003). In contrast, in some group-oriented cultures, shyness-inhibition may be viewed as acceptable, but unsociability or social disinterest is regarded as anticollective and abnormal and thus represents a risk factor in socioemotional development (Casiglia, Lo Coco, & Zappulla, 1998; Chen, Wang, & Cao, 2011; Valdivia, Schneider, Chavez, & Chen, 2005).

CULTURAL VALUES AND SHYNESS-INHIBITION: A CONTEXTUAL-DEVELOPMENTAL PERSPECTIVE

Behavioral patterns reflecting the construct of shyness-inhibition have been found in many countries such as Australia, China, Germany, Italy, Korea, Sweden, and the United States (e.g., Asendorpf, 1991; Broberg, Lamb, & Hwang, 1990; Chung, Rubin, Park, Yoon, & Doh, 2002; Heinrichs et al., 2006; Rapee, 2010; Wang, Chen, & Chen, 2003; Zappulla & Lo Coco, 2003). What is unclear is how culture affects the level of its exhibition and, more important, its functional meaning or adaptational significance. Chen and colleagues (e.g., Chen & French, 2008; Chen, Chung, & Hsiao, 2009) have recently proposed a contextual-developmental perspective on the relations between cultural values and the development of socioemotional characteristics and the role of the social interaction process in mediating the relations. According to this perspective, shy-inhibited behavior is derived from internal anxiety, leading to a low level of spontaneous social engagement, and, at the same time, adequate control to constrain behavioral and emotional reactivity toward self rather than others. Different values may be placed on social initiative and norm-based behavioral control in different cultures; as a result, shy-inhibited behavior may be evaluated differently across societies and communities. In Western individualistic societies in which acquiring independent and assertive social skills is an important socialization goal, social initiative is viewed as an indication of social competence. Consequently, the display of shy-inhibited behavior is perceived as socially immature, incompetent, and maladaptive (Greenfield, Suzuki, & Rothstein-Fisch, 2006; Rubin et al., 2009). In group-oriented societies, social initiative may not be highly appreciated because it does not have apparent positive effects on the harmony and well-being of the group. To maintain interpersonal and group harmony, individuals need to restrain personal desires to address the needs and interests of others (Chen & French, 2008; Triandis, 1995). As a result, shy-inhibited behavior may be positively valued because behavioral restraint and wariness that shy-inhibited children display are conducive to group functioning.

Cultural values may influence children's shyness-inhibition through the social interaction process (Chen, 2012). When children display shy-inhibited behavior in interactions, adults and peers may evaluate it in manners that are consistent with cultural beliefs and values in the society, community, or group. Adults and peers in different cultures may respond differently to this behavior and express different attitudes (e.g., acceptance, rejection) toward the children who display the behavior. To acquire social acceptance, children need to understand the expectations of others and maintain or modify their behavior according to the expectations. Thus, social evaluations and responses serve to regulate children's behavior and ultimately its developmental patterns. The extent to which children can maintain or modify their behaviors according to culturally directed social evaluations is associated with their adjustment outcomes. Children who are sensitive to social expectations and adjust their behaviors accordingly may obtain approval from others, which likely facilitates adaptive development. However, children who fail to modify their behaviors as directed by social evaluations may receive negative evaluations from others, which may elicit distress, frustrations, anger, and other adjustment problems.

THE DISPLAY OF SHYNESS-INHIBITION AMONG CHILDREN ACROSS CULTURES

Cross-cultural researchers have been interested in whether children in different societies display different social behaviors (e.g., Whiting & Edwards, 1988). Edwards (2000), for example, found that children in relatively traditional and agricultural communities (e.g., Kenya and India) scored lower on overall social engagement than children in more open communities (e.g.,

Okinawa and the United States) in which peer interactions were encouraged. Researchers have also found that relative to their Western counterparts, children in some non–Western societies such as Maya (Gaskins, 2000), Bedouin Arab (Ariel & Sever, 1980), Kenya, Mexico, and India (Edwards, 2000; Farver & Howes, 1993) are less likely to engage in sociodramatic activities that require control of social-evaluative anxiety.

Consistent with the cross-cultural research on children's assertive and self-expressive behaviors in social interactions, there is cumulative evidence that East Asian and North American children may differ in the display of shyness-inhibition in the early years (e.g., Farver & Howes, 1988; Kagan, Kearsley, & Zelazo, 1978). For example, Farver, Kim, and Lee (1995) found that compared with European American children, Korean American children displayed more shy and reticent behaviors, and Farver and Shin (1997) found that they also engaged in play with less fantastic and self-expressive themes (i.e., extraordinary actions performed by fantasy characters) and used less self-assertive communicative strategies. Similarly, Rubin et al. (2006) found that Korean and Chinese toddlers exhibited higher inhibition than Australian, Canadian, and Italian toddlers in stressful laboratory sessions. When the children were asked by a female experimenter to touch a scary toy robot, the Korean and Chinese, compared to the Australian, Canadian, and Italian children, were less likely to touch the toy and took longer to do so when they touched the toy. In an analysis of more specific shy-inhibited behavior of Chinese and Canadian children, Chen et al. (1998) found that in mother–child free play sessions, the Chinese toddlers stayed closer to their mothers and were more reluctant to explore the new environment. When the stranger entered the room, the Chinese toddlers displayed more anxious and fearful behavior, as indicated by their higher scores on the latency to approach the stranger and to touch the toys when they were invited to do so. The proportions of toddlers who physically contacted their mothers in the free play and stressful (stranger with toys) sessions in the Chinese sample were almost double those in the Canadian sample. These results indicated that Chinese toddlers were more shy, anxious, and reactive than their Canadian toddler peers.

In short, researchers have observed differences in the display of shy-inhibited behavior among children in different cultures. Cultural values may determine, in part, the display of shyness-inhibition in childhood and adolescence. To understand the processes in which cultural values are involved in the development of shyness-inhibition, it is necessary to examine social interactions, particularly adult and peer evaluations and responses during interactions, in different cultures.

CULTURALLY DIRECTED PARENT AND PEER
ATTITUDES AND RESPONSES

In most North American and Western European societies, parents typically react to children's shy-inhibited behavior with concern, disappointment, and negative emotions (Rubin et al., 2009). The negative attitudes and reactions are related to cultural values of social assertiveness and self-expression, which are reflected in parental socialization goals and practices. For example, Weisz et al. (1988) found that Thai parents appeared to perceive their children's shyness and other internalizing behaviors as less worrisome than did American parents. In a study of parental attitudes and toddlers' inhibition in Canada and China, Chen et al. (1998) found that child inhibition was positively associated with maternal rejection and punishment orientation in Canada. However, the trend was the opposite in China, as child inhibition was positively associated with maternal warm and accepting attitudes and negatively associated with maternal rejection. Positive parental attitudes toward shy-anxious behavior in children and adolescents were also found in China. For example, Chen, Rubin, and Li (1997) examined relations between parent–child relationships and social behaviors and problems in Chinese school-age children and found that children's shyness was associated with maternal acceptance. In a separate study with Chinese children, Chen, Dong, and Zhou (1997) found that shyness was negatively associated with paternal negative attitudes including rejection and power assertion in both boys and girls. Moreover, shyness was negatively associated with maternal negative attitudes in girls.

Cross-cultural differences are also evident in peer evaluations of and responses to children's shy-inhibited behaviors. For example, in a study conducted in the 1990s with groups of 4-year-old normal children, Chen, DeSouza, Chen, and Wang (2006) observed peer interaction in free play settings and found different peer attitudes in Beijing and Shanghai, China, and Southwest Ontario, Canada, toward children who displayed shy and inhibited behaviors. Specifically, relative to nonshy children, shy children in Canada who made passive and low-power social initiations received fewer positive responses and more rejection from peers. However, shy children in China who displayed the same behavior were more likely than others to receive positive responses. Thus, when shy children attempted to initiate social interaction, peers in Canada were more likely to overtly refuse, disagree, and intentionally ignore the initiation, whereas in China, peers tended to respond in a more positive manner by showing approval and support and by controlling their negative actions. The passive and low-power behaviors that were often displayed by shy children were seen by peers as incompetent in Canada but appropriate or desirable in China. In addition, whereas peers were more likely to make negative or high-power voluntary initiations (e.g., direct demands such as "Gimme that" or verbal teasing) to shy children than nonshy children in Canada, peers made similar voluntary initiations to shy and nonshy children in China. These findings suggest that peers are generally unreceptive and antagonistic in Canada but more supportive in China in their interactions with shy-inhibited children.

Cultural values are reflected in dynamic peer interactions as well as general peer attitudes such as acceptance and rejection. In Western societies, shyness-inhibition is associated with peer rejection or isolation; shy-inhibited children are more likely than others to experience difficulties in relationship with their peers (e.g., Rubin et al., 2009). Although research findings are not highly consistent with each other, the evidence indicates that shy children seem to experience fewer problems in peer acceptance in societies in which assertiveness and social initiative are not valued or encouraged. For example, Eisenberg, Pidada, and Liew (2001) found that shyness in Indonesian children was negatively associated with peer nominations of dislike. Similarly, Chen and colleagues found in the early 1990s that whereas shyness was associated with peer rejection in Canadian children, it was associated with peer acceptance in Chinese children (e.g., Chen et al., 1995). In traditional Chinese culture, shy-inhibited behavior is viewed as being associated with virtuous qualities such as modesty and cautiousness (e.g., Liang, 1987). The cultural values may serve as a basis for the social evaluation process in interaction and ultimately affect peer attitudes toward shy-inhibited children.

A more direct and quasi-experimental demonstration of the role of macro-level context in shaping social attitudes is research on the impact of economic and cultural changes on children's socioemotional functioning (Chen, Cen, Li, & He, 2005). For example, China has been changing dramatically since the 1980s toward a competitive market-oriented society, which has led to massive social changes such as increased variation in individual and family income, decline in government control of social welfare, and a rapid rise in competition (Zhang, 2000). Along with the economic reforms, Western individualistic beliefs and values have been gradually appreciated and accepted in the country, especially among the younger generation. Many schools in China have changed their education goals, policies, and practices to facilitate the development of assertive social skills and use a variety of strategies to help students learn these skills (e.g., encouraging students to engage in public debate and to propose their own plans about extracurricular activities). Relative to some other aspects of socioemotional functioning, shyness-inhibition appears to be particularly susceptible to the influence of social and cultural changes. Shy and wary behavior that impedes exploration and initiative taking in stressful situation is incompatible with the requirements of the competitive society. As a result, shyness-inhibition is no longer regarded as competent and is increasingly associated with negative social attitudes (Chang et al., 2005; Hart et al., 2000).

The implications of social change are illustrated in a study conducted by Chen et al. (2005) examining how shyness was associated with peer acceptance and rejection in urban China at different times of the societal transition. The researchers collected data on shyness and peer relationships in three cohorts (1990, 1998, and 2002) of elementary school children. The economic reform in China was initiated in some southern regions in the early 1980s, and the full-scale reform was expanded to major cities in the early 1990s. Whereas children in the 1990 cohort experienced relatively limited influence of the comprehensive reform, children in the 2002 cohort lived in a context in which increased competitiveness and assertiveness were required for adaptation and success. Compared with these cohorts, the 1998 cohort represented an intermediate phase, as children in this cohort might have been exposed to mixed views, values, and lifestyles in the society. Accordingly, Chen et al. (2005) found that shyness was positively associated with peer acceptance in the 1990 cohort but with peer rejection in the 2002 cohort, and both peer acceptance and peer rejection in the 1998 cohort. The analysis using the sociometric classification revealed that whereas shy children were more popular in the 1990 cohort and more rejected in the 2002 cohort than others, shy children in the 1998 cohort received mixed reports; they were both liked and disliked by peers. The ambivalent attitudes of peers toward shy-inhibited children in the 1998 cohort might reflect the conflict between imported Western values of initiative compatible with emerging economic pressures and traditional Chinese values of social wariness and behavioral restraint. These findings seem to indicate a continuous process in which social and historical transition in China influences peer attitudes.

SHYNESS-INHIBITION AND ADJUSTMENT FROM A CULTURAL PERSPECTIVE

The parental and peer attitudes and responses in specific cultures and historical time periods constitute social environments in which children develop, which are likely to result in particular experiences of shy-inhibited children in their social and psychological adjustment. The experiences may be reflected in the relations between shyness-inhibition and adjustment in social, school, and psychological areas.

Concurrent Relations Between Shyness-Inhibition and Adjustment

In Western, particularly North American, societies, shy-inhibited behavior has been found to be associated with difficulties in social, school, and psychological adjustment (e.g., Rubin et al., 2009). Findings from a variety of research programs have indicated that shy-inhibited children, particularly from middle childhood, tend to develop problems in social relationships and school performance (e.g., Asendorpf, 1991; Coplan et al., 2004; Gazelle & Ladd, 2003). When they realize their social difficulties, shy-inhibited children may develop negative self-perceptions and self-feelings and other psychological problems such as anxiety, loneliness, and depression (e.g., Coplan et al., 2004; Crozier, 1995; Kochanska & Radke-Yarrow, 1992; Prior, Smart, Sanson, & Oberklaid, 2000; Rubin, Chen, McDougall, Bowker, & McKinnon, 1995).

Compared with findings from North America, shyness seems to be associated with fewer adjustment problems among children in some Asian countries (Eisenberg et al., 2001). For example, Farver et al. (1995) found that shy and reticent behaviors in Korean children were in accord with cultural values that emphasize group harmony and the school expectation of proper behavior. Chen and colleagues (e.g., Chen, Dong, & Zhou, 1997; Chen, Rubin, & Sun, 1992) also found that shyness was associated with school competence and psychological well-being in the early 1990s in China. Unlike their North American counterparts, shy Chinese children were more likely than others to be rated as competent by teachers, perform well in academic areas, and obtain leadership status and distinguished studentship in the school. Moreover, shy children did not feel lonely or socially dissatisfied or develop negative perceptions of their competence (Chen et al., 2004). However, Chen and colleagues (Chen et al., 2005; Chen, Wang, & Wang, 2009) found that shyness was associated with increasing adjustment problems as China has become more competitive and individualistic during the economic reform. By the early part of the 21st century as the country became more deeply immersed in a market economy, shy-sensitive children, unlike their counterparts in the early 1990s, displayed social and school problems and reported high levels of depression.

There are substantial regional, particularly urban–rural, differences in social and economic development in China. The massive economic reform, such as the opening of stock markets, in China has been largely limited to urban centers and cities. Families in rural China have lived mostly agricultural lives, and rural children do not have as much exposure as urban children to the influence of the dramatic social transformation (Huang & Du, 2007; Li, 2006). In many rural areas, behavioral characteristics that are traditionally endorsed such as self-constraint are still highly valued, whereas the behavioral qualities that are considered important in competitive urban lives such as initiative taking are not endorsed or encouraged in social interactions (e.g., Fuligni & Zhang, 2004; Ming, 2008). Individual behaviors are still evaluated, to a large extent, according to the traditional standards, which may affect the experiences of rural shy-sensitive children. For example, Chen et al. (2011) found that shyness in rural Chinese children was associated with teacher-rated competence, academic achievement, and emotional well-being. Thus, shy rural children in China are still more likely than others to obtain social approval and achieve social and academic success. These results suggest that within-culture variations need to be taken into consideration in the study of the impact of social and cultural conditions and their change on children's behaviors, including shyness-inhibition.

Culture may influence shyness and its meaning in a complicated manner, as indicated by a study conducted by Chen and Tse (2008) among children in Canada with different backgrounds. The results of the study first indicated that Chinese Canadian children (Canadian-born and immigrant Chinese), particularly girls, were rated by others as more shy-inhibited in the school than children with a European background. Moreover, shyness was associated with peer rejection and victimization among European Canadian children, but not among Chinese Canadian children. Although the findings were similar to those found in China (e.g., Chen et al., 1992), Chen and Tse (2008) noted that the processes involved in the relations might be different because the cultural contexts were different between Canadian and Chinese schools. One possibility is that some traditional cultural practices affect socialization experiences of Chinese Canadian children in the family, which in turn help them develop skills to cope with adverse outcomes of their shy-inhibited behavior. Thus, Chinese children may develop relatively advanced regulatory skills in the early years due to family socialization (e.g., Chen et al., 2003; Sabbagh, Xu, Carlson, Moses, & Lee, 2006). These skills may allow them to express their shyness in a relatively acceptable manner. Another possibility is that the group stereotypic reputation (e.g., "Chinese are shy") reduces the pressure that individual shy-inhibited Chinese children face in their interactions with peers.

Developmental Outcomes of Shyness-Inhibition

Shyness-inhibition is considered a major risk factor in maladaptive development (Pennebaker, 1993). Based on longitudinal evidence, childhood shyness-inhibition in Western cultures appears to be associated with negative developmental outcomes (e.g., Asendorpf, Denissen, & van Aken, 2008; Caspi et al., 2003). For example, Schwartz, Snidman, and Kagan (1999) found in a sample of American children that early inhibition predicted later psychopathological symptoms such as social anxiety in adolescence. Similarly, Asendorpf et al. (2008) and Caspi, Elder, and Bem (1988) found that shy-inhibited children, particularly boys, in the United States and Germany developed extensive problems in adulthood such as delayed entry into marriage, parenthood, and stable career. Shy children in North America were also likely to obtain lower occupational achievement and experience greater occupational instability in adulthood. Similar results have been reported in other studies (e.g., Caspi, Moffitt, Newman, & Silva, 1996; Caspi et al., 2003; Gest, 1997).

Shyness-inhibition may be related to fewer negative outcomes in more group-oriented societies. In a sample of children born in a suburb of Stockholm in the mid-1950s, Kerr, Lambert, and Bem (1996) found that shyness was associated with delayed marriage and parenthood but did not affect adulthood careers, including occupational stability, education, or income among Swedish men. Kerr et al. (1996) suggested that due to the social welfare and support systems that evolved from the egalitarian values in Sweden, people did not need to display assertiveness and competitiveness to achieve career success.

Similar to the patterns among Kerr et al.'s (1996) Swedish children, shyness-inhibition in Chinese children has been found to predict positive developmental outcomes. Chen, Chen, Li, and Wang (2009) examined the relations between shyness-inhibition in toddlerhood and social and school outcomes in middle childhood in a Chinese sample. Behavioral inhibition data were collected through laboratory observations from a sample of 2-year-olds and follow-up data were collected 5 years later from multiple sources, including observations of free play peer interactions, interviews, teacher ratings, and school records. The findings indicated that early inhibition positively predicted later cooperative behavior, peer liking, social integration, positive school attitudes, and school competence. Behavioral inhibition also negatively predicted later learning problems. Further analyses revealed that the associations were mainly due to the differences between the highly inhibited children and the other children; the children who were shy-inhibited in toddlerhood were more competent in social and school performance and had fewer problems in middle childhood than the "average" and uninhibited children.

In a longitudinal study from middle childhood to early adolescence conducted in the 1990s in urban China, Chen, Rubin, Li, and Li (1999) assessed shyness using peer evaluations when the children were 8 and 10 years old and collected data on social, school, and psychological adjustment 4 years later from teacher ratings, self-reports, and school records. They found that shyness was not associated with later adjustment problems. Moreover, shyness was positively associated with adolescent adjustment, including teacher-assessed competence, leadership status, academic achievement, and self-perceptions of competence. These findings indicated that shy-inhibited Chinese children continued to be well adjusted in adolescence.

The longitudinal studies of Chinese children (e.g., Chen et al., 1999; Chen et al., 2009) were conducted from 1992 to 1999. It is unclear whether the developmental outcomes of shyness-inhibition are similar in China today. It is also unclear how the new requirements and norms associated with the historical change affected the adulthood adjustment of the shy-inhibited children who were generally adjusted in childhood and adolescence. Was social support that shy children and adolescents received in previous years beneficial to their adjustment in adulthood when social change occurred? Or did the positive experiences reinforce shy-inhibited behavior and impede the development of assertive and self-expressive skills and thus eventually undermine their later adjustment? We speculate that, in general, the early positive experiences may have provided children a basis to acquire competencies and skills to adapt to the changing environment and to effectively cope with new challenges. Moreover, the supportive social relationships they had already established likely constitute resources that continue to guide them to function appropriately in the evolving environment. In addition, some of the shy children, such as those who were able to develop effective coping skills, may have changed their behavior according to the new requirements and became more socially active and assertive during development. These adolescents would continue to be well adjusted in adulthood. However, those who maintained their shy-sensitive behavior in adulthood might develop social and psychological problems. Further research is clearly needed to address these questions.

In summary, findings from various projects suggest that shyness-inhibition in some cultures such as China, Indonesia, and Sweden does not necessarily lead to maladaptive outcomes as it does in North America. In group-oriented cultures, shy-inhibited children may receive social support, which enhances their confidence and ability to participate in social interactions and establish relationships. Social activities in which shy children participate, in turn, provide opportunities for them to learn skills and to display their behaviors according to cultural norms and expectations. Moreover, the relationships that shy-inhibited children form help them develop positive attitudes toward self and others and adjust socially and psychologically in the later years.

FUTURE DIRECTIONS

As one of the major socioemotional characteristics, shyness-inhibition plays a significant role in human development in various areas. Through socialization and social interaction processes, cultural context may affect the exhibition and functional significance of shyness-inhibition. There are several noticeable limitations in the study of shyness-inhibition. First, cultural influence on individual behaviors, particularly their functional meanings, is a highly complex issue that involves various situational and personal factors at multiple levels (Chen & French, 2008). Researchers of culture and shyness-inhibition have relied mostly on direct or indirect comparisons among groups in different societies. Although information about cross-cultural similarities and differences is useful in demonstrating that cultural context plays a role in development, this approach provides little information about the processes of cultural influence. Researchers need to investigate in the future the processes by which macro-level cultural context is involved in development, particularly the processes at the community and societal levels such as policy and social institutions, school atmospheres and practices, and common or shared lifestyles and goals, because how children with a particular behavioral profile are accepted by others and adjust to the environment may depend largely on the general attitudes toward the behavior in the group or community.

Second, shyness-inhibition is considered one of the aspects of social withdrawal (Rubin et al., 2009). It may provide more complete information to study shyness-inhibition along with other aspects such as unsociability or social disinterest and solitude or isolation due to peer rejection (e.g., Masten, Morison, & Pellegrini, 1985; Rubin et al., 2009) in different cultures. For example, unsociable or socially disinterested children are often regarded as being selfish and having negative attitudes toward the collective in group-oriented cultures. Indeed, unsociability has been found to be associated with social, school, and psychological problems in rural Chinese children (Chen et al., 2011). It will be interesting to investigate whether it is associated with less negative social evaluations and response when personal choice, autonomy, and individuality are more encouraged in the society.

Cross-cultural researchers have examined adults' and peers' attitudes and responses and children's shy-inhibited behavior. Little is known about how children perceive and understand this behavior in different cultures. To what extent children's perspectives are similar or different on shyness-inhibition across cultures and how cultural beliefs and values affect children's attitudes and judgments need to be investigated. A cross-cultural study of children's perspectives will help us further understand the mechanisms in which cultural context shapes the development of shyness-inhibition.

REFERENCES

Ariel, S., & Sever, I. (1980). Play in the desert and play in the town: On play activities of Bedouin Arab children. In H. B. Schwartzman (Ed.), *Play and culture* (pp. 164–175). West Point, NY: Leisure Press.

Asendorpf, J. B. (1991). Development of inhibited children's coping with unfamiliarity. *Child Development, 62,* 1460–1474.

Asendorpf, J. B., Denissen, J. J. A., & van Aken, M. A. G. (2008). Inhibited and aggressive preschool children at 23 years of age: Personality and social transition into adulthood. *Developmental Psychology, 44,* 997–1011.

Benedict, R. (1934). Anthropology and the abnormal. *Journal of General Psychology, 10,* 59–82.

Broberg, A., Lamb, M. E., & Hwang, P. (1990). Inhibition: Its stability and correlates in 16- to 40-month-old children. *Child Development, 61,* 1153–1163.

Burger, J. M. (1995). Individual difference in preference for solitude. *Journal of Research in Personality, 29,* 85–108.

Casiglia, A. C., Lo Coco, A., & Zappulla, C. (1998). Aspects of social reputation and peer relationships in Italian children: A cross-cultural perspective. *Developmental Psychology, 34,* 723–730.

Caspi, A., Elder, G. H., Jr., & Bem, D. J. (1988). Moving away from the world: Life-course patterns of shy children. *Developmental Psychology, 24,* 824–831.

Caspi, A., Harrington, H., Milne, B., Amell, J. W., Theodore, R. F., & Moffitt, T. E. (2003). Children's behavioral styles at age 3 are linked to their adult personality traits at age 26. *Journal of Personality, 71,* 495–513.

Caspi, A., Moffitt, T. E., Newman, D. L., & Silva, P. A. (1996). Behavioral observations at age 3 predict psychiatric disorders: Longitudinal evidence from a birth cohort. *Archives of General Psychiatry, 53,* 1033–1039.

Chang, L., Lei, L., Li, K. K., Liu, H., Guo, B., & Wang, Y. et al. (2005). Peer acceptance and self-perceptions of verbal and behavioral aggression and withdrawal. *International Journal of Behavioral Development, 29,* 49–57.

Cheek, J. M., & Buss, A. H. (1981). Shyness and sociability. *Journal of Personality and Social Psychology, 41,* 330–339.

Chen, X. (2012). Culture, peer interaction, and socioemotional development. *Child Development Perspectives, 6,* 27–34.

Chen, X., Cen, G., Li, D., & He, Y. (2005). Social functioning and adjustment in Chinese children: The imprint of historical time. *Child Development, 76,* 182–195.

Chen, X., Chen, H., Li, D., & Wang, L. (2009). Early childhood behavioral inhibition and social and school adjustment in Chinese children: A 5-year longitudinal study. *Child Development, 80,* 1692–1704.

Chen, X., Chung, J., & Hsiao, C. (2009). Peer interactions, relationships and groups from a cross-cultural perspective. In K. H. Rubin, W. Bukowski, & B. Laursen (Eds.), *Handbook of peer interactions, relationships, and groups* (pp. 432–451). New York: Guilford.

Chen, X., DeSouza, A., Chen, H., & Wang, L. (2006). Reticent behavior and experiences in peer interactions in Canadian and Chinese children. *Developmental Psychology, 42,* 656–665.

Chen, X., Dong, Q., & Zhou, H. (1997). Authoritative and authoritarian parenting practices and social and school adjustment. *International Journal of Behavioral Development, 20,* 855–873.

Chen, X., & French, D. (2008). Children's social competence in cultural context. *Annual Review of Psychology, 59,* 591–616.

Chen, X., Hastings, P., Rubin, K. H., Chen, H., Cen, G., & Stewart, S. L. (1998). Childrearing attitudes and behavioral inhibition in Chinese and Canadian toddlers: A cross-cultural study. *Developmental Psychology, 34,* 677–686.

Chen, X., He, Y., De Oliveira, A. M., Lo Coco, A., Zappulla, C., Kaspar, V. et al. (2004). Loneliness and social adaptation in Brazilian, Canadian, Chinese and Italian children. *Journal of Child Psychology and Psychiatry, 45,* 1373–1384.

Chen, X., Rubin, K. H., & Li, B. (1995). Social and school adjustment of shy and aggressive children in China. *Development and Psychopathology, 7,* 337–349.

   (1997). Maternal acceptance and social and school adjustment in Chinese children: A four-year longitudinal study. *Merrill-Palmer Quarterly: Journal of Developmental Psychology, 43,* 663–681.

Chen, X., Rubin, K. H., Li, B., & Li, Z. (1999). Adolescent outcomes of social functioning in Chinese children. *International Journal of Behavioural Development, 23,* 199–223.

Chen, X., Rubin, K. H., Liu, M., Chen, H., Wang, L., Li, D., Gao, X., Cen, G., Gu, H., & Li, B. (2003). Compliance in Chinese and Canadian toddlers. *International Journal of Behavioral Development, 27,* 428–436.

Chen, X., Rubin, K. H., & Sun, Y. (1992). Social reputation and peer relationships in Chinese and Canadian children: A cross-cultural study. *Child Development, 63,* 1336–1343.

Chen, X., & Tse, H. C. (2008). Social functioning and adjustment in Canadian-born children with Chinese and European backgrounds. *Developmental Psychology, 44,* 1184–1189.

Chen, X., Wang, L., & Cao, R. (2011). Shyness-sensitivity and unsociability in rural Chinese children: Relations with social, school, and psychological adjustment. *Child Development, 82,* 1531–1543.

Chen, X., Wang, L., & Wang, Z. (2009). Shyness-sensitivity and social, school, and psychological adjustment in rural migrant and urban children in China. *Child Development, 80,* 1499–1513.

Chung, O. B., Rubin, K., Park, S. Y., Yoon, C. H., & Doh, H. S. (2002). Temperament, parenting, and behavioral inhibition of Korean toddlers. *Korean Journal of Child Studies*, 23, 71–88.

Coplan, R. J., & Armer, M. (2007). A "multitude" of solitude: A closer look at social withdrawal and nonsocial play in early childhood. *Child Development Perspectives*, 1, 26–32.

Coplan, R. J., Prakash, K., O'Neil, K., & Armer, M. (2004). Do you "want" to play? Distinguishing between conflicted-shyness and social disinterest in early childhood. *Developmental Psychology*, 40, 244–258.

Crozier, W. R. (1995). Shyness and self-esteem in middle childhood. *British Journal of Educational Psychology*, 65, 85–95.

Edwards, C. P. (2000). Children's play in cross-cultural perspective: A new look at the six cultures study. *Cross-Cultural Research: The Journal of Comparative Social Science. Special Issue in Honor of Ruth H. Munroe: Part 1*, 34, 318–338.

Eisenberg, N., Pidada, S., & Liew, J. (2001). The relations of regulation and negative emotionality to Indonesian children's social functioning. *Child Development*, 72, 1747–1763.

Eysenck, H. J., & Eysenck, S. B. G. (1969). *Personality structure and measurement.* London: Routledge and Kegan Paul.

Farver, J. A. M., & Howes, C. (1988). Cultural differences in social interaction: A comparison of American and Indonesian children. *Journal of Cross-Cultural Psychology*, 19, 203–315.

Farver, J. A. M., & Howes, C. (1993). Cultural differences in American and Mexican mother child pretend play. *Merrill-Palmer Quarterly*, 39, 344–358.

Farver, J. A. M., Kim, Y. K., & Lee, Y. (1995). Cultural differences in Korean- and Anglo-American preschoolers' social interaction and play behaviors. *Child Development*, 66, 1088–1099.

Farver, J. A. M., & Shin, Y. L. (1997). Social pretend play in Korea- and Anglo-American preschoolers. *Child Development*, 68, 544–556.

Fox, H. A., Henderson, H. A., Marshall, P. J., Nichols, K. E., & Ghera, M. M. (2005). Behavioral inhibition: Linking biology and behavior within a developmental framework. *Annual Review of Psychology*, 56, 235–262.

Fuligni, A. J., & Zhang, W. X. (2004). Attitudes toward family obligation among adolescents in contemporary urban and rural China. *Child Development*, 74, 180–192.

Garcia-Coll, C., Kagan, J., & Reznick, J. S. (1984). Behavioral inhibition in young children. *Child Development*, 55, 1005–1019.

Gaskins, S. (2000). Children's daily activities in a Mayan village: A culturally grounded description. *Cross-Cultural Research*, 34, 375–389.

Gazelle, H., & Ladd, G. W. (2003). Anxious solitude and peer exclusion: A diathesis-stress model of internalizing trajectories in childhood. *Child Development*, 74, 257–278.

Gest, S. D. (1997). Behavioral inhibition: Stability and association with adaptation from childhood to early adulthood. *Journal of Personality and Social Psychology*, 72, 467–475.

Greenfield, P. M., Suzuki, L. K., & Rothstein-Fisch, C. (2006). Cultural pathways through human development. In K. A. Renninger & I. E. Sigel (Eds.),

Handbook of child psychology: Vol. 4. Child psychology in practice (pp. 655–699). New York: Wiley.

Hart, C. H., Yang, C., Nelson, L. J., Robinson, C. C., Olson, J. A., Nelson, D. A., Porter, C. L., Jin, S., Olson, S. F., & Wu, P. (2000). Peer acceptance in early childhood and subtypes of socially withdrawn behavior in China, Russia and the United States. *International Journal of Behavioral Development*, 24, 73–81.

Heinrichs, N., Rapee, R. M., Alden, L. A., Bogels, S., Hofmann, S. G., Oh, K. J., & Sakano, Y. (2006). Cultural differences in perceived social norms and social anxiety. *Behaviour Research and Therapy*, 44, 1187–1197.

Huang, A., & Du, X. (2007). Comparative analysis of urban-rural differences of family education in China. *Journal of Yibin University*, 1, 107–110.

Kagan, J. (1997). Temperament and the reactions to unfamiliarity. *Child Development*, 68, 139–143.

Kagan, J., Kearsley, R. B., & Zelazo, P. R. (1978). *Infancy: Its place in human development*. Cambridge, MA: Harvard University Press.

Kerr, M., Lambert, W. W., & Bem, D. J. (1996). Life course sequelae of childhood shyness in Sweden: Comparison with the United States. *Developmental Psychology*, 32, 1100–1105.

Kleinman, A. (1980). *Patients and healers in the context of culture: An exploration of the borderland between anthropology, medicine, and psychiatry*. Berkeley: University of California Press.

Kochanska, G., & Radke-Yarrow, M. (1992). Inhibition in toddlerhood and the dynamics of the child's interaction with an unfamiliar peer at age five. *Child Development*, 63, 325–335.

Leary, M. R., Herbst, K. C., & McCrary, F. (2003). Finding pleasure in solitary activities: Desire for aloneness or disinterest in social contact? *Personality and Individual Differences*, 35, 59–68.

Li, L. (2006). A study of home education styles in rural areas. *Research on Continuing Education*, 2, 95–97.

Liang, S. (1987). *The outline of Chinese culture*. Shanghai Normal University Press, Shanghai, China: Xue Lin.

Masten, A., Morison, P., & Pellegrini, D. (1985). A revised class play method of peer assessment. *Developmental Psychology*, 21, 523–533.

Ming, Z. (2008). A comparison of urban-rural family education. *Journal of Educational Institute of Jilin Province*, 24, 37–39.

Pennebaker, J. W. (1993). Overcoming inhibition: Rethinking the roles of personality, cognition, and social behaviors. In H. C. Traue & J. W. Pennebaker (Eds.), *Emotion, inhibition and health* (pp. 100–115). Kirkland, WA: Hogrefe & Huber Publishers.

Prior, M., Smart, D., Sanson, A., & Oberklaid, F. (2000). Does shy-inhibited temperament in childhood lead to anxiety problems in adolescence? *Journal of the American Academy of Child and Adolescent Psychiatry* 39, 461–468.

Rapee, R. M. (2010). Temperament and the etiology of social phobia. In K. H. Rubin & R. J. Roplan (Eds.), *The development of shyness and social withdrawal* (pp. 277–299). New York: Guilford Press.

Rubin, K. H., Chen, X., McDougall, P., Bowker, A., & McKinnon, J. (1995). The Waterloo Longitudinal Project: Predicting adolescent internalizing and externalizing problems from early and mid-childhood. *Development and Psychopathology*, 7, 751–764.

Rubin, K. H., Coplan, R. J., & Bowker, J. (2009). Social withdrawal in childhood. *Annual Review of Psychology*, 60, 141–171.

Rubin, K. H., Coplan, R. J., Fox, N. A., & Calkins, S. D. (1995). Emotionality, emotion regulation, and preschoolers' adaptation. *Development and Psychopathology*, 7, 49–62.

Rubin, K. H., Hastings, P. D., Stewart, S., Henderson, H. A., & Chen, X. (1997). The consistency and concomitants of inhibition: Some of the children, all of the time. *Child Development*, 68, 467–483.

Rubin, K.H., Hemphill, S.A., Chen, X., Hastings, P., Sanson, A., Lo Coco, A., et al. (2006). A cross-cultural study of behavioral inhibition in toddlers: East-west-north-south. *International Journal of Behavioral Development*, 30, 219–226.

Sabbagh, M. A., Xu, F., Carlson, S. M., Moses, L. J., & Lee, K. (2006). The development of executive functioning and theory of mind: A comparison of Chinese and U.S. preschoolers. *Psychological Science*, 17, 74–81.

Schmidt, L. A., & Buss, A. H. (2010). Understanding shyness: Four questions and four decades of research. In K. H. Rubin & R. J. Roplan (Eds.), *The development of shyness and social withdrawal* (pp. 23–41). New York: Guilford Press.

Schwartz, C. E., Snidman, N., & Kagan, J. (1999). Adolescent social anxiety as an outcome of inhibited temperament in childhood. *Journal of the American Academy of Child & Adolescent Psychiatry*, 38, 1008–1015.

Stevenson-Hinde, J., Shouldice, A., & Chicot, R. (2011). Maternal anxiety, behavioral inhibition, and attachment. *Attachment & Human Development*, 13, 199–215.

Triandis, H. C. (1995). *Individualism and collectivism*. Boulder, CO: Westview Press.

Valdivia, I. A., Schneider, B. H., Chavez, K. L., & Chen, X. (2005). Social withdrawal and maladjustment in a very group-oriented society. *International Journal of Behavioral Development*, 29, 219–228.

Wang, Z., Chen, H., & Chen, X. (2003). The stability of children's behavioral inhibition: A longitudinal study from two to four years of age. *Acta Psychologica Sinica*, 35, 93–100

Weisz, J. R., Suwanlert, S., Chaiyasit, W., Weiss, B., Walter, B. R., & Anderson, W. W. (1988). Thai and American perspectives on over- and undercontrolled child behavior problems: Exploring the threshold model among parents, teachers, and psychologists. *Journal of Consulting and Clinical Psychology*, 56, 601–609.

Weisz, J. R., Weiss, B., Suwanlert, S., & Chaiyasit, W. (2006). Culture and youth psychopathology: Testing the syndromal sensitivity model in Thai and American adolescents. *Journal of Consulting and Clinical Psychology*, 74, 1098–1107.

Whiting, B. B., & Edwards, C. P. (1988). *Children of different worlds*. Cambridge, MA: Harvard University Press.

Zappulla, C., & Lo Coco, A. (2003). Behavioral inhibition in preschool children. *Età Evolutiva*, 74, 21–32.

Zhang, W. W. (2000). *Transforming China: Economic reform and its political implications*. New York: St. Martin's Press.

4

A Sociocultural Analysis of High-Risk Native American Children in Schools

STEPHANIE A. FRYBERG AND PETER A. LEAVITT

Children characterized as "high risk" constitute one of the most formidable problems of the 21st-century educational system. By "high risk" we refer to children who are immersed in everyday realities characterized by issues such as child abuse, child poverty, teen suicide, teen drug abuse, high school dropout rates, unemployment, limited or no health insurance coverage, food insecurities, and income inequality (Institute for Innovation in Social Policy, 2010). In this chapter, we contend that high-risk Native American children underperform in school, in large part, because their relationship with education is fraught with social, cultural, and historical difficulties (e.g., cultural mismatches, discrimination, historical cycles of low expectations and underperformance) and because attempts to solve these issues have been largely reactive and limited in scope.

The difficulties Native American children experience in education, for example, are too often explained by mainstream, individualist explanations for underperformance. Native students are seen as either not motivated and/or cognitively less skilled, or their home and community contexts are viewed as not adequately fostering positive development. These simple cause-and-effect explanations ignore the fact that history is replete with examples of the ways in which inequality and racism toward Native Americans have been and continue to be fostered by mainstream cultural ideas and practices (Winant, 2004). The legacy of education in the United States, for instance, includes the forced removal of Native American children from their families and placement in government-run boarding schools (Adams, 1988, 1995), which has had a number of pernicious long-term effects on the adaptation of formal, mainstream education in tribal communities (Kawamoto, 2001; Lomawaima & McCarty, 2006).

At issue is not whether the problem lies in the individual Native American child or that the child is an overly deterministic product of history but rather that the lives of Native American children reflect a complicated web of social, cultural, and historical factors. Referring to and understanding the ways in which Native American children are high risk thereby requires a sociocultural approach, an understanding that the bidirectional and dynamic social, cultural, and historical factors shape and are shaped by everyday experiences and actions (Stephens, Markus, & Fryberg, 2012). The bidirectional nature of this approach has been referred to as *mutual constitution* (Adams, Anderson, & Adonu, 2004; Fiske, Kitayama, Markus, & Nisbett, 1998; Markus & Kitayama, 2003; Shweder, 1990). In one direction, individual actions and psychological tendencies (e.g., cognition, emotion, motivation) are influenced by the social and historical structures (e.g., material resources) of the contexts in which individuals participate over time. In the other direction, as individuals interact with their contexts, they play an active role in reinforcing or changing the structures of those contexts (Markus & Kitayama, 2010).

This approach is helpful for thinking about high-risk Native children because it recognizes that individual characteristics and social structural conditions indirectly influence behavior through the socioculturally shaped selves that people bring to a given situation and that inform how they make sense of that situation. These understandings of self allow individuals to make sense of their social worlds and to regulate their behavior (Markus, 2008; Markus & Kitayama, 2010; Oyserman & Markus, 1993). The term "socioculturally shaped" refers to the ways in which understandings of self are not characteristics of individuals but rather emerge in response to the contexts that people interact with in their everyday lives.

Take education as an example. Scholars have written for decades about the underachievement of Native American children. More than six decades ago, Kluckhohn and Leighton (1946/1974) wrote:

> If a teacher who has had great success in teaching White students does not get comparably good results with Navajo children, she thinks this is because the Indian children are less bright. As a matter of fact, the trouble is often that the incentives, which have worked beautifully to make White children bestir themselves, leave Navajo children cold, or even actively trouble and confuse them. For instance, the teacher holds out the hope of a college education with all that this implies for "getting on" in the White world; to at least the younger Navajo child, this means mainly a threat of being taken even further from home and country. (p. 315)

In most tribal communities, this quote would still apply today. The issue is not that Native American children are less bright but rather that we continue to utilize either an individual characteristics approach – to ask why Native children are unmotivated or seemingly have less cognitive ability – or a social structural conditions approach – to decry the social structural factors influencing tribal communities or bemoan the historical injustices imparted upon Native peoples. In this chapter, we offer an integrative socio-cultural approach to thinking about high-risk Native American students. Specifically, we will discuss risk and resilience factors influencing the every-day lives of Native American children more generally and their experiences in the classroom more specifically. Then we will provide evidence-based theories for rethinking how sociocultural contexts influence high-risk Native American children in schools.

RISK AND RESILIENCE FACTORS INFLUENCING NATIVE AMERICAN STUDENTS

When taking a sociocultural model of self-approach, the answer to what makes Native American children high risk is contingent on the social, cul-tural, and historical factors that influence everyday life. Like all students, Native American students bring to the classroom sets of frameworks – tacit assumptions and meanings – for understanding the social world (Resnick, 1994). These frameworks are based on social and developmental experi-ences that shape what it means to be a person in various contexts. In this section, we will address risk and resilience factors from two perspectives. First, we will address the risk and resilience factors contained within Native American contexts, and then we will address how such factors translate into the educational contexts in which Native children participate.

Risk and Resilience Factors Beyond Educational Contexts

While a broad social, cultural, and historical overview exceeds the scope of this chapter, we offer here a few examples of how past historical events contribute to generations of struggle for Native American peoples and how these historical events are reflected in risk and resilience factors that Native American people experience in their everyday lives and that play a role in the ongoing "high-risk" experience of Native American children.

Take as an example the forced removal from families and placement in government-run boarding schools of Native American children for more than 50 years (Adams, 1995). The boarding school experience shaped and continues to shape generations of Native people's attitudes toward formal education. Specifically, the experience created an atmosphere of distrust toward formal education that for many families and communities persists – in varying levels – today. The struggle hinges on whether "buying in" to mainstream educational systems equates to "selling out" cultural traditions and heritage. Although educators today may refute the notion that contemporary educational systems are designed to encourage Native American students to *be* or *act* "White," the reality is that the cultural norms embedded in mainstream educational contexts largely reflect middle-class, European American cultural contexts (Fryberg & Markus, 2007; Li, 2003) and, as a result, success requires adapting to these norms.

Another historical example involves land issues. One need not consider the fairness or appropriateness of reservations or allotted lands to see the role that the geographical segregation that accompanies living on reservations plays in both the preservation of heritage and traditions (LaFromboise, Albright, & Harris, 2010) and, given the under-resourcing of schools on reservations, the persistent achievement gaps (Bissell, 2004; Joffer & Wagner, 1996). For example, Bissell (2004) noted that because of poor infrastructure on some reservations, telephone, cable, and Internet services are much more limited than in urban areas. For example, in 2010, just over half of Native American families reported having Internet access at home and a quarter did not have Internet access at all (Bureau of Census, 2012), the lowest proportion of any ethnic group. In addition, living on a reservation restricts access to some economic opportunities. For instance, some Native Americans head to more urban areas to increase the breadth and financial viability of employment opportunities and then return to the reservation later in life to be closer to family and friends (Joffer & Wagner, 1996). To change these realities requires acknowledging the barriers created by the Western system of reservations and to provide Native communities the educational and social resources to maintain their heritage and traditions and to systematically bridge the academic achievement gap. In fact, research reveals that the preservation of native cultures, languages, and tribal identities provides psychological resources that buffer Native Americans from discrimination and cultural biases (Adams et al., 2006; Demmert, 2005) and increases the likelihood that they will find success in contexts outside their tribal communities.

In addition to historical factors, the contemporary social conditions influencing Native American contexts also play a significant role in Native people's everyday experiences more generally and in their educational experiences more specifically. We will highlight the social conditions by focusing on some of the traditional indicators – poverty rates, income, employment – of social status and success. According to the U.S. Census Bureau, Native

Americans are one of the most impoverished ethnic groups in the United States. In 2009, more than a quarter (27.3%) of Native American individuals and one fifth (22.7%) of Native families lived below the poverty line, which in both cases is approximately double the national average (Bureau of Census, 2012). The median annual income for Native American families in 2009 was $40,552, while the national average was $61,082 (Bureau of Census, 2012). Moreover, in 2009, approximately 11% of Native families lived with an income in the lowest range, $10,000 or less, as compared to only 5% of the general population (Bureau of Census, 2012). Put simply, while there is considerable variation from one tribal community to another, Native Americans in general make less money than the average American.

Income level and poverty are also closely tied to employment outcomes. In 2010, Native Americans had an unemployment rate of 15.2% compared to 9.1% for Whites (Austin, 2010). From 2007 to 2010, the increase in the unemployment rate for Natives was 1.6 times greater than the increase for Whites (Austin, 2010). Furthermore, since unemployment rates refer only to those who are looking for work, it can be helpful to look at employment to population ratio. In the first half of 2010, 51.5% of all Natives were employed compared to 59.3% of Whites (Austin, 2010). While simply being employed is important, the relative quality of one's employment is another important aspect of one's sociocultural context. Only 26% of Native Americans 16 years and older work in management or professional occupations compared to 36% of the general population (Bureau of Census, 2012). In sum, in terms of both the numbers of persons who are employed and the types of positions they occupy, Native Americans seem to be underemployed and working in lower-status jobs compared to the general population.

Poverty rates, income, and employment also influence other life outcomes, such as education and health care. According to the U.S. Census Bureau, in 2009, 76.4% of Native Americans 25 years and older had at least a high school diploma and 13.0% had a bachelor's degree or higher (Bureau of Census, 2012). These figures are significantly lower than the general population, 85.3% and 27.9%, respectively, and are only higher than the figures for Hispanics/Latinos, 60.9% and 12.6%, respectively (Bureau of Census, 2012). Research suggests, however, that these trends may be changing as college enrollment rates for Native Americans are increasing at a faster rate than Native population growth (Bureau of Census, 2012).

When it comes to health care, according to the National Center for Health Statistics, compared to the national average of 18%, nearly half (44%) of Native Americans under age 65 are uninsured (Adams, Martinez, Vickerie, & Kirzinger, 2011). Census data from 2009 also show change show to shows that a greater proportion of Native Americans (21.7%) than Whites (15.1%) do not see health care professionals at all in a 12-month period (Bureau of Census, 2012). In addition to poor involvement in the health care system, Native Americans are also among the least likely ethnic groups to engage in physical exercise, with 49.2% reporting no leisure-time physical activity compared to 34.6% for Whites (Bureau of Census, 2012). One consequence is that approximately 39% of Native Americans are obese, compared to a national average of 27% (Schiller, Lucas, Ward, & Peregoy, 2012). In sum, the data reveal that some of the social institutions in which Americans place so much value and confidence are greatly underutilized by Native Americans.

Other factors influencing Native American sociocultural contexts include a rate of drug and alcohol abuse that is nearly double the national average: 18% of Native American adults in 2008 needed treatment compared to a national average of 9.6% (Substance Abuse and Mental Health Services Administration, 2010). Substance abuse seems to play a role in a host of other social issues. For example, Native Americans comprise about 1% of the population of the United States but comprise 1.9% of people in adult correctional facilities (Bureau of Census, 2012) and 2% of children in foster care (Austin, 2009; Hill, 2007). Native Americans also have higher-than-average suicide rates; from 1999 to 2004, Native American males had a suicide rate of 27.99 per 100,000 compared to Whites, whose suicide rate was 17.54 per 100,000 (Suicide Prevention Resource Center, 2011), and in 2007, suicide accounted for 2.7% of Native deaths, higher than any other ethnic group (Bureau of Census, 2012). The high suicide rates are not only associated with drug and alcohol abuse but rather are due to a loss of traditional cultural values, spurned by government efforts (i.e., forced assimilation of Native children in boarding schools and laws forbidding the practice of traditional ceremonies) and manifested through fragmented families and the lack of traditional cultural activities (LaFromboise & Lewis, 2008). For many of these statistics, the cost to Native children can be inferred, but there is also evidence of direct costs to children as well. For example, Native children experience a higher rate of child abuse (16.5 per 1,000 Native children) compared to White children (10.8 per 1,000; Austin, 2009).

While these sociocultural contexts include a variety of risks and barriers for Native American children that are largely absent from the lives of many other American children, these contexts also proffer a variety of resilience factors that are also not available to other children. Native American children, for instance, often turn to extended family and cultural and spiritual practices as sources of strength and resilience (Belcourt-Ditloff, 2006; Goodluck, 2002; LaFromboise, Hoyt, Oliver, & Whitbeck, 2006). As a result, many

Native American children have been raised in culture-rich environments, with sets of ideas, values, and practices that provide children a clear sense of belonging and identity (i.e., what it means to be a person in that context). LaFromboise and colleagues (2006) found, for example, that perceived community support, a supportive mother, and a high degree of engagement in one's culture were all predictive of prosocial outcomes in Native adolescents. Similarly, Belcourt-Ditloff (2006) showed that social support, hope, and traditional cultural practices were associated with less unpleasant affect and psychological distress in Native Americans, and Mmari, Blum, and Teufel-Shone (2010) found that a supportive relationship with a parent and knowing the tribal language were associated with less juvenile delinquency. The point here is that Native Americans have at their disposal a variety of positive sources from which they can gain resilience.

Risk and Resilience Factors Within Educational Contexts

Having looked at the broader sociocultural context that many Native Americans inhabit and the relevant risk and resilience factors, we now shift to how these contexts influence Native children in the course of their education and what role culture-specific resilience factors play in helping them overcome these obstacles.

Due in large part to the lack of early childhood education and the preponderance of economic and social struggles, when the average Native American child begins school, the outcomes are already bleaker than they are for the average American child. When they enter kindergarten, for instance, they are already further behind in reading, mathematics, and fine motor skills than other children (Snyder & Dillow, 2011). As a result, compared to other ethnic groups, Native children (11%) between the ages of 3 and 17 are more likely to be identified as having a learning disability and as needing special education intervention services (Bureau of Census, 2012). Native American children not only begin school at a disadvantage relative to their peers, but the evidence suggests that they continue to struggle throughout their educational experiences.

The economic and social factors manifest in higher-than-average dropout rates, suspension rates, juvenile delinquency, and absences from school (Bureau of Census, 2012; Devoe & Darling-Churchill, 2008; U.S. Commission on Civil Rights, 2003). For example, in the 12 states with the largest populations of Native American students, fewer than 50% of Native American students graduate from high school while 71.4% of all students graduate (Faircloth & Tippeconic, 2010). The Office of Juvenile Justice and

Delinquency Prevention reports that despite comprising 1% of the population, Native American juveniles are involved in 1.5% of the juvenile court cases (Puzzanchera & Kang, 2011). These outcomes do not constitute a snapshot of one generation of Native students but rather reflect a history of distrust stemming, in large part, from the physical and social abuses experienced during the boarding school era (late 1800s to the mid-1900s) that have been passed down from one generation to the next (i.e., intergenerational trauma; Adams, 1995; Smith, 2005) and the lack of cultural fit for Native American students in mainstream educational institutions (Fryberg, Covarrubias, & Burack, 2013; Fryberg & Markus, 2007; LaFromboise et al., 2006).

As we consider the sociocultural factors that influence Native American students, the school environment itself certainly merits attention. In 2009, 16.5% of Native American high school students, from all kinds of high schools, reported being threatened or injured with a weapon on school property, compared to a national average of 7.7% (Bureau of Census, 2012). School demographics also play a role. Schools in which Native American students make up more than 25% of total enrollment reported more serious problems with absenteeism, tardiness, low family involvement, and low expectations than schools in which Natives make up less than 25% of total enrollment (Devoe & Darling-Churchill, 2008). One school environment factor that may contribute to these outcomes involves the available (or not-so-available) social representations (i.e., ideas and images) regarding school belonging and the belief that Native American students can be successful in education. For instance, Native American students rarely see members of their group represented as primary or secondary teachers (.5% are Native American), as college students (1% are Native American), or as professors (.5% are Native American; Coopersmith, 2009; Snyder, Dillow, & Hoffman, 2009). There has also been, historically, a deficiency in accurate and relevant curriculum for Native American students (Almeida, 1996; Lomawaima & McCarty, 2006). The lack of self-relevant representations in education may subtly convey to Native students that educational contexts are not places for people like them (Fryberg & Townsend, 2008; Gay & Howard, 2000; Ladson-Billings, 1995b; 1996).

Beyond these risk factors, Native American students also draw from various resilience factors related to how they understand themselves and the cultures they inhabit to help them achieve positive educational outcomes. First, Native American students have been shown to hold more interdependent understandings of self (i.e., to place more emphasis on interconnectedness with family and community) as compared to middle-class European Americans, who maintain more independent understandings of self (i.e., understandings of self as separate from others and from the social context). This interdependent view of the self serves as a resilience factor on its own. For Native American students, the more interdependent they feel, the more they trust their teachers and the better grades they achieve (Fryberg et al., 2013; Fryberg & Markus, 2003, 2007; LaFromboise et al., 2006).

Continuing this line of thought, if a Native student has an interdependent view of the self, it suggests that one's culture and community are essential for achieving positive outcomes. Involvement in traditional culture, for example, is positively related to academic achievement for Native American students (Deyhle & Margonis, 1995; Gonzales, Knight, Birman, & Sirolli, 2004). Deyhle (1992, 1995) found that students from more traditional Navajo homes performed better at school than students from less traditional homes. Akee and Yazzie-Mintz (2011) revealed that Native American college students who were exposed to Native cultural activities as children and who spent more time with elders in the community attained higher levels of education. Guillory and Wolverton (2008) identified several cultural factors – including family support, giving back to tribal community, and on-campus social support – that positively influenced persistence for Native American college students. Finally, Guevremont and Kohen (2012) observed that language is another feature of traditional culture that influences education outcomes. Specifically, speaking an Aboriginal language was positively associated with school outcomes for Native Canadian children aged 6 to 14. Note, while Guevremont and Kohen (2012) highlighted the importance of traditional language, another study showed that in 2007, nearly half of Native students in the United States reported never speaking a traditional language at home (Devoe & Darling-Churchill, 2008). This suggests that while language is a resilience factor, in many communities it also symbolizes a loss of culture and tradition dating back to the boarding school era.

In addition to understandings of self and of one's traditional culture, research also reveals that identifying positively with mainstream culture (i.e., being bicultural) yields a variety of protective factors. LaFromboise, Albright, and Harris (2010) found that biculturally competent Native American adolescents and those who lived on a reservation felt more hopeful than those who were not biculturally competent and those who lived in rural or urban nonreservation areas. Similarly, Oyserman, Kemmelmeier, Fryberg, Brosh, and Hart-Johnson (2003) found that Native students who positively incorporate both Native and White culture into their identities demonstrate greater persistence on academic tasks than Native American students who positively identify with one culture or who do not identify (i.e., they are aschematic) with either culture.

The risk factors reveal that Native American students face a variety of obstacles in education but that culture can play an important role in helping them to overcome these obstacles. In fact, the data suggest that Native American students may not "succeed" at the rate of their peers, in part because education is experienced as a place that is "not for me." They are not represented in prominent roles (i.e., as teachers, administrators) nor do they experience the everyday school context as self-relevant. By the same token, the data suggest that Native American students who succeed draw strength from their cultural backgrounds – by knowing who they are and understanding what constitutes the good or right way to be a person in their own culture and in mainstream contexts. These self-understandings buffer them from many of the negative factors (i.e., discrimination, cultural bias, distrusting relationships) that have been historically present in school contexts and that continue to plague schools today. In the next section, we will discuss evidence-based theories or interventions that offer a starting point for addressing the obstacles Native American students confront in schools and for positively building on the strengths that these students bring to the classroom.

RETHINKING HIGH-RISK NATIVE AMERICAN CHILDREN

A sociocultural approach has much to offer high-risk Native American children. For starters, the model provides a social and cultural grounding of psychology. The discipline of psychology often presumes that the methods and theories reflect deeply embedded, natural features of the human psyche that transcend cultural and historical contexts. These presumed universals are viewed as noncontextual and as such ignore the important role that situations and social contexts play in people's everyday experiences. A sociocultural approach attends to the ways in which both the social issues and features of traditional culture are context-specific factors that importantly reflect and shape the social realities of individuals who inhabit those contexts (Duran & Duran, 1995; Greenfield, 1997; Smith, 1999).

As such, a sociocultural approach locates presumed "deficiencies" outside individual minds and *in* the interactions between the individual and the social and cultural worlds that they inhabit (Fryberg, 2012). The integration of both individual and social structural factors gives complexity to indigenous issues. For instance, within a tribe, a Native American may self-identify as a member of a clan or as a member of a particular tribe; among non–Natives, the person may identify as a Native American, American Indian, or "Indian;" and outside the country, he or she may identify as an

"American" (Trimble, 2000). Engaging Indigenous identities in a given context affords Native people a true sense of the complexities of who they are as contemporary people.

Moreover, the approach challenges mainstream interpretations of historical events (e.g., framing Columbus Day as a commemoration of genocide rather than a celebration of "discovery"; Nagel, 1996; Yellow Bird, 2004) and provides opportunities to redefine individual manifestations of distress in terms of intergenerational rather than individual trauma (Duran & Duran, 1995). The linking of individual psychological tendencies and behaviors to the context gives breadth to the content associated with different understandings of self and may ultimately yield positive psychological resources (i.e., self-esteem; Adams et al., 2006) that help individual Native Americans cope with everyday life, particularly if the individual moves between Native and non–Native contexts.

In the classroom, this approach also integrates individual and social structural factors. For instance, efforts to close the achievement or opportunity gap focus on everything from eliminating negative stereotypes and low expectancies of underrepresented racial-ethnic minority students to enhancing understandings of cultural differences. A sociocultural approach contends that when the school environment is free from negative or limiting stereotypes (Davies, Spencer, & Steele, 2005; Fryberg & Townsend, 2008; Markus, Steele, & Steele, 2000) and the curriculum is perceived as self-relevant (Gay, 2004; Ladson-Billings, 1995a; Maehr, 2008), students will feel identity safety – they will perceive school as a place they belong (i.e., school is "for me") and can be successful (Purdie-Vaughns, Steele, Davies, Ditlmann, & Crosby, 2008).

By acknowledging the powerful role that school contexts can play in individual educational experiences, we legitimate the difficulties Native American students face in education. At issue is not whether Native American students are motivated but whether the school may be conveying subtle cues about belonging and the potential to succeed that ultimately undermine academic performance (Cohen, Garcia, Apfel, & Master, 2006; Stephens, Fryberg, Markus, Johnson, & Covarrubias, 2012; Walton & Cohen, 2007).

For instance, Stephens and colleagues (2012) found that a simple reframing of the college environment serves to alleviate the underperformance of first-generation college students whose parents do not have 4-year college degrees. Specifically, over the first 2 years of college, they found that when students' goals "match," as they did for continuing-generation students, whose parents have 4-year college degrees, they performed better in school (i.e., higher grades) than when they did "not match," as was the case for

first-generation college students. Then, to reduce the performance disparity between first-generation and continuing-generation college students,
Stephens and colleagues provided a culture-relevant message that subtly
framed the university context as more interdependent. The small change
in framing alleviated the discrepancies in performance between these two
groups.

The situation for high-risk Native American students is much the same.
They bring to the classroom tacit frameworks for understanding the world
that highlight their own historical, social, and cultural realities (Resnick,
1994). That is, if they grew up in a home in which their grandparent was
forcibly removed to a boarding school or in which a parent dropped out
because of prejudice and discrimination, then they arrive at the classroom with some meaningful distrust for the school environment. These
frameworks of understanding have been referred to as "cultural models"
(D'Andrade, 1981, 1995; Holland & Quinn, 1987; Shore, 1996; Sperber, 1985),
but in school contexts, Fryberg and Markus (2007, p. 237) coined the term
"cultural models of education."

These models of education refer to the patterns of ideas and practices
that are implicit in education contexts (i.e., who is a good student, the
purpose of getting an education, and the nature of the teacher–student
relationship) and thus serve to challenge the "neutrality" of mainstream
educational contexts. For example, Stephens and colleagues (2012) found
that university administrators endorsed the notion that college students
should be independent; they should ascribe to a view of the self as separate
from others and from the social context. This view of self has been termed
the *independent* representation of self (Markus & Kitayama, 2010; Markus,
Mullally, & Kitayama, 1997).

In classrooms that reflect and foster independent representations of self,
being a learner is equated to becoming an independent thinker (Bellah
et al., 1985; Bruner, 1996; Greenfield, Trumbull, & Keller, 2006; Greenfield,
Trumbull, & Rothstein-Fisch, 2003; Tharp, 1994). Students should be indi-
vidually motivated, engage their own sense of individuality, strive to differentiate themselves from others, and take responsibility for their choices and
actions (Plaut & Markus, 2005; Tobin, Wu, & Davidson, 1989).

In contrast, East Asian, Latino, Native American, and African cultural
contexts foster an interdependent view of the self, an understanding of the
self as fundamentally connected and responsive to the needs and expectations of close others and of the surrounding contexts (Markus & Kitayama,
2003). In classrooms that foster interdependence, the process of learning
is a social project that occurs largely in interactions with others (Boykin

et al., 2005; Escalante & Dirmann, 1990; Greenfield et al., 2003; Tobin et al., 1989; Trumbull, Rothstein-Fisch, & Greenfield, 2000). Similarly, individual motivation and achievement are positively influenced by role models, mentorship, strong connections to the community, and trusting relationships with teachers (Cole, Matheson, & Anisman, 2007; Cummins, 1992; Deyhle & Margonis, 1995; Fryberg et al., 2013; Fryberg & Markus, 2007; Gloria & Kurpius, 2001). For example, as the theory of independent and interdependent representations of self would predict, independent representation of self positively predicted grades for European American high school students, whereas trust for teachers and interdependent representations of self positively predicted grades for Native American students (Fryberg et al., 2013).

Although the interdependent representation of self has a presence in mainstream educational contexts, its frequent relegation to the "other" model has a variety of consequential implications for psychological well-being and academic success. Cultural mismatch theory (Stephens et al., 2012), for instance, revealed that mainstream educational contexts often reflect the pervasive middle-class norms of independence and that the effect of the educational context on students depends, in large part, on the implicit cultural frameworks or models of self that students bring with them to the learning environment. Specifically, students were advantaged when they experienced a cultural match between their own norms and the norms represented in the educational context but were disadvantaged when they experienced a cultural mismatch. The extent to which students experience a match or mismatch depends not only on cues in the immediate situation (e.g., the classroom) but also on the norms that were typically included or valued in the larger educational context.

According to cultural mismatch theory, when high-risk Native students interact with the school context, they are often asked to act and relate in ways that feel foreign to them; the context does not match their individual models of self. This experience conveys to them that they do not belong and cannot be successful in that context. If we then factor in other features associated with being "high risk" (e.g., child abuse, child poverty, teen suicide, teen drug abuse, high school dropout rates, unemployment, limited or no health insurance coverage, food insecurities, and income inequality; Institute for Innovation in Social Policy, 2010), we begin to see that what is often construed as cognitive or motivational "deficits" may merely be a result of a long list of factors that convey to high-risk Native American children that students like them do not belong and cannot be successful in educational contexts. By including other ways of being as viable (i.e., by creating more opportunities for "cultural matches"), educators can do more to legitimate the experiences of high-risk Native American students in the classroom.

Beyond facing educational contexts that do not cohere with Native American students' cultural frameworks for getting an education or with their own understandings of what it means to be a "good" person or self, Native students also face a severe lack of contemporary representations or role models in education. A sociocultural approach suggests that providing such representations is not as simple as providing role models but rather requires carefully attending to and challenging the implicit and explicit messages about education that exist in the social contexts that students inhabit. For example, one cannot simply reject the notion that education is a tool used to assimilate Natives into White culture and/or that getting an education is a "White thing to do" (Fordham & Ogbu, 1986), but rather educators must challenge these ideas with culture-relevant messages. Fryberg et al. (2013), for instance, conducted a study in which Native American middle school students were shown a picture of either an European American college student role model with an independent message (i.e., "Getting an education will benefit you in the future"), a Native American college student role model with the same independent message, a Native American college student role model with an interdependent message (i.e., "Getting an education will benefit your tribe in the future"), or no role model/message control condition. The Native American college student role model was intended to challenge the notions that getting an education is a "White thing to do" and that Natives are not and cannot be successful in school, whereas the message that "getting an education is good for your tribe" was intended to confront the belief that education is a tool used to assimilate Natives into White culture.

The studies revealed that challenging the prevalent social messages about education with inclusive culture-relevant messages increased motivation for Native American students. Specifically, Native students who were exposed to the Native American role model with an interdependent message (benefit your tribe) reported greater motivation than Native students exposed to the European American or Native American role model with the independent message (benefit you). The results revealed that a simple reframing of education countered preconceived notions and reaffirmed the self-relevancy of education.

Finally, a sociocultural approach to creating positive learning environments for high-risk Native American students importantly involves attending to how Native American students think about themselves as students and how others, such as teachers, think about them. Native American students, much like other racial-ethnic minorities in the United States, have had to contend with negative stereotypes about their group as having "less innate mental ability" than White students (Mihesuah, 1996; Steele, 1997). This particular ideology is representative of the persistent debate about the under-performance of racial-ethnic minority students (Gould, 1996; Herrnstein & Murray, 1994), which centers on whether the "achievement gap" is the result of cognitive deficiencies (Herrnstein & Murray, 1994; Jensen, 1969; Manly et al., 2002; Rushton & Jensen, 2005) or the inability of educational institutions to teach racial-ethnic minority students (Banks, 2006; Gay & Howard, 2000; Ladson-Billings, 1995a, 1996). One issue in attempting to clarify this debate is that innate ability and environmental or cultural factors cannot be measured independent of one another (Heaton, Ryan, & Grant, 2009). For example, the most basic neurological tests (i.e., circle drawing, finger tapping, motor skills) are quite sensitive to social and cultural factors (Ardila, 2005; Arnold et al., 1994). Thus, changing sociocultural factors (i.e., quality of education) can greatly improve mental ability (Krohn & Lamp, 1989; Manly et al., 2002; Vincent, 1991) and thereby reduce the achievement gap (Cohen et al., 2006; Flores, 2007; McKown & Weinstein, 2008).

Moreover, in contrast to the fixed nature of innate mental ability, the malleability of environmental and cultural factors affords researchers and school professionals optimism that changing learning environments can positively influence academic performance. For example, students with a growth mindset (i.e., belief that intelligence can grow with effort) respond to negative feedback by increasing effort, whereas students with a fixed mindset (i.e., belief that intelligence is fixed and cannot grow with effort) respond to negative feedback by decreasing effort (Dweck, 2006; Kamins & Dweck, 1999). Building on this work, Covarrubias, Fryberg, Dweck, and Pauker (2013) examined the impact of growth and fixed mindsets on academic self-views (i.e., understandings of self as student) and grades (i.e., official report cards in math, reading, and writing) for Native American elementary school students (grades K-2). They found that a growth mindset positively predicted grades for these students, and that this relationship was mediated or explained by positive academic self-views. That is, the more students endorsed a growth mindset, the more they personally endorsed or saw as self-relevant academic attributes, which, in turn, led to better grades at the end of the year. Thus, the relationship between growth mindset and academic performance was explained by changes in Native students' academic self-views. They then replicated these findings with Native American 3rd through 5th graders at two different elementary schools and with Native American middle school students (6th through 8th grade).

These studies suggests that teaching Native American students about the malleability of their brains (i.e., instilling a growth mindset) can undermine negative stereotypes about intelligence and ultimately change the attitudes and expectations of school administrators, teachers, and students alike. This is one example of how learning environments can be changed to explicitly contend with the social, cultural, and historical factors influencing main-stream educational contexts. Moreover, a growth mindset has been shown to benefit everyone, so there are no adverse effects of implementing such an approach broadly. All students are viewed as having the potential to learn and succeed. As we rethink high-risk Native American students, we can utilize growth mindset ideologies and practices as a means of creating identity-safe learning environments or more specifically schools and class-rooms in which all Native students feel they belong and can be successful (Markus et al., 2000; Purdie-Vaughns et al., 2008).

In theory, all students can benefit from identity-safe contexts, but given the underperformance of Native American students, innovative strategies are needed to lessen the achievement gap. Learning contexts can be changed to optimize academic performance by holistically addressing the social, cultural, and historical factors influencing education for Native American students. This means actively attending to and confronting the institutional values and practices that subtly convey who belongs and who does not, the prevalent ideas and beliefs held by Native American students and others in their families and communities about the purpose of education, and the everyday realities of Native students both in and out of school. If we do not develop learning environments that address all of these factors, then, as the saying goes, "If you always do what you've always done, you'll always get what you've always got." In other words, we will fail to disrupt the cycle of underperformance that has been plaguing high-risk Native American students and their families for generations.

CONCLUSION

Understanding high-risk Native American children begins with acknowl-edging the pervasiveness of social inequality for all historically underrep-resented and underserved groups in American society and thereby the fact that the unequal attainment of these groups more generally and of Native American children more specifically is not a coincidence. When we overlook the historical, social, and cultural factors that shape how children under-stand themselves, others, and their social worlds, we presume a "one size fits all" school will work for all. Yet, as Kluckholn and Leighton (1946/1974) taught us decades ago, "the trouble is often that the incentives, which have worked beautifully to make White children bestir themselves, leave Navajo children cold, or even actively trouble and confuse them." Native American children do not approach education with the same cultural framework that White children do.

A sociocultural approach suggests that what will disrupt or break the cycle of underperformance is 1) a meaningful recognition and incorporation of the historical events impacting the educational experience for Native students, 2) an acknowledgment that history is replete with examples of historical injustices that feed the social inequity that Native people experience in their everyday lives, and 3) a sincere belief that all children, including high-risk Native American children, have the potential to learn and succeed. Researchers and theoreticians alike have been examining the protective or resilience factors that help high-risk Native students overcome the many barriers before them. Educators, for instance, could harness the protective effects of social support, connectedness, culture- and self-relevancy, traditional knowledge, and the collective will to succeed that exists within Native communities. Unfortunately, these factors are too often overlooked by the dominant ideologies and beliefs that pervade mainstream educational contexts in the United States.

The benefit of a sociocultural approach is that small changes can have big effects (e.g., see Cohen et al., 2006; Stephens et al., 2011; Walton & Cohen, 2007). Whether normalizing Native American students' experiences or simply reframing the cultural context, giving Native students a reason to believe that the school context is "for them" can have huge effects on their school experience and performance. If educators couple these small interventions with an acknowledgment that the personal and cultural beliefs Native students hold are viable ways of being a person, then the outcomes may be exponentially greater. At the end of the day, educators cannot change everything for high-risk Native students, but they can begin the process of disrupting the cycle of underperformance and thus helping these students chart a new course for themselves and for future generations of Native American students.

REFERENCES

Adams, D. W. (1988). Fundamental considerations: The deep meaning of Native American schooling, 1880–1900. *Harvard Educational Review*, 58(1), 1–28.
  (1995). *Education for extinction: American Indians and the boarding school experience 1875–1928*. Lawrence: University Press of Kansas.
Adams, G., Anderson, S. L., & Adonu, J. K. (2004). The cultural grounding of closeness and intimacy. In D. J. Mashek & A. Aron (Eds.), *Handbook of closeness and intimacy* (pp. 321–339). Mahwah, NJ: Erlbaum.

Adams, G., Fryberg, S. A., Garcia, D. M., & Delgado-Torres, E. U. (2006). The psychology of engagement with Indigenous identities: A cultural perspective. *Cultural Diversity and Ethnic Minority Psychology*, 12, 493–508.

Adams, P. F., Martinez, M. E., Vickerie, J. L., & Kirzinger, W. K. (2011). Summary health statistics for the U.S. population: National Health Interview Survey, 2010. National Center for Health Statistics. *Vital and Health Statistics*, 10(251), 1–126.

Akee, R. Q., & Yazzie-Mintz, T. (2011). "Counting experience" among the least counted: The role of cultural and community engagement on educational outcomes for American Indian, Alaska Native, and Native Hawaiian students. *American Indian Culture and Research Journal*, 35(3), 119–150.

Almeida, D. A. (1996). Countering prejudice against American Indians and Alaska Natives through antibias curriculum and instruction. *ERIC Digest* ED400146. Retrieved from http://www.eric.ed.gov/PDFS/ED400146.pdf

Ardila, A. (2005). Cultural values underlying psychometric cognitive testing. *Neuropsychology Review*, 15, 185–195.

Arnold, B. R., Montgomery, G. T., Castaneda, I., & Longoria, R. (1994). Acculturation and performance of Hispanics on selected Halstead-Reitan neuropsychological tests. *Assessment*, 1, 239–248.

Austin, A. (2010). Different race, different recession: American Indian unemployment in 2010. *EPI Issue Brief*, 289.

Austin, L. (2009). Serving Native American children in foster care. *The Connection*. Winter 2009, 6–11.

Banks, J. (2006). *Cultural diversity and education: Foundations, curriculum and teaching* (5th ed.). Boston, MA: Pearson, Allyn & Bacon.

Belcourt-Ditloff, A. E. (2006). Resiliency and risk in Native American communities: A culturally informed investigation. (Doctoral dissertation). *Retrieved from ProQuest. (3244363).*

Bellah, R. N., Madsen, R., Sullivan, W. M., Swidler, A., & Tipton, S. M. (1985). *Habits of the heart: Individualism and commitment in American life* (pp. 142–153). New York: Harper Row.

Bissell, T. (2004). The digital divide dilemma: Preserving Native American culture while increasing access to information technology on reservations. *Journal of Law, Technology, & Policy*, 2004(1), 129–150.

Boykin, A. W., Albury, A., Tyler, K., Hurley, E., Bailey, C. T., & Miller, O. A. (2005). Culture-based perceptions of academic achievement among low-income elementary students. *Cultural Diversity and Ethnic Minority Psychology*, 11, 339–350.

Bruner, J. (1996). *The culture of education*. Cambridge, MA: Harvard University Press.

Bureau of Census. (2012). *Statistical abstract of the U.S., 2012: social statistics.* Retrieved from http://web.lexisnexis.com/statuniv

Cohen, G. L., Garcia, J., Apfel, N., & Master, A. (2006). Reducing the racial achievement gap: A social-psychological intervention. *Science*, 313, 1307–1310.

Cole, B., Matheson, K., & Anisman, H. (2007). The moderating role of ethnic identity and social support on relations between well-being and academic performance. *Journal of Applied Social Psychology*, 37, 592–615.

Coopersmith, J. (2009). *Characteristics of public, private, and Bureau of Indian Education elementary and secondary school teachers in the United States: Results from the 2007–08 Schools and Staffing Survey. First Look. NCES 2009–324.* National Center for Education Statistics.

Covarrubias, R., Fryberg, S., Dweck, C., & Pauker, K. (2013). *To be fixed or growth? Students' mindsets impact classroom behavior, academic self-views and performance.* Newark: University of Delaware Press.

Cummins, J. (1992). The empowerment of Indian students. In J. Reyhner (Ed.), *Teaching American Indian students* (pp. 3–12). Norman: University of Oklahoma Press.

D'Andrade, R. (1981). The cultural part of cognition. *Cognitive Science, 5,* 179–195.
   (1995). *The development of cognitive anthropology.* Cambridge, MA: Cambridge University Press.

Davies, P., Spencer, S., & Steele, C. (2005). Clearing the air: Identity safety moderates the effects of stereotype threat on women's leadership aspirations. *Journal of Personality and Social Psychology, 88,* 276–287.

Demmert, W. G. (2005). The influences of culture on learning and assessment among Native American students. *Learning Disabilities Research & Practice, 20*(1), 16–23.

DeVoe, J. F., & Darling-Churchill, K. E. (2008). *Status and trends in the education of American Indians and Alaska Natives: 2008* (NCES 2008–084). Washington, DC: National Center for Education Statistics, Institute of Education Sciences, U.S. Department of Education.

Deyhle, D. (1992). Constructing failure and maintaining cultural identity: Navajo and Ute school leavers. *Journal of American Indian Education, 31,* 24–47.
   (1995). Navajo youth and Anglo racism: Cultural integrity and resistance. *Harvard Educational Review, 65,* 403–444.

Deyhle, D., & Margonis, F. (1995). Navajo mothers and daughters: Schools, jobs, and the family. *Anthropology & Education Quarterly, 26,* 135–167.

Duran, E., & Duran, B. (1995). *Native American postcolonial psychology.* Albany: SUNY Press.

Dweck, C. S. (2006). *Mindset.* New York: Random House.

Escalante, J., & Dirmann, J. (1990). The Jaime Escalante math program. *Journal of Negro Education, 59,* 407–423.

Faircloth, S. C., & Tippeconic, J. W., III. (2010). *The dropout/graduation crisis among American Indian and Alaska Native students: Failure to respond places the future of Native peoples at risk.* Published report in collaboration with the Civil Rights Project at UCLA and the Center for the Study of Leadership in American Indian Education at Pennsylvania State University. Retrieved from http://civilrightsproject.ucla.edu/research/k-12-education/school-dropouts/the-dropout-graduation-crisis-among-american-indian-and-alaska-native-students-failure-to-respond-places-the-future-of-native-peoples-at-risk/faircloth-tippeconnic-native-american-dropouts.pdf.

Fiske, A. P., Kitayama, S., Markus, H. R., & Nisbett, R. (1998). The cultural matrix of social psychology. In D. Gilbert, S. Fiske, & G. Lindzey (Eds.), *Handbook of social psychology* (pp. 915–981). New York: McGraw-Hill.

Flores, A. (2007). Examining disparities in mathematics education: Achievement gap or opportunity gap. *The High School Journal*, 91(1), 29–42.

Fordham, S., & Ogbu, J. U. (1986). Black students' school success: Coping with the "burden of 'acting White.'" *The Urban Review*, 18(3), 176–206.

Fryberg, S. A. (2012). Cultural psychology as a bridge between anthropology and cognitive science. *Topics in Cognitive Science*, 4, 437–444.

Fryberg, S. A., Covarrubias, R., & Burack, J. (2013). Cultural models of education and academic performance for Native American and European American students, *School Psychology International*, 34(4), 439–452.

Fryberg, S. A., & Markus, H. R. (2003). On being American Indian: Current and possible selves. *Journal of Self and Identity*, 2, 325–344.

(2007). Cultural models of education in American Indian, Asian American, and European American contexts. *Social Psychology of Education*, 10, 213–246.

Fryberg, S. A., & Townsend, S. M. (2008). The psychology of invisibility. In G. Adams, M. Biernat, N. Branscombe, C. Crandall, & L. Wrightsman (Eds.), *Commemorating Brown: The social psychology of racism and discrimination* (pp. 173–193). Washington, DC: American Psychological Association.

Gay, G. (2004). Beyond brown: Promoting equality through multicultural education. *Journal of Curriculum and Supervision*, 19, 193–216.

Gay, G., & Howard, T. C. (2000). Multicultural teacher education for the 21st century. *The Teacher Educator*, 36, 1–16.

Gloria, A. M., & Kurpius, S. E. R. (2001). Influences of self-beliefs, social support, and comfort in the university environment on the academic nonpersistence decisions of American Indian undergraduates. *Cultural Diversity and Ethnic Minority Psychology*, 7, 88–102.

Gonzales, N. A., Knight, G. P., Birman, D., & Sirolli, A. A. (2004). Acculturation and enculturation among Latino youth. In M. Kenneth, C. Schellenback, et al., *Investing in children, youth, families, and communities: Strengths-based research and policy* (pp. 285–302). Washington, DC: American Psychological Association.

Goodluck, C. (2002). *Native American children and youth well-being indicators: A strengths perspective*. Seattle, WA; Flagstaff: Casey Family Programs; Northern Arizona University Press.

Gould, S. (1996). *The mismeasure of man*. New York: Norton.

Greenfield, P. M. (1997). You can't take it with you: Why ability assessments don't cross cultures. *American Psychologist*, 52, 1115–1124.

Greenfield, P. M., Trumbull, E. T., & Keller, H. (2006). Cultural conceptions of learning and development. In P. A. Alexander & P. H. Winne (Eds.), *Handbook of educational psychology* (pp. 675–692). Mahwah, NJ: Lawrence Erlbaum Associates Publishers.

Greenfield, P. M., Trumbull, E. T., & Rothstein-Fisch, C. (2003). Bridging cultures. *Cross-Cultural Psychology Bulletin*, 37, 6–16.

Guevremont, A., & Kohen, D. E. (2012). Knowledge of an aboriginal language and school outcomes for children and adults. *International Journal of Bilingual Education and Bilingualism*, 15(1), 1–27.

Guillory, R. M., & Wolverton, M. (2008). It's about family: Native American student persistence in higher education. *Journal of Higher Education*, 79(1), 58–87.

Heaton, R. K., Ryan, L., & Grant, I. (2009). Demographic influences and use of demographically corrected norms in neuropsychological assessment. In I. Grant & K. M. Adams (Eds.), *Neuropsychological assessment of neuropsychiatric disorders* (pp. 127–158), New York: Oxford University Press.

Herrnstein, R. J., & Murray, C. (1994). *The bell curve*. New York: Free Press.

Hill, R. B. (2007). *An analysis of racial/ethnic disproportionality and disparity at the national, state, and county levels.* Center for the Study of Social Policy. Available from http://www.aecf.org/KnowledgeCenter.aspx.

Holland, D., & Quinn, N. (Eds.). (1987). *Cultural models in language and thought.* New York: Cambridge University Press.

Institute for Innovation in Social Policy. (2010). *The index of social health.* Institute for Innovation in Social Policy, Vassar College. Poughkeepsie, NY. Retrieved from http://iisp.vassar.edu/ish.html

Jensen, A. R. (1969). How much can we boost IQ and scholastic achievement? *Harvard Educational Review, 39,* 1–123.

Joffer, P. A., & Wagner, M. K. (1996). Native American return migration to reservation areas. *Great Plains Sociologist, 9*(1), 57–71.

Kamins, M., & Dweck, C. (1999). Person versus process praise and criticism: Implications for contingent self-worth and coping. *Developmental Psychology, 36,* 835–847.

Kawamoto, W. T. (2001). Community mental health and family issues in sociohistorical context. *American Behavioral Scientist, 44,* 1482–1491.

Kluckhohn, C., & Leighton, D. (1946/1974). *The Navajo* (rev. ed.). Cambridge, MA: Harvard University Press.

Krohn, E. J., & Lamp, R. E. (1989). Concurrent validity of the Stanford-Binet fourth edition and K-ABC for Head Start children. *Journal of School Psychology, 27*(1), 59–67.

Ladson-Billings, G. J. (1995a). But that's just good teaching! The case for culturally relevant pedagogy. *Theory into Practice, 34,* 159–165.

Ladson-Billings, G. J. (1995b). Toward a theory of culturally relevant pedagogy. *American Education Research Journal, 35,* 465–491.

Ladson-Billings, G. J. (1996). Silences as weapons: Challenges of a black professor teaching white students. *Theory into Practice, 35,* 79–85.

LaFromboise, T. D., Albright, K., & Harris, A. (2010). Patterns of hopelessness among American Indian adolescents: Relationships by levels of acculturation and residence. *Cultural Diversity and Ethnic Minority Psychology, 16,* 68–76.

LaFromboise, T. D., Hoyt, D., Oliver, L., & Whitbeck, L. (2006). Family, community, and influences on resilience among American Indian adolescents in the upper Midwest. *Journal of Community Psychology, 34,* 193–209.

LaFromboise, T. D., & Lewis, H. A. (2008). The Zuni Life Skills Development Program: A school/community-based suicide prevention intervention. *Suicide and Life-Threatening Behavior, 38*(3), 343–353.

Li, J. (2003). U.S. and Chinese cultural beliefs about learning. *Journal of Educational Psychology, 95*(2), 258–267.

Lomawaima, K. T., & McCarty, T. L. (2006). *To remain an Indian: Lessons in democracy from a century of Native American education.* New York: Teachers College Press.

Maehr, M. (2008). Culture and achievement motivation. *International Journal of Psychology*, 43, 917–918.

Manly, J. J., Jacobs, D. M., Touradji, P., Small, S. S., & Stern, Y. (2002). Reading level attenuates differences in neuropsychological test performance between African American and White elders. *Journal of the International Neuropsychological Association*, 8, 341–348.

Markus, H. R. (2008). Identity matters: Ethnicity, race, and the American dream. In R. Shweder, M. Minow, & H. R. Markus (Eds.), *Just schools: Pursuing equal education in societies of difference*. New York: Russell Sage Foundation.

Markus, H. R., & Kitayama, S. (2003). Culture, self, and the reality of the social. *Psychological Inquiry*, 14, 277–283.

   (2010). Cultures and selves: A cycle of mutual constitution. *Perspectives on Psychological Science*, 5, 420–430.

Markus, H. R., Mullally, P., & Kitayama, S. (1997). Selfways: Diversity in modes of cultural participation. In U. Neisser & D. Jopling (Eds.), *The conceptual self in context: Culture, experience, self-understanding* (pp. 13–61). New York: Cambridge University Press.

Markus, H. R., Steele, C. M., & Steele, D. M. (2000). Colorblindness as a barrier to inclusion: Assimilation and nonimmigrant minorities. *Daedalus*, 129, 233–259.

McKown, C., & Weinstein, R. (2008). Teacher expectations, classroom context, and the achievement gap. *Journal of School Psychology*, 46(3), 235–261.

Mihesuah, D. A. (1996). *American Indians: Stereotypes and realities*. Atlanta, GA: Clarity Press.

Mmari, K. N., Blum, R. W., & Teufel-Shone, N. (2010). What increases risk and protection for delinquent behaviors among American Indian youth? Findings from three tribal communities. *Youth & Society*, 41(3), 382–413.

Nagel, J. (1996). *American Indian ethnic renewal: Red power and the resurgence of identity and culture*. New York: Oxford University Press.

Oyserman, D., Kemmelmeier, M., Fryberg, S., Brosh, H., & Hart-Johnson, T. (2003). Racial-ethnic self-schemas [Special issue]. *Social Psychology Quarterly*, 66, 333–347.

Oyserman, D., & Markus, H. R. (1993). The sociocultural self. In J. Suls & A. Pratkanis (Eds.), *Psychological perspectives on the self Vol. 4* (pp. 187–220). Hillsdale, NJ: Erlbaum.

Plaut, V. C., & Markus, H. R. (2005). The "inside" story: A cultural-historical analysis of being smart and motivated, American style. In A. J. Elliot & C. S. Dweck (Eds.), *Handbook of competence and motivation* (pp. 457–488). New York: Guilford Press.

Purdie-Vaughns, V., Steele, C. M., Davies, P. G., Ditlmann, R., & Crosby, J. R. (2008). Social identity contingencies: How diversity cues signal threat or safety for African Americans in mainstream institutions. *Journal of Personality and Social Psychology*, 94(4), 615–630.

Puzzanchera, C., & Kang, W. (2011). *Easy access to juvenile court statistics: 1985–2009*. Retrieved from: http://www.ojjdp.gov/ojstatbb/ezajcs/.

Resnick, L. B. (1994). Situated rationalism: Biological and social preparation for learning. In L. A. Hirschfeld & S. A. Gelman (Eds.), *Mapping the mind: Domain specificity in cognition and culture* (pp. 474–493). New York: Cambridge University Press.

Rushton, J., & Jensen, A. (2005). Thirty years of research on race differences in cognitive ability. *Psychology, Public Policy, and Law*, 11(2), 235–294.

Schiller, J. S., Lucas, J. W., Ward, B. W., & Peregoy, J. A. (2012). Summary health statistics for U.S. adults: National Health Interview Survey, 2010. *Vital and Health Statistics*, 10(252), 1–207. Retrieved from http://www.cdc.gov/nchs/data/series/sr_10/sr10_252.pdf.

Shore, B. (1996). *Culture in mind: Cognition, culture, and the problem of meaning*. New York: Oxford University Press.

Shweder, R. A. (1990). Ethical relativism: Is there a defensible version?. *Ethos*, 18(2), 205–218.

Smith, A. (2005). *Conquest: Sexual violence and American Indian genocide*. Cambridge, MA: South End Press.

Smith, L. T. (1999). *Decolonizing methodologies: Research and indigenous peoples*. London: Zed Books.

Snyder, T. D., & Dillow, S. A. (2011). *Digest of education statistics 2010* (NCES 2011–015). Washington, DC: National Center for Education Statistics, Institute of Education Sciences, U.S. Department of Education.

Snyder, T. D., Dillow, S. A., & Hoffman, H. M. (2009). *Digest of education statistics 2008* (NCES 2009020). Washington, DC: National Center for Education Statistics, Institute of Education Sciences, U.S. Department of Education.

Sperber, D. (1985). Anthropology and psychology: Towards an epidemiology of representations. *Man*, 20, 73–89.

Steele, C. M. (1997). A threat in the air: How stereotypes shape intellectual identity and performance. *American Psychologist*, 52, 613–629.

Stephens, N. M., Fryberg, S. A., Markus, H. R., Johnson, C. S., & Covarrubias, R. (2012). Unseen disadvantage: How American universities' focus on independence undermines the academic performance of first-generation college students. *Journal of Personality and Social Psychology*, 102(6), 1178–1197.

Stephens, N. M., Markus, H. R., & Fryberg, S. A. (2012). Social class disparities in health and education: Reducing inequality by applying a sociocultural model of behavior. *Psychological Review*, 119, 723–744.

Substance Abuse and Mental Health Services Administration (HHS). (2010). *Substance use among American Indian or Alaska Native adults*. Retrieved from http://web.lexisnexis.com/statuniv

Suicide Prevention Resource Center. (2011). *Suicide among American Indians/Alaska Natives*. Education Development Center, Inc. Retrieved from http://www.sprc.org/sites/sprc.org/files/library/ai.an.facts.pdf.

Tharp, R. (1994). Intergroup differences among Native Americans in socialization and child cognition: An ethnogenetic analysis. In P. Greenfield & R. Cocking (Eds.), *Cross-cultural roots of minority child development* (pp. 87–105). Hillsdale, NJ: Lawrence Erlbaum.

Tobin, J. J., Wu, D. Y., & Davidson, D. H. (1989). *Preschool in three cultures: Japan, China, and the United States*. New Haven, CT: Yale University Press.

Trimble, J. E. (2000). Social psychological perspectives on changing self-identification among American Indians and Alaska Natives. In R. H. Dana (Ed.),

Handbook of cross-cultural and multicultural personality assessment (pp. 197–222). Hillsdale, NJ: Erlbaum.

Trumbull, E., Rothstein-Fisch, C., & Greenfield, P. M. (2000). Bridging cultures in our schools: New approaches that work. Retrieved June 16, 2007 from http://www.wested.org/online_pubs/lcd-99-01.pdf.

U.S. Commission on Civil Rights. (2003). *A quiet crisis: Federal funding and unmet needs in Indian Country.* Washington, DC. Retrieved from http://www.usccr.gov/pubs/na0703/na0731.pdf.

Vincent, K. R. (1991). Black/white IQ differences: Does age make the difference? *Journal of Clinical Psychology, 47,* 266–270.

Walton, G. M., & Cohen, G. L. (2007). A question of belonging: Race, social fit, and achievement. *Journal of Personality and Social Psychology, 92,* 82–96.

Winant, H. (2004). "Behind blue eyes": Whiteness and contemporary U.S. racial politics. *Off White: Readings on power, privilege, and resistance, 225,* 3–16.

Yellow Bird, M. (2004). Cowboys and Indians: Toys of genocide, icons of colonialism. *Wicazo Sa Review, 18,* 33–48.

AUTHOR NOTE

My thanks to Anikka Castle for help with the references.

5

Developmental Perspectives on the Role of Cultural Identity in Well-Being: Evidence from Aboriginal Communities in Canada

JACOB A. BURACK, AMY BOMBAY, HEIDI FLORES, JILLIAN STEWART, AND VLADIMIR PONIZOVSKY

The study of the outcome of Aboriginal youths in Canada reflects the incredible complexity in understanding developmental risk and well-being and the many different ways that they can be influenced by context and culture. It is also an example of the way in which the translation of scientific knowledge can and should inform society at large. We use the guiding themes of this volume, cultural and contextual perspectives on developmental risk and well-being, to challenge the clichéd narrative of Aboriginal communities to which virtually all Canadians are exposed by the media – a grim narrative of high rates of suicide, substance abuse, school dropout, unemployment, incarceration, and family discord. Based on case studies of youths at the most extreme risk from specific communities or on population statistics from across the country, these broad brushstrokes of failure make for compelling reporting, but alas, not for an accurate or a representative portrayal of the reality of most Aboriginal youths. Rather, the story that needs to be told is that of success and well-being of so many of these youths despite the history of colonization and oppression that so drastically disrupted the course of their peoples' histories, societies, and families over the last few hundred years, albeit in different ways across the many different communities. The focus should be on the positive influences and processes that promote these successes with an emphasis on both those that have wide-ranging relevance to Aboriginal communities across the country and those that are unique to specific communities or even individuals (Kirmayer, Dandeneau, Marshall, Phillips, & Williamson, 2011). Thus, in articulating this strength-based focus, we identify historic and contemporary risks to the development of Aboriginal youths across Canada while emphasizing the need to acknowledge the uniqueness of each community with regard to history, geography, culture, language, challenges, and resources, and of each individual in understanding the basis of resilience and paths to well-being. In particular, this discussion of well-being is framed within the context of the promotive and protective influences of identification with one's own ancestral culture.

As elsewhere in the Americas, the detrimental effects of the oppression of the Aboriginal peoples of Canada are not limited to the physical and health sequelae of atrocities, such as warfare, the deportations of children to residential schools, or forced geographic relocation. Rather, the goal of these actions by the European invaders was the diminishment and even obliteration of many of the Aboriginal cultures and ways of being. No community survived entirely intact. Even in the communities in which many aspects of the culture were maintained, the simple domination of the European invaders led to "mismatches" of values and ways of being that disadvantage Aboriginal persons on many different indexes of success according to the majority culture, including those related to educational performance and job attainment, two aspects that are essential to the integrity and long-term well-being of communities and their members (Fryberg et al., 2013; Fryberg et al., in press). Yet despite, or possibly because of, this history of oppression and suppression of culture, identification with a community's or one's own indigenous culture is seen as essential to well-being. In this chapter, we consider a range of evidence in support of this link between cultural identity and well-being among the Aboriginal youths of Canada. As neither cultural identity nor well-being is a monolithic concept, we present a variety of studies that highlight the unique relationships between them for specific communities and individuals. These studies differ with regard to the conceptualizations of both cultural identity and well-being, the level of analysis (e.g., individual or community), and the ages of the participants.

A BRIEF HISTORY OF CANADA'S ABORIGINAL PEOPLES

In Canada, the term "Aboriginal" refers to the country's original inhabitants, which comprise First Nations (the indigenous peoples of the Americas located within the boundaries of Canada, excluding the Arctic), Inuit (indigenous peoples located in the Arctic), and Métis (descendents of a group established in the 17th and 18th centuries from mixed First Nations and European heritage). Like virtually all of the indigenous peoples across the Americas, those in Canada experienced a long history of attempted genocide, oppression, marginalization, geographic displacement, forced assimilation, and ultimately the profound disruption and loss of their traditional life course

(Wilson, Rosenberg, & Abonyi, 2010; Wright, 1992). The nature and timing of the encounters between the different Aboriginal societies and the invaders, who arrived primarily from France and the British Isles, varied considerably over the past 500 years. Whereas some Aboriginal groups met Europeans hundreds of years ago, others did not make contact until the past half century. Similarly, some cultural groups co-existed relatively peaceably with the settlers, albeit in the context of a colonizer–colonizee relationship, whereas others were obliterated from existence (Wright, 1992; for a brief discussion of a similar history in the United States, please see Fryberg & Leavitt, this volume).

The European newcomers' approach to the Aboriginal peoples of Canada was exemplified by that of the 17th- and 18th-century missionaries, who described Aboriginal values and practices as "savage," "uncivilized," and "immature" and who went to great lengths to abolish them from practice and the collective memory of the communities (Kirkness, 1999). They viewed traditional Aboriginal education as perpetuating an archaic and "inferior" way and as the main barrier to the inclusion of Aboriginal people into Western society. The situation did not improve with the establishment of the nation of Canada in 1867, as the Indian Act that was passed in 1876 provided the government with the exclusive authority to define "Indian" status and to designate specific areas of land that were to be used by Aboriginal people (Royal Commission on Aboriginal Peoples [RCAP], 1996). The prevailing notion was that only the "complete training [of the young] in industries and domestic economy" could emancipate the Aboriginal peoples from their "present state of ignorance, superstition and helplessness" (RCAP, 1996). Subsequent amendments to the Indian Act further promoted the abolishment of both traditional cultural gatherings and ceremonies and the creation and implementation of residential schools for Aboriginal children, widely considered the saddest and most destructive legacy in Canadian history.

Residential schools and their deleterious legacy on the history of the Aboriginal peoples within the borders of Canada. As part of the broader goal of assimilation, the establishment of the residential school system was initiated in the late 1800s to enforce a systematic social and educational policy based on the suppression of the Aboriginal culture, language, and traditions in hopes of Christianizing, "civilizing," and resocializing Aboriginal children so that they and future generations would fit into modern Canadian society (Milloy, 1999; RCAP, 1996). Church and government agents travelled widely to forcibly remove children of Aboriginal descent (aged 5–15 years) from their families and communities and place them in the boarding schools operated by the Roman Catholic Church, the

Church of England, the United Church, the Presbyterian Church, and later by the Canadian government (Elias et al., 2012). In just more than a century, at least 150,000 students were forced into residential schools, with a peak enrollment of 8,900 children in the 1940s (Milloy, 1999). Although the schools began to close in the 1950s, the final government-run school was not shut down until 1996 (Troniak, 2011).

In addition to the traumatic forced removal of the children from their homes, the residential school experience was characterized by other extreme trauma involving inadequate health care and neglect, physical, emotional and sexual abuse (Blacksmith, 2010; Blackstock, 2003), and even elevated rates of deaths – most of which were from preventable causes of disease (Bryce, 1922; Milloy, 1999). As a consequence of being taken from their families and of the multitude and severity of the traumas that they endured, children who attended residential schools often suffered a loss of culture, language, tradition, family ties, life and parenting skills, self-respect, and respect for others, which filtered down to subsequent generations. Although each child's experience of the residential schools was unique, the physical and psychological harm inflicted on the generations of Aboriginal children was colossal (Blacksmith, 2010). Furthermore, the suffering of these children often continued upon their return home at the end of each year of separation from their families and communities, as they were often viewed and treated as social outcasts because they brought with them a foreign language, culture, and way of living. These experiences continued to deleteriously affect the survivors throughout their lives as well as their relationships with their descendants (Blacksmith, 2010), and continue to have a lasting impact on present-day Aboriginal communities (Bombay, Matheson, & Anisman, 2013a; Gone, 2010).

The deleterious outcomes of residential schools on those who attended and on subsequent generations are highlighted in the 2008 official apology articulated by Stephen Harper, the prime minister of Canada. On behalf of his country, he asked forgiveness for the government's central role in this atrocity and acknowledged the legacy of family and cultural disruption created by the removal of children from their homes and communities (Harper, 2008). Among the many wrongs imposed on the Aboriginal persons who were forced to attend the residential schools, their families, and descendants, Harper (2008) noted that

> We now recognize that in separating children from their families, we undermined the ability of many to adequately parent their own children and sowed the seeds for generations to follow, and we apologize for having done this. We now recognize that far too often these institutions gave

rise to abuse or neglect and were inadequately controlled, and we apologize for failing to protect you. Not only did you suffer these abuses as children, but as you became parents, you were powerless to protect your own children from suffering the same experience, and for this we are sorry.

The apology just touches on the extensiveness of the long-term sequelae of the residential school experiences. For example, survivors of the residential schools have reported issues of isolation, low self-esteem, suicidal behaviors, and alcohol and drug abuse, which, combined with continued systemic and structural discrimination, left them at even greater risk of being perceived in a negative way (Evans-Campbell et al., 2006; Stout & Peters, 2011). The intergenerational transmission of the negative effects observed among survivors is evidenced in the finding that the children of those who attended were more likely than Aboriginal children whose parents did not experience residential schools to have experienced various forms of childhood neglect, abuse, and household dysfunction (Bombay, Matheson, & Anisman, 2011). Children of residential school survivors were also more likely to have grown up in households with lower incomes and food security concerns, which, in turn, partially accounted for the reduced school success observed among these children (Bougie & Senécal, 2010). Linked with their adverse early-life experiences, children of residential school survivors also reported experiencing greater exposure to trauma and discrimination in adulthood, which were associated with higher levels of depressive symptoms relative to Aboriginal adults without a familial history of residential school attendance (Bombay et al., 2011). The practice and sequelae of removing Aboriginal children from their homes to be placed in residential schools still taints every aspect of the relationship between the Canadian government and the Aboriginal peoples of Canada, but it is only one aspect of a systemic and pervasive approach to ridding the country of its indigenous cultures and ways of being.

Beyond residential schools: The widespread negative impact of the European invasion on Aboriginal peoples within the borders of Canada. The sufferings of the Aboriginal peoples in Canada were certainly not limited to the atrocities of the residential schools. Even among communities that did not experience the deportation of their children to residential schools, encounters with the Europeans (and eventually the Canadians) and their government involved assaults on virtually every aspect of life, including (but not limited to) commerce, relationship with the land, language, religion and spirituality, family integrity, health, diet, and education. Many of these cases entailed the forceful relocation of communities through which the Aboriginal peoples were ripped from the contexts of their histories, cast aside as impediments to the framework of the developing nation, and ultimately abandoned and even, in some cases, annihilated. As with the residential school policy, the intended and inevitable outcome was that the intergenerational transmission of traditional ways of life that had been practiced for generations was severely disrupted and even severed, and, as a result, ties to cultures and histories were often lost or abandoned. Considering the extreme adversity faced by all Aboriginal groups in Canada, the general question, then, is how these communities and the individuals survived and even thrived. Specifically, how does the identification with the remnants of these cultures, in their modern and revitalized forms, buffer and promote positive development and well-being despite the centuries of oppression, particularly among the youths?

A DEVELOPMENTAL FRAMEWORK ON RISK AND WELL-BEING

Against this backdrop of relentless long-term oppression and discrimination, we delineate issues of risk and well-being among Aboriginal youths through the lens of a developmental framework (e.g., Burack, 1997; Cicchetti, 1984; Cicchetti & Cohen, 2006; Luthar, 2006; Sroufe & Rutter, 1984) in which the notion of risk represents some type of challenge to well-being in any one or more domains of life functioning in relation to societal or communal expectations at any given developmental stage. We acknowledge that each component of this framework is fraught with ambiguity and complexity (for a discussion, see Burack, Blidner, Flores, & Fitch, 2007). For example, risk is clearly an amorphous concept that is typically discussed within the context of some statistical likelihood of outcome that is of concern because it reflects lower levels of adaptation or well-being than that of the general population or of some other relevant comparison group. However, this conceptualization is further obscured by cultural, societal, communal, and individual perspectives on risk and the determination of what constitutes problematic or deleterious outcomes (Iarocci, Root, & Burack, 2009; Kirmayer, Dandeneau, Marshall, Phillips, & Williamson, 2011; Markstrom, 2011). Although concerns about certain types of risk and outcome may be virtually universal, such as those associated with early death, disease, and malnutrition, most are determined by societal and community values at specific times in history (for discussions, see Burack et al., 2007; Fisher, Storck, & Bacon, 1999; Luthar & Burack, 2000). The same is true for the other end of the spectrum, as the notion of well-being is virtually entirely dependent on contextual values and perspectives. Even the old-clichéd refrain of "as long as you have your health" needs to be qualified, as notions of health and mental health can vary dramatically in relation to context. In some contexts, just staying alive might be considered well-being, whereas in others, a life that does not involve a prestigious university education, a high-paying job, and a comfortable lifestyle might be considered a failure. Different determinants of well-being across mainstream and Aboriginal cultures might explain why, despite their lower average income and higher unemployment and poverty rates, Aboriginal peoples living in urban cities were as likely to report being happy as non–Aboriginal peoples in Canada (more than 90% in each group; Gross & Richards, 2012).

The complexity of these issues is not just a matter of individual and group differences but is further complicated by the systemic and dynamic nature of the developmental change of the individual as part of a transactional relationship with the environment (Burack et al., 2007). Just as level of adaptation, or well-being, for an individual is judged in relation to societal expectations regarding the navigation of the salient developmental issues for a given age (Sroufe & Rutter, 1984), the level of success of a community varies in relation to the salient issues at a specific moment in its history. For both an individual and a community, a protective factor at one moment in time can be a risk factor at another, and heroic behavior in one moment can be criminal in another. This role of context in understanding the benefits and pitfalls of a specific behavior is highlighted by Bombay, Matheson, and Anisman (2014a), who argue that disruptive behaviors that are typically viewed both as negative outcomes and as risk factors for later social maladaptation could be seen as adaptive in the appalling conditions experienced by the residential school students. Due to the neglect and maltreatment suffered by the students, these behaviors were viewed by some as "a way of saying 'I'm not a victim'. Stealing was resilience. Lying was resilience." According to former residential school students, stealing food was necessary, and even heroic, as they were not adequately fed by the school staff.

The intricacy in delineating the issues of risk, well-being, context, and cultural identity is further highlighted by the realization that, despite the shared history of invasion, oppression, and discrimination, even the focus of this chapter on the youths from Aboriginal communities within the boundaries of Canada is a misnomer because of the differences in culture, language, geographic locale, resources, histories, experiences of colonization, economies, and many other factors across the communities. As communities continue to evolve and change in their own unique ways, the differences among them, including with regard to developmental risk and well-being, also continue to grow.

Amid this recognition of a disparate national mosaic of Aboriginal peoples in Canada, we highlight that certain very general commonalities of historical and political significance are implicated in such a way that the construction of some universal narrative about developmental risk and well-being is informative but that the evidence needs to be pieced together from specific communities and individuals. Thus, we note that the impact of culture and context on the developmental outcome of Canada's Aboriginal peoples at both the community and individual levels might have some universal implications but needs to be considered within the integrity and nuance of individual persons and communities. One powerful example of the way that the more global picture may be misleading is the often-reported high rates of suicide in First Nations communities, especially among the youths. However, these rates do not imply that all Indigenous adolescents are at the same level of risk or even that all Indigenous adolescents are at any risk at all. The complexity of this issue is highlighted by Chandler and Lalonde's (1998) findings that the rates of suicide between 1987 and 1992 among the approximately 200 First Nations bands in British Columbia ranged from 0 to 800 times the national average. Although the rate of 800 times the national average is magnified considerably because of the small number of people in certain affected bands, the variability points to the utility of specifically fine-tuning the conceptualizations of suicide in Indigenous populations, as well as to the complexity of evaluating risk and well-being. For example, Chandler and Lalonde (1998) highlight that the experience and effects of "Aboriginality" can vary dramatically even among persons from a relatively defined geographic region and from communities with relatively comparable histories of persecution and oppression. Thus, the experience of events or situations is not straightforward and the sequelae are largely dependent on the individuals' history, development, environment, and the transactions among all these prior to, during, and following their encounters with the event or context.

Developmental Perspectives on Cultural Identity

As communities and individuals strive to participate and succeed in the majority culture, their ancestral cultures and ways of being are often abandoned or deemphasized by persecution, necessity, or as a way of adaptation within the majority culture. In contemporary times, these challenges lead to the rather precarious survival of indigenous language, history, or culture with implications for the development of Aboriginal youths. For example, educators of Aboriginal youths typically need to comply with government curricular requirements and are, as a result, able to devote little, if any, time to these foundational components of cultural identity. This dearth of opportunity to educate about the students' ancestral heritage is the case in urban schools in which the Aboriginal youths represent only one of many possible populations but even characterizes schools based in Aboriginal communities that are also regulated by government curricula and regulations. Within this context of government-mandated education, the maintenance and continuity of the cultural identity of the many different Aboriginal groups and of their youths are threatened.

Devoid of contact with anyone from the outside, the identification with one's ancestral culture is inevitable, unchallenged, and maybe even unnecessary – in such cases, the community members are inherently linked to the one culture that they know. However, to the extent that we know, no Aboriginal communities in Canada and few, if any, Aboriginal individuals remain completely isolated from the Western world. All have some, and most have considerable, contact with other Canadians and with various levels and aspects of government. The focus, then, is on these encounters and the extent to which they affect and are affected by the identification with one's or a community's indigenous culture in relation to the majority culture.

One possible outcome of the meeting of cultures is that the ancestral culture and its components are obliterated either by forced oppression and persecution, as attempted by the proponents of the residential schools, or by the abandonment of culture that occurs either in the face of external or internal pressure to conform to the majority culture. Even in scenarios in which the indigenous culture survives, the pressures to conform to the values and ways of being of the majority culture virtually always relegate the indigenous culture in a minimal and subsidiary role in the lives of individuals and communities. The individuals in these types of communities are faced with, and must navigate between, at least two, often incompatible, cultures and associated ways of being. Typically, any mismatches between the cultures with regard to values and ways of being disadvantages those who are most connected to and engaged in their own nonmajority culture. In one simple example, persons who learn and speak their ancestral language may be delayed and less proficient in speaking the language of the majority culture, which is inevitably essential to competence and success in so many aspects of the larger society. Similarly, persons from the minority culture are judged and assessed negatively in essential contexts, as in the case of school settings in which students are evaluated by teachers from the majority culture who, even when well-meaning, depend on the Western values and guidelines for teaching and behavior imbued in them through personal life experiences and professional training (Fryberg, Leavitt, & Burack, 2013; Fryberg & Markus, 2007a; Fryberg et al., 2013). For example, as assertiveness is typically valued in mainstream education and positively associated with academic success (Calarco, 2011) but not among many North American Aboriginal cultures, Aboriginal students who behave in ways that represent their ancestral values may be perceived in deleterious ways by teachers trained in the mainstream culture (Cheah & Nelson, 2004; Fryberg et al., 2013).

Despite these not-infrequent instances of disadvantage, the identification with and maintenance of ancestral culture and ways of being are generally depicted as a source of resilience (Luthar, 2006; Masten, Best, & Garmezy, 1990) and promotive of well-being (Luthar & Burack, 2000) in the developmental outcome of minority youths. Thus, in light of the historical transgressions against the Aboriginal peoples of Canada and the contemporary reports of all sorts of developmental risk in these groups, the benefits and pitfalls of identifying with ancestral culture have begun to be studied among their youths. This research reflects much of the diversity of ideas and conceptualizations regarding this construct and differences in focus across studies with regard to societal level (i.e., community or individual), source of data, age, and index of outcome. Although these types of disparities across studies are often decried because they limit generalizability or comparisons across studies, they reflect the complexity of a construct that, rather than being a monolithic one with a single imposed operationalization or measure, varies meaningfully in relation to culture and context.

In one commonly used framework, the emphasis is on the relations between enculturation, the degree to which a member of an ethnic minority group retains their culture of origin, and acculturation, the extent to which an individual modifies their attitudes or behavior in order to adapt to the majority culture (Berry, 1997; LaFromboise, Coleman, & Gerton, 1993). These concepts are typically operationalized in self-reports of the extent of exposure and embeddedness within the values, traditions, and practices of both the ancestral and mainstream cultures, although the orientation toward one culture can be independent of that with any other culture such that any combination of levels of identification with one or more cultures is possible (Oetting & Beauvais, 1991). For example, an Aboriginal youth might identify highly with mainstream Canadian culture (i.e., acculturated) but at the same time remain well integrated within their traditional indigenous culture (i.e., enculturated). These youths who identify with both cultures are considered to be "bicultural," which is often thought to be the optimal way of being for minority youths, as it entails the successful navigation of the demands in both the minority and mainstream societies (e.g., David, Okazaki, & Saw, 2009; LaFromboise et al. 1993; Luthar & Burack, 2000). Conversely, individuals and communities who are not aligned with the values and ideology of either their own or mainstream society are thought to be the most at risk (e.g., Oetting & Beauvais, 1991; Phinney, 1989; Yoon et al., 2013).

Cultural identity has also been framed to involve the centrality of group membership, the collective esteem based on positive or negative evaluation or feelings ascribed to group membership, and the perceptions of cohesion, commonality, and belongingness with other group members (Cameron, 2004). These more cognitive and affective dimensions of identity are conceptually as well as empirically distinct, and can vary independently (Ellemers, Kortekaas, & Ouwerkerk, 1999; Jackson & Smith, 1999). Thus, being Aboriginal might be very salient to an individual's self-concept but may be associated with feelings of either pride or negativity about being Aboriginal. Concordantly, either positive or negative feelings about being Aboriginal may also be linked to feelings of being disconnected or isolated from other Aboriginal people.

With this background, we attempt to provide some overarching, general conclusions about the role of identification with and maintenance of ancestral culture in the protection and well-being of Aboriginal youths in Canada while respecting the considerable diversity across studies of both communities and individuals. The sources of information and inference concerning cultural identity, in its disparate forms and contexts, are wide ranging and include communal activities, self-report, and the simple percentage of Aboriginal persons in a setting. Similarly, the foci of the study, the ages of the participants, and the outcome measures differ across the studies. Yet, through these differences, cultural identity appears to be essential to developmental well-being of Aboriginal youths and adults despite their shared history of persecution and colonization.

Communal cultural identity and continuity as a protective factor in emotional well-being. In challenging the clichéd representation or "actuarial fiction" of uniformly elevated suicide rates across Aboriginal communities with evidence of great diversity in rates of suicide, ranging from none to 800 times the national average, across the 196 First Nations communities of British Columbia, Chandler and Lalonde (1998) argued for "cultural continuity as a hedge against suicide." In their theoretical framework, commitment to the future and a sense of one's own continuity in time is essential to their care and concern for their own well-being (also see

Chandler et al., 2003). Accordingly, First Nations youths are at particular risk for suicide and other deleterious outcomes as their experience of the dramatic upheaval common to virtually all adolescents and young adolescents may be exacerbated by the lack of a sense of cultural continuity in their communities in which the ancestral cultures were radically changed and undermined. Conversely, Chandler and Lalonde hypothesized that communal engagement in the preservation and rehabilitation of ancestral culture would be associated with less deleterious outcomes for the youth. In order to test this notion, they identified six factors thought to reflect communities' efforts in the rehabilitation and maintenance of their ancestral culture – they included communal attempts to (i) secure the title to their ancestral lands; (ii) reclaim aspects of self-governance; (iii) take some control of education; (iv) take some control of the police and fire-protection services; (v) take some control of health services; and (vi) establish "cultural facilities" intended to preserve and enrich the ancestral culture. Consistent with Chandler and Lalonde's (1998) hypothesis, the engagement in these activities by communities was related to lower rates of suicide. As all First Nations youths are at risk due to the disruption of their ancestral culture by the majority culture, these findings provided powerful initial evidence that communal engagement in the rehabilitation and preservation of cultural identity and the promotion of cultural continuity can protect against deleterious outcomes among individual community members (Chandler & Lalonde, 1998, 2009; Chandler et al., 2003).

Chandler and Lalonde (2009) extended their initial study (Chandler & Lalonde, 1998) by including (i) data from the additional 8-year period between 1993 and 2000; (ii) information on adult as well as youth suicide; and (iii) the factors of the number of council seats occupied by women and the provision of child and family services within the community to their index of cultural continuity. Although Chandler and Lalonde's original conceptualization was focused on the struggle for identity formation despite the radical changes that are concomitant with the adolescent years, they added adults to this later study in consideration of the possibility that adults may experience identity problems similar to adolescents. As in the previous study, the rates of suicide by band and tribal council varied considerably, with some communities evidencing no deaths by suicide and others suffering suicide rates several times higher than the respective provincial average. Their list of cultural continuity factors was expanded from six to a total of eight with the addition of the number of council seats occupied by women and the provision of child and family services within the community. The participation of women in local governance can be seen as an essential index of cultural rehabilitation of the historically matrilineal First Nations communities of the west coast of Canada. The information on child and family services is a telling indicator in the progress of communities in acquiring control of child custody and protection services following an era, especially, the 1960s, in which many of their children were placed in the care of non–Aboriginal persons and institutions.

Individual cultural identity and health outcomes. Taylor (1997, 2002) addresses the notion of cultural identity as a protective factor against emotional problems among Aboriginal youths in his conceptual and empirical analyses of the relations among identity, esteem, self, and mood. Based on major theoretical distinctions between identity and esteem ("what am I" versus "how worthy am I") as two parts of the self (Campbell, 1990) and between individual and social aspects of the self ("I am intelligent, stupid, shy, or brave" versus "I am a young white middle-class university student"; Tajfel & Turner, 1986), Taylor proposes a four-component conceptualization that includes self-concept of personal identity, personal self-esteem, collective identity, and collective self-esteem. In an assessment of these factors, Taylor argues that personal self-esteem, which is the most proximal to some health outcomes and generally considered the most important, is the least important theoretically. Rather, he emphasizes that personal self-esteem is untenable without a personal identity and that a personal identity is impossible without a clear collective identity, because the attributes that comprise individual identity are always defined against a collective identity through which the norms or standards that impact self-esteem are understood. According to Taylor, cultural identity is a kind of a collective identity that, like the notion of cultural continuity forwarded by Chandler and Lalonde (1998, 2009), is a prerequisite for personal continuity and ultimately for well-being.

In applying Taylor's model, Usborne and Taylor (2010) examined the role of cultural identity clarity for self-concept clarity, self-esteem, and subjective well-being among persons from several culturally distinct groups in Canada, including 76 members of the Yellowknives Dene First Nation (ages ranging from 18 to 64 years old). Similar to the findings among other groups (e.g., undergraduates at an urban university, Anglophone Canadians, Chinese Canadians, and Francophone Canadians), the evidence from the members of the Yellowknives Dene First Nation indicated that cultural identity clarity predicted personal identity clarity and was a marginal predictor of self-esteem and mood and that personal identity clarity, in its turn, was a strong predictor of self-esteem and mood. A test of a mediation model indicated that personal identity clarity mediated the relationship between cultural identity clarity and self-esteem/mood.

Individual cultural identity and psychosocial functioning. Using an enculturation/acculturation framework, Gfellner and Armstrong (2012a) examined relations among cultural identity, ego development, and ego strengths among 227 First Nation children and adolescents in grades 5 through high school (weighted to more participants in the younger grades) from four First Nation communities in the central Midwest of Canada. Ego development, as conceptualized by Loevinger (1976) on the basis of Erikson's psychosocial model, refers to the evolvement of the ego across the lifespan due to interactions with one's self and the surrounding environment. Ego strengths include factors such as hope, will, purpose, competence, fidelity, love, care, and wisdom and refer to developing outcomes throughout the lifespan that represent progress and resolution of Erikson's psychosocial stages of development. The First Nations youths who were highly enculturated with their ancestral heritage demonstrated greater ego strengths than the adolescents who identified with both First Nation and Canadian cultures (i.e., bicultural) and those who identified with only Canadian culture (i.e., acculturated). Those who were considered to be of marginal status because they identified with neither culture had the lowest ego strengths among the groups (Gfellner & Armstrong, 2012a).

Because aggression is a behavioral aspect of psychosocial development of particular relevance to Aboriginal youths who both perpetrate and are victims of aggressive behaviors at rates considerably higher than those of other minority groups in the United States (Perry, 2004), Flanagan et al. (2011) examined perceptions of physical and relational aggression in relation to self-reported cultural identity among almost the entire population of adolescents in the Naskapi community of Kawawachikamach, an Aboriginal community in Northern Québec. The Naskapi adolescents who scored higher on their preference for their native culture were perceived by their peers as being less aggressive, both physically and relationally, suggesting a protective role for identification with ancestral identity against aggressive behaviors and the potential deleterious sequelae. The findings from both this study and the one by Gfellner and Armstrong (2012a) highlight the strength of affiliation with traditional culture as a promotive and protective factor in two divergent manifestations of psychosocial functioning, one as self-report of internal ego strengths and the other as peer report of both relational and physical aggressive behaviors.

These results were consistent with findings from a subsequent study by Gfellner and Armstrong (2012b) in which the bicultural First Nations youths did not appear to be better off than highly enculturated or acculturated youth in relation to prosocial behaviors (e.g., homework completion, avoided fighting), but all three of these groups had higher scores in this regard compared to youth classified as marginal (i.e., those who did not identify with either culture). Based on the findings from both of their studies, Gfellner and Armstrong (2012a, 2012b) argued that enculturated and bicultural youth appear to demonstrate the most adaptive functioning but that a lack of identification to any culture confers the most risk. However, pointing to the complexity of developmental and gender issues in understanding the effects of cultural identity, this conclusion did not apply across all outcomes that were considered in these studies. For example, males classified as marginal who were not identified with either culture had relatively high ego strength scores (Gfellner & Armstrong, 2012a), which was attributed to the older age of the males in this group.

The findings from the two studies by Gfellner and Armstrong (2012a, 2012b) were partially inconsistent with evidence among other minority youths suggesting that biculturalism is the most protective identity status, even compared to enculturated adolescents (e.g., David et al., 2009; Luthar & Burack, 2000; Wei et al., 2010). Gfellner and Armstrong (2012a) suggested that the lack of support for the protectiveness of a bicultural orientation in their group might reflect the unique history of assimilation of Aboriginal groups. Alternatively, they suggested that biculturalism and/or acculturation may be more beneficial for older youth and for those who live off-reserve or attend integrated schools (Gfellner & Armstrong, 2012a). Indeed, bicultural American Indian adolescents reported the lowest levels of self-reported hopelessness, but the beneficial effect of being acculturated to mainstream culture was particularly relevant for those who lived in urban areas (LaFromboise, Albright, & Harris, 2010).

In addition to the importance of contextual factors such as living on- versus off-reserve to the influence of cultural identity, the relations among enculturation, acculturation, and various outcomes may also be dependent on the values of the culture in relation to the specific outcome being considered. Enculturation and acculturation have both been studied in relation to behaviors associated with health risks linked to peer pressure. For example, Currie et al. (2011) examined associations between Aboriginal enculturation, Canadian acculturation, and alcohol problems among 60 Aboriginal university students from the University of Alberta in Edmonton who self-identified as First Nation, Métis, Inuit, or Aboriginal. They found that higher levels of Aboriginal enculturation were associated with reduced alcohol problems, whereas Canadian acculturation was not significantly associated with alcohol problems. These findings suggest that Aboriginal enculturation may have both direct and indirect impacts on the reduction of alcohol use. With regard to direct influences, the participants described Aboriginal ceremonies as a key component of cultural practice and articulated that participation in these ceremonies may have had a direct effect on the reduction of alcohol problems, since they are often based on spiritual practices and beliefs that prohibit alcohol use or recommend moderation. Enculturation may also have indirect effects by reducing the motivation to drink, as cultural practice apparently enabled the students to better cope with stress, enhance mood, and obtain social rewards, all of which are commonly cited motivators for alcohol use among adolescents (Currie et al., 2011).

In contrast to the finding that enculturation was associated with fewer alcohol problems among Aboriginal university students (Currie et al., 2011), Greaves et al. (2011) found that levels of acculturation to Canadian society but not enculturation with Aboriginal culture were associated with a reduced likelihood of smoking among 123 First Nations (and 1 Métis) middle and high school–aged youth in British Columbia (no information was provided as to whether the participants lived on- or off-reserve). They suggested that the protective effect of acculturation may stem from the anti-smoking norm in the mainstream Canadian population. The differences between these findings and those presented by Currie et al. (2011) regarding alcohol problems likely also reflect the complexity in understanding, operationalizing, and testing enculturation and acculturation, the protective and promotive powers of each, and the extent to which outcomes can vary in relation to them.

To further complicate matters, the benefits associated with having high levels of cultural identity can be limited in some cases due to the consistent positive relationship between cultural identity centrality and perceived discrimination, as reported in other stigmatized groups (e.g., African Americans; Sellers, Caldwell, Schmeelk-Cone, & Zimmerman, 2003). This was evident among a group of 399 Aboriginal adults from across Canada living predominately off-reserve (most were First Nations, with a smaller number of Métis and Inuit adults), as those who considered their Aboriginal identity as a central component of their self-concept (i.e., identity centrality) reported more frequent past experiences with discriminatory treatment, were more likely to attribute scenarios depicting negative intergroup encounters as being due to discrimination, and attributed greater threat appraisals to these encounters (Bombay, Matheson, & Anisman, 2014b). Although the relevance of these findings to First Nations persons living on-reserve is unclear, they demonstrate the importance of a group's history in relation to identity and well-being. In this regard, the participants who had a parent who had attended residential school reported higher levels of identity centrality compared to the adults whose parents did not attend, which in turn translated into greater levels of perceived discrimination in these adults (Bombay et al., 2014b).

Individual cultural identity and educational outcomes. Fryberg et al. (2013) followed up on the notion of the potential detrimental effects of the *cultural mismatch* between *White* teachers who teach a majority-culture curriculum and promote ways of being that are consistent with the values of the majority culture and First Nations students in another study of virtually all the adolescents in the Naskapi community of Kawawachikamach. According to cultural matching theory (Stephens et al., 2012), a *cultural mismatch* occurs in a school setting when the norms and values promoted by the school or teacher are not similar to those of the student. In this type of setting, students feel that they do not belong or that they cannot be successful, and as a result, their potential for success is undermined. One example of a source of cultural mismatch is that Western models of education focus on independence and assertiveness, which are incompatible with the interdependence and collectivistic ways of being among Aboriginal persons in North America (Cheah & Nelson, 2004). Thus, whereas individuality and assertiveness may foster persistence and academic achievement in mainstream contexts, perceived social support, mentorship, maintaining strong connections to the community, and trusting relationships with teachers promote persistence and academic achievement in Aboriginal contexts (Fryberg & Markus, 2007; Fryberg et al., 2013; LaFromboise et al., 2010).

In focusing on the teachers' perceptions of assertiveness and academic outcome in relation to the youths' cultural identification, Fryberg et al. (2013) found that high identification with either Aboriginal or White culture was related to higher grades, regardless of whether the students were perceived as assertive by their teacher. Conversely, with low levels of cultural identification toward Aboriginal or White culture, the teachers' perceptions of the students' assertiveness was essential to school performance – being perceived as low in assertiveness by the teacher predicted lower grades, but being perceived as high in assertiveness predicted higher grades. Thus, both high cultural identification, regardless of whether to the ancestral or majority culture, and assertiveness can contribute to enhancing the educational outcomes of Aboriginal students, but Aboriginal students with low levels of both cultural identification and assertiveness are at particular risk as they both are mismatched with the culture of mainstream schools and do not benefit from the protective effects of identity with a culture.

Based on provincial data of 366 nonreserve schools with 30 Aboriginal students over a continuous 5-year period, Richards et al. (2010) examined the performance of Aboriginal students on a standardized test of cognitive skills in relation to both the performance of their non-Aboriginal peers, which was thought to indicate the overall quality of the school, and percentage of Aboriginal children in the school, which was thought to reflect the cultural competence/promotion of Aboriginal culture in the school. The initial analysis indicated a relationship between socioeconomic status and performance on standardized tests for both the Aboriginal and non–Aboriginal students. In subsequent multivariate analyses, the performance of non–Aboriginal students was positively related to performance of Aboriginal students, suggesting that either these were better schools or that the encounters with non–Aboriginal peers provided for higher expectations, better models for academic achievement, or some combination of them. In addition, the number of Aboriginal students in school was negatively associated with test scores, as the students in the schools with higher numbers of Aboriginal students scored lower on the standardized tests. Richards et al. (2010) suggested that grouping Aboriginal students together may induce a "culture of low expectations" – both from teachers regarding the success of their students and from students regarding their peers' achievement.

The findings by Fryberg et al. (2013) highlight the potential power of identification with both ancestral and majority culture, albeit for very different reasons, in promoting academic success among Aboriginal youths. However, both their findings and those of Richards et al. (2010) highlight complex ways that teachers' perceptions and the meeting of cultures can affect, usually deleteriously, the educational outcomes of these students and, in turn, the types of policy changes that might optimize success. Fryberg et al.'s (2013) message is clearly that increased cultural programming and sensitivity can enhance student outcomes both by fostering two essential predictors, the students' identity with ancestral culture and an increased cultural match between the teachers, who are virtually all trained in the majority culture, and the students. Although Richards et al.'s (2010) suggestion of a tradeoff in which the provision of more culturally competent services is associated with decreased academic achievement, at least on standardized tests, by Aboriginal students seems inconsistent with this policy plan. However, their findings highlight the complementary notion that modifying teachers' perceptions of Aboriginal students' styles and abilities may be the key to the academic success of these youths.

SUMMARY

The long history of Aboriginal people living in the borders of Canada changed profoundly with their encounters with the European invaders to the Americas. The subsequent story includes generations of marginalization, geographic displacement, forced assimilation, and the resultant disruption and loss of tradition. Despite this history of centuries of oppression, many of the Aboriginal peoples were and are able to survive and thrive. In this chapter, we highlight ways that these successes, particularly among the youths, can be linked to the identification with ancestral culture. Although cultural identity, like so many psychological constructs, is too nuanced to be encapsulated in a single statement, the initial evidence certainly supports the notion that identification with and maintenance of ancestral culture is largely adaptive and essential to the well-being of Aboriginal youths in Canada. The identification with ancestral culture largely appears to be adaptive when it is their primary cultural orientation but also often when it is part of a bicultural identification with the majority culture. And for some Aboriginal people and in some instances, the abandonment of the ancestral culture in favor of the Canadian culture may be a way to survive and even succeed. The level of complexity does not end there because, as is the case with all developmental issues, the role of identity with ancestral and mainstream culture is dynamic and ever changing in relation to each individual's developmental level, social and emotional challenges that are faced, familial and communal input, and more general environmental factors (Burack et al., 2007). In the face of this developmental complexity, evidence supporting the strong influence of identification with ancestral culture on positive outcomes for so many youths in so many contexts highlights the power of the continuity of Aboriginal cultures in Canada in promoting well-being among so many.

REFERENCES

Berry, J. W. (1997). Immigration, acculturation, and adaptation. *Applied Psychology,* 46(1), 5–34.
Blacksmith, G. (2010). *The intergenerational legacy of the Indian residential school system on the Cree communities of Mistissini, Oujebougamau and Waswanipi: An investigative research on the experiences of three generations of the James Bay Cree of northern Quebec.* Unpublished doctoral dissertation. McGill University, Montreal.
Blackstock, C. (2003). First Nations child and family services: Restoring peace and harmony in First Nations communities. In K. Kufeldt & B. McKenzie (Eds.), *Child welfare: Connecting research policy and practice* (pp. 331–343). Waterloo, IA: Wilfrid Laurier University Press.

Bombay, A., Matheson, K., & Anisman, H. (2011). The impact of stressors on second generation Indian residential school survivors. *Transcultural Psychiatry*, 48, 367–391.

(2013). The intergenerational effects of Indian Residential Schools: Implications for the concept of historical trauma. *Transcultural Psychiatry*. Advanced online publication. d.o.i. **10.1177/1363461513503380**

(2014a). *An exploratory investigation of student-to-student abuse in residential schools and the implications of this phenomenon.* Ottawa: Aboriginal Healing Foundation.

(2014b). Appraisals of discriminatory events among adult offspring of Indian Residential School Survivors: The influences of identity centrality and past perceptions of discrimination. *Cultural Diversity and Ethnic Minority Psychology*, 20, 75–86. Advanced online publication. d.o.i. 10.1037/a0033352

Bougie, E., & Senécal, S. (2010). Registered Indian children's school success and intergenerational effects of residential schooling in Canada. *International Indigenous Policy Journal*, 1, 5.

Bryce, P. H. (1922). *The story of a national crime: An appeal for justice to the Indians of Canada.* Ottawa: James Hope & Sons, Limited.

Burack, J. A. (1997). The study of atypical and typical populations in developmental psychopathology: The quest for a common science. In S. S. Luthar, J. A. Burack, D. Cicchetti, & J. R. Weisz (Eds.), *Developmental psychopathology: Perspectives on adjustment, risk and disorder* (pp. 139–165). New York: Cambridge University Press.

Burack, J. A., Blidner, A., Flores, H., & Fitch, T. (2007). Constructions and deconstructions of risk, resilience and wellbeing: A model for understanding the development of Aboriginal adolescents. *Australasian Psychiatry*, 15, S18–S23.

Calarco, J. M. (2011). "I need help!" Social class and children's help-seeking in elementary school. *American Sociological Review*, 76, 862–882.

Cameron, J. E. (2004). A three-factor model of social identity. *Self and Identity*, 3, 239–262.

Campbell, J. D. (1990). Self-esteem and clarity of the self-concept. *Journal of Personality and Social Psychology*, 59, 538.

Chandler, M. J., & Lalonde, C. E. (1998). Cultural continuity as a hedge against suicide in Canada's First Nations. *Transcultural Psychiatry*, 35, 191–219.

(2009). Cultural continuity as a moderator of suicide risk among Canada's First Nations. In L. Kirmayer & G. Valaskakis (Eds.), *Healing traditions: The mental health of Aboriginal peoples in Canada* (pp. 221–248). Vancouver: University of British Columbia Press.

Chandler, M. J., Lalonde, C. E., Sokol, B. W., Hallett, D., & Marcia, J. E. (2003). Personal persistence, identity development, and suicide: A study of native and non-native North American adolescents. *Monographs of the Society for Research in Child Development*, 68.

Cicchetti, D. (1984). The emergence of developmental psychopathology. *Child Development*, 55, 1–7.

Cicchetti, D., & Cohen, D. (Eds.). (2006). *Developmental psychopathology.* New York: Wiley.

Currie, C. L., Wild, T. C., Schopflocher, D. P., Laing, L., Veugelers, P. J., Parlee, B., & McKennitt, D. W. (2011). Enculturation and alcohol use problems among aboriginal university students. *Canadian Journal of Psychiatry. Revue Canadienne de psychiatrie*, 56, 735.

David, E. J. R., Okazaki, S., & Saw, A. (2009). Bicultural self-efficacy among college students: Initial scale development and mental health correlates. *Journal of Counseling Psychology*, 56, 211–226.

Elias, B., Mignone, J., Hall, M., Hong, S. P., Hart, L., & Sareen, J. (2012). Trauma and suicide behaviour histories among a Canadian indigenous population: An empirical exploration of the potential role of Canada's residential school system. *Social Science Medicine*, 74, 1560–1569.

Ellemers, N., Kortekaas, P., & Ouwerkerk, J. W. (1999). Self-categorisation, commitment to the group and group self-esteem as related but distinct aspects of social identity. *European Journal of Social Psychology*, 29, 371–389.

Evans-Campbell, T., Lindhorst, T., Huang, B., & Walters, K. L. (2006). Interpersonal violence in the lives of urban American Indian and Alaska Native women: Implications for health, mental health, and help-seeking. *American Journal of Public Health*, 96, 1416–1422.

Fisher, P. A., Storck, A., & Bacon, J. G. (1999). In the eye of the beholder: Risk and protective factors in rural American Indian and Caucasian adolescents. *American Journal of Orthopsychiatry*, 69, 294–304.

Flanagan, T., Iarocci, G., D'Arrisso, A., Mandour, T., Tootoosis, C., Robinson, S., & Burack, J. A. (2011). Reduced ratings of physical and relational aggression for youths with a strong cultural identity: Evidence from the Naskapi people. *Journal of Adolescent Health*, 49, 155–159.

Fryberg, S. A., & Markus, H. R. (2007). Cultural models of education in American Indian, Asian American, and European American contexts. *Social Psychology of Education*, 10, 213–246.

Fryberg, S. A., Troop-Gordon, W., D'Arrisso, A., Flores, H., Ponizovsky, V., Ranney, J. D., Mandour, T., Tootoosis, C., Robinson, S., Russo, N., & Burack, J. A. (2013). Cultural mismatch and the education of Aboriginal youth: The interplay of cultural identities and teacher ratings. *Developmental Psychology*, 49, 72–79.

Gfellner, B. M., & Armstrong, H. D. (2012a). Ego development, ego strengths, and ethnic identity among First Nation adolescents. *Journal of Research on Adolescence*, 22, 225–234.

(2012b). Racial-ethnic identity and adjustment in Canadian indigenous adolescents. *Journal of Early Adolescence*, 33, 635–662.

Gone, J. P. (2010). Psychotherapy and traditional healing for American Indians: Exploring the prospects for therapeutic integration. *The Counselling Psychologist*, 38, 166–235.

Greaves, L., Poole, N., Okoli, C. T. C., Hemsing, N., Qu, A., Bialystok, L., & O'Leary, R. (2011). *Expecting to quit: A best practices review of smoking cessation interventions for pregnant and post-partum women* (2nd ed.). Vancouver: British Columbia Centre of Excellence for Women's Health.

Gross, D. & Richards, J. (2012). Breaking the stereotype: Why urban Aboriginals score highly on "happiness" measures. *CD Howe Institute Commentary*, 354.

Harper, S. (2008). Statement of apology – to former students of Indian Residential Schools. Aboriginal Affairs and Northern Development Canada. Retrieved December 29, 2013, from http://www.aadnc-aandc.gc.ca/eng/1100100015644/1100100015649.

Iarocci, G., Root, R., & Burack, J. A. (2009). Social competence and mental health among Aboriginal youth: An integrative developmental perspective. In L. Kirmayer & G. Valaskakis (Eds.), *Healing traditions: The mental health of Aboriginal peoples in Canada* (pp. 80–106). Vancouver: UBC Press.

Jackson, J. W., & Smith, E. (1999). Conceptualizing social identity: A new framework and evidence for the impact of different dimensions. *Personality and Social Psychology Bulletin*, 25, 120–135.

Kirkness, V. J. (1999). Aboriginal education in Canada: A retrospective and a prospective. *Journal of American Indian Education*, 39, 14–30.

Kirmayer, L. J., Dandeneau, S., Marshall, E., Phillips, M. K., & Williamson, K. J. (2011). Rethinking resilience from indigenous perspectives. *Canadian Journal of Psychiatry*, 56, 84–91.

LaFromboise, T. D., Albright, K., & Harris, A. (2010). Patterns of hopelessness among American Indian adolescents: Relationships by levels of acculturation and residence. *Cultural Diversity and Ethnic Minority Psychology*, 16, 68–76.

LaFromboise, T. D., Coleman, H. L. K., & Gerton, J. (1993). The psychological impact of biculturalism: Evidence and theory. *Psychological Bulletin*, 114, 395–412.

Loevinger, J. (1976). *Ego development: Conceptions and theories*. San Francisco: Jossey-Bass.

Luthar, S. S. (2006). Resilience in development: A synthesis of research across five decades. In D. Cicchetti & D. Cohen (Eds.), *Developmental psychopathology: Risk, disorder, and adaptation* (pp. 739–795). New York: Wiley.

Luthar, S. S., & Burack, J. A. (2000). Adolescent wellness: In the eye of the beholder? In D. Cicchetti, J. Rappaport, I. Sandler, & R. P. Weissberg (Eds.), *The promotion of wellness in children and adolescents* (pp. 29–57). Washington, DC: Child Welfare League of America.

Markstrom, C. A. (2011). Identity formation of American Indian adolescents: Local, national, and global considerations. *Journal of Research on Adolescence*, 21, 19–35.

Masten, A. S., Best, K. M., & Garmezy, N. (1990). Resilience and development: Contributions from the study of children who overcome adversity. *Development and Psychopathology*, 2, 425–444.

Milloy, J. S. (1999). *A national crime: The Canadian government and the residential school system*. Winnipeg: University of Manitoba Press.

Oetting, E. R., & Beauvais, F. (1991). Orthogonal cultural identification theory: The cultural identification of minority adolescents. *International Journal of the Addictions*, 25, 655–685.

Perry, S. W. (2004). *American Indians and crime: A BJS statistical profile, 1992–2002*. Washington, DC: U.S. Department of Justice.

Phinney, J. S. (1989). Stages of ethnic identity development in minority group adolescents. *Journal of Early Adolescence*, 9, 34–49.

Richards, J. G., Vining, A. R., & Weimer, D. L. (2010). Aboriginal performance on standardized tests: Evidence and analysis from provincial schools in British Columbia. *Policy Studies Journal*, 38, 47–67.

Royal Commission on Aboriginal Peoples (RCAP) (1996). *Looking Forward, Looking Back: Report of the Royal Commission on Aboriginal Peoples, Volume 1.* Ottawa, ON: Communication Group Publishing.

Sellers, R. M., Caldwell, C. H., Schmeelk-Cone, K. H., & Zimmerman, M. A. (2003). Racial identity, racial discrimination, perceived stress, and psychological distress among African American young adults. *Journal of Health and Social Behavior*, 302–317.

Sroufe, A. L., & Rutter, M. (1984). The domain of developmental psychopathology. *Child Development*, 55, 17–29.

Stephens, N. M., Fryberg, S. A., Markus, H. R., Johnson, C. S., & Covarrubias, R. (2012). Unseen disadvantage: How American universities' focus on independence undermines the academic performance of first-generation college students. *Journal of Personality and Social Psychology*. Advance online publication. doi:10.1037/a0027143.

Stout, R., & Peters, S. (2011). *Kiskinohamâtôtâpânâsk: Inter-generational effects on professional First Nations women whose mothers are residential school survivors.* Winnipeg, MB: Prairie Women's Centre for Research.

Tajfel, H., & Turner, J. C. (1986). The social identity theory of intergroup behaviour. In S. Worchel & W. G. Austin (Eds.), *Psychology of intergroup relations* (pp. 7–24). Chicago: Nelson-Hall.

Taylor, D. M. (1997). The quest for collective identity: The plight of disadvantaged ethnic minorities. *Canadian Psychology/Psychologie canadienne*, 38, 174.

   (2002). *The quest for identity: From minority groups to generation Xers.* Westport, CT: Praeger.

Troniak, S. (2011). *Addressing the legacy of residential schools.* Background paper 76-E, Social Affairs Division, Parliament of Canada. Retrieved from http://www.parl.gc.ca/Content/LOP/Research Publications/2011-76-e.htm.

Usborne, E., & Taylor, D. M. (2010). The role of cultural identity clarity for self-concept clarity, self-esteem, and subjective well-being. *Personality and Social Psychology Bulletin*, 36, 883–897.

Wei, M., Liao, K. Y., Chao, R. C., Mallinckrodt, B., Tsai, P., & Botellow-Zammarron, R. (2010). Minority stress, perceived bicultural competence and depressive symptoms among ethnic minority college students. *Journal of Counseling Psychology*, 57, 411–422.

Wilson, K., Rosenberg, M. W., & Abonyi, S. (2010). Aboriginal peoples, health and healing approaches: The effects of age and place on health. *Social Science Medicine*, 72, 355–364.

Wright, R. (1992). *Stolen continents: The "New World" through Indian eyes.* Boston, MA: Houghton-Mifflin.

Yoon, E., Chang, C., Kim, S., Clawson, A., Cleary, S. A., Hansen, M., Bruner, J. P., et al. (2013). A meta-analysis of acculturation/enculturation and mental health. *Journal of Counseling Psychology*, 60, 15–30.

PART II

CONTEXTUAL PERSPECTIVES ON
DEVELOPMENTAL RISK AND WELL-BEING

6

Peer Victimization: Understanding the Developmental Correlates of At-Risk Children and Youth

JENNIFER M. KNACK, TRACY VAILLANCOURT,
AMANDA KRYGSMAN, STEVEN ARNOCKY,
IRENE VITOROULIS, JENNIFER HEPDITCH, AND
CHRISTINE BLAIN-ARCARO

Humans have an innate need to form meaningful, lasting relationships with others (Baumeister & Leary, 1995). The necessity of forming significant relationships is evident when considering (1) the multiple developmental domains impacted by social experiences including cognitive, moral, language, emotional, and social development as well as (2) the various outcomes associated with negative social experiences including psychological and physical health problems. When social experiences are negative, development is negatively impacted. For example, cognitive developmental disruption can be seen in poor academic performance among youth who experience peer victimization (e.g., Vaillancourt Brittain, McDougall, & Duku, 2013).

In this chapter, we examine the correlates associated with the negative social experience of being victimized by peers. Although peer victimization occurs throughout the lifespan from early preschool age through later adulthood, in this chapter we focus on peer victimization research during childhood through emerging adulthood. We consider individual (e.g., sex, genetic risk) and contextual-level (e.g., numerical ethnic majority versus minority, friendships) risk and protective factors for peer victimization. We highlight the poor mental and physical health associated with peer victimization; we also briefly discuss how a person's biology may play an integral role in the expression of these risk factors. Throughout the chapter, where possible, we present literature considering whether ethnicity alters the experience of peer victimization.

Peer victimization, also called peer abuse and bullying, occurs when a person is the target of repeated aggression by a peer(s) who has more power (Olweus, 1993). Power differences are often seen in social status, physical size, and sex (McKenney, Pepler, Craig, & Connolly, 2006). Peer victimization can take different forms including physical (e.g., hitting), verbal (e.g., name calling), relational/social/indirect (e.g., shunning), or cyber (e.g., email, text message) abuse and can occur through direct/overt (e.g., verbal attacks) or indirect/covert (e.g., rumors) means. Estimates of the prevalence of peer victimization among school-age children tend to converge around the figures of 10% for those who are frequently bullied and 30% for those who are occasionally bullied (Limber & Small, 2003; Nansel et al., 2003; Vaillancourt et al., 2010). Although Craig and colleagues (2009) found on average across 40 countries that 12.6% adolescents reported being bullied, 10.7% reported bullying others, and 3.6% reported being a bully-victim (i.e., both bullied and bullying others), the estimates of bullying varied both by country and sex. For example, in Sweden, 8.6% of boys reported bullying involvement compared to 4.8% of girls; in Lithuania, 45.2% of boys reported bullying involvement compared to 35.8% of girls. Marginalized populations (e.g., lesbian, gay, bisexual, or transgendered youth, those with a disability) seem to be particularly at risk for peer abuse (Swearer, Espelage, Vaillancourt, & Hymel, 2010).

DEVELOPMENTAL PATTERNS OF PEER VICTIMIZATION

During childhood and adolescence, youth are socialized, form friendships, and learn how to get along with others (Parker et al., 2006). However, the social skills of children and adolescents are far from refined compared to the social skills of adults, and accordingly, peer difficulties are fairly frequent. For example, in early childhood, peer aggression is not uncommon as children learn social etiquette (e.g., taking turns, sharing), learn to resolve conflict, and develop language and cognitive skills (Côté et al., 2006, 2007; Vaillancourt et al., 2007). A positive association between peer aggression and peer victimization is seen during childhood; children who are aggressive toward their peers also tend to be victimized by their peers (e.g., Barker, Arseneault, Brendgen, & Maughan 2008; Burk et al., 2011; Haynie et al., 2001). As one example, Ostrov (2007) found this pattern for both relational and physical aggression/victimization, suggesting that children socialize each other with regard to acceptable social interactions by punishing those who are overly aggressive. Alternatively, this relationship between victimization and aggression could indicate a deficiency of self-regulatory skills or social skills.

During later childhood and adolescence, youth are better able to take others' perspectives, predict consequences of their own actions, and understand the dynamics of the peer group. In turn, peer victimization, especially physical victimization, should decrease as youth learn more socially appropriate ways of handling conflict. However, relational victimization may remain stable or even increase as children develop more sophisticated social skills and learn to maneuver and manipulate the peer group. Because children who are bullied may be the target of multiple forms of bullying or solely one form of bullying, overall victimization levels as well as the degree of physical and nonphysical (e.g., relational, verbal, cyber) forms of victimization need to be considered. As expected, as children grow older, overall victimization and physical victimization decrease while nonphysical forms of victimization increase (Craig, 2004). This shift in the form of victimization matches the increased cognitive functioning of older children and adolescents. The increase in nonphysical forms of victimization is also not surprising given that youth spend more time with their peers and, in turn, learn to manipulate the social network and begin to form more clear-cut social hierarchies (e.g., Buhrmester & Furman, 1987; Hartup, 1993; Vaillancourt, Hymel, & McDougall, 2003). As children develop, physical aggression becomes less socially acceptable, and children learn to be assertive and handle conflict without being physically aggressive. Indeed, Schwartz, Dodge, and Coie (1993) found that 6- and 8-year-old boys were more likely to be victimized if they were unable to assert themselves (e.g., lack effective persuasion techniques or were submissive), suggesting that being the target of early peer victimization may be an indication of developmental difficulties in social or cognitive development.

Patterns of peer victimization seem to be in line with the above noted developmental changes in aggression. First, peer victimization and bullying often coincide with changes in the structure of the peer group, such as when children transition from elementary to middle school (Pellegrini, 2004; Pellegrini & Long, 2002; Pepler et al., 2006), which may be a function of the shifting social hierarchy within peer groups, and an indication that youth are jockeying for positions within the social structure of their school. Second, during this transition period, youth tend to target same-sex peers rather than cross-sex peers (Pellegrini & Long, 2002). This type of targeting makes sense because children spend the majority of their time with same-sex peers; youth only begin to spend more time with cross-sex peers in early adolescence (e.g., 7th and 8th grade; e.g., Arndorfer & Stormshak, 2008).

Although peer victimization remains fairly stable throughout childhood and adolescence (Kochel, Ladd, & Rudolph, 2012; Pedersen, Vitaro, Barker, & Borge, 2007; van Lier et al., 2012), being victimized early in childhood is not a sure indication that one will be victimized at a later time. Rueger,

Malecki, and Demaray (2011) found that approximately half of 7th- and 8th-grade students who reported victimization by peers in the fall semester also reported peer victimization in the spring semester; the other half of the students who reported victimization were either victimized only in the fall quarter *or* victimized only in the spring quarter. Similarly, Scholte, Engles, Overbeek, de Kemp, and Haselager (2007) found that 43% of adolescents (around age 14) who were rated by peers as victimized were also rated as victimized in childhood (around age 11); about half of the children who were rated as victimized in childhood were not victimized in adolescence, and only 7% of youth were rated as victims only in adolescence. Although Sourander, Helstela, Helenius, and Piha (2000) found that on average youth who reported being victimized by peers at age 8 also reported being victimized at age 16, the stability rates differed considerably for boys and girls. Ninety percent of the boys who were victimized at age 8 were also victimized at age 16, whereas only 48.5% of the girls who were victimized at age 8 were also victimized at age 16. There is also some evidence that stability of peer victimization may differ by ethnicity. Hanish and Guerra (2000) found that peer victimization was less stable across a 2-year period for black children than for Hispanic or white children; however, the risk of being victimized in late childhood was lower for black children than for white children, suggesting that the patterns of stability may differ by ethnicity. Although these studies collectively suggest that individuals who are victimized in childhood are likely to also be victimized in adolescence, the studies also highlight heterogeneity in developmental pathways. In the sections that follow, we consider factors that may contribute to these differences in victimization trajectories and discuss how peer victimization impacts the developing person.

PEER VICTIMIZATION AND ETHNICITY

In multicultural societies, it seems feasible that peer victimization would occur between youth of different ethnic backgrounds. It is also likely that there would be differences in patterns of peer victimization (e.g., time of onset, severity), as well as differences in the severity of outcomes associated with being victimized. Surprisingly, however, differences in peer victimization based on ethnicity are rarely reported in the empirical literature, although immigrant and ethnic minority youth are involved in bullying, peer victimization, and peer aggression (e.g., Nansel et al., 2001; Putallaz et al., 2007). For example, contrary to expectations, McKenney et al. (2006) did not find significant differences in reports of general peer victimization between Canadian immigrant youth and nonimmigrant youth. However, differences in peer victimization were seen when researchers focused on ethnicity-based victimization, which is experienced more often by ethnic minority and immigrant youth than their ethnic majority counterparts (e.g., Boulton, 1995; Verkuyten & Thijs, 2002). Indeed, although McKenney et al. (2006) did not find differences between Canadian immigrant and nonimmigrant youth for general victimization, they did find evidence for ethnic victimization, especially for first-generation Canadian youth.

Research is indicating that understanding ethnicity-based victimization requires a nuanced examination of the ethnic composition of social contexts rather than simply looking at distinct ethnic groups. Having a numerical majority, regardless of ethnicity, plays a key role in predicting which students are bullied (Graham, Bellmore, & Mize, 2006). For example, contrary to expectations, Vervoort, Scholte, and Overbeek (2010) found that ethnic minority adolescents were *less* likely to be victimized than native Dutch majority adolescents when the ethnic composition of the classes was controlled. Interestingly, classrooms where at least 25% of students were from an ethnic minority had higher overall levels of reported peer victimization than classrooms in which fewer than 25% of students were from an ethnic minority. Graham and Juvonen (2002) found that students from numerical minority ethnic groups were more likely to be nominated as a victim than students from the numerical majority ethnic groups regardless of which groups they belonged to (i.e., being European-American or not). Similarly, Hanish and Guerra (2000) found that white children who attended schools in which white students were a numerical minority (i.e., predominantly non–white school) were at a higher risk of being victimized than white students attending schools in which white students were a numerical majority (i.e., predominantly white school). In contrast, Hanish and Guerra (2000) found that black children who were in schools where black students were a numerical majority were *more* likely to be victimized than black students attending school where black students were the numerical minority. Finally, Hanish and Guerra (2000) found that the rate of victimization did not differ for Hispanic children regardless of the ethnic composition of the school. This finding suggests that peer victimization may be a function of an imbalance of power or size of ethnic groups. Conversely, ethnically diverse friendships can act as a buffer against peer victimization in contexts where ethnic groups are equally distributed (Juvonen, Nishina, & Graham, 2006). Thus, ethnicity alone does not place students at a higher risk for peer victimization. Rather, peer victimization needs to be considered in the overall social context to include factors such as ethnicity (e.g., ethnic composition, balance of ethnicity).

When examining ethnic differences in peer victimization, it is important to consider how victimization is being measured. Peer victimization is typically assessed using either a definition-based measure (i.e., the definition of bullying is provided and people indicate the frequency that they were bullied) or a behavior-based measure (i.e., people are asked about how frequently they experience specific behaviors associated with bullying such as being teased, being left out, being hit/slapped/kicked). Sawyer, Bradshaw, and O'Brennan (2008) found that minority youth (including African Americans and Asians) in the United States (specifically Maryland) were *less* likely to report being bullied compared to white youth when peer victimization was assessed using a *definition-based* measure. However, minority youth were *more* likely to report being bullied compared to white youth when peer victimization was assessed using a *behavior-based* measure. It is possible that the stigma of being bullied differs across ethnic groups, thereby resulting in differences across ethnic groups in how willing people are to classify their experiences as "being bullied."

PEER VICTIMIZATION AND MENTAL HEALTH

Peer victimization is associated with a host of psychosocial difficulties both concurrently and longitudinally (for reviews, see Swearer et al., 2010; Vaillancourt et al., 2010). Children who are bullied have lower self-esteem and self-worth than children who are not bullied; they are also more lonely, withdrawn, socially anxious, avoidant, depressed, and suicidal (Hawker & Boulton, 2000; Klomek, Marrocco, Kleinman, Schonfeld, & Gould, 2008). People who experience peer victimization also have more externalizing problems such as hyperactivity, delinquency, and aggression. In terms of school functioning, children and youth who are victimized by their peers report being unhappy at school, like school less, and feel more unsafe than those who are not victimized (Vaillancourt et al., 2010). They also perform worse on academics, are absent from school more often, and drop out at a higher rate than their nonbullied peers. Some research indicates that mental health outcomes may be qualified by the form of peer victimization that children experience. For example, physical victimization tends to be associated with externalizing problems (Cullerton-Sen & Crick, 2005; Prinstein, Boergers, & Vernberg, 2001), whereas relational/indirect and verbal peer victimization tend to be associated with internalizing problems (Baldry, 2004; Hawker & Boulton, 2001; van der Wal et al., 2003).

•

The relationship between peer victimization and poor mental health initially appeared to be directional (from victimization to psychopathology; e.g., Arseneault et al., 2006; Kim, Koy, & Leventhal, 2005; Sourander, Helstela, Helenius, & Piha, 2000; Vaillancourt, Hymel, & McDougall, 2011). For example, in a longitudinal study, Schreier et al. (2009) found that children who were victimized by their peers were more likely to have psychotic symptoms as adolescents than those children who were not victimized by their peers. Schreier and colleagues also found that youth with stable experiences of peer victimization (i.e., victimized both in childhood and adolescence) and who experienced both overt and relational peer victimization were more likely to have psychotic symptoms than youth who were only victimized during childhood or adolescence or who experienced only one form of victimization. Based on their meta-analytic review, Ttofi, Farrington, Losel, and Loeber (2011) reported that peer victimization was a unique risk factor for later depression after controlling for major childhood risk factors. However, other studies have indicated that the relationship between peer victimization and poor mental health is bidirectional (Reijntjes, Kamphuis, Prinzie, Boelen, van der Schoot, & Telch, 2011; Reijntjes, Kamphuis, Prinzie, & Telch, 2010). For example, Sweeting, Young, West, and Der (2006) found the relationship between peer victimization and depression was bidirectional. However, their study suggests that the strength of the relationship between peer victimization and depression may depend on one's developmental period. For example, in early adolescence at age 13, Sweeting et al. (2006) found peer victimization more strongly predicted depression compared to depression predicting peer victimization (although both pathways were significant); by 15 years of age, the association between peer victimization and depression was primarily driven by depression predicting peer victimization.

There is limited evidence that the psychosocial and mental health outcomes associated with peer victimization differ by ethnicity. Spriggs et al. (2007) found that black, Hispanic, and white students who experienced peer victimization were all more likely to feel socially isolated at school and have difficulty communicating with their parents than students who were bullies. However, only white students who were victimized reported feeling unsafe at school; there was no evidence that black or Hispanic students, even those who were peer victimized, felt unsafe.

One potential explanation for the limited evidence of ethnicity differences for the association between peer victimization and mental health may be the samples included in studies examining ethnicity and peer victimization. Instead of comparing the association between peer victimization and mental health by ethnicity or race, several researchers (e.g., Nadeem & Graham, 2005; Storch, Nock, Masia-Warner, & Barlas, 2003) have examined the relationship between peer victimization and mental health problems within specific ethnic groups. Most commonly, Hispanic and black youth are selected by researchers who want to examine ethnicity and peer victimization. For example, Storch, Nock, Masia-Warner, and Barlas' (2003) study indicated higher rates of peer victimization in their sample of Hispanic children than the rates of peer victimization in studies with Caucasian participants; they suggested that this higher incidence of peer victimization in their sample may be due to the high exposure to violence and crime of living in an urban inner city. However, their study did not statistically examine whether the associations between peer victimization and mental health differed by ethnicity; rather, they examined the association between peer victimization and mental health in a sample composed primarily of Hispanic and black youth. Although examination of the association between peer victimization and mental health in specific ethnic groups is necessary, such a study provides little information about differences between different ethnic groups.

Friendships seem to be an important developmental context that provides some protection against the negative mental health outcomes associated with peer victimization. For example, Hodges, Boivin, Vitaro, and Bukowski (1999) found that the association between peer victimization and internalizing problems was weaker in 4th- and 5th-grade children with a high-quality best friend than in children with a low-quality best friend or without a best friend. Even in preschoolers, social context is important. Although friendships were not linked with peer victimization, Hanish, Ryan, Martin, and Fabes (2005) found that playing with aggressive peers and exposure to aggressive peers predicted peer victimization in preschoolers. In kindergarteners, being liked by peers and having friends was associated with lower levels of peer victimization, whereas exposure to aggressive peers predicted higher levels of peer victimization. Similarly, Malcolm, Jensen-Campbell, Rex-Lear, and Waldrip (2006) found that having high-quality friendships was associated with lower levels of peer victimization. In their short-term longitudinal study, Malcolm et al. (2006) found that high-quality friendships in the fall predicted lower levels of peer victimization in the spring, whereas fall peer victimization was not associated with spring friendship quality. Together, these findings demonstrate the importance of considering the social context when examining the outcomes associated with peer victimization. Furthermore, having ethnically diverse friendships may protect children from peer victimization more than having same-ethnicity friendships do (Kawabata & Crick, 2011).

PEER VICTIMIZATION AND BIOLOGICAL FUNCTIONING

Children and adolescents who are bullied report more health problems such as headaches, abdominal pain, sore throats, and mouth sores than those who are not bullied (e.g., Greco, Freeman, & Dufton, 2007; Williams, Chambers, Logan, & Robinson, 1996; Wolke, Woods, Bloomfield, & Karstadt, 2001). Evidence from short-term longitudinal studies suggests that frequent experiences of peer victimization in the fall predict poorer physical health in the spring (e.g., Knack, Iyer, & Jensen-Campbell, 2012; Nishina, Juvonen, & Witkow, 2005). Among college-age students, peer victimization was associated with severe health problems such as heart problems, bone/joint problems, chest pain, and high blood pressure (Knack, Iyer, & Jensen-Campbell, 2012). College-age students who reported being frequently victimized by their peers also reported using more pain medication, having more visits to the doctor, and experiencing more impairment in day-to-day activities than students who reported less peer victimization (Knack, Gomez, & Jensen-Campbell, 2010).

Researchers have begun to examine associations between peer victimization and neuroendocrine functioning (e.g., hypothalamic-pituitary-adrenal [HPA] axis and neuronal functioning) in an effort to understand the relationship between victimization and poor health. To examine the activity of the HPA axis in response to experiencing the stress of being victimized by peers, cortisol is commonly assessed because it is one of the end products of HPA axis activation. Both girls (Vaillancourt et al., 2008) and adults (Hansen et al., 2006) who were bullied by their peers or colleagues have lower levels of salivary cortisol in the morning. In contrast, Vaillancourt et al. (2008) found that boys who were bullied had higher morning cortisol levels than boys who were not bullied. Knack, Jensen-Campbell, and Baum (2011) found that cortisol levels mediated the relationship between peer victimization and poor health; adolescents who reported being bullied had a flattened cortisol awakening response, which predicted poor physical health. In addition to differences in daily levels of salivary cortisol, Knack and colleagues found that adolescents who were bullied had lower cortisol levels 30 minutes after an acute social stressor (i.e., preparing and delivering a speech), which predicted more visits to health-care professionals.

Friendships are an important context often considered as a buffer for the negative outcomes associated with peer victimization. Similar to the previous studies, Peters, Riksen-Walraven, Cillessen, and de Weerth (2011) found that being excluded (one specific form of peer victimization) predicted salivary cortisol levels in 4th-grade children. Contrary to those studies, Peters et al. (2011) found that being excluded predicted *higher* salivary cortisol levels at school but a flatter diurnal pattern across the school day (no direct associations were found between peer victimization and cortisol levels). This flattened diurnal pattern was strongest for children with fewer friends or low-quality friends compared to children with more friends or high-quality friends. This finding suggests that having more friends and high-quality friends may lessen the neuroendocrine stress response of being socially excluded.

In addition to examining the neuroendocrine correlates of peer victimization, other researchers have explored neural correlates. For example, Vaillancourt et al. (2011) reviewed the evidence of an overlap in the neural substrates that are activated during social and physical pain (e.g., Burklund, Eisenberger, & Lieberman, 2007; Eisenberger et al., 2007). This neural overlap is also evident in pain sensitivity (e.g., Eisenberger et al., 2006). Evidence of neural activation during social pain experiences is important because the brain is continuing to develop during childhood and adolescence. Given that experience influences brain development and function (e.g., dendritic pruning, neuronal organization), repeated peer victimization during childhood and adolescence may alter brain development (e.g., Vaillancourt, 2010, 2011, 2013) and, in turn, impact development in other domains (e.g., cognitive). Thus, these changes in biological functioning may affect how subsequent peer victimization is experienced (Knack, Gomez, & Jensen-Campbell, 2010), suggesting that biological functioning (i.e., neural activation, HPA axis functioning) differs between individuals who experience peer victimization and those who do not. These differences may account for poorer physical health among people who experience peer victimization. Future research will need to examine the directionality of these relationships, namely whether differences in biological functioning (e.g., neural activation, HPA axis functioning) or experiences of peer victimization occur first.

FACTORS THAT MAY ALTER EXPERIENCES OF PEER VICTIMIZATION

Not all youth who are victimized by their peers suffer from mental or physical problems and academic difficulties. Thus, the question exists as to why some people experience psychosocial, physical, and academic problems whereas other people appear resilient. Factors associated with poorer outcomes among bullied children and adolescents compared with those youth who are not bullied include genetic predisposition and sex. In the following subsections, we discuss these two factors.

Genetic Predisposition. In a Canadian study on twins in kindergarten, the relationship between aggression (i.e., an externalizing problem) and victimization depended on children's genetic vulnerability for aggressive behavior in girls but not boys (Brendgen et al., 2008); the link between peer victimization and aggressive behavior was stronger for girls who had high genetic risk for aggressive behavior than those who did not. For boys, greater peer victimization was strongly associated with high levels of aggression regardless of genetic risk. Given that the association between peer victimization and aggression existed regardless of genetic risk, Brendgen et al. (2008) concluded that peer victimization (assessed via peer nominations) was primarily environmentally driven and not related to genetic disposition.

Other researchers have sought to understand why some people who are victimized experience internalizing problems whereas others do not. There is some evidence that the serotonin transporter gene (5-HTTLPR) is linked with internalizing problems such as depression. In a British twin study, 5-HTTLPR was found to moderate the relationship between peer victimization and emotional problems (Benjet, Thompson, & Gotlib, 2010; Sugden et al., 2010). Children with two short alleles of 5-HTTLPR who were victimized were at greater risk for developing emotional problems than children with heterogeneous alleles (short-long) or two long alleles. This finding was observed even after controlling for emotional problems prior to victimization and other shared environment risk factors. Iyer, Dougall, and Jensen-Campbell (2013) also found that 5-HTTLPR moderated the relationship between peer victimization and depression; adolescents with a short allele of 5-HTTLPR (short-short or short-long) who experienced peer victimization were more likely to experience depression than adolescents with two long alleles who experienced peer victimization (see also Benjet et al., 2010). These studies suggest that some people who are victimized may be at higher risk for experiencing adjustment problems such as depression than others.

Sex Differences in Peer Victimization. Boys and girls vary in their experiences of peer victimization regarding the (1) type of abuse experienced, (2) consequences of abuse, and (3) level of support available. Boys are more likely than girls to experience physical victimization (Crick & Nelson, 2002; Underwood, Galen, & Paquette, 2001), whereas girls typically use and target other girls with relational/indirect aggression (Gallup, O'Brien, White, & Wilson, 2009; Österman et al., 1998), thus placing them at particular risk of experiencing indirect forms of victimization. Distinctions between the sexes can also be made regarding the relationship between the child who bullies and the victim; boys are more likely to be victimized by strangers or acquaintances, whereas girls are more frequently victimized within closer social affiliations such as friendships (Turkel, 2007).

Physical victimization, typically experienced more by boys, is associated with higher risk of physical injury than relational victimization (Sullivan, Farrell, & Kliewer, 2006). Accordingly, Miller and Spicer (1998) found that boys were generally physically injured more often than were girls. Although experiences of relational/indirect victimization can be deleterious to boys, boys typically rate physical victimization as being more harmful than girls. In contrast, girls, compared to boys, rate social victimization as being more harmful than physical victimization (Galen & Underwood, 1997). When boys and girls were exposed to similar levels of social aggression, Paquette and Underwood (1999) found that girls thought about being victimized more and were more distressed by it. Archer and Coyne (2005) argued that adolescent girls may be hurt more by indirect aggression due to the impetus placed on social status and having friends during this stage of development.

With regard to the social support that is available to victims, boys are less commonly the target of prosocial behavior from peers than girls (Crick & Grotpeter, 1996). Cowie (2000) found that boys are underrepresented as peer supporters, and because many children prefer a peer supporter to be of the same sex, boys may be particularly at risk of receiving less support. A sizeable number of boys refrain from reporting their victimization to anyone (Cowie, 2000), which can further exacerbate the lack of support provided.

In addition to the above sex differences in how peer victimization is experienced, the relationship between peer victimization and poor mental health is qualified by the sex of the person being victimized, consistent with literature on the development of psychopathology in response to stressors (Achenbach & Edelbrock, 1983; Crick & Zahn-Waxler, 2003). For example, Rueger, Malecki, and Demaray (2011) found that girls who were victimized by their peers experienced residual internalizing and academic difficulties after the abuse had stopped whereas for boys, residual problems were not found. However, sex differences are not always found, as indicated by the longitudinal study of elementary school-age children by Rudolph, Troop-Gordon, Hessel, and Schmidt (2011), who reported that peer victimization similarly predicted depressive symptoms and overt aggression for girls and boys.

The relationship between victimization and maladjustment may depend on the form of peer victimization experienced; girls tend to experience more maladjustment when socially victimized and boys tend to experience more maladjustment when physically victimized (Crick & Grotpeter, 1995; Sullivan, Farrell, & Kliewer, 2006). Vuijk, van Lier, Crijnen, and Huizink (2007) provide support for this idea with their findings that reductions in relational victimization were associated with reduced anxiety and depression for girls but that reductions in physical victimization were associated with reduced anxiety and panic for boys.

CONCLUSIONS

In this chapter, we discussed peer victimization within a developmental framework to examine risk factors and negative outcomes associated with being the target of peer aggression. Where possible, we highlighted differences by ethnicity and where developmental contexts such as friendship altered the experience or outcomes of being peer victimized. Peer victimization is associated with mental and physical health problems as well as possible changes in biological functioning. Sex and genetics are two factors that affect experiences of peer victimization. However, even when considering sex differences and genetic risk, it should be clear from this review that being the target of peers' aggression is associated with a number of substantial problems that have negative developmental implications. Given the negative ramifications of poor social experiences, it is encouraging that researchers are seeking ways to identify youth who may be at risk for developmental disruptions due to peer victimization (e.g., genetic predisposition to internalizing problems). We encourage researchers to continue examining whether the outcomes of peer victimization differ by ethnic group.

REFERENCES

Achenbach, T. M., & Edelbrock, C. (1983). *Manual for the child behavior checklist and revised child behavior profile*. Burlington, VT: Queen City Printers.

Archer, J., & Coyne, S. (2005). An integrated review of indirect, relational, and social aggression. *Personality and Social Psychology Review*, 9, 212–230.

Arndorfer, C. L., & Stormshak, E. A. (2008). Same-sex versus other-sex best friendships in early adolescence: Longitudinal predictors of antisocial behavior throughout adolescence. *Journal of Youth and Adolescence*, 37, 1059–1070.

Arseneault, L., Walsh, E., Trzesniewski, K., Newcombe, R., Caspi, A., & Moffitt, T. E. (2006). Bullying victimization uniquely contributes to adjustment problems in young children: A nationally representative cohort study. *Pediatrics*, 118, 130–138.

Baldry, A. C. (2004). The impact of direct and indirect bullying on the mental and physical health of Italian youngsters. *Aggressive Behavior*, 30, 343–355.

Barker, E. D., Arseneault, L., Brendgen, M., Fontaine, N., & Maughan, B. (2008). Joint development of bullying and victimization in adolescence: Relations to delinquency and self-harm. *Journal of the American Academy of Child and Adolescent Psychiatry, 47*, 1030–1038.

Baumeister, R. F., & Leary, M. R. (1995). The need to belong: Desire for interpersonal attachments as a fundamental human motivation. *Psychological Bulletin, 117*, 497–529.

Benjet, C., Thompson, R. J., & Gotlib, I. H. (2010). 5-HTTLPR moderates the effect of relational peer victimization on depressive symptoms in adolescent girls. *Journal of Child Psychology and Psychiatry, 51*, 173–179.

Boulton, M. J. (1995). Patterns of bully/victim problems in mixed race groups of children. *Social Development, 4*, 277–293.

Brendgen, M., Boivin, M., Vitaro, F., Girard, A., Dionne, G., & Pérusse, D. (2008). Gene-environment interaction between peer victimization and child aggression. *Development and Psychopathology, 20*, 455–471.

Buhrmester, D., & Furman, W. (1987). The development of companionship and intimacy. *Child Development, 58*, 1101–1113.

Burk, L. R., Armstrong, J. M., Park, J., Zahn-Waxler, C., Klein, M. H., & Essex, M. J. (2011). Stability of early identified aggressive victim status in elementary school and associations with later mental health problems and functional impairments. *Journal of Abnormal Child Psychology, 39*, 225–238.

Burklund, L., Eisenberger, N. I., & Lieberman, M. D. (2007). The face of rejection: Rejection sensitivity moderates dorsal anterior cingulate cortex activity to disapproving facial expression. *Social Neuroscience, 2*, 238–253.

Côté, S., Vaillancourt, T., Barker, E. D., Nagin, D., & Tremblay, R. E. (2007). The joint development of physical and indirect aggression: Predictors of continuity and change during childhood. *Development and Psychopathology, 19*, 37–55.

Côté, S., Vaillancourt, T., LeBlanc, J. C., Nagin, D. S., & Tremblay, R. E. (2006). The development of physical aggression from toddlerhood to pre-adolescence: A nation wide longitudinal study of Canadian children. *Journal of Abnormal Child Psychology, 34*, 62–82.

Cowie, H. (2000). Bystanding or standing by: Gender issues in coping with bullying in English schools. *Aggressive Behavior, 26*, 85–97.

Craig, W., Harel-Fisch, Y., Fogel-Grinvald, H., Dostaler, S., Hetland, J., Simons-Morton, B., Molcho, M., de Mato, M. G., Overpeck, M., Due, P., Pickett, W., the HBSC Violence & Injuries Prevention Focus Group, & the HBSC Bullying Writing Group. (2009). A cross-national profile of bullying and victimization among adolescents in 40 countries. *International Journal of Public Health, 54*, S216–S224.

Craig, W. M. (2004). Bullying in Canada in the Canadian World Health Organization Report on the Health of youth in Canada. *Health Canada.*

Crick, N. R., & Grotpeter, J. K. (1995). Relational aggression, gender, and social–psychological adjustment. *Child Development, 66*, 710–722.

(1996). Children's treatment by peers: Victims of relational and overt aggression. *Development and Psychopathology, 8*, 367–380.

Crick, N. R., & Nelson, D. A. (2002). Relational and physical victimization within friendships: Nobody told me there'd be friends like this. *Journal of Abnormal Child Psychology, 30*, 599–607.

Crick, N., & Zahn-Waxler, C. (2003). The development of psychopathology in females and males: Current progress and future challenges. *Development and Psychopathology*, 15, 719–742.

Cullerton-Sen, C., & Crick, N. R. (2005). Understanding the effects of physical and relational victimization: The utility of multiple perspectives in predicting social-emotional adjustment. *School Psychology Review*, 34, 147–160.

Eisenberger, N. I., Jarcho, J. M., Lieberman, M. D., & Naliboff, B. D. (2006). An experimental study of shared sensitivity to physical pain and social rejection. *Pain*, 126, 132–138.

Eisenberger, N. I., Way, B. M., Taylor, S. E., Welch, W. T., & Lieberman, M. D. (2007). Understanding genetic risk for aggression: Clues from the brain's response to social exclusion. *Biological Psychiatry*, 61, 1100–1108.

Galen, B. R., & Underwood, M. K. (1997). A developmental investigation of social aggression among children. *Developmental Psychology*, 33, 589–600.

Gallup, A. C., O'Brien, D. T., White, D. D., & Wilson, D. S. (2009). Peer victimization in adolescence has different effects on the sexual behavior of male and female college students. *Personality and Individual Differences*, 46, 611–615.

Graham, S., Bellmore, A. D., & Mize, J. (2006). Peer victimization, aggression, and their co-occurrence in middle school: Pathways to adjustment problems. *Journal of Abnormal Child Psychology*, 34, 363–378.

Graham, S., & Juvonen, J. (2002). Ethnicity, peer harassment, and adjustment in middle school: An exploratory study. *Journal of Early Adolescence*, 22, 173–199.

Greco, L. A., Freeman, K. E., & Dufton, L. (2007). Overt and relational victimization among children with frequent abdominal pain: Links to social skills, academic functioning, and health service use. *Journal of Pediatric Psychology*, 32, 319–329.

Hanish, L. D., & Guerra, N. G. (2000). The roles of ethnicity and school context in predicting children's victimization by peers. *American Journal of Community Psychology*, 28, 201–223.

Hanish, L. D., Ryan, P., Martin, C. L., & Fabes, R. A. (2005). The social context of young children's peer victimization. *Social Development*, 14, 2–19.

Hansen, A. M., Hogh, A., Persson, R., Karlson, B., Garde, A. H., Orbaek, P. (2006). Bullying at work, health outcomes, and physiological stress response. *Journal of Psychosomatic Research*, 60, 63–72.

Hartup, W. W. (1993). Adolescents and their friends. *New Directions for Child and Adolescent Development*, 60, 3–22.

Hawker, D. S., & Boulton, M. J. (2000). Twenty years' research on peer victimization and psychological maladjustment: A meta-analytic review of cross sectional studies. *Journal of Child Psychology and Psychiatry*, 41, 441–455.

Hawker, D. S. J., & Boulton, M. J. (2001). Subtypes of peer harassment and their correlates: A social dominance perspective. In J. Juvonen & S. Graham (Eds.), *Peer harassment in school: The plight of the vulnerable and victimized* (pp. 378–397). New York: Guilford.

Haynie, D. L., Nansel, T., Eitel, P., Davis Crump, A., Saylor, K., Yu, K., & Simons-Morton, B. (2001). Bullies, victims, and bully/victims: Distinct groups of at-risk youth. *Journal of Early Adolescence*, 21, 29–49.

Hodges, E. V., Boivin, M., Vitaro, F., & Bukowski, W. M. (1999). The power of friendship: Protection against an escalating cycle of peer victimization. *Developmental Psychology*, 35, 94–101.

Iyer, P. A., Dougall, A. L., & Jensen-Campbell, L. A. (2013). Are some adolescents differentially susceptible to the influence of bullying on depression? *Journal of Research in Personality*, 47, 272–281.

Juvonen, J., Nishina, A., & Graham, S. (2006). Ethnic diversity and perceptions of safety in urban middle schools. *Psychological Science*, 17, 393–400.

Kawabata, Y., & Crick, N. R. (2011). The significance of cross-racial/ethnic friendships: Associations with peer victimization, peer support, sociometric status, and classroom diversity. *Developmental Psychology*, 47, 1763–1775.

Kim, Y. S., Koh, Y. J., & Leventhal, B. (2005). School bullying and suicidal risk in Korean middle school students. *Pediatrics*, 115, 357–363.

Klomek, A. B., Marrocco, F., Kleinman, M., Schonfeld, I. S., & Gould, M. S. (2008). Peer victimization, depression, and suicidality in adolescents. *Suicide and Life-Threatening Behaviour*, 38, 166–180.

Knack, J. M., Gomez, H., & Jensen-Campbell, L. A. (2010). Bullying and its long-term health implications. In G. MacDonald & L. A. Jensen-Campbell (Eds.), *Social pain: Neuropsychological and health implications of loss and exclusion* (pp. 215–236). Washington, DC: American Psychological Association.

Knack, J. M., Iyer, P. A., & Jensen-Campbell, L. A. (2012). Not simply "in their heads:" Being bullied predicts health problems above and beyond known individual differences associated with victimization and health. *Journal of Applied Social Psychology*, 42, 1625–1650.

Knack, J. M., Jensen-Campbell, L. A., & Baum, A. (2011). Worse than sticks and stones? Bullying is linked with altered HPA axis functioning and poorer health. *Brain and Cognition*, 77, 183–190.

Kochel, K. P., Ladd, G. W., & Rudolph, K. D. (2012). Longitudinal associations among depressive symptoms, peer victimization, and low peer acceptance: An interpersonal process perspective. *Child Development*, 83, 637–650.

Limber, S. P., & Small, M. A. (2003). State laws and policies to address bullying in schools. *Social Psychology Review*, 32, 445–455.

Malcolm, K. T., Jensen-Campbell, L. A., Rex-Lear, M., & Waldrip, A. (2006). Divided we fall: Children's friendships and peer victimization. *Journal of Social and Personal Relationships*, 23, 721–740.

McKenney, K. S., Pepler, D., Craig, W. M., & Connolly, J. (2006). Peer victimization and psychosocial adjustment: The experiences of Canadian immigrant youth. *Electronic Journal of Research in Educational Psychology*, 9, 239–264.

Miller, T. R., & Spicer, R. S. (1998). How safe are our schools? *American Journal of Public Health*, 88, 413–418.

Nadeem, E., & Graham, S. (2005). Early puberty, peer victimization, and internalizing symptoms in ethnic minority adolescents. *Journal of Early Adolescence*, 25, 197–222.

Nansel, T. R., Overpeck, M., Silla, R. S., Ruan, W. J., Simons-Morton, B., & Scheidt, P. (2001). Bullying behaviors among US youth: Prevalence and association with psychosocial adjustment. *Journal of the American Medical Association*, 285, 2094–2100.

Nansel, T. R., Overpeck, M. D., Haynie, D. L., Ruan, W. J., & Scheidt, P. C. (2003). Relationships between bullying and violence among U.S. youth. *Archives of Pediatric Adolescent Medicine*, 157, 348–353.

Nishina, A., Juvonen, J., & Witkow, M. R. (2005). Sticks and stones may break my bones, but names will make me feel sick: The psychosocial, somatic, and scholastic consequences of peer harassment. *Journal of Clinical Child and Adolescent Psychology*, 34, 37–48.

Olweus, D. (1993). *Bullying at school: What we know and what we can do*. Cambridge, MA: Blackwell.

Österman K., Björkqvist, K., Lagerspetz, K. M. J., Kaukiainen, A., Landau, S. F., Frączek, A., & Caprara, G. V. (1998). Cross-cultural evidence of female indirect aggression. *Aggressive Behavior*, 24, 1–8.

Ostrov, J. M. (2007). Forms of aggression and peer victimization during early childhood: A short-term longitudinal study. *Journal of Abnormal Child Psychology*, 36, 311–322.

Parker, J. G., Rubin, K. H., Erath, S. A., Wojslawowicz, J. C., & Buskirk, A. A. (2006). Peer relationships, child development, and adjustment: A developmental psychopathology perspective. In D. Cicchetti & D. J. Cohen (Eds.), *Developmental psychopathology. Vol. 2: Theory and method* (2nd ed., pp. 96–161). Hoboken, NJ: John Wiley & Sons.

Paquette, J. A., & Underwood, M. K. (1999). Gender differences in young adolescents' experiences of peer victimization: Social and physical aggression. *Merrill-Palmer Quarterly*, 45, 242–266.

Pedersen, S., Vitaro, F., Barker, E. D., & Borge, A. I. H. (2007). The timing of middle-childhood peer rejection and friendship: Linking early behavior to early-adolescent adjustment. *Child Development*, 78, 1037–1051.

Pellegrini, A. D. (2004). Bullying during the middle school years. In C. E. Sanders & G. D. Phye (Eds.), *Bullying: Implications for the classroom* (pp. 177–202). New York: Elsevier.

Pellegrini, A. D., & Long, J. D. (2002). A longitudinal study of bullying, dominance, and victimization during the transition from primary school through secondary school. *British Journal of Development Psychology*, 20, 259–280.

Pepler, D. J., Craig, W. M., Connolly, J. A., Yuile, A., McMaster, L., & Jiang, D. (2006). A developmental perspective on bullying. *Aggressive Behavior*, 32, 376–384.

Peters, E., Riksen-Walraven, J. M., Cillessen, A. H. N., & de Weerth, C. (2011). Peer rejection and HPA activity in middle childhood: Friendship makes a difference. *Child Development*, 82, 1906–1920.

Prinstein, M. J., Boergers, J., & Vernberg, E. M. (2001). Overt and relational aggression in adolescents: Social-psychological functioning of aggressors and victims. *Journal of Clinical Child Psychology*, 30, 477–489.

Putallaz, M., Grimes, C. L., Foster, K. J., Kupersmidt, J. B., Coie, J. D., & Dearing, K. (2007). Overt and relational aggression and victimization: Multiple perspectives within the school setting. *Journal of School Psychology*, 45, 523–547.

Reijntjes, A., Kamphuis, J. H., Prinzie, P., Boelen, P. A., van der Schoot, M., & Telch, M. J. (2011). Prospective linkages between peer victimization and externalizing problems in children: A meta-analysis. *Aggressive Behaviour*, 37, 215–222.

Reijntjes, A., Kamphuis, J. H., Prinzie, P., & Telch, M. J. (2010). Peer victimization and internalizing problems in children: A meta-analysis of longitudinal studies. *Child Abuse & Neglect*, 34, 244–252.

Rudolph, K. D., Troop-Gordon, W., Hessel, E. T., & Schmidt, J. D. (2011). A latent growth curve analysis of early and increasing peer victimization as predictors of mental health across elementary school. *Journal of Clinical Child & Adolescent Psychology*, 40, 111–122.

Rueger, S. Y., Malecki, C. K., & Demaray, M. K. (2011). Stability of peer victimization in early adolescence: Effects of timing and duration. *Journal of School Psychology*, 49, 443–464.

Sawyer, A. L., Bradshaw, C. P., & O'Brennan, L. M. (2008). Examining ethnic, gender, and developmental differences in the way children report being a victim of "bullying" on self-report measures. *Journal of Adolescent Health*, 43, 106–114.

Scholte, R. H. J., Engels, R. C. M. E., Overbeek, G., de Kemp, R. A. T., & Haselager, G. J. T. (2007). Stability in bullying and victimization and its association with social adjustment in childhood and adolescence. *Journal of Abnormal Child Psychology*, 35, 217–228.

Schreier, A., Wolke, D., Thomas, K., Horwood, J., Hollis, C., Gunnell, D., Lewis, G., Thompson, A., Zammit, S., Duffy, L., Salvi, G., & Harrison, G. (2009). Prospective study of peer victimization in childhood and psychotic symptoms in a nonclinical population at age 12 years. *Archive of General Psychiatry*, 66, 527–536.

Schwartz, D., Dodge, K. A., & Coie, J. D. (1993). The emergence of chronic peer victimization in boys' play groups. *Child Development*, 64, 1755–1772.

Sourander, A., Helstela, L., Helenius, H., & Piha, J. (2000). Persistence of bullying from childhood to adolescence: A longitudinal 8-year follow-up study. *Child Abuse and Neglect*, 24, 873–881.

Spriggs, A. L., Iannotti, R. J., Nansel, T. R., & Haynie, D. L. (2007). Adolescent bullying involvement and perceived family, peer and school relations: Commonalities and differences across race/ethnicity. *Journal of Adolescent Health*, 41, 283–293.

Storch, E. A., Nock, M. K., Masia-Warner, C., & Barlas, M. E. (2003). Peer victimization and social-psychological adjustment in Hispanic and African-American children. *Journal of Child and Family Studies*, 12, 439–452.

Sugden, K., Arseneault, L., Harrington, H., Moffit, T. E., Williams, B., & Caspi, A. (2010). Serotonin transporter gene moderates the development of emotional problems among children following bullying victimization. *Journal of the American Academy of Child & Adolescent Psychiatry*, 49, 830–840.

Sullivan, T. N., Farrell, A. D., & Kliewer, W. (2006). Peer victimization in early adolescence: Associations between physical and relational victimization and drug use, aggression, and delinquent behaviors among urban middle school students. *Development and Psychopathology*, 18, 119–137.

Swearer, S., Espelage, D. L., Vaillancourt, T., & Hymel, S. (2010). What can be done about school bullying? Linking research to educational practice. *Educational Researcher*, 39, 38–47.

Sweeting, H., Young, R., West, P., & Der, G. (2006). Peer victimization and depression in early-mid adolescence: A longitudinal study. *British Journal of Educational Psychology*, 76, 577–594.

Ttofi, M. M., Farrington, D. P., Losel, F., & Loeber, R. (2011). Do victims of school bullying tend to become depressed later in life? A systematic review and meta-analysis of longitudinal studies. *Journal of Aggression, Conflict and Peace Research*, 3, 63–73.

Turkel, A. R. (2007). Sugar and spice and puppy dog's tails: The psychodynamics of bullying. *Journal of the American Academy of Psychoanalysts and Dynamic Psychiatry*, 35, 243–258.

Underwood, M. K., Galen, B. R., & Paquette, J. A. (2001). Top ten challenges for understanding gender and aggression in children: Why can't we all just get along? *Social Development*, 10, 248–266.

Vaillancourt, T., Brittain, H. L., McDougall, P., & Duku, E. (2013). Longitudinal links between childhood peer victimization, internalizing and externalizing problems, and academic functioning: Developmental cascades. *Journal of Abnormal Child Psychology*, 41, 1203–1215

Vaillancourt, T., Clinton, J., McDougall, P., Schmidt, L. A., & Hymel, S. (2010). The neurobiology of peer victimization and rejection. In S. R. Jimerson, S. M. Swearer, & D. L. Espelage (Eds.), *Handbook of bullying in schools: An international perspective* (pp. 293–304). New York: Routledge.

Vaillancourt, T., Duku, E., Becker, S., Schmidt, L., Nicol, J., Muir, C., & MacMillan, H. (2011). Peer victimization, depressive symptoms, and high salivary cortisol predict poor memory in children. *Brain and Cognition*, 77, 191–199.

Vaillancourt, T., Duku, E., deCantzaro, D., MacMillan, H., Muir, C., & Schmidt, L. A. (2008). Variation in hypothalamic-pituitary-adrenal axis activity among bullied and non-bullied children. *Aggressive Behavior*, 34, 294–305.

Vaillancourt, T., Hymel, S., & McDougall, P. (2003). Bullying is power: Implications for school-based intervention strategies. Special issue: *Journal of Applied School Psychology*, 19, 157–176.

(2011). Why does being bullied hurt so much? Insights from neuroscience. In D. Espelage & S. W. Swearer (Eds.), *Bullying in North American schools* (2nd ed., pp. 23–33). New York: Taylor & Francis Group, Inc.

(2013). The biological underpinnings of peer victimization: Understanding why and how the effects of bullying can last a lifetime. *Theory into Practice*, 52, 241–248.

Vaillancourt, T., Miller, J. L., Fagbemi, J., Côté, S., & Tremblay, R. E. (2007). Trajectories and predictors of indirect aggression: Results from a nationally representative longitudinal study of Canadian children aged 2–10. *Aggressive Behavior*, 33, 314–326.

Vaillancourt, T., Trinh, T., McDougall, P., Duku, E., Cunningham, L., Cunningham, C., Hymel, S., & Short, K. (2010). Optimizing population screening of bullying in school-aged children. *Journal of School Violence*, 9, 233–250.

van der Wal, M. F., de Wit, C. A. M., & Hirasing, R. A. (2003). Psychosocial health among young victims and offenders of direct and indirect bullying. *Pediatrics*, 111, 1312–1317.

van Lier, P. A. C., Vitaro, F., Barker, E. D., Brendgen, M., Tremblay, R. E., & Boivin, M. (2012). Peer victimization, poor academic achievement, and the link between childhood externalizing and internalizing problems. *Child Development*, 83, 1775–1788.

Verkuyten, M., & Thijs, J. (2002). Racist victimization among children in the Netherlands: The effect of ethnic group and school. *Ethnic and Racial Studies*, 25, 310–331.

Vervoort, M. H. M., Scholte, R. H. J., & Overbeek, G. (2010). Bullying and victimization among adolescents: The role of ethnicity and ethnic composition of school class. *Journal of Youth and Adolescence*, 39, 1–11.

Vuijk, P., van Lier, P., Crijnen, A., & Huizink, A. (2007). Testing sex-specific pathways from peer victimization to anxiety and depression through a randomized intervention trial. *Journal of Affective Disorders*, 100, 221–226.

Williams, K., Chambers, M., Logan, S., & Robinson, D. (1996). Association of common health symptoms with bullying in primary school children. *British Medical Journal*, 3, 17–19.

Wolke, D., Woods, S., Bloomfield, L., & Karstadt, L. (2001). Bullying involvement in primary school and common health problems. *Archives of Disease in Childhood*, 85, 197–201.

7

The Potential Risks and Adaptive Contributions of Elite Social Status to Youth Development

WENDY TROOP-GORDON

When examining the cultural and contextual forces on the developing child, one would be remiss not to address one of the most proximal and influential of those contexts: the peer group. A complex network of friendships dyads, cliques, antipathies, and acquaintances, each peer group has a hierarchical power structure and its own culture that dictates the group's values, goals, and standards with which to evaluate group members. Success within the peer context is not merely a marker of healthy development. Forging satisfying and supportive peer relationships has been identified by developmentalists and clinical psychologists as vital for youths' mental and physical well-being. This is evidenced by the prominence of social competence and peer relationships in recent theories of developmental psychopathology (e.g., Masten & Cicchetti, 2010; Rudolph et al., 2000), and more than three decades of research bridging success in peer contexts with greater mental health, behavioral adjustment, academic achievement, and physical well-being (Ladd, 2005; Rubin, Bukowski, & Parker, 2006).

Based on this evidence, the prevailing view has been that success in peer relationships fosters mental health and adjustment. Being liked by agemates, establishing close dyadic friendships, and avoiding negative interactions with peers (e.g., peer victimization) have all been heralded as hallmarks of healthy social development (Ladd, 2005; Ladd & Ladd, 2001; Rubin, Bukowski, & Laursen, 2009). However, what it means to be socially successful to children and adolescents may be quite different than what has been reflected in the research literature. For example, children do not merely seek to be accepted; they also strive to be powerful (Jarvinen & Nicholls, 1996; Ojanen, Grönroos, & Salmivalli, 2005). They not only want intimate, supportive friendships; they seek to be central members of prestigious social cliques (Adler, Kless, & Adker, 1992; Eder, 1985; LaFontana & Cillessen, 2010). They do not avoid confrontation at all costs; they challenge peers who threaten their status in the social hierarchy (Adler & Adler, 1998; Merten, 1994, 1997; Sippola, Paget, & Buchanan, 2007). Put plainly, youth want to be "popular." However, unlike acceptance from peers and friendships, which have almost universal positive effects on the individual, striving for status may simultaneously jeopardize and bolster health and well-being. It is the seemingly incongruous effects elite status has on youths' development that is the focus of this chapter.

Among developmental psychologists, the entire meaning of "popularity" and "status" has undergone a relatively recent transformation. Historically, when examining youths' social standing within their peer group, investigators have equated popularity with likeability. Using sociometric measures of who is "liked most" and who is "liked least," popular children and adolescents have been identified as those youth who are highly liked, and rarely disliked, by their peers (Coie, Dodge, & Coppotelli, 1982). This sociometric view of popularity contrasts sharply with sociological perspectives on the meaning of status in peer cultures (Asher & McDonald, 2009; Cairns, 1983; Lease, Musgrove, & Axelrod, 2002), as well as children's and adolescents' own conceptions of social success (e.g., LaFontana & Cillessen, 1998; Parkhurst & Hopmeyer, 1998), where popularity is viewed as indicative of prestige, power, and social centrality. In order to distinguish this prestige-based popularity from "sociometric popularity" or likeability (i.e., popularity defined as being well-liked by peers), investigators have begun to use terms such as "reputation-based popularity" (Wang, Houshyar, & Prinstein, 2006), "consensual popularity" (de Bruyn & van den Boom, 2005), or "perceived popularity" (e.g., LaFontana & Cillessen, 2002). In this chapter, I use the terms "elite social status" or "high social status" to refer to this form of popularity and to synthesize research that has examined the developmental and health implications of social prestige and stature using disparate theoretical perspectives and methodological paradigms.

A major impetus for studying socially elite youth is that, despite their enviable position within their peer group's social hierarchy, these youths are not necessarily high in sociometric popularity. Socially elite youth enjoy a number of positive social provisions including being emulated by others, sought after for friendship, and viewed by others as possessing valued traits (e.g., "coolness," physical attractiveness, athletic ability; Adler & Adler, 1998; Cillessen & Rose, 2005; Dijkstra, Cillessen, Lindenberg, & Veenstra, 2010; Eder, 1985). However, they are not necessarily liked by their peers (Cillessen & Rose, 2005). Correlations between nominations as "popular" and traditional measures of sociometric popularity are often modest and decrease with age (Cillessen & Borch, 2006; Rose & Swenson, 2009). For example, Cillessen and Mayeux (2004) found a correlation of .73 between sociometric popularity and nominations as popular among a sample of 5th graders. However, this association had steadily decreased to .40 by the time the children were in the 9th grade.

The weak relation between being liked by peers and being identified as "popular" further confirms the distinctiveness of these two forms of peer success and has sparked substantial interest in identifying those characteristics that contribute to high social status within children's and adolescents' peer groups. This work has yielded a fairly consistent picture of the traits characteristic of socially elite youth. Similar to children and adolescents identified as well accepted using sociometric nominations of liking, those who attain elite social status are often prosocial in their interactions with agemates (e.g., LaFontana & Cillessen, 2002; Parkhurst, & Hopmeyer, 1998; Rodkin, Farmer, Pearl, & van Acker, 2000). They also tend to be highly socially skilled, athletic, physically attractive, and wealthy relative to peers and are leaders within their peer groups (Adler & Adler, 1998; Lease et al., 2002; Meisinger, Blake, Lease, Palardy, & Olejnik, 2007; Xie, Li, Boucher, Hutchins, & Cairns, 2006). However, they can also be snobbish, manipulative, and overtly and relationally aggressive (e.g., Bowker, Rubin, Buskirk-Cohen, Rose-Krasnor, & Booth-LaForce, 2010; Cillessen & Rose, 2005; Eder, 1985; Parkhurst & Hopmeyer, 1998; Rodkin et al., 2000). Consequently, these youth are often disliked by peers who have been hurt by their more destructive behaviors (Parkhurst & Hopmeyer, 1998).

Elite status has also sparked the interest of investigators because of the importance placed on it by children and adolescents. High social status is a salient goal for many youth (Adler & Adler, 1998; Corsaro & Eder, 1990; Jarvinen & Nicholls, 1996; LaFontana & Cillessen, 2010; Ryan & Shim, 2008), suggesting that much is to be gained from achieving elite status. Yet the immediate benefits procured from elite social status may not lead to long-term gains in youths' psychosocial adjustment. Furthermore, heightened concerns regarding social standing may come at a cost, as children and adolescents may set aside other important goals and personally held values in the quest for social stature. Thus, explicating the risks and benefits of achieving elite status within one's peer group remains an important objective within the field of developmental psychopathology.

In this chapter, I explore how high social status may be beneficial as well as detrimental to children's development. I start with the premise that efforts to understand the developmental implications of social stature can be aided by greater specificity in the definition of terms such as "perceived" or "consensual popularity" and by distinguishing the defining features of social status from those correlates that either aid in the attainment and maintenance of elite status or are the consequence of having achieved high social standing within the peer group. Beyond the question of definition, understanding why achieving or protecting elite status is a high priority for so many children and adolescents can help elucidate the benefits status confers. To this end, three theoretical perspectives are presented to illuminate why goals to be "popular" are salient during childhood and adolescence and why elite status may beneficially impact youths' development. However, achieving or maintaining high social standing may come at a cost. Children and adolescents may engage in risky behaviors and compromise personal values and goals in the quest to be prominent members of prestigious cliques (LaFontana & Cillessen, 2010; Mayeux, Sandstrom, & Cillessen, 2008). Elite status as a risk factor, therefore, is addressed next with a particular emphasis on how a desire for high social status can lead to compromised behavioral and school adjustment. Recent research addressing the consequences of attaining social stature is then reviewed in light of these theoretical perspectives, and future directions for the study of status-adjustment linkages are proposed.

WHAT IS "POPULARITY"? DEFINING ELITE SOCIAL STATUS

Investigators vary as to which characteristics of youth they identify as being indicative of elite social status. This is due, in part, to the genesis of the construct. Early investigations into elite social status were premised on the assumption that "popularity" had a different meaning to children and adolescents than it did to peer relations researchers (LaFontana & Cillessen, 2002; Parkhurst & Hopmeyer, 1998; Vaillancourt & Hymel, 2006). To address this concern, researchers began asking children to identify who was popular in their classroom or grade without providing a definition of the term (e.g., LaFontana & Cillessen, 2002; Parkhurst & Hopmeyer, 1998). Thus, popularity was conceived as socially constructed within the peer culture and, therefore, to study it, meaning was not to be imposed by investigators (Rose, Swenson, & Waller, 2004).

The proliferation of studies on elite social status has resulted in a multitude of methods for identifying high-status youth. Most commonly, investigators have adopted the peer nomination method of having youth identify their "popular" (e.g., Rose, Swenson, & Waller, 2004) or "most popular" and "least popular" peers (e.g., de Bruyn & Van den Boom, 2005; Meijs, Cillessen, Scholte, Segers, Spijkerman, 2010; Prinstein & Cillessen, 2003; Vaillancourt, Hymel, & McDougall, 2003). Less frequently, investigators use teacher nominations or rankings (Farmer, Estell, Bishop, O'Neal, & Cairns, 2003; Rodkin et al., 2000; Rodkin & Roisman, 2010), or peer ratings (Troop-Gordon, Visconti, & Kuntz, 2011) of popularity and related traits (e.g., is popular with boys, has lots of friends, is "cool"). Others rely on children's or adolescents' nominations of peers on traits characteristic of high-status youth (e.g., someone everyone likes to be with; e.g., Bowker et al., 2010; Dijkstra, Lindenberg, Verhulst, Ormel, & Veenstra, 2009). More pronounced departures from the peer-nomination tradition of identifying peer status can be seen in the sociological work of such investigators as Adler and Adler (Adler & Adler, 1998; Adler et al., 1992), Eckert (1989), Eder (Eder, 1985; Evans & Eder, 1993), and Merten (1996, 1997, 2004). In this work, the meaning of popularity is derived from conversations and direct observations of youth. Others identify high-status youth through the use of social network analysis, which provides assessments of youths' clique membership, their location within the clique (i.e., central vs. peripheral), and the status of their clique within the larger social structure of the peer group (e.g., Gest, Graham-Bermann, & Hartup, 2001; Rodkin et al., 2000).

Consequently, a precise definition of "popularity," separate from sociometric popularity, has yet to be established. Rather, investigators use a variety of terms to describe high-status youth, reflecting the particular theoretical perspective on which their research is based, as well as their preferred method for identifying popular youth. Popularity is often equated with *status, power, prestige, prominence, social visibility, dominance, social centrality, influence, access to resources,* and *impact* (Cohen & Prinstein, 2006; de Bruyn & van den Boom, 2005; Farmer et al., 2003; LaFontana & Cillessen, 2002). High-status youth are further perceived as those children and adolescents who are sought after for affiliation and friendship, are members of prestigious crowds and cliques, and are emulated by peers (Cillessen & Mayeux, 2004; Dijkstra et al., 2009; Puckett, Aikins, & Cillessen, 2008).

The identification of the benefits of achieving elite social status, however, necessitates distinguishing the state of being popular from the advantages that high social status may confer (e.g., dominance, resources, visibility, influence, admiration). To this end, I propose that popularity might best be conceived as membership and centrality in a prestigious social clique. The prestige of a clique depends on a reputational consensus that clique members exemplify those characteristics that are valued by the peer group at large. Thus, rather than reflecting characteristics specific to the individual, elite social status may be conceived as solely a function of one's affiliative ties.

To illustrate this point, imagine a girl named Kemerie, a bright, outgoing, athletic, attractive, and socially skilled student. In elementary school, she and her friends had the reputation for being the most "popular" girls in the class. They garnered others' admiration, were imitated by other girls, and received attention from the most popular boys. After transitioning to middle school, however, Kemerie no longer saw her old friends. She made new friends who were nice, but her new clique never gained high status within the social hierarchy of her middle school. Although remaining as attractive, socially competent, bright, and athletic as she had been in elementary school, Kemerie failed to receive the same level of admiration from her peers as she had before the school transition, and she was no longer as well known, influential, or sought after by peers as she had once been.

Conceptualizing popularity as a function of one's clique and one's position in that clique is in line with sociological perspectives on popularity that have informed much of the current research on elite social status. As the term "elite social status" implies, being part of a prestigious clique is a strong desire for many children and adolescents, and socially elite youth are, in turn, careful to limit clique membership (Adler et al., 1992; Eder, 1985; Merten, 1996). This definition also allows for multiple pathways to social stature. For example, two subtypes of high-status youth have been identified – one with a reputation for engaging primarily in prosocial interactions with peers and one that exhibits a combination of hostile, coercive, and prosocial behaviors toward others (e.g., Farmer et al., 2003; Hawley, 2003; Rodkin et al., 2000; Rodkin & Roisman, 2010), suggesting that children and adolescents may rely on both prosocial and coercive tactics to gain entry into prestigious cliques and maintain their position within the social hierarchy. This definition also takes into account recent findings that the characteristics associated with elite social status may vary across developmental and cultural contexts (Kennedy, 1995; LaFontana & Cillessen, 2002; Meisinger et al., 2007).

THE APPEAL OF ELITE SOCIAL STATUS

During early and middle childhood, social motivations center on having friends and being liked by others (Buhrmester & Furman, 1986; Parker & Gottman, 1989). At these younger ages, nominations of popularity are highly correlated with measures of liking (Cillessen & Borch, 2006; Cillessen & Mayeux, 2004). Late childhood (i.e., 10 or 11 years of age) ushers in substantial changes in the social structure of the peer group and in the social goals of greatest importance to youth. Cliques begin to form (Cairns, Xie, & Leung, 1998; Corsaro & Eder, 1990) and concerns emerge regarding one's standing within this newly formed social hierarchy (Adler & Adler, 1998;

Corsaro & Eder, 1990; Jarvinen & Nicholls, 1996; LaFontana & Cillessen, 2010 Ryan & Shim, 2008; Sullivan, 1953). Many youth report that achieving popularity is one of their primary goals (Jarvinen & Nicholls, 1996; Ojanen et al., 2005). For example, LaFontana and Cillessen (2010) found that beginning in the elementary school years, children begin to prioritize status goals over concern for others' welfare, romantic relationships, friendships, and academic success. Concerns regarding social status peak during middle school and then begin to wane, although obtaining elite social status can remain a prominent social goal for many youth throughout late adolescence (Brown, Eicher, & Petrie, 1986; Buhrmester & Furman, 1986; LaFontana & Cillessen, 2010).

What provisions do youth in elite social cliques enjoy that makes high social status a central goal to so many youth? In this section, I review three theoretical perspectives that may illuminate the desire for elite status. I begin with evolutionary psychology, which has been used extensively to understand how high social status can lead to greater access to social and instrumental resources. I then turn to two theories – self-determination theory and symbolic interaction theory – to address the psychological benefits that may be accrued from elite social status.

Evolutionary perspectives. From the perspective of evolutionary psychology, success in the peer group is a function of one's ability to compete for resources (Bjorklund & Blasi, 2005; Cummins, 2005; Hawley, 1999). For both animals (de Waal, 1982; Dunbar, 1988; Duntley, 2005; Hausfater, Altmann, & Altmann, 1982) and humans (Strayer & Strayer, 1976), dominant group members excel within competitive contexts (e.g., physical confrontations), yielding greater access to potential mates and other valued resources (de Waal, 1982; Dunbar, 1988; Duntley, 2005; Hausfater et al., 1982; Pellegrini & Bartini, 2001). Over time, a dominance hierarchy is established with those at the lower echelons yielding greater access to mates, social affiliations, and other material rewards to more dominant group members (Bernstein, 1981; Pellegrini, 2001; Strayer, 1980). Consequent to this dynamic, intragroup agonism is diminished.

Investigators addressing dominance consistent with zoological and ethological approaches have primarily focused on coercive means of achieving dominance and power (see Hawley, 2007; Pellegrini, 2008, for background). This agonism-leads-to-power approach stands in contrast to peer relations research, which has historically underscored the role of low rather than high levels of agonism in garnering popularity, social impact, and status (Asher & McDonald, 2009; Newcomb, Bukowski, & Pattee, 1993). Developments within both fields have allowed for a bridging of these contradictory perspectives on social hierarchies. Child development researchers versed in evolutionary theory have noted that power over others can be achieved through multiple, diverse means, including methods that are indirect and enhance cooperation among group members (Charlesworth, 1996; LaFreniere & Charlesworth, 1983). Hawley's (1999, 2007) resource control theory expands upon this proposition, proposing two equally successful routes to social dominance and resource attainment – one in which individuals enlist the aid and support of others through affiliative behaviors and a second in which individuals utilize more antagonistic strategies. Applying this principle to human children and adolescents, Hawley has identified two types of socially elite youth – prosocial controllers who embody positive social skills (i.e., those who use cooperation, help, and prosocial means of eliciting resources from others) and bistrategic controllers (i.e., those who obtain resources using a combination of prosocial and coercive means). Although they employ different tactics to achieve social dominance, prosocial and bistrategic controllers enjoy similarly high levels of peer regard (Hawley, 2003).

Within the peer relations literature, a complementary set of findings began to emerge in the mid to late 1990s with the identification of high-status youth who engage in overt and relational aggression (Luthar & McMahon, 1996; Parkhurst & Hopmeyer, 1998; Rodkin et al., 2000). Thus, assumptions regarding the prosocial basis of popularity were challenged, as investigators began to identify the use of aggressive and manipulative behaviors in the service of obtaining social standing. Consequently, a more complex understanding of status during childhood and adolescence emerged that included not only being liked by others but also having a position of prestige. This confluence of findings across literatures has allowed for a reconceptualization of the meaning of social status amenable to evolutionary perspectives.

Social status and dominance are related, leading researchers to question whether elite social status is one of many social resources procured by dominant youth, or, conversely, whether elite social status imparts power and influence over others. Empirical evidence from longitudinal studies on the association between social status and one means of dominating peers, aggression, indicates that social stature forecasts subsequent increases in aggressive behavior (Cillessen & Mayeux, 2004; Prinstein & Cillessen, 2003; Puckett et al., 2008; Rose, Swenson, & Waller, 2004; Sandstrom & Cillessen, 2006; although see Cillessen & Mayeux, 2004; Puckett et al., 2008; and Rose, Swenson, & Waller, 2004 for findings showing reciprocal associations). Thus, elite social status may be a route to increased aggression and resource control, making the obtainment of high social status an attractive goal to children and adolescents. These data are limited, however, to aggressive behaviors. The possibility remains that elite status may also foster socially valued resource control strategies (e.g., prosocial behaviors) that are typically perceived as indicative of adaptive development.

Although developmental shifts occur in the types of resources for which humans compete (e.g., access to toys during toddlerhood and preschool; Hawley & Little, 1999; Pellegrini, 2001, 2008), sexual competition and access to desirable mates remain at the forefront in evolutionary psychology circles focusing on adults (e.g., Buss, 1995). High-status children's advantages in cross-sex relationships are well documented. During middle childhood and preadolescence, these youth are often the first to cross sex-segregation boundaries (Adler & Adler, 1998; Adler et al., 1992). Such interactions are often playful in nature and involve teasing, communicating through friends, and other safe interactions that protect youth from the appearance of romantic interest (i.e., borderwork, Thorne, 1986). As comfort with cross-sex engagement increases, socially elite youth are leaders in initiating contact and social activity between cross-sex cliques (Adler et al., 1992) and are among the first in their age group to engage in dating relationships (Adler & Adler, 1998; Carlson & Rose, 2007; Dunphy, 1963).

Aggression and other acts of agonism (e.g., toughness) may be one way that high-status youth secure access to cross-sex peers (Pellegrini & Long, 2003). For example, girls are attracted to more aggressive males (Bukowski, Sippola, & Newcomb, 2000; Pellegrini & Bartini, 2001). In their observations of early adolescent boys, Evans and Eder (1993) witnessed frequent use of sexually based insults against less dominant peers, including questioning others' sexual orientation and masculinity. Similarly, whether girls are attractive to boys as dating partners is significantly related to their use of relational aggression (Pellegrini & Long, 2003), perhaps reflecting competition among girls for males' romantic interests (Sippola et al., 2007). However, membership in high-status cliques may provide additional advantages in securing potential cross-sex mates. Centrality in high-status peer groups communicates that one embodies peer-valued characteristics, and although culture-specific correlates of social status are noted (Kennedy, 1995; Meisinger et al., 2007), the characteristics often associated with being socially elite may signal reproductive fitness to cross-sex peers. For example, toughness, athleticism, and leadership are associated with elite status among males; physical attractiveness and wealth are associated with elite status among females (Adler & Adler, 1998; Hopmeyer & Parkhurst, 1998; LaFontana & Cillessen, 2002). Furthermore, as high-status youth tend to befriend and socialize with other high-status youth (Eder, 1985; Peters, Cillessen, Riksen-Walraven, & Haselager, 2010), affiliating with socially elite peers may increase opportunities to interact with potential, desirable mates.

Youth may also seek out elite social status as a means of seeming more attractive to potential romantic partners. Hawley, Johnson, Mize, and McNamara (2007) found that, when asked to rate the attractiveness of their students, preschool teachers showed a bias toward bistrategic and proso- cial controllers, students who typically also enjoy power and status among their peers. However, these same children were not viewed as more attrac- tive than their peers when evaluated by adults with whom they were unac- quainted. Although these findings were limited to preschool children and evaluations of physical attraction, one implication is that elite social sta- tus may positively bias how individuals are seen by others, increasing their chances of establishing romantic relationships.

Increased opportunities for cross-sex relationships may not be the only benefit socially elite youth gain from their privileged status. Sociologists note that high-status children and adolescents enjoy greater visibility and influence among peers, larger social circles, and greater social activity (e.g., Adler &Adler, 1998). Thus, elite social status may help fulfill a range of social and intrapsychic needs (Hawley, 1999; Pellegrini, 2008). Whereas evolutionary psychology has provided a solid basis for examining status as a means of obtaining desired resources, self-determination and symbolic interaction theories provide conceptual frameworks well suited for expli- cating the psychological benefits of obtaining an elite position in one's peer group.

Self-Determination Theory. Although evolutionary psychologists are primarily known for stressing adaptive behaviors and group structures in the service of satisfying physiological necessities (e.g., procuring mates, protection, food), they also point to status and dominance as means of sat- isfying psychological needs (e.g., cognitive stimulation, companionship; Hawley, 1999). From the perspective of self-determination theory (SDT), three basic psychological needs have evolved that aid in species' adaptation to environmental changes and challenges: competence, relatedness, and autonomy (Deci & Ryan, 2000). Individuals strive to satisfy these needs through the pursuit of culturally valued activities and personal goals. When all three needs are fulfilled, behaviors become intrinsically motivated, and extrinsic pressures become fully integrated into one's sense of self, resulting in an autonomy orientation (i.e., sense of one's behavior as encompassing volitional, self-determined acts that reflect a congruent self-identity). Thus, through the satisfaction of psychological needs, personal well-being and growth are achieved. In contrast, when psychological needs are thwarted, extrinsic or impersonal (i.e., amotivated) orientations develop, compromising mental health and overall adjustment. Consistent with this premise, obstacles to fulfillment of relatedness, competence, or autonomy result in reduced well-being, including less positive affect and self-esteem and more health disturbances (Deci & Ryan, 2000).

Although SDT has been applied most widely to achievement and health domains, within the peer culture of childhood and adolescence, elite social status may be a salient means with which to satisfy basic psychological needs. For example, Stump, Ratliff, Wu, and Hawley (2009) noted that bistrategic controllers, who often receive high peer regard, are able to successfully fulfill competence, relatedness, and autonomy needs. Elite status may play a particularly important role in the fulfillment of competence needs within social domains, as social stature enhances visibility and influence over peers (Vaillancourt & Hymel, 2006). For example, socially elite youth set group opinions and determine peer clique boundaries (Adler et al., 1992; Eder, 1985; Farmer et al., 2003). This ability to successfully navigate and direct their peer ecology can foster a heightened sense of social efficacy among elite youth (Cillessen & Mayeux, 2007; Puckett et al., 2008). In addition, high-status youth, through their social ties and influence over others, may have greater opportunity to engage in competence-enhancing activities (e.g., cheerleading, athletics, student government).

Evidence points to greater satisfaction of relatedness needs among high-status youth as well (Stump et al., 2009). High-status youth are often the recipients of others' bids for friendship and affiliation (Adler et al., 1992; Dijkstra et al., 2009; Eder, 1985; see also Hawley et al., 2007). They have more friends than less popular youth and engage in more fun and social activities (Adler & Adler, 1998; Rose, Swenson, & Carlson, 2004). Although some question whether high-status youth form genuine and mutually satisfying friendships with peers (Eder, 1985; Lesko, 1988), greater social prestige is positively associated with friendship quality (Rose, Swenson, & Carlson, 2004). Thus, elite social status may provide a means of satisfying relatedness needs at both the group and dyadic levels.

Attainment of prestigious social status should also allow for greater fulfillment of autonomy needs. Rather than yielding to the will of others, socially elite youth have greater freedom to act on their own volition, leading peers rather than being led (Hawley, 2003). Capitalizing on their social centrality and leadership roles, high-status youth have greater liberty to determine with whom they affiliate and, as decision makers, may direct the clique's activities, resulting in heightened feelings of autonomy (Stump et al., 2009). Not all members of elite cliques, however, may have equal fulfillment of autonomy needs. Some high-status youth may feel external control as they strive to emulate peer group norms and values (e.g., group standards regarding physical fitness, attractiveness, toughness, and maturity). Peripheral members of elite cliques may be particularly vulnerable to the thwarting of autonomy goals as they may submit to the explicit and implicit social demands of more socially prominent peers in order to maintain their fragile role in the status hierarchy (see Cohen & Prinstein, 2006, for the role of status on peer contagion). Thus, by trying to attain or hold on to elite social status, youths may in advertently undermine rather than enhance their own autonomy.

Symbolic Interactionism. From a symbolic interaction framework, elite status may have a substantial impact on youths' developing identity and assessment of self-worth. Symbolic interactionism (for a review, see Stryker & Vryan, 2006) stresses the constructive and fluid process of self-identity development through interactions with social others. Within the context of social interactions, individuals derive shared meanings, or symbols, which serve to organize human behavior and systems of understanding. The self and other become significant symbols often understood through recognized social categories and roles. Self-understanding is construed from individuals' perceptions of how they are appraised by others and the roles others and the self are seen as occupying (Mead, 1934). Drawing from these basic tenets of symbolic interactionism, peer relationship researchers have explicated the important role of peer acceptance, friendships, and peer victimization in youths' self-concept development and self-esteem (e.g., Cole, Maxwell, Dukewich, & Yosick, 2010; Ladd & Troop-Gordon, 2003; Salmivalli & Isaacs, 2005 Troop-Gordon & Ladd, 2005).

Within the peer group, elite status is a highly salient social category around which relationships and behaviors are organized (Adler et al., 1992; Eder, 1985). As high social status engenders attainment of valued characteristics and competencies, incorporation of "popular" into one's identity may boost one's sense of self-worth and assessment of one's capabilities in a variety of domains (e.g., appearance, scholastics, athletics). In addition, the relative status of individuals leads to predictable patterns of interaction. For example, Eder (1985) observed that girls wishing to elevate their own social status often flatter socially elite girls in an effort to win their favor. Thus, high-status youth may receive more positive appraisals from others and less criticism, thereby leading to heightened feelings of self-worth and competence (Adler et al., 1992; de Bruyn & Cillessen, 2006; Sandstrom &

Cillessen, 2010). Consistent with this proposition, within late childhood and adolescence, high-status youth have more positive assessments of their social relationships and abilities than their peers (de Bruyn & van den Boom, 2005; Hawley, 2003; Lease et al., 2002). The implications for youths' mental health development are far reaching as greater social self-esteem and more positive self-perceptions within peer domains have been found to protect against later internalizing problems such as depression and anxiety (e.g., Cole, Peeke, Dolezal, Murray, & Canzoniero, 1999; Ladd & Troop-Gordon, 2003; Troop-Gordon & Ladd, 2005). However, heightened social self-esteem may simultaneously contribute to increased aggression directed toward peers, particularly when feelings of competence are threatened (Diamantopoulou, Rydell, & Henricsson, 2008).

THE POTENTIAL FOR ELITE STATUS TO BE AN ASSET AND A LIABILITY

In order to garner the benefits of elite status, youth must exemplify those characteristics valued by their peer group. This, in itself, can be a promotive or risky endeavor. To the extent that the traits and characteristics valued by peers are concordant with adults' goals for youths' development, efforts to obtain or maintain elite status should have a positive effect on long-term behavioral and health outcomes. Indeed, many of the traits correlated with high social status overlap with the goals parents and teachers have for children's and adolescents' development. For example, these youth often are socially intelligent (Adler & Adler, 1998; Andreou, 2006; Meijs et al., 2010), prosocial in their interactions with peers (e.g., Cillessen & Rose, 2005; LaFontana & Cillessen, 2002; Luthar & McMahon, 1996; Rodkin et al., 2000), have a good sense of humor (Vaillancourt & Hymel, 2006), and are athletic (Adler & Adler, 1998; LaFontana & Cillessen, 2002; Rodkin et al., 2000). They also display leadership skills (Farmer et al., 2003; Lease et al., 2002; Rodkin et al., 2000) and, at least during late childhood, are academically successful (Farmer et al., 2003; Kennedy, 1995; LaFontana & Cillessen, 2002); success in school may be particularly associated with perceived popularity among girls (Adler & Adler, 1998; Adler et al., 2002).

To the extent that peer-valued characteristics serve in opposition to societally held values for youth, efforts to obtain or protect one's status may compromise healthy development. Beginning in late childhood, a divergence emerges between what youth see as attractive in peers and what adults value (Allen, Weissberg, & Hawkins, 1989). For example, in contrast to the prosocial orientation adults often try to instill in youths, children increasingly view aggression, delinquency, defiance of adults, and toughness positively (Becker & Luthar, 2007; Bukowski et al., 2000; Coie, Dodge, & Kupersmidt, 1990; Corsaro & Eder, 1990). In response to pressure to conform to gender norms during early adolescence, boys often come to value aggression in their peer interactions, and girls may feel pressure to become less assertive, less academically inclined, and more concerned about physical appearance and pleasing others (see Galambos, Almeida, & Petersen, 1990; Galambos, Berenbaum, & McHale, 2009; Hill & Lynch, 1983). Therefore, in an effort to maintain membership and social centrality in prestigious cliques, youth may display hostile, delinquent, and oppositional behaviors, may disengage from academic pursuits, and may experiment with behaviors that place their health and well-being at risk.

This valuing of antisocial and risky behavior co-occurs with a temporary rise in aggressive and delinquent behaviors during adolescence. This increased oppositional and delinquent activity has been attributed to *a maturity gap* beginning in early adolescence such that adult-imposed restrictions on youths' freedoms are discordant with adolescents' increasing physiological maturity, desire and ability to take on adult-like roles, and psychological need for autonomy (Moffitt, 1993). Adolescents' delinquent behavior serves as a means of exerting their maturity and, therefore, is seen as a relatively normative process during adolescence. However, as youth may disengage from school activities, aggress against others, and become involved in risky and delinquent behaviors, such exertions of their maturity may place their health and development and the well-being of others at risk. Moreover, as maturity and autonomy become increasingly valued by the larger peer group, high-status youth may feel the greatest pressure to engage in delinquent behaviors and to move away from adult-sanctioned activities and behaviors in order to protect their social status (Mayeux et al., 2008; Prinstein, Meade, & Cohen, 2003; Troop-Gordon, Visconti, & Kuntz, 2011).

EMPIRICAL EVIDENCE OF THE BENEFITS AND RISKS ASSOCIATED WITH ELITE SOCIAL STATUS

As the preceding review suggests, attaining high social status can be a rewarding experience yielding increased access to resources, fulfillment of basic psychological needs, and increased sense of competency and self-esteem, resulting in increased mental health and positive personal growth. However, elite status might also come at a cost. High-status youth may engage in aggressive and risky behaviors in an effort to prove their maturity and conform to peer expectations. In this section, I review the empirical evidence addressing the role of status in four domains of youth development: emotional well-being, aggression, risky behaviors, and school adjustment.

Emotional well-being. Youth with elite social status are as emotionally adjusted as their peers. Even those who are aggressive in their peer interactions are no more depressed or anxious than socially prestigious children and adolescents who are not aggressive. In illustration of this point, Luthar and McMahon (1996) found, with a sample of inner-city adolescents of primarily African-American and Hispanic backgrounds, no differences between popular-prosocial and popular-aggressive adolescents with regard to depression and anxiety, and these two groups were no more depressed or anxious than a normative comparison group. Relatively low levels of internalizing problems have also been found among "model" (i.e., popular-prosocial) and "tough" (i.e., popular-aggressive) youth in two studies, the first examining an ethnically diverse sample of 4th- through 6th-grade boys from urban, rural, and suburban communities (Rodkin et al., 2000) and the second focused on male and female rural African-American early adolescents (Farmer et al., 2003). Similarly, in a study on high social status and internalizing problems using a sample of 7th and 9th graders from the Midwestern United States, Rose and Swenson (2009) found that high social status was associated with less internalizing symptomology and protected relationally aggressive adolescents from heightened levels of emotional distress. Furthermore, bistrategic and prosocial controllers, two groups of youth often well regarded by peers, report greater-than-average levels of positive affect (Hawley, 2003).

Thus, not only does it seem that elite status does not hinder youths' well-being, these findings suggest that elite social status may actually bolster youths' emotional adjustment. However, as it is equally possible that high status is a consequence rather than a cause of a positive disposition and low levels of negative affect, investigators have begun testing the longitudinal associations between social status and emotional health. For example, Sandstrom and Cillessen (2006) found among a sample of American early adolescents that being identified as popular in the 5th grade predicted lower levels of internalizing problems 3 years later among boys. In a follow-up study with this same sample, the investigators found that boys who had been relationally aggressive in high school were less likely to report higher levels of depressive symptoms and psychopathology in early adulthood if they had high social status as adolescents (Sandstrom & Cillessen, 2010). Therefore, consistent with the theoretical perspectives discussed in this chapter that point to social stature as a source of enhanced emotional well-being, these findings suggest that elite status leads to improved mental health and happiness.

Yet some investigators speculate that socially elite youth have poor-quality friendships, leading to heightened emotional distress. High-status girls in particular have been reported to be less loyal to friends and more likely to discontinue friendships in order to affiliate with other high-status peers (Eder, 1985; Lesko, 1988). Hawley and colleagues (2007) have also found greater levels of aggression and conflict within the friendships of adolescents identified as bistrategic controllers. Competition and increased use of relational aggression could conceivably detract from the quality of popular youths' friendships, reducing the social support available to them and increasing emotional distress.

Why then do we not find heightened levels of depression and negative affect among high-status youth? One clue may be culled from recent findings showing that high-status youth have a large number of friends and that their friendships are high in intimacy and companionship (Hawley, Little, & Card, 2007; Rose, Swenson, & Carlson, 2004). One possibility is that socially elite youth engage in a pattern of forming highly intimate friendships with peers. These friendships, however, are relatively short in duration due to competition and the use of agonism to retain social standing. When these friendships end, socially elite youth may quickly form new, equally intimate friendships, allowing for continued fulfillment of relatedness and affiliation needs and sustained mental health and well-being.

Aggressive behavior. The use of aggression by high-status youth is a primary reason this group of children and adolescents is so interesting to investigators. Whereas aggression is traditionally seen as antithetical to the development of positive peer relationships, high-status youth are able to adeptly use hostile behaviors while still being admired, sought after, and emulated by peers (see Cillessen & Rose, 2005; Hawley, 2007). This has raised a number of questions regarding the role of aggression in peer relationships: Under what circumstances is aggression conducive to achieving positive peer regard? Are there developmental shifts in the relation between aggression and status over the course of childhood and adolescence? And how is aggression used in the service of obtaining or protecting social prestige?

Descriptions of aggressive behavior are rife within sociological examinations of social status (e.g., Adler & Adler, 1998; Adler et al., 1992; Eder, 1985; Merten, 1997). Based on their observations of children, Adler and Adler (1998) viewed toughness as a core characteristic of high-status boys, and the exclusionary and covertly aggressive behaviors of high-status girls are well documented (e.g., Eder, 1985; Merten, 1997). However, correlations between social status and aggression tend to be modest, suggesting that aggressiveness may not be characteristic of all high-status youth. This has been confirmed in a number of studies in which children have been categorized as a function of their personal characteristics, including aggressive and disruptive behaviors, and their social status or prominence. For example, Farmer, Rodkin, and their colleagues (e.g., Farmer et al., 2003; Rodkin et al., 2000; Rodkin & Roisman, 2010) have identified two subgroups of high-status children – model youth, who engage in low levels of delinquency and aggression, and tough youth, who are more hostile and defiant in their interactions with others. These groupings match nicely onto the prosocial and bistrategic controllers identified by Hawley (2003) who similarly enjoy stature among peers. However, only those categorized as bistrategic display agonistic behaviors.

The link between elite social status and aggression also strengthens as children get older. During early and middle childhood, correlations between status, as indicated by peer nominations of popularity, and aggression are quite modest and may even be negative, but these links become stronger and more positive during early adolescence (Cillessen & Mayeux, 2004; Rose et al., 2004). Greater prevalence of aggression among high-status adolescents may reflect the increasing concern that the youth of this age have regarding their social standing. Others point to school transitions, such as the move to a middle or junior high school, as a precipitating factor in the increase in aggression during early adolescence, as youth struggle to reestablish a dominance hierarchy with a new set of peers (Pellegrini & Bartini, 2001).

Relational aggression, hostile behaviors used to damage others' friendships, reputations, and social standing (Crick & Grotpeter, 1995), may be particularly well suited for obtaining and protecting elite social status. Relationally aggressive acts include spreading negative gossip about someone, excluding a peer from activities, and threatening to end a relationship in order to get one's way. When relational and more overt forms of aggression (e.g., hitting, kicking, calling names) are simultaneously tested as correlates of being nominated by peers as popular, only relational forms of aggression show an independent association with high social status (Prinstein & Cillessen, 2003; Rose et al., 2004). Similarly, Cillessen and Mayeux (2004) have shown that among American youth, relational aggression is more strongly associated with social status than physical aggression and that this difference is stronger among somewhat older children and among girls.

There are a number of reasons why socially elite youth may draw upon relationally aggressive behaviors to manipulate their social environment and harm those who threaten their status. For example, social exclusion and negative gossip may be particularly effective at determining clique membership and boundaries (Cillessen & Rose, 2005), therefore securing one's clique's reputation as being exclusive and limited to only those youth who exemplify peer-valued characteristics. Furthermore, because of its often indirect nature, relational aggression maybe well suited for targeting aggression against others without damaging one's reputation for being kind and cooperative (Rose et al., 2004; Xie, Swift, Cairns, & Cairns, 2002). This may be particularly important for girls, who tend to see covert forms of aggression as more morally justifiable than the use of overtly aggressive behaviors (Evans & Eder, 1993).

Although some youths may use aggression as a means of obtaining social stature, findings from longitudinal studies provide evidence for the reverse direction of effect, that is, that the attainment of high social status is a contributing factor in the development of aggression and externalizing problems (Cillessen & Mayeux, 2004; Prinstein & Cillessen, 2003; Puckett et al., 2008; Rose et al., 2004; Sandstrom & Cillessen, 2006). Moreover, consistent with the premise that covert forms of aggression that damage others' relationships might be well suited for the maintenance of elite status, there is evidence suggesting that obtaining high social status may be more strongly associated with future relational aggression than future overt aggression (Cillessen & Mayeux, 2004; Rose et al., 2004). Elite social status may protect youth from the negative social repercussions that normally follow acts of aggression, allowing high-status youth to use hostile means against those who they believe have harmed them or threaten their social standing (Cillessen & Mayeux, 2004; Rose & Swenson, 2009; Rose et al., 2004; Wang et al., 2006). Indeed, awareness of one's privileged social status, and, therefore, one's power over others, amplifies the likelihood that socially elite youth will become aggressive (Mayeux & Cillessen, 2008). Having established their status in the peer group, they can then further use aggression as a means of drawing self-enhancing comparisons between themselves and those peers seen as failing to display traits valued by the peer group (e.g., approved gender norms; see Evans & Eder, 1993, for a discussion of youths' derision of lower-status peers to enhance their own self-worth), and as a way to show their toughness, a trait that can garner the esteem of older children and adolescents (Becker & Luthar, 2007; Bukowski, Sippola, & Newcomb, 2000; Corsaro & Eder, 1990).

Engagement in risky behaviors. Socially elite youths' deviant behaviors are not limited to aggression against others. Consistent with the proposition that high-status youth assert their maturity and garner the respect of peers through engaging in high-risk behaviors (Mayeux et al., 2008; Prinstein et al., 2003; Troop-Gordon et al., 2011), elite status in adolescence has been linked to engaging in a range of activities that place their health and well-being at risk (e.g., Dolcini & Adler, 1994; Veenstra, Huitsing, Dijkstra, & Lindenberg, 2010; Xie et al., 2006). Substance use is one such behavior. Adolescents who view themselves as being "popular" are more likely than other youth to have used alcohol, cigarettes, and marijuana (Alexander, Piazza, Mekos, & Valente, 2001; Diego, Field, & Sanders, 2003), and adolescents who are viewed by schoolmates as being highly sought after by peers for friendship and affiliation are more likely to have used alcohol and other substances than youth who are seen as receiving fewer friendship bids (Dijkstra et al., 2009). Although it is possible that substance use is a route to gaining social prestige, elite status appears to precede and forecast increased alcohol and substance use among high school students (Mayeux et al., 2008).

In addition to substance use, socially elite youth are also seen by peers as being sexually active (Xi et al., 2006), and investigations into the link between elite status and sexual behaviors confirm these perceptions (e.g., Dolcini & Adler, 1994; Mayeux et al., 2008; Prinstein et al., 2003). Meschke, Zweig, Barber, and Eccles (2000) found, using a sample of Caucasian youth from the Midwest of the United States, that age of first intercourse was negatively associated with placing importance on popularity for boys, providing further support for the proposition that sexual behavior may be a means of asserting one's maturity and sustaining one's social status. However, not all sexual behavior may be related to enhanced social stature. For example, Prinstein et al. (2003) found that promiscuity (i.e., having a number of sexual partners) is not characteristic of socially elite youth, although high social status in adolescence is positively related to engaging in oral sex and sexual intercourse. Thus, sexual behaviors may be seen as an index of maturity, but only respectable in the context of a monogamous relationship.

Socially elite youth may also feel increased pressure to conform to societal standards for physical attractiveness. Physical attractiveness is strongly associated with social standing, particularly among girls (Adler & Adler, 1998; Vaillancourt & Hymel, 2006; Xie et al., 2006). Being overweight may be an especially salient social liability (Fox & Farrow, 2009; Hasler et al., 2005). Perhaps due to felt pressure to conform to peers' expectations regarding physical attractiveness, greater social status is positively associated with engaging in weight-control behaviors (e.g., dieting, exercising; Wang et al., 2006), as well as greater concern for one's body type (Rancourt & Prinstein, 2010). As a result, elite social status may leave youth at risk for eating disorders and associated health-related consequences.

Behavioral and health-related risks associated with elite status may persist beyond adolescence and even after adult peer groups have formed. Sandstrom and Cillessen (2010) found that high-status adolescents continue to show heightened levels of deviant behaviors (i.e., substance use, sexual activity) in the 3 years following high school. These findings suggest that the delinquency exhibited by high-status youth may not be limited to adolescence, as is often assumed. Perhaps due to being socially intelligent (Meijs et al., 2010) and strategic in their ability to garner interpersonal and instrumental resources (Hawley, 2007), some elite youth are able to excel in their professional and personal lives despite engaging in behaviors that would otherwise compromise their well-being. Such possibilities speak to the potential for divergent trajectories in adulthood for previously socially elite youth and the need to examine a range of indicators of adjustment in adulthood (e.g., occupational success, marital adjustment) in order to better understand how status in childhood and adolescence relates to development across the lifespan.

School adjustment and academic success. During childhood and early adolescence, high social status has been associated with a positive orientation toward school and academic success. For example, LaFontana and Cillessen (2002) found, using a sample of low-income, ethnically diverse early adolescents, that identification as "popular" by peers is positively associated with being seen by schoolmates as academically competent, and academic achievement has been found to be positively associated with girls' social status (Adler et al., 1992; Farmer et al., 2003). Furthermore, when transitioning to middle school or high school, youth with higher social status report more positive expectations regarding their future academic performance than their less socially prestigious peers (Cillessen & Mayeux, 2007).

However, during early adolescence, youth increasingly lose admiration for academically oriented peers and increasingly see scholastic achievement as uncharacteristic of high-status youth (Allen et al., 1989; Xie et al., 2006). Low academic achievement may become particularly characteristic of socially elite youth who are relatively high in aggression. Among youth who show high levels of aggressive and disruptive behaviors, academic disengagement may be valued as a means of demonstrating one's maturity and independence from adults' expectations and rules. For these children and adolescents, therefore, decreased academic motivation and effort may be a means of garnering peer regard and status. Consistent with this proposition, socially elite aggressive youth display poor school adjustment and academic problems (de Bruyn & Cillessen, 2006; Farmer et al., 2003; Luthar & McMahon, 1996; Rodkin et al., 2000). In contrast, high-status youth who engage primarily in prosocial interactions with others show average or above-average levels of academic performance (de Bruyn & Cillessen, 2006; Farmer et al., 2003).

Negative associations between status and academic performance among aggressive youth raise the question as to whether the academic difficulties of high-status aggressive youth are attributable to problems associated with being aggressive (e.g., attentional difficulties, conduct problems) or whether high social status is a contributing factor in these students' academic problems. To address this issue, Schwartz, Gorman, Nakamoto, and McKay (2006) and Troop-Gordon and colleagues (2011) investigated whether higher social status predicts trajectories of increased or compromised academic adjustment among aggressive and nonaggressive youth. Schwartz and colleagues (2006) found that high social status predicted declines in GPA and increased unexcused absences from school between the 9th and 10th grades among aggressive adolescents. Similarly, Troop-Gordon and colleagues found that elite social status predicts declines in teacher-rated academic performance and increased school avoidance between the 4th and 5th grades, but only among aggressive youth. Together, these studies suggest that the lower academic performance and school problems of aggressive youth cannot be attributed solely to problems associated with their aggressive behavior.

CONCLUSIONS

The objective of this chapter was to examine the developmental implications of social success from the standpoint of status and prestige rather than acceptance and likeability. However, this task could not be accomplished without first examining how this conceptual distinction and the subsequent increased attention to elite status emerged, resulting in substantial methodological and conceptual variance in the treatment of popularity within the peer relations literature. In this chapter, I have used "elite social status" and "high social status" as umbrella terms with which to synthesize work in this field. The assumption is that, despite widely varying assessment tools and items, the set of studies reviewed here has captured related, if not always completely overlapping, aspects of social status. That is, despite the various ways in which status has been operationalized, each study taps into the extent to which children and adolescents are "socially elite." The viability of this assumption needs to be tested. For example, are the children who are nominated or rated by peers as "popular" the same as those identified as tough or model by adults? Are youth seen as being popular by schoolmates the same as those who are viewed as being someone that others want to be associated with? Tests of the extent to which these varying methods for assessing status converge on the same underlying social phenomenon would help clarify the nature and defining features of elite social status.

The implications of high social status also cannot be fully understood without a clear definition of the meaning of elite status and what its defining features are. To address the lack of a clear definition of terms such as "popularity," I proffered a definition of elite social status as membership and greater centrality in a social clique regarded by peers as exemplifying those characteristics valued by the larger peer group. This is premised on the notion that individuals gain power, prestige, and visibility through membership in prestigious, socially exclusive cliques. This definition of elite status has methodological implications, including the need to use social network analysis to identify social cliques and the status and reputation of each clique. As with other measures of social status, the extent to which this definition is consistent with youths' understanding of popularity needs to be tested in future research. For example, would the children identified as members in elite social cliques be the same as those that are nominated as "popular" by peers? Inevitably, the meaning of terms such as "elite status" and "popularity" will continue to be debated and refined. Such conversations will move the field forward and further our understanding of the role of social status in youths' development.

Evolutionary, self-determination, and symbolic interactionism theories were then presented as potential perspectives with which to understand the motive for elite social status. These theories provide a framework for understanding recent evidence pointing to the potential benefits of elite social status for children's mental health and emotional well-being. Future studies should be focused on whether the mechanisms outlined in the theories reviewed account for the greater emotional health of high-status youth. These theories also provide a framework for understanding why the thwarting of status motives can jeopardize youths' well-being. For example, less central members of prestigious cliques may show heightened levels of negative affect stemming from a constant struggle to maintain or improve their standing in the social hierarchy.

Indeed, the implications of failing to attain or maintain high social status also deserve further attention in the research literature. Brown and Lohr (1987) showed that adolescents who are dissatisfied with their crowd membership have lower self-esteem than adolescents content with the status of their crowd. Thus, thwarting of important social goals, such as popularity, may exacerbate emotional difficulties and serve as a sign that a child or adolescent is at risk for behavioral problems in and out of school. However, as the literature reviewed in this chapter illustrates, finding that unsuccessful obtainment of status goals results in deleterious outcomes does not necessitate that attainment of status goals leads to long-term health and well-being. Elite status is predictive of declining school performance, substance abuse, and sexual activity, all of which can all have long-term repercussions for youths' health and well-being. However, for many youth, the psychosocial benefits of obtaining elite social status outweigh the risks associated with engaging in these behaviors.

An overarching theme for this chapter has been that the implications of elite status are dependent upon the peer culture. If status is obtained by exemplifying the values of the larger peer group, the consequences of high status will be a direct function of the nature of those peer values. In this chapter, the peer context was examined as a function of developmental changes, including an increased emphasis on maturity, autonomy, and risk taking. The consequence is that elite status becomes progressively intertwined with greater delinquency, sexual activity, and, among more aggressive youth, declining academic performance and school orientation. Such normative developmental shifts, however, do not preclude the possibility that elite status may impact youth differently depending on other peer-culture differences, including those related to ethnicity, geographical location, or community values. Integrating knowledge of the local peer culture into the study of child and adolescent social hierarchies remains a challenging but ultimately necessary step in elucidating the risks and benefits of elite status to youth development.

REFERENCES

Adler, P. A., & Adler, P. (1998). *Peer power: Preadolescent culture and identity.* Piscataway, NJ: Rutgers University Press.

Adler, P. A., Kless, S. J., & Adler, P. (1992). Socialization to gender roles: Popularity among elementary school boys and girls. *Sociology of Education, 65,* 169–187.

Alexander, C., Piazza, M., Mekos, D., & Valente, T. (2001). Peers, schools, and adolescent cigarette smoking. *Journal of Adolescent Health, 29,* 22–30.

Allen, J. P., Weissberg, R. P., & Hawkins, J. A. (1989). The relation between values and social competence in early adolescence. *Developmental Psychology, 25,* 458–464.

Andreou, E. (2006). Social preference, perceived popularity, and social intelligence: Relations to overt and relational aggression. *School Psychology International*, 27, 339–351.

Asher, S. R., & McDonald, K. L. (2009). The behavioral basis of acceptance, rejection, and perceived popularity. In K. H. Rubin, W. M. Bukowski, & B. Larsen (Eds.), *Handbook of peer interactions, relationships, and groups* (pp. 232–248). New York: Guilford Press.

Becker, B. D., & Luthar, S. S. (2007). Peer-perceived admiration and social preference: Contextual correlates of positive peer regard among suburban and urban adolescents. *Journal of Research on Adolescence*, 17, 117–144.

Bernstein, I. (1981). Dominance: The baby and the bathwater. *Behavioral and Brain Sciences*, 4, 419–457.

Bjorklund, D. F., & Blasi, C. H. (2005). Evolutionary developmental psychology. In D. M. Buss (Ed.), *The handbook of evolutionary psychology* (pp. 828–850). Hoboken, NJ: John Wiley & Sons Inc.

Bowker, J. C., Rubin, K. H., Buskirk-Cohen, A., Rose-Krasnor, L., & Booth-LaForce, C. (2010). Behavioral changes predicting temporal changes in perceived popular status. *Journal of Applied Developmental Psychology*, 31, 126–133.

Brown, B. B., Eicher, S. A., & Petrie, S. (1986). The importance of peer group ("crowd") affiliation in adolescence. *Journal of Adolescence*, 19, 73096.

Brown, B. B., & Lohr, M. J. (1987). Peer-group affiliation and adolescent self-esteem: An integration of ego-identity and symbolic-interaction theories. *Journal of Personality and Social Psychology*, 52, 47–55.

Buhrmester, D., & Furman, W. (1986). The changing functions of children's friendships: A neo-Sullivan perspective. In V. Derlega & B. Winstead (Eds.), *Friendships and social interaction* (pp. 41–62). New York: Springer.

Bukowski, W. M., Sippola, L. K., & Newcomb, A. F. (2000). Variations in patterns of attraction of same- and other-sex peers during early adolescence. *Developmental Psychology*, 36, 147–154.

Buss, D. M. (1995). Psychological sex differences: Origins through sexual selection. *American Psychologist*, 50, 164–168.

Cairns, R., Xie, H., & Leung, M. (1998). The popularity of friendship and the neglect of social networks: Toward a new balance. In W. M. Bukowski & A. H. Cillessen (Eds.), *Sociometry then and now: Building on six decades of measuring children's experiences with the peer group* (pp. 25–53). San Francisco: Jossey-Bass.

Cairns, R. B. (1983). Sociometry, psychometry, and social structure: A commentary on six recent studies of popular, rejected, and neglected children. *Merrill-Palmer Quarterly*, 29, 429–438.

Carlson, W., & Rose, A. J. (2007). The role of reciprocity in romantic relationships in middle childhood and early adolescence. *Merrill-Palmer Quarterly*, 53, 262–290.

Charlesworth, W. R. (1996). Co-operation and competition: Contributions to an evolutionary and developmental model. *International Journal of Behavioral Development*, 19, 25–38.

Cillessen, A. H. N., & Borch, C. (2006). Developmental trajectories of adolescent popularity: A growth curve modeling analysis. *Journal of Adolescence*, 29, 935–959.

Cillessen, A. H. N., & Mayeux, L. (2004). From censure to reinforcement: Developmental changes in the association between aggression and social status. *Child Development*, 75, 147–163.

(2007). Expectations and perceptions at school transitions: The role of peer status and aggression. *Journal of School Psychology*, 45, 567–586.

Cillessen, A. H. N., & Rose, A. J. (2005). Understanding popularity in the peer system. *Current Directions in Psychological Science*, 14, 102–105.

Cohen, G. L., & Prinstein, M. J. (2006). Peer contagion of aggression and health risk behavior among adolescent males: An experimental investigation of effects of public conduct and private attitudes. *Child Development*, 77, 967–983.

Coie, J. D., Dodge, K. A., & Coppotelli, H. (1982). Dimensions and types of social status: A cross-age perspective. *Developmental Psychology*, 18, 557–570.

Coie, J. D., Dodge, K. A., & Kupersmidt, J. B. (1990). Peer group behavior and social status. In S. R. Asher & J. D. Coie (Eds.), *Peer rejection in childhood* (pp. 17–59). New York: Cambridge University Press.

Cole, D. A., Maxwell, M. A., Dukewich, D. L., & Yosick, R. (2010). Targeted peer victimization and the construction of positive and negative self-cognitions: Connections to depressive symptoms in children. *Journal of Clinical Child & Adolescent Psychology*, 39, 421–435.

Cole, D. A., Peeke, L., Dolezal, S., Murray, N., & Canzoniero, A. (1999). A longitudinal study of negative affect and self-perceived competence in young adolescents. *Journal of Personality and Social Psychology*, 77, 851–862.

Corsaro, W. A., & Eder, D. (1990). Children's peer cultures. *Annual Review of Sociology*, 16, 197–220.

Crick, N. R., & Grotpeter, J. K. (1995). Relational aggression, gender, and social-psychological adjustment. *Child Development*, 66, 710–722.

Cummins, D. (2005). Dominance, status, and social hierarchies. In D. Buss (Ed.), *The handbook of evolutionary psychology* (pp. 676–697). Hoboken, NJ: John Wiley & Sons, Inc.

de Bruyn, E. H., & Cillessen, A. H. N. (2006). Heterogeneity of girls' consensual popularity: Academic and interpersonal behavioral profiles. *Journal of Youth and Adolescence*, 35, 435–445.

de Bruyn, E. H., & van den Boom, D. C. (2005). Interpersonal behavior, peer popularity, and self-esteem in early adolescence. *Social Development*, 14, 555–573.

de Waal, F. (1982). *Chimpanzee politics*. New York: John Hopkins.

Deci, E. L., & Ryan, R. M. (2000). The "what" and "why" of goal pursuits: Human needs and the self-determination of behavior. *Psychological Inquiry*, 11, 227–268.

Diamantopoulou, S., Rydell, A., & Henricsson L. (2008). Can both low and high self-esteem be related to aggression in children? *Social Development*, 17, 682–698.

Diego, M., Field, T. M., & Sanders, C. E. (2003). Academic performance, popularity, and depression predict adolescent substance use. *Adolescence*, 38, 35–42.

Dijkstra, J. K., Cillessen, A. H. N., Lindenberg, S., & Veenstra, R. (2010). Basking in reflected glory and its limits: Why adolescents hang out with popular peers. *Journal of Research on Adolescence*, 20, 942–958.

Dijkstra, J. K., Lindenberg, S., Verhulst, F. C., Ormel, J., & Veenstra, R. (2009). The relation between popularity and aggressive, destructive, and norm-breaking behaviors: Moderating effects of athletic abilities, physical attractiveness, and prosociality. *Journal of Research on Adolescence*, 19, 401–413.

Dolcini, M., & Adler, N. E. (1994). Perceived competencies, peer group affiliation, and risk behavior among early adolescents. *Health Psychology*, 13, 496–506.

Dunbar, R. I. M. (1988). The evolutionary implications of social behavior. In H. C. Plotkin (Ed.), *The role of behavior in evolution* (pp. 165–188). Cambridge, MA: MIT Press.

Dunphy, D. C. (1963). The social structure of urban adolescent peer groups. *Sociometry*, 26, 230–246.

Duntley, J. D. (2005). Adaptations to dangers from humans. In D. Buss (Ed.), *The handbook of evolutionary psychology* (pp. 224–249). New York: Wiley.

Eckert, P. (1989). *Jocks and burnouts: Social categories and identity in the high school*. New York: Teachers College Press.

Eder, D. (1985). The cycle of popularity: Interpersonal relations among female adolescents. *Sociology of Education*, 58, 154–165.

Evans, C., & Eder, D. (1993). "No exit": Processes of social isolation in the middle school. *Journal of Contemporary Ethnography*, 22, 139–170.

Farmer, T. W., Estell, D. B., Bishop, J. L., O'Neal, K. K., & Cairns, B. D. (2003). Rejected bullies or popular leaders? The social relations of aggressive subtypes of rural African American early adolescents. *Developmental Psychology*, 39, 992–1004.

Fox, C. L., & Farrow, C. V. (2009). Global and physical self-esteem and body dissatisfaction as mediators of the relationship between weight status and being a victim of bullying. *Journal of Adolescence*, 32, 1287–1301.

Galambos, N. L., Almeida, D. M., & Petersen, A. C. (1990). Masculinity, femininity, and sexrole attitudes in early adolescence: Exploring gender intensification. *Child Development*, 61, 1905–1914.

Galambos, N. L., Berenbaum, S. A., & McChale, S. M. (2009). Gender development in adolescence. In R. M. Lerner & L. Steinberg (Eds.), *Handbook of adolescent psychology, Vol. 1: Individual bases of adolescent development* (pp. 305–357). Hoboken, NJ: John Wiley & Sons, Inc.

Gest, S. D., Graham-Bermann, S. A., & Hartup, W. W. (2001). Peer experience: Common and unique features of number of friendships, social network centrality, and sociometric status. *Social Development*, 10, 23–40.

Hasler, G., Pine, D. S., Kleinbaum, D. G., Gamma, A., Luckenbaugh, D., Ajdacic, V., Eich, D., Rossler, W., & Angst, J. (2005). Depressive symptoms during childhood and adult obesity: The Zurich Cohort Study. *Molecular Psychiatry*, 10, 842–850.

Hausfater, G., Altmann, J., & Altmann, S. (1982). Long-term consistency of dominance relations among female baboons (*Papio cynocephalus*). *Science*, 217, 752–755.

Hawley, P. H. (1999). The ontogenesis of social dominance: A strategy-based evolutionary perspective. *Developmental Review*, 19, 97–132.

   (2003). Prosocial and coercive configurations of resource control in early adolescence: A case for the well-adapted Machiavellian. *Merrill-Palmer Quarterly*, 49, 279–309.

(2007). Social dominance in childhood and adolescence: Why social competence and aggression may go hand in hand. In P. H. Hawley, T. D. Little, & P. Rodkin (Eds.), *Aggression and adaptation: The bright side of bad behavior* (pp. 1–29). Hillsdale, NJ: Lawrence Erlbaum and Associates.

Hawley, P. H., Johnson, S. E., Mize, J. A., & McNamara, K. A. (2007). Physical attractiveness in preschoolers: Relationships with power, status, aggression and social skills. *Journal of School Psychology, 45*, 499–521.

Hawley, P. H., & Little, T. D. (1999). On winning some and losing some: A social relations approach to social dominance in toddlers. *Merrill-Palmer Quarterly, 45*, 185–214.

Hawley, P. H., Little, T. D., & Card, N. A. (2007). The allure of a mean friend: Relationship quality and processes of aggressive adolescents with prosocial skills. *International Journal of Behavioral Development, 31*, 170–180.

Hill, J. P., & Lynch, M. E. (1983). The intensification of gender-related role expectations during early adolescence. In J. Brooks-Gunn & A. C. Petersen (Eds.), *Girls at puberty: Biological and psychosocial perspectives* (pp. 201–228). New York: Plenum.

Jarvinen, D. W., & Nicholls, J. G. (1996). Adolescents' social goals, beliefs about the causes of social success, and satisfaction in peer relations. *Developmental Psychology, 32*, 435–441.

Kennedy, E. (1995). Correlates of perceived popularity among peers: A study of race and gender differences among middle school students. *Journal of Negro Education, 64*, 186–195.

Ladd, B. K., & Ladd, G. W. (2001). Variations in peer victimization: Relations to children's maladjustment. In J. Juvonen & S. Graham (Eds.), *Peer harassment in school: The plight of the vulnerable and victimized.* New York: Guildford Press.

Ladd, G. W. (2005). *Children's peer relations and social competence: A century of progress.* New Haven, CT: Yale University Press.

Ladd, G. W., & Troop-Gordon, W. (2003). The role of chronic peer difficulties in the development of children's psychological adjustment problems. *Child Development, 74*, 1344–1367.

LaFontana, K. M., & Cillessen, A. H. N. (1998). The nature of children's stereotypes of popularity. *Social Development, 7*, 301–320.

(2002). Children's perceptions of popular and unpopular peers: A multimethod assessment. *Developmental Psychology, 38*, 635–647.

(2010). Developmental changes in the priority of perceived status in childhood adolescence. *Social Development, 19*, 130–147.

LaFreniere, P., & Charlesworth, W. R. (1983). Dominance, attention, and affiliation in a preschool group: A nine-month longitudinal study. *Ethology & Sociobiology, 4*, 55–67.

Lease, A. M., Musgrove, K. T., & Axelrod, J. L. (2002). Dimensions of social status in preadolescent peer groups: Likability, perceived popularity, and social dominance. *Social Development, 11*, 508–533.

Lesko, N. (1988). *Symbolizing society: Stories, rites, and structure in a Catholic high school.* Philadelphia: Falmer Press.

Luthar, S. S., & McMahon, T. J. (1996). Peer reputation among inner-city adolescents: Structure and correlates. *Journal of Research on Adolescence*, 6, 581–603.

Masten, A. S., & Cicchetti, D. (2010). Developmental cascades. *Development and Psychopathology*, 22, 491–495.

Mayeux, L., & Cillessen, A. H. N. (2008). It's not just being popular, it's knowing it, too: The role of self-perceptions of status in the associations between peer status and aggression. *Social Development*, 17, 871–888.

Mayeux, L., Sandstrom, M. J., & Cillessen, A. H. N. (2008). Is being popular a risky proposition? *Journal of Research on Adolescence*, 18, 49–74.

Mead, G. H. (1934). *Mind, self, and society*. Chicago: University of Chicago Press.

Meijs, N., Cillessen, A. H. N., Scholte, R. H. J., Segers, E., & Spijkerman, R. (2010). Social intelligence and academic achievement as predictors of adolescent popularity. *Journal of Youth and Adolescence*, 39, 62–72.

Meisinger, E. B., Blake, J. J., Lease, A. M., Palardy, G. J., & Olejnik, S. F. (2007). Variant and invariant predictors of perceived popularity across majority-Black and majority-White classrooms. *Journal of School Psychology*, 45, 21–44.

Merten, D. E. (1994). The cultural context of aggression: The transition to junior high school. *Anthropology & Education*, 25, 29–43.

(1996). Burnout as cheerleader: The cultural basis for prestige and privilege in junior high school. *Anthropology & Education Quarterly*, 27, 51–70.

(1997). The meaning of meanness: Popularity, competition, and conflict among junior high school girls. *Sociology of Education*, 70, 175–191.

(2004). I. Securing her experience: Friendship versus popularity. *Feminism & Psychology*, 14, 361–365.

Meschke, L. L., Zweig, J. M., Barber, B. L., & Eccles, J. S. (2000). Demographic, biological, psychological, and social predictors of the timing of first intercourse. *Journal of Research on Adolescence*, 10, 315–338.

Moffitt, T. E. (1993). Adolescence-limited and life-course-persistent antisocial behavior: A developmental taxonomy. *Psychological Review*, 100, 674–701.

Newcomb, A. F., Bukowski, W. M., & Pattee, L. (1993). Children's peer relations: A meta-analytic review of popular, rejected, neglected, controversial, and average sociometric status. *Psychological Bulletin*, 113, 99–128.

Ojanen, T., Grönroos, M., & Salmivalli, C. (2005). An interpersonal circumplex model of children's social goals: Links with peer reported behavior and sociometric status. *Developmental Psychology*, 41, 699–710.

Parker, J. G., & Gottman, J. M. (1989). Social and emotional development in a relational context: Friendship interaction from early childhood. In T. J. Berndt & G. W. Ladd (Eds.), *Peer relationships in child development* (pp. 95–131). Oxford: John Wiley & Sons Inc.

Parkhurst, J. T., & Hopmeyer, A. (1998). Sociometric popularity and peer-perceived popularity: Two distinct dimensions of peer status. *Journal of Early Adolescence*, 18, 125–144.

Pellegrini, A. D. (2001). The roles of dominance and bullying in the development of early heterosexual relationships. *Journal of Emotional Abuse*, 2, 63–73.

(2008). The roles of aggressive and affiliative behaviors in resource control: A behavioral ecological perspective. *Developmental Review*, 28, 461–487.

Pellegrini, A. D., & Bartini, M. (2001). Dominance in early adolescent boys: Affiliative and aggression dimensions and possible functions. *Merrill-Palmer Quarterly*, 47, 142–163.

Pellegrini, A. D., & Long, J. D. (2003). A sexual selection theory longitudinal analysis of sexual segregation and integration in early adolescence. *Journal of Experimental Child Psychology*, 85, 257–278.

Peters, E., Cillessen, A. H. N., Riksen-Walraven, M. J., & Haselager, G. T. (2010). Best friends' preference and popularity: Associations with aggression and prosocial behavior. *International Journal of Behavioral Development*, 34, 398–405.

Prinstein, M. J., & Cillessen, A. H. N. (2003). Forms and functions of adolescent peer aggression associated with high levels of peer status. *Merrill-Palmer Quarterly*, 49, 319–342.

Prinstein, M. J., Meade, C. S., & Cohen, G. L. (2003). Adolescent oral sex, peer popularity, and perceptions of best friends' sexual behavior. *Journal of Pediatric Psychology*, 28, 243–249.

Puckett, M. B., Aikins, J. W., & Cillessen, A. H. N. (2008). Moderators of the association between relational aggression and perceived popularity. *Aggressive Behavior*, 34, 563–576.

Rancourt, D., & Prinstein, M. J. (2010). Peer status and victimization as possible reinforcements of adolescent girls' and boys' weight-related behaviors and cognitions. *Journal of Pediatric Psychology*, 35, 354–367.

Rodkin, P. C., Farmer, T. W., Pearl, R., & Van Acker, R. (2000). Heterogeneity of popular boys: Antisocial and prosocial configurations. *Developmental Psychology*, 36, 14–24.

Rodkin, P. C., & Roisman, G. I. (2010). Antecedents and correlates of the popular-aggressive phenomenon in elementary school. *Child Development*, 81, 837–850.

Rose, A. J., & Rudolph, K. D. (2006). A review of sex differences in peer relationship processes: Potential trade-offs for the emotional and behavioral development of girls and boys. *Psychological Bulletin*, 132, 98–131.

Rose, A. J., & Swenson, L. P. (2009). Do perceived popular adolescents who aggress against others experience adjustment problems themselves? *Developmental Psychology*, 45, 868–872.

Rose, A. J., Swenson, L. P., & Carlson, W. (2004). Friendships of aggressive youth: Considering the influences of being disliked and of being perceived as popular. *Journal of Experimental Psychology*, 88, 25–45.

Rose, A. J., Swenson, L. P., & Waller, E. M. (2004). Overt and relational aggression and perceived popularity: Developmental differences in concurrent and prospective relations. *Developmental Psychology*, 40, 378–387.

Rubin, K. H., Bukowski, W. M., & Laursen, B. (2009). *Handbook of peer interactions, relationships, and groups*. New York: Guilford Press.

Rubin, K. H., Bukowski, W. M., & Parker, J. G. (2006). Peer interactions, relationships, and groups. In N. Eisenberg, W. Damon, & R. M. Lerner (Eds.), *Handbook of child psychology: Vol. 3, Social, emotional, and personality development* (6th ed., pp. 571–645). Hoboken, NJ: John Wiley & Sons Inc.

Rudolph, K. D., Hammen, C., Burge, D., Lindberg, N., Herzberg, D., & Daley, S. E. (2000). Toward an interpersonal life-stress model of depression: The developmental context of stress generation. *Development and Psychopathology*, 12, 215–234.

Ryan, A. M., & Shim, S. S. (2008). An exploration of young adolescents' social achievement goals and social adjustment in middle school. *Journal of Educational Psychology*, 100, 672–687.

Salmivalli, C., & Isaacs, J. (2005). Prospective relations among victimization, rejection, friendlessness, and children's self- and peer-perceptions. *Child Development*, 76, 1161–1171.

Sandstrom, M. J., & Cillessen, A. H. N. (2006). Likeable versus popular: Distinct implications for adolescent adjustment. *International Journal of Behavioral Development*, 30, 305–314.

(2010). Life after high school: Adjustment of popular teens in emerging adulthood. *Merrill-Palmer Quarterly*, 56, 474–499.

Schwartz, D., Gorman, A. H., Nakamoto, J., & McKay, T. (2006). Popularity, social acceptance, and aggression in adolescent peer groups: Links with academic performance and school attendance. *Developmental Psychology*, 42, 1116–1127.

Sippola, L. K., Paget, J., & Buchanan, C. M. (2007). Praising Cordelia: Social aggression and social dominance among adolescent girls. In P. H. Hawley, T. D. Little, & P. C. Rodkin (Eds.), *Aggression and adaptation: The bright side to bad behavior* (pp. 157–183). Mahwah, NJ: Lawrence Erlbaum Associates Publishers.

Strayer, F. F. (1980). Child ethology and the study of preschool social relations. In H. C. Foot, A. J. Chapman, & J. R. Smith (Eds.), *Friendship and social relations in children* (pp. 235–265). Piscataway, NJ: Transaction Publishers.

Strayer, F. F., & Strayer, J. (1976). An ethological analysis of social agonism and dominance relations among preschool children. *Child Development*, 47, 980–989.

Stryker, S., & Vryan, K. D. (2006). The symbolic interactionist frame. In J. Delamater (Ed.), *Handbook of social psychology* (pp. 3–28). New York: Springer.

Stump, K. N., Ratliff, J. M., Wu, Y. P., & Hawley, P. H. (2009). Theories of social competence from the top-down to the bottom-up: A case for considering human needs. In J. L. Matson (Ed.), *Social behavior and skills in children* (pp. 23–37). New York: Springer Science + Business Media.

Sullivan, H. S. (1953). *The interpersonal theory of psychiatry.* New York: Norton.

Thorne, B. (1986). Girls and boys together but mostly apart: Gender arrangements in elementary schools. In W. W. Hartup & Z. Rubin (Eds.), *Relationships and development* (pp. 167–184). Hillsdale, NJ: Erlbaum.

Troop-Gordon, W., & Ladd, G. W. (2005). Trajectories of peer victimization and perceptions of the self and schoolmates: Precursors to internalizing and externalizing problems. *Child Development*, 76, 1072–1091.

Troop-Gordon, W., Visconti, K. J., & Kuntz, K. J. (2011). Perceived popularity during early adolescence: Links to declining school adjustment among aggressive youth. *Journal of Early Adolescence*, 31, 125–151.

Vaillancourt, T., & Hymel, S. (2006). Aggression and social status: The moderating roles of sex and peer-valued characteristics. *Aggressive Behavior*, 32, 369–408.

Vaillancourt, T., Hymel, S., & McDougall, P. (2003). Bullying is power: Implications for school-based intervention strategies. *Journal of Applied School Psychology*, 19, 157–176.

Veenstra, R., Huitsing, G., Dijkstra, J. K., & Lindenberg, S. Friday on my mind: The relation of partying with antisocial behavior of early adolescents. The TRAILS Study. *Journal of Research on Adolescence*, 20, 420–431.

Wang, S. S., Houshyar, S., & Prinstein, M. J. (2006). Adolescent girls' and boys' weight-related health behaviors and cognitions: Associations with reputation- and preference-based peer status. *Health Psychology*, 25, 658–663.

Xie, H., Li, Y., Boucher, S. M., Hutchins, B. C., & Cairns, B. D. (2006). What makes a girl (or a boy) popular (or unpopular)? African American children's perceptions and developmental differences. *Developmental Psychology*, 42, 599–612.

Xie, H., Swift, D. J., Cairns, B., & Cairns, R. B. (2002). Aggressive behaviors in social interaction and developmental adaptation: A narrative analysis of interpersonal conflicts during early adolescence. *Social Development*, 11, 205–224.

8

Culture and Context Modify Neural Correlates of Adolescent Risk-Taking Behavior

CHRISTINE L. LACKNER AND SIDNEY J. SEGALOWITZ

Psychological development during adolescence can be conceptualized as stemming from two opposing perspectives. One is physiological and reductionist, focusing on developmental brain factors. The other involves the cultural and holistic factors that are the focus of the present volume and focus on the individual's motivation to fit into a rapidly changing social cohort. We sometimes think of these contrasting views as representing differences with respect to a bottom-up versus a top-down approach, or a medical versus a social model. However, these perspectives are increasingly integrated in contemporary neuroscience, and we outline one such integration in this chapter – how neural systems and the culture of the adolescent interact to predict risk-taking behavior.

Traditional neuroscience emphasizes a mechanistic flow of information from sensory input to conceptual coding to decision making and ultimately to behavior. However, there is much literature on top-down processes at the psychological and sociological levels that have effects on behavior. Top-down psychological processes, such as strategy selection, have an obvious effect on behavior, and traditional sociological perspectives emphasize the role of top-down processes, including social context, in driving behavior. In this chapter, we focus on the notion that top-down processes can exert a powerful influence on some bottom-up processes, including sensory information processing, automatic reward processing, and reward-system-related risk-taking behaviors. The challenge is how to conceptualize a mechanical neural system that incorporates both perspectives of an individual as a purposeful goal-directed agent and as being driven by outside forces.

Traditional sociological theory emphasizes the role of culture and the social group in predicting behavior at all developmental stages. Culture has been described in a wide variety of ways throughout history (see Kroeber & Kluckhohn, 1952, for a review of 164 distinct uses of the word). However, for our purposes, culture can be described as the distinctive patterns of thought (e.g., attitudes, beliefs, values) and behavior (e.g., choice of clothing, risk propensity, rituals) that differentiate social groups from one another. These characteristic patterns are dynamic and can change over time and importantly can drive behavior in a top-down fashion. For example, culturally mediated cognitive schemas can influence mental health behavior in adolescence. Anxious adolescents from Mexican, Mexican-American, and American backgrounds differ significantly in symptom presentation, with Mexican adolescents displaying significantly more physiological and worry symptoms than American adolescents with these symptom differences being strongly correlated with cultural variables such as *simpatia* (a traditional Mexican cultural value that results in refraining from sharing health problems with others) and degree of cultural assimilation (Varela et al., 2004). Thus, top-down cultural values can influence mental health–related behavior and likely influence a wide variety of other behaviors as well.

Smaller cultural groups can form within particular ethnicities and the behavior of group members can be influenced by these somewhat specialized cultural values. Adolescents, at least in Western society, have formed such a cultural subgroup by creating cultural markers that symbolize their membership, such as particular communication patterns, clothing, music, and choice of usage for free time. One salient aspect of adolescent peer culture is a culture of risk taking. Adolescents, or at least some large subset of them, engage in risky behaviors more than persons in other age groups. They have some of the highest rates of dangerous driving, hard drug and alcohol use, risky sexual behavior, and violence (Blum & Nelson-Mmari, 2004; Reyna & Farley, 2006; Williams, Holmbeck, & Greenley, 2002), despite the fact that, at least for some categories of risky behavior, adolescents in general understand and evaluate the consequences of these actions in an adult-like manner (Cohn, Macfarlane, Yanez, & Imai, 1995; Diblasio, 1986; Fischhoff, 2008; Reyna & Farley, 2006). Of course, some adolescents high in risk taking may tend to associate with other adolescents high in risk taking, thereby forming their own subculture in which risky behavior is more normative (Arnett, 1992; Jaccard, Blanton, & Dodge, 2005; Kandel, 1978).

Yet risk taking holds a paradoxical or ambiguous status in adolescence. Risk taking, by its very nature, presents an increased probability for physical or emotional harm yet also provides substantial benefits to the adolescent. Humans are not the only species in which the adolescent period is one characterized by increased risk taking or sensation/novelty seeking. When given a choice, adolescent mice prefer to explore novel environments whereas their adult counterparts prefer familiar environments

(Adriani, Chiarotti, & Laviola, 1998). Adolescent rats self-administer greater quantities of cocaine and alcohol than rats of other ages (Brunell & Spear, 2005; Doremus, Brunell, Rajendran, & Spear, 2005; Schramm-Sapyta et al., 2011). Adolescent vervet monkeys engage in socially impulsive behavior in response to an unfamiliar "intruder" male, a behavioral pattern that declines with age (Fairbanks, Melega, Jorgensen, Kaplan, & McGuire, 2001). Therefore, from an evolutionary psychology perspective, increased risk taking in adolescence confers a fitness and social utility function, increasing the adolescents' likelihood of survival and development (Spear, 2003) as well their opportunities for reproduction and social status within the group (Nell, 2002).

However, not all types of risk are equivalently motivated. Kloep, Güney, Çok, and Simsek (2009) outline several types of risk-taking behavior, each with its own drives. Social motives in particular may be especially salient for adolescents. Adolescents are motivated to engage in risky behaviors for reasons of security and/or fear. They fear a loss of social support or approval within an esteemed social group with its own cultural norms. In at least one sample, risk-taking behavior was positively correlated with the number of friends and presence of at least one close friendship (quantity) and also positively correlated with trust, positive communication, support, and acceptance (quality) of peer relationships (Engels & ter Bogt, 2001), a finding consistent with the proposed benefits of risky behavior (Nell, 2002). Even in countries in which risk-taking rates are lower than they are in North America (e.g., Turkey and Wales), adolescents engage in audience-controlled motivated risk taking (Kloep et al., 2009). From an adolescent's perspective, the point of some risky behaviors is lost without an audience. As Kloep et al. (2009) note, "What fun is there in trying an 'ollie' on a skateboard, if there is no one to applaud or disapprove?" (137). Adolescents, more than adults, are influenced by the presence of peers to take risks (Gardner & Steinberg, 2005). Adolescent behavior is both driving and being driven by the cultural norms of their rapidly changing social cohort. Yet, as the following section details, behavior is also driven in a mechanistic way by the brain, and it is here that bottom-up and top-down influences come together (or perhaps even collide).

A NEUROSCIENTIFIC PERSPECTIVE

Over the past several decades, neuroscientists have mapped out how bottom-up perception occurs and have begun to understand how relatively simple top-down influences may impact this perception. When a stimulus is detected in the external environment, it is first encoded by a set of sensory neurons (e.g., olfactory receptors, mechanoreceptors, photoreceptors). These sensory neurons then project this information to a number of structures, including the thalamus, the brain's "relay station," which then sends this information onward to primary sensory areas of the neocortex, with the exception of olfaction, which may occur without thalamic rerouting. Regions supporting these stages of processing are sometimes viewed as the neural substrates of bottom-up activity. However, primary sensory information is also fed forward to "higher" cortical levels (e.g., parietal cortex, prefrontal cortex; Cauller, 1995; Mechelli, Price, Friston, & Ishai, 2004). According to one theory, these higher cortical structures are then responsible for top-down influence on perception, exerting their influence via reciprocal connections to primary sensory regions (see Angelucci et al., 2002; Shmuel et al., 2005). Primary visual cortex, or V1, for example, receives such re-entrant feedback from many other brain regions including V2 and V4, which in turn receive feedback from higher cortical areas including the temporal lobe (Gilbert & Sigman, 2007). Therefore, the neural structures subserving bottom-up and top-down cognition are highly interconnected and not mutually exclusive, thereby giving rise to the possibility that culture can influence bottom-up perception.

More generally, mechanisms have been advanced to explain this pronounced interaction between top-down and bottom-up processes, particularly in the visual domain. Later processing stages in vision involving the fusiform cortex may be influenced by input from much "higher" centers such as those in the prefrontal cortex (Bar, 2003). Low spatial frequency "gist" information is projected rapidly from early visual processing regions forward to the prefrontal cortex. This is then used by the prefrontal cortex to make predictions and exert top-down influence on other visual processing regions (Bar, 2003). Moreover, context-based top-down influences can come from the parahippocampal cortex and the retrosplenial complex, two structures known to show larger activations to objects with strong contextual associations than those with weak contextual associations (Fenske, Aminoff, Gronau, & Bar, 2006). These provide predictive contextual information and thus have top-down influence on the perceptive process.

At a cellular level, we have also begun to understand the mechanisms of top-down and bottom-up interactions. Forward projections from primary somatosensory regions to higher-order areas terminate in layer IV of the cortex (sensory receiving area), and backward projections from higher-order areas to somatosensory regions terminate in layers I/II (computational levels). These backward projections constitute the neural substrate of top-down influence (both from other sensory regions and attentional control regions) on bottom-up processing (Cauller, 1995; Larkum, Senn, & Luscher, 2004; Olson, Chun, & Allison, 2001). Activity in any given neuron or cortical area is influenced by a network of brain regions including the local circuit itself as well as feedback and feedforward cortical connections (Gilbert & Sigman, 2007). Future research is required to determine if these same neural pathways contribute to top-down (e.g., cultural) influence on bottom-up processing.

Often top-down influences are thought of as occurring when conscious strategy choices influence low-level neural processing, such as when attending to the motion aspects of colored stimuli activates the visual movement cortex and reduces activation in cortex sensitive to color and vice versa when color is attended to (Chawla, Rees, & Friston, 1999; Corbetta, Miezin, Dobmeyer, Shulman, & Petersen, 1990). However, there is no reason the top-down influence needs to be conscious or strategic. An acquired attitude can also alter cortical processing of stimuli. For example, we recently examined early cortical responses to faces before and after participants have somewhat arbitrarily learned to consider them as belonging to their own social group or not. We found out-group assignment significantly delayed an early event-related potential component that is particularly sensitive to structural processing of faces – the N170 – all within a short training session (Zheng & Segalowitz, 2013). That this early stage of perceptual could be so easily manipulated in an arbitrary manner points to a basic flexibility of cortical processes in response to social contexts.

Overall, there is extensive behavioral, neuroimaging, and neurophysiological evidence to suggest that top-down influences can profoundly affect bottom-up processing. In fact, Gilbert and Sigman (2007) state that information flowing from higher- to lower-order cortical regions plays an equally important role in perception as feedforward pathways do. The pre-existing "brain state" and expectations of a perceiver influence subsequent perception via top-down influence (Gilbert & Sigman, 2007). We now have reason to believe that the physiological substrate exists for top-down influences to impact bottom-up processes. In the remainder of the chapter, we will explore how these processes may interact in shaping risky adolescent behavior. We are interested in understanding how top-down processes influence somewhat automatic neural activation and behavior, especially during adolescence.

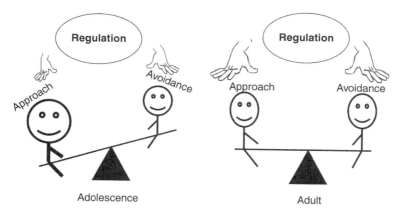

FIGURE 8.1. Triadic Model patterned after Ernst, Pine, and Hardin (2006). The regulatory capacity of the medial prefrontal cortex is diminished in adolescence, in comparison to during adulthood, while the approach drive of the ventral striatum is amplified and the avoidance drive of the amygdala is diminished. The adolescent pattern is shifted toward the approach system compared to the balanced pattern in the adult.

A Neuroscientific Model of Risk

From a behavioral neuroscience perspective, Ernst and Fudge's Triadic model (2009) provides a useful framework for conceptualizing neural substrates of the self-regulatory system, a system that must be functioning optimally to successfully withhold the temptation to engage in risk (Ernst, Pine, & Hardin, 2006) and a system with both top-down control of behavior and bottom-up activations to stimuli. In this model, approach (reward-driven) and avoidance (harm-avoidant) tendencies are seen as lying opposite to one another on a balance beam. The relative balance of the two systems is controlled by the third node – a largely top-down modulating system (see Figure 8.1). The physiological representatives of these three systems include the amygdala for avoidance, the ventral striatum (a forebrain structure strongly associated with positive emotional and motivational aspects of behavior) for approach, and the prefrontal cortex for the modulation or regulation of the other two systems. Activation of the ventral striatum and amygdala are considered automatic (and thus bottom-up) evolutionarily significant responses to important environmental stimuli, whereas later responses of the prefrontal cortex are seen as a modulatory top-down self-regulatory component.

Significant developmental differences are observed in this system. The adult pattern of regulated behavior is a balanced system, whereas the pattern expected in adolescents is disproportionately weighted toward approach behavior. During adolescence, the prefrontal cortex (especially medial and/or ventral portions) is unable to appropriately inhibit the strong approach tendencies of the ventral striatum (Ernst & Fudge, 2009; Ernst et al., 2006), although there may be striking individual differences in the balance of the system, and as is discussed later, this system is heavily influenced by contextual factors, including the presence of peers. We would argue that the imbalance in this system is not entirely maladaptive – while it may contribute to increased rates of risk taking during adolescence, such elevated levels of risk taking afford the adolescent numerous developmental opportunities for growth, including the chance to try out new roles. Recent neurophysiological research supports this conjecture. Frontal white matter connectivity, indicative of more adult-like cortices, is positively associated with risk taking in adolescents ages 14 to 18 (Berns, Moore, & Capra, 2009). Increased levels of risk taking may confer social and neurobiological benefits to adolescents.

This regulatory system undergoes significant maturational changes over the adolescent period in terms of both structure and neurotransmitter functioning. Specifically, dramatic changes are observed within the mesocortical dopamine system, which projects from approach-related regions such as the striatum forward to the modulatory prefrontal cortex. There is evidence that in adolescence, the dopamine activity in the prefrontal cortex overshoots adult levels and subsequently reduces in late adolescence or early adulthood (Anderson, Classey, Conde, Lund, & Lewis, 1995; Wahlstrom et al., 2007), resulting in inefficient functioning during the heightened dopamine period (Wahlstrom, White, & Luciana, 2010). The same mesocortical dopamine system in subcortical structures, including the ventral striatum's central reward system, also overshoots the final adult pattern of dopamine receptors in adolescence with a subsequent reduction to adult levels (Tarazi & Baldessarini, 2000). Thus, during adolescence there appears to be a heightened activation of the ventral striatum (leading to more reward-seeking behavior) together with an inefficient prefrontal cortex. Since the prefrontal cortex exerts top-down control to help regulate the behaviors being driven by the reward system (e.g., risky behaviors), it would have a greater challenge when the increased activation of ventral striatum influences behavior. However, the fact that the prefrontal cortex maturation does not keep pace with the reward system has implications for a variety of control systems involving both emotion and cognition, including those systems involved in risky behavior. This situation contrasts considerably, of course, with the system during childhood, when the prefrontal cortex may be even less sophisticated but so too are the pressures from the reward system. In children, much risky behavior may be more a result of curiosity blended with poor judgment than a result of a pressure for novelty or sensation seeking.

The prefrontal cortex, the region upon which the regulatory function is highly dependent, has many subcomponents. The primary characteristic of relevance here is its ability to be molded to meet environmental demands through massive pruning of synapses, a hypothesis first articulated by Rakic et al. (1994). The growth and subsequent pruning in gray matter volumes seem to be regionally specific and are major indicators of the maturation process. Some areas of frontal gray matter reach peak volumes by approximately 12 years of age, while others lag significantly behind, reaching peak levels during early adulthood. Specifically, the dorsolateral prefrontal cortex, a region of the brain heavily involved in impulse control, does not reach full gray matter maturity until the early 20s. However, nonpurely sensory cortex such as the temporal cortex, a region of the brain that exerts less top-down influence, reaches full maturity earlier, in this case at age 16 (Giedd, 2004). In contrast, the striatum, an integral part of Ernst and Fudge's (2009) approach system, undergoes significant pruning beginning in early adolescence (Lenroot et al., 2007). Gogtay et al. (2010) describe the pattern of gray matter development as one of ontogeny recapitulating phylogeny – the oldest evolutionary structures maturing earlier in the course of development, with the phylogenetically newer structures maturing later in development, loosely from bottom-up to top-down regions. Thus, unsurprisingly, evidence from MRI studies indicates that anterior and superior regions of the frontal cortex are some of the last regions to mature, at between 12 and 30 years of age (Paus et al., 1999; Sowell et al., 1999).

A different maturational pattern is seen in white matter. A relatively linear increase in white matter volume is observed across all brain regions during adolescence (Giedd, 2004; Giedd et al., 1999; Giorgio et al., 2008). These increases are thought to reflect either the process of increased myelination, involving the wrapping of neuronal axons in lipid sheaths, a process that greatly increases the speed of neuronal firing (Giedd, 2004), and/or an increase in axon size (Paus, 2010). White matter changes during adolescence are associated with increased directional connectivity, particularly within the frontal lobes, the key regulatory node of the triadic model (Schmithorst & Yuan, 2010). Prefrontal-striatal connections involved in top-down executive control over behavior do not reach adult-like maturity until at least 18 years of age (Asato, Terwilliger, Woo, & Luna, 2010). With respect to the harm-avoidance node of the triadic model, Cunningham, Bhattacharyya, and Benes (2002) found that amygdalo-cortical fibers increase in density throughout adolescence, perhaps allowing the adolescent to have greater regulatory control over harm-avoidant behavior. Despite this increased connectivity with frontal regions, the overall amygdala volume actually decreases between ages 10 and 21 (Chen et al., 2004).

Neurochemical changes to this system are also observed in adolescence. While gonadal hormones themselves (e.g., estrogen, testosterone) do not appear to be at the root of changes in adolescent risky behavior, the effects of gonadal hormones on oxytocin, a neuromodulator associated with the onset of pleasant feelings in social situations, may be strongly linked to changes in adolescent behavior (see Steinberg, 2008 for a review). In particular, gonadal steroids increase at the onset of puberty and subsequently influence the proliferation of oxytocin receptors in the amygdala and nucleus accumbens, two neural structures that, as previously mentioned, are heavily involved in the brain's socioemotional system. Increased responsiveness to oxytocin ultimately influences emotional and behavioral responses to top-down social stimuli (see Nelson, Leibenluft, McClure, & Pine, 2005). Steinberg (2008) hypothesizes that this increase in oxytocin explains adolescents' increased sensitivity to social-contextual stimuli, and in conjunction with imbalances in the triadic nodes, it may make engaging in audience-controlled risk taking particularly salient for adolescents.

Thus, all of the structures so key to regulating adolescent risk-taking behavior in the triadic model of regulated behavior, including those that are automatically activated and those that require effortful engagement, undergo important developmental changes directly related to their functioning during adolescence. Gray and white matter changes and changes in connectivity and neurochemistry are all observed. Periods of such rapid neurophysiological development are often thought of as critical or sensitive periods. Perturbations of these ongoing processes due to external (e.g., social stressors) or internal (e.g., disease) forces could therefore have long-lasting consequences (Dahl, 2004). Adolescence can be conceptualized as a sensitive period of brain development with heightened vulnerability to both positive and negative influences of social context (Steinberg, 2005). Therefore, top-down cultural and contextual influences may impact both the neurophysiological substrates of risk taking and ultimately the observed behavior.

NEURAL SUBSTRATES OF RISK TAKING IN ADOLESCENCE

During risk-taking behavior, adolescents display characteristic patterns of neural activation that may differ from the neural activation displayed by adults who choose to make those same risky decisions, an idea consistent with the tenets of the triadic model (Ernst et al., 2006). Galvan et al. (2007) used a cross-sectional design to investigate the neural correlates of risk-taking behavior, focusing specifically on activation of the nucleus accumbens, the largest segment of the ventral striatum, in children, adolescents, and adults while they anticipated receiving a monetary reward. Nucleus accumbens activity was then correlated with real-world scores on a variety of risk-taking measures. Across all the participants, but primarily among the adults and adolescents, nucleus accumbens activity was correlated with the likelihood of engaging in risky behavior in the next 6 months. Moreover, adolescents and adults who anticipated experiencing positive consequences from engaging in risky behavior in the future activated the nucleus accumbens to a greater extent during reward anticipation. Thus, anticipation of outcome (a top-down cognitive process) can drive the extent of seemingly automatic neural activity in the reward system during both adolescence and adulthood.

Furthermore, the activation levels of these systems during risky decision making appear to be particularly different during adolescence. For example, Van Leijenhorst, Zanolie et al. (2010) had children, adolescents, and young adults engage in a slot-machine gambling game while in a fMRI scanner. More than the other two groups, the adolescents showed increased levels of activation in the ventral striatum during the receipt of rewards. In a second study, using a different risky decision-making paradigm but with three similarly aged participant groups, Van Leijenhorst, Moor et al. (2010) found that risk-related activation of the anterior cingulate cortex, part of the modulatory system, decreased with age while reward activation of the caudate to gains peaked in adolescence. Moreover, across age groups, activation of the modulatory system was associated with individual differences in propensity to take risks during the task (Van Leijenhorst, Moor et al., 2010). Thus, this system is differentially active in adults versus adolescents, and individual differences in the activation of this system may be indicative of levels of risk-taking personality traits.

Within the adolescent age group, striking individual differences in the activation of these systems are observed. For example, Shad et al. (2011) administered a gambling game in which some decisions were relatively more or less risky to a group of adolescents. The adolescents who were not risk averse (i.e., made risky gambling choices frequently) showed lower activation levels in the frontal cortex modulatory system (specifically the anterior cingulate cortex, orbitofrontal cortex, and medial prefrontal cortex) than those who engaged in this behavior less frequently. Such wide individual differences in the neural correlates of top-down control are often observed.

Thus, group-level analyses have frequently shown that adolescents engage the reward-related system to a greater extent during risky behavior in the lab than adults do and that individual differences in the ability to recruit modulatory regions correlate with individual differences in risk-taking behavior. Both reward and modulatory systems are activated, though to different extents, during risk taking. Given the elevated reward value placed on peers in adolescence (Hand & Furman, 2009), risk taking in the presence of peers might be exceptionally consequential for the functioning of these systems (Chein, Albert, O'Brien, Uckert, & Steinberg, 2010), a finding we discuss in more detail later.

COMBINING LEVELS OF ANALYSIS: CULTURE, CONTEXT, AND PHYSIOLOGY INFLUENCE RISKY BEHAVIOR

Some scholars have understandably raised concerns about "brain overclaim" (see Steinberg, 2008), and it is highly reasonable to speculate that factors other than brain activation levels influence adolescent risk taking (such as a more specific influence of peer culture discussed above). Furthermore, there might be potentially informative interactions between peer influence and the development/activation of the modulatory system in predicting risky behavior. To this end, Romer and Hennessy (2007) proposed a biosocial-affect model of risk taking. This three-part model outlines an interaction among three systems. The affective component of the model involves the evaluation of the emotional valence attached to a particular behavior. The social component of the model highlights the role of peers in risky behavior, with some biological factors influencing outcomes. For example, peer acceptance of risk and affect evaluation of potential risks predicted experimentation with drugs (tobacco, alcohol, and marijuana) in a sample of 14- to 22-year-olds, with this effect moderated by the biological factor of sex (Romer & Hennessy, 2007). Consistent with evidence that male and female adolescents have different rates of neurodevelopment during adolescence, Romer and Hennessy (2007) found that females showed earlier peak levels of risk taking. Males reported greater levels of social approval of risk by their peers and reported less negative affect associated with engaging in risky behaviors than did females. The first two components of the model together predicted slightly more variance in males' risk-taking behavior than in that of females. Biology (sex), social (peers), and affect (evaluation) all influenced the likelihood of engaging in risky behavior. Therefore, Romer and Hennessey (2007) point out that reductionistic models, whether from a physiological ("brain overclaim") or sociological perspective, are inadequate to explain adolescent risk and that all three levels should be included in investigations of adolescent risk. Yet their description of the biological component to the model is understandably shallow due to their methods of investigation. fMRI and EEG methodologies are ideally suited for understanding the biological processes that may modulate adolescent risk-taking behavior.

PEER PRESENCE INFLUENCES NEURAL SUBSTRATES OF DECISION MAKING

Given the changes in the dopamine system during adolescence, the adolescent propensity to engage in risk taking, and the highly rewarding nature of peer interaction to the adolescent, Segalowitz et al. (2012) investigated the impact that the presence of peers would have on an adolescent's behavior in a risk-taking situation and its associated modifications to activity in dopamine-rich brain regions (e.g., medial prefrontal cortex). Building on a behavioral study by Gardner and Steinberg (2005) and Steinberg's (2007) model of the social network during adolescence engaging the reward system, they asked 15-year-old boys to play a video game that involved driving a car along a road and accumulating points as they proceeded. The participants were allowed to drive for as long as they wished and they kept all the points that they had accumulated upon stopping safely; however, at some unexpected time a brick wall appeared, and they would crash into the wall and lose all the points that they had accumulated on that trial. Points were later converted to prizes. The participants completed this task under "alone" and "together" conditions, that is, in the presence of two same-aged friends. Segalowitz et al. (2012) examined the event-related potential responses elicited by the appearance of the wall. The major electrocortical event to this feedback that the player has driven too long is a component called the feedback-related negativity (FRN). The FRN is a negative deflection occurring 250 ms after performance feedback and has been localized to a generator in dopamine-rich regions of the medial prefrontal cortex (Nieuwenhuis, Slagter, von Geusau, Heslenfeld, & Holroyd, 2005). According to Holroyd and Coles (2002), the FRN is thought to reflect activation of the anterior cingulate cortex following unexpected (usually negative) environmental feedback. The research question was whether this prefrontal monitoring response would be affected by peer presence.

Overall, behavioral performance did not differ between the alone and together conditions because peer presence increased the number of car crashes for some participants but decreased them for others. However, this

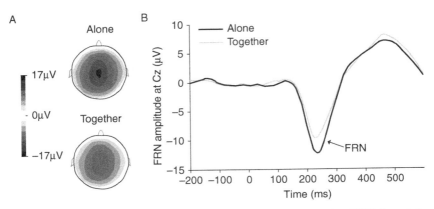

FIGURE 8.2. Topographic maps and waveforms depicting the FRN found in Segalowitz et al. (2012). (A) Group average topographic maps of the FRN period while alone (top) and with peers (bottom); (B) group averaged ERP waveforms at Cz from 200 ms before to 600 ms after the presentation of feedback indicating that a "crash" is imminent while alone (heavy line) and with peers (light line).

was not the case when personality factors were taken into consideration. Participants who were high on surgency, a composite trait characterizing a tendency toward approach (as opposed to avoidance) of situations, along with sensation seeking and positive affect, made significantly more crashes in the together relative to the alone condition. Electrophysiological differences were found in the two conditions. When in the alone condition, these participants showed a much larger FRN than participants in the together condition (see Figure 8.2). The FRN was 28% larger in the alone condition, suggesting that the presence of peers diminishes the salience to the regulatory module of negative feedback. Current source densities (CSDs) extracted from the rostral anterior cingulate cortex, dorsal anterior cingulate cortex, and ventromedial prefrontal cortex showed evidence of deactivation during the together condition. This suggests that top-down inhibitory control may not be as strong in the presence of peers (Segalowitz et al., 2012). Therefore, context effects predict the neural activation in reward-sensitive regions of the adolescent brain during risky decision making. Individual differences were also found. CSD activation levels were associated with surgency scores, as those highest in surgency showed lower levels of activation in prefrontal cortex structures than those lower in surgency, but only in the together condition (Segalowitz et al., 2012). Thus, personality and the presence of peers together modulate the likelihood of taking risks and/or the neural correlates of risk taking. As has been articulated elsewhere in this volume, contextual variables influence the functioning of neural systems related to at-risk development.

Recent fMRI work has further supported the general effect of peer presence. For example, Chein et al. (2010) measured brain activation in incentive-processing regions (ventral striatum, orbitofrontal cortex) and in cognitive-control regions (lateral prefrontal cortex) in adolescents, young adults, and adults during a similar driving task performed while in a fMRI scanner. All the participants completed the tasks under two conditions: alone and with the presence of two same-aged, same-sex friends. In their version of the task, the adolescents as a group engaged in more risks in the presence of peers than when alone. Findings from fMRI indicated higher levels of activity in the ventral striatum and orbitofrontal cortex among the adolescents in the together condition in comparison to other age groups under either of the two conditions. They also indicated an increased reward center response when taking risks in the adolescents but not for the other age groups (Chein et al., 2010). These findings powerfully illustrate the impact of top-down contextual influences on the neural substrates of adolescent affective incentive processing. The picture emerging is that individual differences in neural activation in response to risky decisions are correlated with the likelihood of taking risks themselves, and both the probability of engaging in risk as well as the neural activations associated with that risk are profoundly influenced by the social context.

Less direct evidence for our assertion that peer context influences the neural substrates of risky decision making is also beginning to amass and can be integrated into a framework that we propose in Figure 8.3. Peer rejection is a common experience in the lives of many adolescents, and the experience of peer rejection may be inversely related to risk taking (Engels & ter Bogt, 2001). Peer acceptance, the converse of peer rejection, is positively associated with risk-taking behavior in adolescence (including substance use and minor deviant acts; Engels & ter Bogt, 2001) and is positively correlated with increases in problem behavior (including substance use and antisocial behavior) during the transition to early adolescence (Maggs, Almeida, & Galambos, 1995). This is consistent with evolutionary psychology principles asserting that risk taking leads to increases in social status (Nell, 2002). However, there are substantial individual differences in responses to peer rejection, and these individual differences may in part have a neural basis in the social network. Masten et al. (2009) simulated peer rejection and inclusion using a virtual game called Cyberball and measured brain activations in social cognitive regions of the brain. Individual differences in activity in many regions associated with the social network were

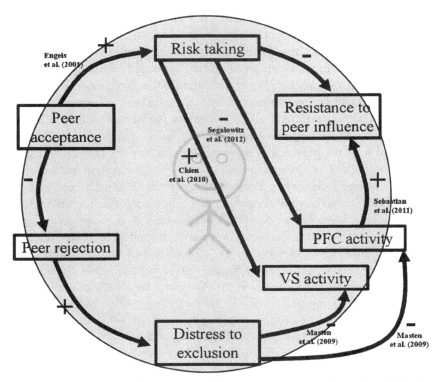

FIGURE 8.3. A proposed integration of the interactive nature of social and biological variables that contribute to risk-taking activity in adolescents. Plus and minus signs indicate the direction of the correlation between the two variables.

correlated with the degree of subjective distress reported by adolescents in the exclusion condition. Higher levels of distress during exclusion were associated with decreased levels of activity in both prefrontal cortex and ventral striatum. Similarly, Sebastian et al. (2011) reported that increased activity in the medial prefrontal cortex during the exclusion condition was related to increased self-reported resistance to peer influence. Thus, individual differences in the experience of social exclusion are associated with individual differences in activation of the social cognitive network, which is also involved in risk taking.

Risk taking appears to be multiply determined by both social and neural factors. These include peer presence, susceptibility to peer influence versus peer acceptance, and prefrontal and ventral striatum activity. In addition, the connectivity across the regions has also been shown to be important in a variety of contexts, although mainly so far with adults (Hermans et al.,

2011; Nagano-Saito et al., 2008; Tu, Hsieh, Li, Bai, & Su, 2012). Similarly, reduced PFC activity can occur in both peer accepted and rejected groups, but for different reasons. Perhaps the distress related to social exclusion leads to low PFC activity mediated through the amygdala and anterior temporal regions, while the risk taking related to high peer acceptance is associated with low PFC moderated through high ventral striatum activity, that is, a high reward reactivity coupled with low prefrontally mediated self-regulation disposes individuals to higher peer-accepted risk-taking behaviors. Given the feedback loops, it is not at all clear that the neural components always lead the social-reactivity factors or vice versa. There are likely other factors that influence these relations, so at present we are only able to document correlations.

As we have shown, bottom-up processing of the instinctual reward value of risk taking is influenced by the top-down influence of social context, variables that differ dramatically across individuals. Thus, top-down and bottom-up influences on risk taking and self-regulation are symbiotic with one another. We agree with biosocial-affect models of adolescent risk taking (e.g., Romer & Hennessy, 2007) in which the bottom-up (instinctual affective evaluation) factors are combined with top-down (social) factors in producing risky behavior, and we look forward to more direct neurophysiological support for this approach of the type outlined in this chapter. Because social context influences both socially rewarding adolescent behavior and the neural correlates of reward-system activity, more studies that directly manipulate the social context during potentially rewarding and risky behaviors are required. For instance, we need to conduct studies integrating the factor of peer presence and peer influence on reactivity of the neural social network in the context of a wider variety of risk-taking opportunities and behaviors.

CONCLUSIONS

Top-down and bottom-up influences on behavior are becoming increasingly integrated in contemporary neuroscience. The processing of both basic sensory and complex socially relevant stimuli are influenced by context. So-called top-down influences are dramatically impacted by culture and context, and these effects can occur in what normally are seen as being at an automatic level of brain responses. Thus, behavioral control required to self-regulate (e.g., to avoid risk taking) does not map clearly onto the top-down versus bottom-up distinction. Self-regulation involves a dynamic interplay of top-down and bottom-up processes and may involve automatic responses reconfiguring as strategic "controlled" responses. In this chapter, we provided one example of how adolescent peer culture, a top-down influence, may impact the neural correlates of adolescent risk-taking behavior. In the presence of peers, the neural structures associated with rewarding behavior (i.e., those that are conceptualized as being under bottom-up automatic control) are active to a greater extent than they are in peers' absence. Moreover, the regulatory capacity of the medial prefrontal cortex is also diminished in the presence of peers, a context that is exceptionally salient to the developing adolescent. Thus, the magnitude of top-down influence on bottom-up processing is dependent on context, and contexts can vary greatly depending on social affiliations.

Given these interacting factors, we can see risk-taking behavior as driven by a set of variables whose influence changes developmentally. We see risk taking in childhood as typically being a sign of poor judgment. In adolescence it is more ambiguous, potentially being the result of new social demands and a growing internal drive for novelty associated with more mature brain development. This naturally results in an increased "window of vulnerability" that is, in many senses, a healthy sign of growth, but it of course suggests the need for supervision and care from others. Adult risk taking is much more complex to categorize, because maturation rates and end points of brain growth are so highly variable and social and professional demands create contexts that are highly variable across adults.

REFERENCES

Adriani, W., Chiarotti, F., & Laviola, G. (1998). Elevated novelty seeking and peculiar d-amphetamine sensitization in periadolescent mice compared with adult mice. *Behavioral Neuroscience*, 112(5), 1152–1166.

Anderson, S. A., Classey, J. D., Conde, F., Lund, J. S., & Lewis, D. A. (1995). Synchronous development of pyramidal neuron dendritic spines and parvalbumin-immunoreactive chandelier neuron axon terminals in layer III of monkey prefrontal cortex. *Neuroscience*, 67(1), 7–22.

Angelucci, A., Levitt, J. B., Walton, E. J., Hupe, J. M., Bullier, J., & Lund, J. S. (2002). Circuits for local and global signal integration in primary visual cortex. *Journal of Neuroscience*, 22(19), 8633–8646.

Arnett, J. (1992). Reckless behavior in adolescence: A developmental perspective. *Developmental Review*, 12(4), 339–373.

Asato, M. R., Terwilliger, R., Woo, J., & Luna, B. (2010). White matter development in adolescence: A DTI study. *Cerebral Cortex*, 20(9), 2122–2131.

Bar, M. (2003). A cortical mechanism for triggering top-down facilitation in visual object recognition. *Journal of Cognitive Neuroscience*, 15(4), 600–609.

Berns, G. S., Moore, S., & Capra, C. M. (2009). Adolescent engagement in dangerous behaviors is associated with increased white matter maturity of frontal cortex. *PloS One*, 4(8), e6773.

Blum, R. W., & Nelson-Mmari, K. (2004). The health of young people in a global context. *Journal of Adolescent Health*, 35(5), 402–418.

Brunell, S. C., & Spear, L. P. (2005). Effect of stress on the voluntary intake of a sweetened ethanol solution in pair-housed adolescent and adult rats. *Alcoholism: Clinical & Experimental Research*, 29(9), 1641–1653.

Cauller, L. (1995). Layer I of primary sensory neocortex: Where top-down converges upon bottom-up. *Behavioral Brain Research*, 71(1–2), 163–170.

Chawla, D., Rees, G., & Friston, K. J. (1999). The physiological basis of attentional modulation in extrastriate visual areas. *Nat Neurosci*, 2(7), 671–676.

Chein, J., Albert, D., O'Brien, L., Uckert, K., & Steinberg, L. (2010). Peers increase adolescent risk taking by enhancing activity in the brain's reward circuitry. *Developmental Science*, 14(2), F1–F10.

Chen, B. K., Sassi, R., Axelson, D., Hatch, J. P., Sanches, M., Nicoletti, M., et al. (2004). Cross-sectional study of abnormal amygdala development in adolescents and young adults with bipolar disorder. *Biological Psychiatry*, 56(6), 399–405.

Cohn, L. D., Macfarlane, S., Yanez, C., & Imai, W. K. (1995). Risk-perception – differences between adolescents and adults. *Health Psychology*, 14(3), 217–222.

Corbetta, M., Miezin, F. M., Dobmeyer, S., Shulman, G. L., & Petersen, S. E. (1990). Attentional modulation of neural processing of shape, color, and velocity in humans. *Science*, 248(4962), 1556–1559.

Cunningham, M. G., Bhattacharyya, S., & Benes, F. M. (2002). Amygdalo-cortical sprouting continues into early adulthood: Implications for the development of normal and abnormal function during adolescence. *Journal of Comparative Neurology*, 453(2), 116–130.

Dahl, R. E. (2004). Adolescent brain development: A period of vulnerabilities and opportunities. Keynote address. *Annals of the New York Academy of Sciences*, 1021, 1–22.

Diblasio, F. A. (1986). Drinking adolescents on the roads. *Journal of Youth and Adolescence*, 15(2), 173–188.

Doremus, T. L., Brunell, S. C., Rajendran, P., & Spear, L. P. (2005). Factors influencing elevated ethanol consumption in adolescent relative to adult rats. *Alcoholism: Clinical & Experimental Research*, 29(10), 1796–1808.

Engels, R. C. M. E., & ter Bogt, T. (2001). Influences of risk behaviors on the quality of peer relations in adolescence. *Journal of Youth and Adolescence*, 30(6), 675–695.

Ernst, M., & Fudge, J. L. (2009). A developmental neurobiological model of motivated behavior: Anatomy, connectivity and ontogeny of the triadic nodes. *Neuroscience and Biobehavioral Reviews*, 33, 367–382.

Ernst, M., Pine, D. S., & Hardin, M. (2006). Triadic model of the neurobiology of motivated behavior in adolescence. *Psychological Medicine*, 36(3), 299–312.

Fairbanks, L. A., Melega, W. P., Jorgensen, M. J., Kaplan, J. R., & McGuire, M. T. (2001). Social impulsivity inversely associated with CSF 5-HIAA and fluoxetine exposure in vervet monkeys. *Neuropsychopharmacology*, 24(4), 370–378.

Fenske, M. J., Aminoff, E., Gronau, N., & Bar, M. (2006). Top-down facilitation of visual object recognition: Object-based and context-based contributions. *Progress in Brain Research*, 155, 3–21.

Fischhoff, B. (2008). Assessing adolescent decision-making competence. *Developmental Review*, 28(1), 12–28.

Galvan, A., Hare, T., Voss, H., Glover, G., & Casey, B. J. (2007). Risk-taking and the adolescent brain: Who is at risk? *Developmental Science*, 10(2), F8-F14.

Gardner, M., & Steinberg, L. (2005). Peer influence on risk taking, risk preference, and risky decision making in adolescence and adulthood: An experimental study. *Developmental Psychology*, 41(4), 625–635.

Giedd, J. N. (2004). Structural magnetic resonance imaging of the adolescent brain. *Annals of the New York Academy of Sciences*, 1021, 77–85.

Giedd, J. N., Blumenthal, J., Jeffries, N. O., Castellanos, F. X., Liu, H., Zijdenbos, A., et al. (1999). Brain development during childhood and adolescence: A longitudinal MRI study. *Nature Neuroscience*, 2(10), 861–863.

Gilbert, C. D., & Sigman, M. (2007). Brain states: Top-down influences in sensory processing. *Neuron*, 54(5), 677–696.

Giorgio, A., Watkins, K. E., Douaud, G., James, A. C., James, S., De Stefano, N., et al. (2008). Changes in white matter microstructure during adolescence. *Neuroimage*, 39(1), 52–61.

Gogtay, N., & Thompson, P. M. (2010). Mapping gray matter development: Implications for typical development and vulnerability to psychopathology. *Brain and Cognition*, 72(1), 6. doi: 10.1016/j.bandc.2009.08.009.

Hand, L. S., & Furman, W. (2009). Rewards and costs in adolescent other-sex friendships: Comparisons to same-sex friendships and romantic relationships. *Social Development*, 18(2), 270–287.

Hermans, E. J., van Marle, H. J., Ossewaarde, L., Henckens, M. J., Qin, S., van Kesteren, M. T., et al. (2011). Stress-related noradrenergic activity prompts large-scale neural network reconfiguration. *Science*, 334(6059), 1151–1153.

Holroyd, C. B., & Coles, M. G. H. (2002). The neural basis of human error processing: Reinforcement learning, dopamine, and the error-related negativity. *Psychological Review*, 109(4), 679–709.

Jaccard, J., Blanton, H., & Dodge, T. (2005). Peer influences on risk behavior: An analysis of the effects of a close friend. *Developmental Psychology*, 41(1), 135–147.

Kandel, D. B. (1978). Homophily, selection, and socialization in adolescent friendships. *American Journal of Sociology*, 84(2), 427–436.

Kloep, M., Güney, N., Çok, F., & Simsek, O. F. (2009). Motives for risk-taking in adolescence: A cross-cultural study. *Journal of Adolescence*, 32(1), 135–151.

Kroeber, A. L., & Kluckhohn, C. (1952). Culture: A critical review of concepts and definitions. *Papers. Peabody Museum of Archaeology & Ethnology, Harvard University*, 47(1), 223.

Larkum, M. E., Senn, W., & Luscher, H. R. (2004). Top-down dendritic input increases the gain of layer 5 pyramidal neurons. *Cereb Cortex*, 14(10), 1059–1070.

Lenroot, R. K., Gogtay, N., Greenstein, D. K., Wells, E. M., Wallace, G. L., Clasen, L. S., et al. (2007). Sexual dimorphism of brain developmental trajectories during childhood and adolescence. *Neuroimage*, 36(4), 1065–1073.

Maggs, J. L., Almeida, D. M., & Galambos, N. L. (1995). Risky business: The paradoxical meaning of problem behavior for young adolescents. *Journal of Early Adolescence*, 15(3), 344–362.

Masten, C. L., Eisenberger, N. I., Borofsky, L. A., Pfeifer, J. H., McNealy, K., Mazziotta, J. C., et al. (2009). Neural correlates of social exclusion during adolescence: Understanding the distress of peer rejection. *Social Cognitive and Affective Neuroscience*, 4(2), 143–157.

Mechelli, A., Price, C. J., Friston, K. J., & Ishai, A. (2004). Where bottom-up meets top-down: Neuronal interactions during perception and imagery. *Cerebral Cortex*, 14(11), 1256–1265.

Nagano-Saito, A., Leyton, M., Monchi, O., Goldberg, Y. K., He, Y., & Dagher, A. (2008). Dopamine depletion impairs frontostriatal functional connectivity during a set-shifting task. *J Neurosci*, 28(14), 3697–3706.

Nell, V. (2002). Why young men drive dangerously: Implications for injury prevention. *Current Directions in Psychological Science*, 11(2), 75–79.

Nelson, E. E., Leibenluft, E., McClure, E. B., & Pine, D. S. (2005). The social re-orientation of adolescence: A neuroscience perspective on the process and its relation to psychopathology. *Psychological Medicine*, 35(2), 163–174.

Nieuwenhuis, S., Slagter, H. A., von Geusau, N. J., Heslenfeld, D. J., & Holroyd, C. B. (2005). Knowing good from bad: Differential activation of human cortical areas by positive and negative outcomes. *European Journal of Neuroscience*, 21(11), 3161–3168.

Olson, I. R., Chun, M. M., & Allison, T. (2001). Contextual guidance of attention: Human intracranial event-related potential evidence for feedback modulation in anatomically early, temporally late stages of visual processing. *Brain*, 124, 1417–1425.

Paus, T. (2010). Growth of white matter in the adolescent brain: Myelin or axon? *Brain and Cognition*, 72(1), 26–35.

Paus, T., Zijdenbos, A., Worsley, K., Collins, D. L., Blumenthal, J., Giedd, J. N., et al. (1999). Structural maturation of neural pathways in children and adolescents: In vivo study. *Science*, 283(5409), 1908–1911.

Rakic, P., Bourgeois, J. -P., & Goldman-Rakic, P. S. (1994). Synaptic development of the cerebral cortex: Implications for learning, memory, and mental illness. *Progress in Brain Research*, 102, 227–243.

Reyna, V. F., & Farley, F. (2006). Risk and rationality in adolescent decision making – implications for theory, practice, and public policy. *Psychological Science*, 1–44.

Romer, D., & Hennessy, M. (2007). A biosocial-affect model of adolescent sensation seeking: The role of affect evaluation and peer-group influence in adolescent drug use. *Prevention Science*, 8(2), 89–101.

Schmithorst, V. J., & Yuan, W. (2010). White matter development during adolescence as shown by diffusion MRI. *Brain and Cognition*, 72(1), 16–25.

Schramm-Sapyta, N. L., Cauley, M. C., Stangl, D. K., Glowacz, S., Stepp, K. A., Levin, E. D., et al. (2011). Role of individual and developmental differences in voluntary cocaine intake in rats. *Psychopharmacology (Berl)*, 215(3), 493–504.

Sebastian, C. L., Tan, G. C., Roiser, J. P., Viding, E., Dumontheil, I., & Blakemore, S. J. (2011). Developmental influences on the neural bases of responses to social rejection: implications of social neuroscience for education. *Neuroimage*, 57(3), 686–694.

Segalowitz, S. J., Santesso, D. L., Willoughby, T., Reker, D. L., Campbell, K., Chalmers, H., et al. (2012). Adolescent peer interaction and trait surgency weaken medial prefrontal cortex responses to failure. *Social Cognitive and Affective Neuroscience* 7(1), 115–124.

Shad, M. U., Bidesi, A. S., Chen, L. A., Thomas, B. P., Ernst, M., & Rao, U. (2011). Neurobiology of decision-making in adolescents. *Behavioral Brain Research*, 217(1), 67–76.

Shmuel, A., Korman, M., Sterkin, A., Harel, M., Ullman, S., Malach, R., et al. (2005). Retinotopic axis specificity and selective clustering of feedback projections from V2 to V1 in the owl monkey. *J Neurosci*, 25(8), 2117–2131.

Sowell, E. R., Thompson, P. M., Holmes, C. J., Batth, R., Jernigan, T. L., & Toga, A. W. (1999). Localizing age-related changes in brain structure between childhood and adolescence using statistical parametric mapping. *Neuroimage*, 9(6 Pt 1), 587–597.

Spear, L. P. (2003). Neurodevelopment during adolescence. In D. Cicchetti & E. F. Walker (Eds.), *Neurodevelopmental mechanisms in psychopathology* (pp. 62–83). Cambridge: Cambridge University Press.

Steinberg, L. (2005). Cognitive and affective development in adolescence. *Trends in Cognitive Sciences*, 9, 69–74.

   (2008). A social neuroscience perspective on adolescent risk-taking. *Developmental Review*, 28(1), 78–106.

Steinberg, L., & Monahan, K. C. (2007). Age differences in resistance to peer influence. *Developmental Psychology*, 43(6), 1531–1543.

Tarazi, F. I., & Baldessarini, R. J. (2000). Comparative postnatal development of dopamine D(1), D(2) and D(4) receptors in rat forebrain. *International Journal of Developmental Neuroscience*, 18(1), 29–37.

Tu, P. C., Hsieh, J. C., Li, C. T., Bai, Y. M., & Su, T. P. (2012). Cortico-striatal disconnection within the cingulo-opercular network in schizophrenia revealed by intrinsic functional connectivity analysis: A resting fMRI study. *Neuroimage*, 59(1), 238–247.

Van Leijenhorst, L., Moor, B. G., de Macks, Z. A. O., Rombouts, S. A. R. B., Westenberg, P. M., & Crone, E. A. (2010). Adolescent risky decision-making: Neurocognitive development of reward and control regions *Neuroimage*, 51(1), 345–355.

Van Leijenhorst, L., Zanolie, K., Van Meel, C. S., Westenberg, P. M., Rombouts, S. A. R. B., & Crone, E. A. (2010). What motivates the adolescent? Brain regions mediating reward sensitivity across adolescence. *Cerebral Cortex*, 20(1), 61–69.

Varela, R. E., Vernberg, E. M., Sanchez-Sosa, J. J., Riveros, A., Mitchell, M., & Mashunkashey, J. (2004). Anxiety reporting and culturally associated interpretation biases and cognitive schemas: a comparison of Mexican, Mexican American, and European American families. *Journal of Clinical Child and Adolescent Psychology*, 33(2), 237–247.

Wahlstrom, D., White, T., Hooper, C. J., Vrshek-Schallhorn, S., Oetting, W. S., Brott, M. J., et al. (2007). Variations in the catechol O-methyltransferase polymorphism and prefrontally guided behaviors in adolescents. *Biol Psychiatry*, 61(5), 626–632.

Wahlstrom, D., White, T., & Luciana, M. (2010). Neurobehavioral evidence for changes in dopamine system activity during adolescence. *Neuroscience and Biobehavioral Reviews, 34*(5), 631–648.

Williams, P. G., Holmbeck, G. N., & Greenley, R. N. (2002). Adolescent health psychology. *Journal of Consulting and Clinical Psychology, 70*(3), 828–842.

Zheng, X., & Segalowitz, S. J. (2013). Putting a face in its place: In- and out-group membership alters the N170 response. *Social Cognitive and Affective Neuroscience.* Advanced online publication. doi:10.1093/scan/nst069.

PART III

CONTEXTUAL PERSPECTIVES ON ATYPICALITY

9

Prematurity as a Context of Development at Risk

LAUREN DRVARIC, JORDANA WAXMAN,
RYAN J. VAN LIESHOUT, AND LOUIS A. SCHMIDT

The search for contextual influences on socioemotional developmental processes has a long and rich history in the field of human development. Indeed, the chapters in this volume illustrate the broad range and multiple meanings of what is meant by context in the study of risk. One contextual factor that provides promise for investigation in the study of risk is the prenatal environment and the impact of being born extremely preterm (< 28 weeks) or at extremely low birth weight ([ELBW]; < 1,000 g) has on socioemotional development.

The burgeoning interest in the study and conceptualization of prematurity as a contextual factor within the field of human development can be attributed to at least three issues. One, there has been a fundamental shift in the *Zeitgeist* over the last several decades in terms of how we conceptualize what is meant by context and environment. For example, until recently, in the case of prematurity, the phenomenon was largely viewed as an individual-level predictor variable for outcome studies. Traditionally, individual-level variables are viewed as static or fixed, limiting the range of possibilities of how we then studied developmental outcomes. Conversely, if one conceptualizes prematurity from an environmental approach, the range and ways of studying the phenomenon are enhanced, given that from this approach the environment is quite dynamic and multidetermined.

A second issue that contributed to the limited use of prematurity as a contextual factor in the study of socioemotional development was that, until the last 30 years, there was little opportunity to examine survivors of preterm birth and low birth weight longitudinally. With the advent of advances occurring in fetal and neonatal medicine in the past 30 years,

Author Note: The first two authors contributed equally to the writing of this chapter and are listed here alphabetically.

183

many of the tiniest and most at-risk infants have gone on to survive into childhood and adulthood, making it possible to examine these survivors from a developmental perspective.

A third issue is related to limitations in theory, methods, and designs that have been used over the years in the study of prematurity and socio-emotional outcomes. Most of these studies have been atheoretical and descriptive in nature and involved cross-sectional designs and subjective measures. This too is now changing. As a result of lengthened lifespan and their increased life expectancies, we now can incorporate longitudinal and prospective designs. As well, theoretical advances from the field of neuroscience provide us with new theories about how early adversity may impact brain development and which putative brain areas are likely to hold promise for the investigation of the relevant mechanism(s) of action. Collaborations across different scientific disciplines that incorporate longitudinal designs and objective measures, including behavioral and physiological indices, and provide a less biased approach to measurement have now begun to emerge.

In this chapter, we argue that prematurity and low birth weight might provide additional contexts of development at risk. We focus on an extreme form of early prematurity (i.e., ELBW: < 1,000 grams), with the caveat that the vast majority but not all of ELBW babies are born extremely prematurely (i.e., < 28 weeks gestation). Infants born at ELBW are the tiniest and most at-risk babies in the extremely preterm group. Because of advances in neonatal and fetal medicine over the past several decades, many infants who would not have survived in the past now thrive into their adult years and live relatively free of physical and mental impairments. As such, ELBW provides a unique and naturally occurring model in nature of how exposure to early adversity may impact brain–behavioral relations.

We utilize ELBW as a model to understand how exposure to early adversity impacts the development of socioemotional problems. We review literature that suggests two putative stress vulnerability systems, neuroendocrine and frontal brain-autonomic, that underlie emotion regulatory processes and may be perturbed as a result of being born at ELBW and why such perturbations may account for the increased prevalence of socioemotional problems observed in ELBW survivors.

The chapter is organized around three sections. In the first section, we review literature linking a putative central and peripheral nervous system circuit, the neuroendocrine system, to emotion regulation and dysregulation. In the second section, we review the frontal brain-autonomic system, one that links the prefrontal cortex (PFC) and autonomic nervous system (ANS) activity to emotion regulatory and dysregulatory processes. In the third section, we then use the information reviewed in the prior two sections to develop a preliminary and integrated model of how these systems might be conceptually and statistically affected by or interact with extreme prematurity and ELBW to confer an increased risk for the development of socioemotional problems.

EARLY ADVERSITY, THE NEUROENDOCRINE SYSTEM, AND SOCIOEMOTIONAL PROBLEMS

Stress is labeled as toxic when levels of exposure are high and prolonged (Shonkoff, Boyce, & McEwen, 2009). Toxic stress experienced *early* in life can be particularly deleterious, as certain biological, psychological, homeostatic, and behavioral adaptations are made that can cause the brain and other physiological systems (including the neuroendocrine system) to be altered in ways that are maladaptive (Rutter & O'Connor, 2004). Preterm birth (and low birth weight) is a model of early adversity that exemplifies how stress can affect biological mechanisms and ultimately lead to negative physiological and psychological outcomes (Phillips, 2007). In this section, we discuss (1) the neuroendocrine system and its development in typical populations, (2) early adversity, in particular prematurity, and its effects on the neuroendocrine system, (3) the relation between prematurity and psychopathology, and (4) the potential mediating and moderating effects of the neuroendocrine system on links between prematurity and later psychopathology.

The Neuroendocrine System

The neuroendocrine system is composed of two interrelated physiological systems, the ANS and the hypothalamic-pituitary-adrenal (HPA) axis. These work in synchrony to increase the likelihood of an organism's short-term survival in the face of danger (Sanchez, 2006). The ANS is a fast-acting system that is composed of the sympathetic (SNS) and parasympathetic nervous systems (PNS; Rudolph, Troop-Gordon, & Granger, 2011). The sympathetic branch is referred to as the "fight or flight" system, which defends against controllable threats, while the parasympathetic system is the "brake" of the ANS. The parasympathetic system enforces negative feedback control in order to make the sympathetic response brief (Rudolph et al., 2011).

The HPA axis is the slower-acting stress response system that controls a number of bodily functions and is activated by both physiological and psychological stressors (Rudolph et al., 2011). In humans, these stressors trigger the hypothalamus to release the corticotrophin-releasing hormone (CRH; Schulkin, Gold, & McEwen, 1998). CRH binds to receptors in the anterior pituitary gland and stimulates secretion of the adrenocorticotropic hormone (ACTH). ACTH then causes the adrenal cortex to release cortisol, a glucocorticoid hormone (McCrory, De Brito, & Viding, 2010). Cortisol prepares the body to meet the energy demands associated with stressful events and triggers a negative feedback loop that suppresses CRH and ACTH production (Rudolph et al., 2011). When the HPA axis becomes dysregulated, the body cannot return to its baseline state (McCrory et al., 2010; Schulkin et al., 1998). If the HPA axis is chronically activated, its protective effects are diminished and the system can cause damage (Schulkin et al., 1998).

Development of the HPA axis. In early postnatal life, typically developing human infants are said to be in a stress-hyporeactive period (SHRP). The SHRP is defined as the first 4 to 14 postnatal days, during which it is difficult to produce elevated levels of ACTH and cortisol in response to stressors (Slattery & Neumann, 2008). After postnatal day 14, however, infants demonstrate significant increases in stress-reactive cortisol levels, as well as the emergence of a diurnal cortisol rhythm (Rivkees, 2003). This diurnal rhythm is defined as the normal daily variation in cortisol levels over typical 24-hour periods, with the highest levels of cortisol experienced in early morning, followed by a significant decrease at midmorning and a gradual decline over the remainder of the day (Rivkees, 2003; Watamura, Donzella, Kertes, & Gunnar, 2004).

At 2 years of age, diurnal cortisol rhythm is still immature in humans, but there is a distinct daytime rhythm in cortisol production (Watamura et al., 2004). Throughout early childhood, the diurnal cortisol rhythm becomes increasingly stable, although increases in cortisol levels in response to mild stressors are difficult to attain (Dettling, Gunnar, & Donzella, 1999; Tarullo & Gunnar, 2006; Watamura et al., 2004). By adolescence, the adult diurnal cortisol rhythm is achieved, but baseline and stress-reactive cortisol levels remain higher than in adults (Lupien, McEwen, Gunnar, & Heim, 2009). As the neuroendocrine system continues to develop throughout infancy, childhood, and adolescence, toxic stress exposure during development can perturb the HPA axis permanently, with lasting effects on the individual.

Early Adversity and the Neuroendocrine System

Early adversity can be defined as challenges to emotional and/or physical well-being in early life that can reduce one's ability to cope and lead to chronic stress (Gunnar & Quevedo, 2007). When one experiences a chronically or intensely stressful early environment, permanent reorganization may occur in hormonal, physiological, and behavioral systems, which can increase vulnerability to psychiatric disorders later in life (Grunau et al., 2007).

The neuroendocrine axis has been identified as a biological system that can be perturbed due to adversities in pre- and postnatal life (Field et al., 2004; Gunnar & Vazquez, 2001). Approximately 10 to 20% of maternal glucocorticoids can pass through the placenta and lead to structural changes in the child's neuroendocrine system (McEwen, 2003; Seckl, 2004). Changes to the neuroendocrine system appear to be stable, as individuals whose mothers experienced negative life events during pregnancy experience lower baseline and higher stress-reactive cortisol levels than controls in adulthood (Entringer, Kumsta, Hellhammer, Wadhwa, & Wüst, 2009). Prenatal depression also has been shown to affect infants' postnatal cortisol levels, with infants of depressed mothers experiencing higher baseline cortisol levels than typically developing infants (Entringer et al., 2009).

Postnatal stressors, such as maltreatment, neglect, and deprived rearing environments also have been shown to permanently disturb the neuroendocrine system (Gunnar & Donzella, 2002; Gunnar & Vazquez, 2001; Tarullo & Gunnar, 2006). Lower early-morning cortisol levels and a blunted diurnal cortisol rhythm have been demonstrated in those who experienced early adversity (Gunnar & Vazquez, 2001; Kliewer, Reid-Quinones, Shields, & Foutz, 2008; MacMillan et al., 2009; Tarullo & Gunnar, 2006). These atypical cortisol levels may be explained by early activation of the HPA axis combined with suboptimal adaptations and coping strategies adopted in order to cope with the chronic stress associated with these negative life events (Compas, 2006).

Prematurity and the neuroendocrine system. Premature birth is thought to reflect exposure to adverse intrauterine conditions, which may leave the infant at risk for a variety of negative outcomes, including inadequate time for the attainment of important developmental milestones (Schäffer et al., 2009). Coupled with additional stressful postnatal events such as blood sampling, steroid exposure, suctioning, and routines such as weighing and clustered nursing (Glover, Miles, Matta, Modi, & Stevenson, 2005; Holsti, Weinberg, Whitfield, & Grunau, 2007), those born prematurely often have accelerated HPA axis maturation, which alters the timing of the SHRP (Schäffer et al., 2009). The body may reset baseline cortisol levels when the SHRP is perturbed, and this can have long-term adverse effects on the HPA axis (Grunau et al., 2007; Schäffer et al., 2009).

Risk gradients. Children born prematurely may have altered baseline and stress-reactive cortisol levels, with a gradient of risk becoming apparent for decreasing birth weight and size for gestational age (Field et al., 2006; Grunau et al., 2007; Kajantie et al., 2002). In early infancy, the level of perturbation in the neuroendocrine system has been shown to be due in part to birth weight, as inverse associations between birth weight and baseline cortisol levels have been reported by at least two groups (Grunau et al., 2007; Kajantie et al., 2002).

Infants classified as low birth weight (LBW; < 2,500 g) also have been shown to manifest higher levels of cortisol in early infancy, which may be due to changes in the expression of steroid receptors in the limbic system caused by the multitude of stressors experienced by LBW infants in early life (Field et al., 2006). Very-low-birth-weight (VLBW; < 1,500 g) infants also tend to have heightened cortisol and ACTH levels that persist to 1 month of age relative to normal-birth-weight (NBW) controls. Babies born at ELBW are born at the limits of survivability and tend to experience many stresses which leave them prone to extreme perturbations in their neuroendocrine system, specifically a blunted diurnal cortisol rhythm in early infancy and heightened cortisol production at 8 and 18 months (Aucott, Watterberg, Shaffer, & Donohue, 2008; 2010).

The inverse relation between birth weight and cortisol levels is not fleeting and can even persist into adulthood. Kajantie et al. (2002) reported that HPA axis function during a standardized psychosocial stress challenge in elderly participants was predicted by birth weight. In particular, they found that the highest ACTH and cortisol concentrations were found in those born at the lowest quintile of birth weight. These results suggest that the developmental programming effect of premature birth on the neuroendocrine system persists into adulthood and that the physical and mental health risks associated with a dysregulated neuroendocrine system may also continue into the later stages of life.

Although decreasing birth weight has been established as a risk factor for neuroendocrine dysregulation, size for gestational age has also proven to be an important factor in predicting both baseline and stress-reactive cortisol in infancy and early childhood (Brummelte et al., 2011; Grunau et al., 2007; Schäffer et al., 2009; Verkauskiene et al., 2007). Size for gestational age is another useful proxy for intrauterine stress exposure (Brummelte et al.,

2011) and a gradient of risk has emerged that predicts the greatest cortisol dysregulation in those born small for gestational age (SGA; birth weights < 10th percentile for gestational age; Brummelte et al., 2011; Grunau et al., 2007; Schäffer et al., 2009; Verkauskiene et al., 2007).

In research on newborn infants' umbilical cord cortisol levels, lower baseline cortisol levels were found in babies experiencing intrauterine growth restriction than NBW infants (Verkauskiene et al., 2007). Similar findings were present in SGA neonates, as they were found to have blunted baseline and stress-reactive cortisol levels compared to those born at an appropriate birth weight for gestational age (AGA; > 10th percentile for gestational age; Schäffer et al., 2009).

Abnormally blunted responses to stress, as well as baseline levels of cortisol that seem to be irregular from birth, can convert to a hyperreactive system later in life (Brummelte et al., 2011; Grunau et al., 2007). Infants born extremely prematurely tend to show significantly lower baseline cortisol levels at 3 months and higher baseline cortisol levels at both 8 and 18 months compared to very-low-gestational-age (VLGA; 29–32 weeks gestation) and NBW infants (Brummelte et al., 2011). These results suggest a switch from higher to lower cortisol levels in extremely preterm infants, which persists throughout the first 2 years of life. These abnormal cortisol levels may be due to adrenal hypersecretion following adverse intrauterine environments, as well as postnatal stress (Grunau et al., 2007). As a result, immaturity of physiological systems may contribute to the higher cortisol set points in extremely preterm/SGA infants compared to NBW/AGA controls (Grunau et al., 2007). A variety of negative outcomes have been shown to accompany premature birth, which may be due to perturbations in the HPA axis caused by immature physiological systems and early-life stressors. Indeed, a gradient of risk for mental health outcomes has been shown to exist depending on birth weight as well as size for gestational age.

Prematurity and Later Mental Health Outcomes

Decreased weight at birth is commonly associated with an elevated risk for psychopathology (Crombie, Clark, & Stansfeld, 2011; Hack et al., 2002; Nomura et al., 2007; Schlotz & Phillips, 2009). Individuals born at VLBW tend to experience increased emotionality and internalizing problems in young adulthood compared to NBW control groups (Aarnoudse-Moens, Weisglas-Kuperus, van Goudoever, & Oosterlaan, 2009; Bhutta, Cleves, Casey, Cradock, & Anand, 2002; Boyle et al., 2011). Individuals born at

ELBW also tend to have persistent problems with internalizing problems into young adulthood, and those born SGA appear to have the most severe problems (Boyle et al., 2011; Raikkonen et al., 2008). Appropriateness of birth weight for gestational age also seems to play a significant role in determining the severity of internalizing disorders within these LBW groups, (e.g., Monfils Gustafsson, Josefsson, Ekholm Selling, & Sydsjö, 2009; Raikkonen et al., 2008).

The risk for other mental health problems also increases significantly as one's birth weight and size for gestational age decrease. Individuals born at ELBW are at increased risk for attention deficit hyperactive disorder (ADHD) and autism spectrum disorders during childhood (Johnson et al., 2010), and those born SGA are found to have higher parent-rated behavioral symptom scores of ADHD at 56 months of age compared to those born AGA. ELBW/SGAs are also three times more likely to receive a diagnosis of ADHD than those born AGA (Johnson et al., 2010). These data raise the possibility that early physiological adaptation, specifically in the HPA axis, to adverse intrauterine and early postnatal environments may underlie the association between premature birth and later risk for mental health problems.

Prematurity and Mental Health Outcomes: The Role of the Neuroendocrine System

The neuroendocrine system is a potential conceptual and statistical mediating and/or moderating factor that affects the relation between preterm birth and later psychiatric risk (Bagner, Sheinkopf, Vohr, & Lester, 2010; Betts, Williams, Najman, & Alati, 2011; Brummelte et al., 2011; Raikkonen et al., 2008). Both maternal and fetal cortisol concentrations have been linked to low birth weight, more specifically birth weight for gestational age, and dysregulation of the HPA axis has been associated with a variety of internalizing disorders (Betts et al., 2011). These associations may be due to individuals born prematurely experiencing early physiological adaptation, which may increase their vulnerability to HPA axis dysregulation and later onset of internalizing problems (Raikkonen et al., 2008).

Early physiological adaptation in the HPA axis appears to have long-lasting and potentially permanent effects on the behavior of premature children (Bagner, Pettit, Lewinsohn, & John, 2011; Brummelte et al., 2011). For example, Brummelte et al. (2011) reported a gradient of risk for internalizing behavior problems based on baseline cortisol levels and size for gestational age. In this work, a child's inability to regulate both baseline and stress-reactive cortisol levels contributed to increased levels of anxiety and depressive symptoms at 18 months of age in children born at extremely preterm and, to a lesser degree, VLGA.

Bagner et al. (2011) reported that dysregulation of the HPA axis due to prematurity has the ability to affect children's behavior into their school-age years. Children born prematurely who had increased cortisol reactivity to a stressor had significantly more problems with attention, emotional reactivity, anxiety, depression, and overall internalizing behavior problems when compared to children who had decreases in cortisol reactivity following a stressor. Bagner et al. suggest that stress-reactive cortisol levels may be a physiological indicator of comorbid mental health problems (Bagner et al., 2011).

Summary

In this section, we briefly described the neuroendocrine system and its development in both typical and atypical populations. Exposure to early-life stress and in particular prematurity have been found to increase one's risk for HPA axis dysregulation, which may be due in part to exposure to intrauterine and postnatal stressors that result in fetal growth restriction and low birth weight. Early dysregulation of the HPA axis has long-lasting and potentially permanent effects and may underlie associations between prematurity and mental health problems.

EARLY ADVERSITY, CENTRAL AND AUTONOMIC SYSTEMS, AND SOCIOEMOTIONAL PROBLEMS

The influence of early experience on human development has been well established. From the earliest stages of development, humans are malleable to changes from sources other than genetic influences. Indeed, environmental factors play a crucial role in shaping the development of the human brain, both structurally and functionally. From the perspective of developmental psychopathology, the role of early-life adversity in affecting emotional reactivity and increasing the risk of various mental disorders in adolescence and adulthood has been well-documented. The elucidation of indices that measure emotion reactivity and regulation is essential to understanding the impact of early adversity on underlying neural circuits and brain systems in shaping behavior and behavioral responses.

In this section, we provide a brief overview of the neural circuitry that is involved in emotion expression and regulation. This involves a discussion of PFC, amygdala, and autonomic substrates. Next, we review some of the recent work on noninvasive central and peripheral psychophysiological measures indexing emotion reactivity and regulation: specifically, frontal Electroencephalography (EEG) asymmetry and cardiac vagal tone (CVT). Here we provide a literature review linking these measures to early adversity (with a specific focus on prematurity), emotion reactivity and regulation, and psychiatric outcome. The goal of this section is to highlight the importance of noninvasive psychophysiological measures in human studies to help provide a link between early adversity (especially extreme prematurity) and clinical health-related outcomes.

Central-Peripheral Nervous System Involvement in Emotion Reactivity and Regulation: Prefrontal Cortex, Amygdala, and Autonomic Substrates

In this section, we provide a brief overview of two brain systems that are involved in emotion reactivity and regulation, the PFC and the amygdala. The PFC and amygdala are both fundamental to emotion reactivity and regulation. The PFC has largely been regarded as the center of cognitive control and the amygdala the center of emotion. Both brain regions function in dynamic coordination in order to express and regulate emotion (Salzman & Fusi, 2010).

The PFC modulates activity in the limbic system, particularly the amygdala, either increasing or decreasing activity in congruence with the direction of emotion reactivity and/or regulation (e.g., suppression or activation; Davidson et al., 2003; Pitskel et al., 2011). The amygdala is fundamental in recruiting and coordinating cortical arousal, though the amygdala's core function is to rapidly assess threat-related stimuli. Essentially, the amygdala is the reactivity component of a much larger emotional network that responds to threat-related stimuli.

The PFC and surrounding cortical regions act in concert as part of a larger emotion-cognitive process that functions in a context-appropriate manner. These cortical regions guide planning and anticipation of they so that emotion-related goals (e.g., appetitive goals) can be coordinated with appropriate affective and behavioral responses (e.g., approach-related responses; Davidson, Fox, & Kalin, 2007).

The PFC is one of the last cortical structures to reach maturity. As it continues to develop throughout our life, it remains vulnerable to environmental risk factors/life stressors, which can have long-lasting adverse effects (Pitskel et al., 2011). Functionally, then, normative development of emotion regulation may in part rely on normative development of the PFC and surrounding cortical structures.

Both the PFC and amygdala are interconnected in specific ways in order to create bidirectional feedback for the expression and regulation of emotion. Primarily, the function of the PFC in emotion is its cognitive control function, which inhibits the rapid threat appraisals of the excitatory role of the amygdala (Thayer & Lane, 2000). The PFC acts to control the activation of the amygdala from which information is then relayed to the PFC. The goal of both the PFC and amygdala is to effectively regulate emotion by implementing a coordinated balance through feedback from each system.

Central-peripheral nervous system involvement in emotion reactivity and regulation. The central-autonomic network (CAN) is where basic autonomic control of the heart is modulated by a functional network of cortical and subcortical brain regions (Thayer and Lane, 2009; Benarroch, 1993, 1997). The CAN influences autonomic regulation by allowing responses that are fundamental to goal-directed behavior and adaptability. In this section, the PFC and amygdala are the only cortical structures involved in this network that are discussed, as they are the most relevant to the current description (for a broader discussion of the CAN, see Thayer & Lane, 2009).

PFC modulation of autonomic functioning is largely inhibitory (Ahern et al., 2001), and the amygdala is primarily excitatory (Benarroch, 1993). The amygdala accelerates HR in order for the individual to respond to stimuli. The heart provides information to brain systems by providing HR feedback to the CNS. This connection carries bidirectional communication between central and peripheral nervous systems.

Central and Autonomic Measures in Emotion Regulation

Frontal brain asymmetry and emotion. There is an array of emotions that individuals can experience and express; however, research has demonstrated that there are two main motivational circuits, approach and withdrawal, around which emotions are organized (Fox, 1991). Asymmetry in the functioning of left and right sides of the PFC are differentially associated with approach- and withdrawal-related emotions. The two systems vary in valence, where left hemispheric PFC regions are oriented toward approach-related goals and positive emotions and right hemispheric PFC regions are oriented toward withdrawing from situations and influencing individuals to respond in a withdrawal-related manner. Right PFC regions also tend to be associated with negative emotions (Davidson et al., 2003). Empirical evidence from the past three decades indicates that the resting patterns of frontal EEG asymmetry reflect emotion expression and regulation by

(1) indexing individual differences in affective style and (2) predicting the effects of insults leading to psychopathology across development.

Germane to the present discussion, the presence of relative right frontal EEG asymmetry has been found in those exposed to various forms of early adversity (e.g., in infants of women with postpartum depression; Field, 1992), institutionalized children (McLaughlin, 2011), adolescents exposed to maltreatment (Miskovic et al., 2009), and adults born at ELBW (Schmidt et al., 2010). Furthermore, this pattern of right frontal asymmetry has been linked to various forms of psychopathology, specifically anxiety and depression (Blackhart, Minnix, & Kline, 2006; Coan & Allen, 2004; Feng et al., 2012; Hannesdottir et al., 2010; McLaughlin et al., 2011; Smit et al., 2007; Thibodeau, Jorgensen, & Kim, 2006). As such, the outcomes related to patterns of greater relative right frontal EEG asymmetry may index associations between being exposed to early-life adversity and the development of psychopathology later in life.

Over the past few decades, numerous studies have examined how early adversity affects the developing brain, emotion reactivity and regulation, and risk for psychopathology. The majority of these studies have utilized subjective measures (i.e., self-report measures), although biological correlates of early-life adversity must also be explored in depth. These studies have recently begun to use measures of frontal EEG asymmetry to index emotion reactivity and regulation and are capable of determining whether emotion regulation can mediate or moderate the association between exposure to early-life adversity (including being born at ELBW), and the risk of developing psychopathology later in life. For example, Schmidt et al. (2010) examined the development of psychopathology in a group of young adults born at ELBW and found that these individuals exhibited greater relative right frontal EEG asymmetry compared to their NBW counterparts, suggesting that ELBWs have a tendency to experience difficulties in regulating mental stress. This study suggests that those exposed to various forms of early adversity show greater relative right frontal PFC activity compared to typically developing individuals. This raises the possibility that developmentally atypical functioning of emotion regulation as indexed by the presence of relative right hemisphere activity in the PFC may mediate the associations observed between exposure to early adversity and psychiatric impairment.

Another example of early adversity is children reared in institutions (i.e., orphanages). These children are at a developmental disadvantage due to the limited resources in their environment, and this can adversely affect normative development of cognitive and emotional functions. For example, in a study of frontal EEG symmetry among institutionalized infants,

McLaughlin (2011) found a prolonged period of increased right hemisphere activity overall, demonstrating greater withdrawal behavior in response to novel stimuli (i.e., poorer emotion regulation). Similar results were found among children of parents with depression (Forbes et al., 2006). The mother–child relationship is an especially significant context within which children learn effective emotion regulation, and successful development of affect regulation can help combat aversive experiences. In children of depressed parents, these emotional regulatory processes may be perturbed.

Cardiac vagal tone and emotion. Exposure to early adverse life events can also lead to the atypical development of ANS regulation and thereby of emotion expression and regulation. The ANS is primarily responsible for the process of self-regulation of bodily functions. The SNS and PNS are the two main branches of the ANS. The SNS functions to prepare an organism to direct energy to engage in either physical or mental activity. The PNS functions to conserve and restore energy. Both systems work in dynamic balance, with each system making adjustments when the human body and/or mind is stressed. Thus, ANS activity enables an individual to respond adaptively to different environmental challenges – where one can either engage with the environment or retreat from potentially threatening environmental stimuli. Here we provide a brief review of the literature examining early adversity, difficulties in emotion regulatory functioning, and the development of psychopathological impairment, using measures of CVT (a measure of PNS activity) to demonstrate its role as a potential mediator.

A number of studies have examined the relation between ANS measures and atypical development. For example, Oosterman et al. (2010) examined the effects of the quality of caregiver–child relationship and past experiences of neglect on foster children. They focused on the relation between ANS reactivity and quality of attachment in foster children and found that the children categorized as ordered attachment exhibited greater vagal regulation than children with disordered attachment style.

Hae-Kyung (2009) examined ANS functioning (i.e., emotion regulation functioning) in premature infants and found that healthy newborns exhibited significantly greater CVT than premature infants. Similarly, Doussard-Roosevelt et al. (1997) found that high CVT was associated with better developmental outcomes in social functioning, and greater CVT maturation was associated with better outcomes in cognitive and executive functioning among a group of VLBW. High CVT was associated with better social functioning, and greater CVT maturation was associated with better cognitive and executive functioning. Lower HR was associated with better behavioral regulation, social skills, and motor skills. Doussard-Roosevelt et al. (1997) found that those categorized as ELBW demonstrated poorer functioning than heavier infants, stressing the importance of birth weight in development.

These studies suggest that individuals exposed to various forms of early adversity show greater autonomic regulation difficulties compared to typically developing individuals who are not exposed to such adversities. Moreover, they suggest that these vulnerable and at-risk populations (including those born at ELBW) show developmentally atypical functioning of emotion regulation (as is evidenced by the presence of decreased HRV), and that decreased autonomic regulation possibly mediates links with psychopathological impairment.

Summary

Exposure to early adversity affects both physiological and behavioral development. Various behavioral responses have been shaped not only by exposure to adverse experience but also through alterations at a biological level, where physiological systems (i.e., brain and peripheral and systemic physiology) have been affected by such adversities. In order to examine the origins of psychopathology in individuals exposed to early adversity such as ELBW, we may need to consider examining the biological markers underlying the central and peripheral nervous systems. By using these biological measures, we can begin to understand psychological disorders at a deeper behavioral and symptom level by identifying physiological mechanisms underlying them.

LINKING PREMATURITY, STRESS VULNERABILITY, AND PSYCHOPATHOLOGY: POSSIBLE MODELS

In this section, we discuss two possible conceptual and statistical models that may underlie the links among exposure to early adversity, stress vulnerability, and psychopathology (see Figure 9.1). We use extreme prematurity as an example of exposure to early adversity. We define stress vulnerability as hypersensitivity in at least two biological systems: the neuroendocrine system and frontal brain–autonomic system, which are known to underlie emotion regulatory and dysregulatory processes. We use cortisol, frontal EEG activity, and CVT measures to index these two systems, respectively. In Figure 9.1 (top panel), we provide an example of how these stress vulnerability measures may mediate the relation between prematurity

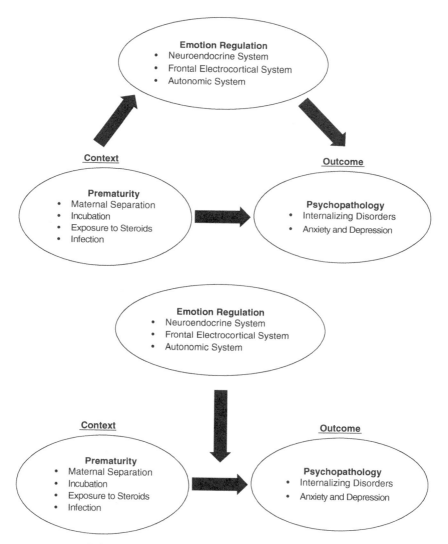

FIGURE 9.1. Relations among exposure to early adversity, stress vulnerability substrates/measures, and psychopathology (top panel, illustrating a mediation model; bottom panel, illustrating a moderation model).

and mental health problems. Prematurity may affect the neuroendocrine and frontal-autonomic systems rendering them hypersensitive to stress, which can then lead to mental health problems. Alternatively, these stress vulnerability measures may moderate the relation between prematurity and mental health problems (bottom panel). Here, sensitivity in these stress vulnerability systems may have developed independently of the effects of exposure to prematurity and may interact with prematurity to confer mental health problems.

Theoretical and practical implications. These models provide avenues for future research and hypothesis testing of risk and resiliency outcomes. For example, the model would predict that a combination of exposure to early adversity in combination with right frontal EEG activity, high and stable heart rate, and high cortisol levels would place one at risk for mental health problems. On the other hand, individuals exposed to early adversity who display left frontal EEG activity, low and variable heart rate, and relatively lower cortisol levels might be relatively protected from mental health problems. These models could be tested using a variety of exposures to early adversity. These models also inform practice, as the biological measures used in the model are malleable in response to psychotherapy and psychopharmacology. Thus, interventions directed at the biological (middle) level that are malleable may possibly help to prevent and/or mitigate the deleterious effects of exposure to early adversity and later risk for mental health problems.

CONCLUSION

The origins of mental health problems are undoubtedly complex and multidetermined. No single context, gene, and/or biological measure accounts for all of the variance in the development of mental illness. In this chapter, we argued that extreme prematurity provides one contextual factor that represents early adversity and that it is often overlooked in the field of developmental psychopathology. We also discussed the putative brain and peripheral substrates that underlie stress vulnerability and how these substrates can be measured noninvasively using cortisol, regional EEG, and cardiovascular measures. These integrated conceptual and statistical models can potentially be used by researchers and clinicians to inform theory and practice in understanding risk and resiliency outcomes in individuals exposed to early adversity.

ACKNOWLEDGMENTS

Work on the chapter was supported by operating grants from the Natural Sciences and Engineering Research Council of Canada (NSERC), the Social Sciences and Humanities Research Council of Canada (SSHRC), and the Canadian Institutes of Health Research (CIHR) awarded to Louis Schmidt.

REFERENCES

Aarnoudse-Moens, C. S. H., Weisglas-Kuperus, N., van Goudoever, J. B., & Oosterlaan, J. (2009). Meta-analysis of neurobehavioral outcomes in very preterm and/or very low birth weight children. *Pediatrics*, 124, 717–728.

Ahern, G. L., Sollers, J. J., Lane, R. D., Labiner, D. M., Herring, A. M., Weinand, M. E., Hutzler, R., et al. (2001). Heart rate and heart rate variability changes in the intracarotid sodium amobarbital test. *Epilepsia*, 42, 912–921.

Aucott, S. W., Watterberg, K. L., Shaffer, M. L., & Donohue, P. K. (2008). Do cortisol concentrations predict short-term outcomes in extremely low birth weight infants? *Pediatrics*, 122, 775–781.

(2010). Early cortisol values and long-term outcomes in extremely low birth weight infants. *Journal of Perinatology*, 30, 484–488.

Bagner, D. M., Pettit, J. W., Lewinsohn, P. M., & John, R. (2011). Effect of maternal depression on child behavior: A sensitive period? *Journal of Child Psychology and Psychiatry and Allied Disciplines*, 49, 699–707.

Bagner, D. M., Sheinkopf, S. J., Vohr, B. R., & Lester, B. M. (2010). A preliminary study of cortisol reactivity and behavior problems in young children born premature. *Developmental Psychobiology*, 52, 574–582.

Benarroch, E. E. (1993). The central autonomic network: Functional organization, dysfunction, and perspective. *Mayo Clinic Proceedings*, 68, 988–1001.

(1997). The central autonomic network. In *Clinical autonomic disorders* (2nd ed., pp. 73–82). Philadelphia: Lippincott-Raven Publishers.

Betts, K. S., Williams, G. M., Najman, J. M., & Alati, R. (2011). The association between birth weight and anxiety disorders in young adults. *Journal of Anxiety Disorders*, 25, 1060–1067.

Bhutta, A. T., Cleves, M. A., Casey, P. H., Cradock, M. M., & Anand, K. J. S. (2002). Cognitive and behavioral outcomes of school-aged children who were born preterm. *Journal of American Medical Association*, 288, 728–737.

Blackhart, G. C., Minnix, J. A., & Kline, J. P. (2006). Can EEG asymmetry patterns predict future development of anxiety and depression? A preliminary study. *Biological Psychology*, 72, 46–50.

Boyle, M. H., Miskovic, V., Lieshout, R. V., Duncan, L., Schmidt, L. A., & Hoult, L. (2011). Psychopathology in young adults born at extremely low birth weight. *Psychological Medicine*, 41, 1763–1774.

Brummelte, S., Grunau, R. E., Zaidman-Zait, A., Weinberg, J., Nordstokke, D., & Cepeda, I. L. (2011). Cortisol levels in relation to maternal interaction and child internalizing behavior in preterm and full-term children at 18 months corrected age. *Developmental Psychobiology*, 53, 184–195.

Coan, J. A., & Allen, J. J. B. (2004). Frontal EEG asymmetry as a moderator and mediator of emotion. *Biological Psychology*, 67, 7–49.

Compas, B. E. (2006). Psychobiological processes of stress and coping: Implications for resilience in children and adolescents. *Annals of the New York Academy of Sciences*, 1094, 226–234.

Crombie, R., Clark, C., & Stansfeld, S. A. (2011). Environmental noise exposure, early biological risk and mental health in nine to ten year old children: A cross-sectional field study. *Environmental Health*, 10, 1–8.

Davidson, R. J., Fox, A., & Kalin, N. H. (2007). Neural bases of emotion regulation in nonhuman primates and humans. In J. J. Gross (Ed.), *Handbook of Emotion Regulation* (pp. 47–68). New York: Guildford Press.

Davidson, R. J., Pizzagalli, D., Nitschke, J. B., & Kalin, N. H. (2003). Parsing the subcomponents of emotion and disorders of emotion: Perspectives from affective neuroscience. In R. J. Davidson, K. R. Scherer, & H. H. Goldsmith (Eds.), *Handbook of affective sciences* (pp. 8–24). New York, NY: Oxford University Press.

Dettling, A. C., Gunnar, M. R., & Donzella, B. (1999). Cortisol levels of young children in full-day childcare centers: Relations with age and temperament. *Psychoneuroendocrinology, 24*, 519–536.

Doussard-Roosevelt, J. a, Porges, S. W., Scanlon, J. W., Alemi, B., & Scanlon, K. B. (1997). Vagal regulation of heart rate in the prediction of developmental outcome for very low birth weight preterm infants. *Child Development, 68*, 173–186.

Entringer, S., Kumsta, R., Hellhammer, D. H., Wadhwa, P. D., & Wüst, S. (2009). Prenatal exposure to maternal psychosocial stress and HPA axis regulation in young adults. *Hormones and Behavior, 55*, 292–298.

Feng, X., Forbes, E. E., Kovacs, M., George, C. J., Lopez-Duran, N. L., Fox, N. A., & Cohn, J. F. (2012). Children's depressive symptoms in relation to EEG frontal asymmetry and maternal depression. *Journal of Abnormal Child Psychology, 40*, 265–276.

Field, T. (1992). Infants of depressed mothers. *Development and Psychopathology, 4*, 49–66.

Field, T., Diego, M., Dieter, J., Hernandez-Reif, M., Schanberg, S., Kuhn, C., Yando, R., et al. (2004). Prenatal depression effects on the fetus and the newborn. *Infant Behavior & Development, 27*, 216–229.

Field, T., Hernandez-Reif, M., Diego, M., Figueiredo, B., Schanberg, S., & Kuhn, C. (2006). Prenatal cortisol, prematurity and low birthweight. *Infant Behavior & Development, 29*, 268–275.

Forbes, E. E., Shaw, D. S., Fox, N. A., Cohn, J. F., Silk, J. S., & Kovacs, M. (2006). Maternal depression, child frontal asymmetry, and child affective behavior as factors in child behavior problems. *Journal of Child Psychology and Psychiatry, and Allied Disciplines, 47*, 79–87.

Fox, N. A. (1991). If it's not left, it's right: Electroencephalograph asymmetry and the development of emotion. *American Psychologist, 46*, 863–872.

Glover, V., Miles, R., Matta, S., Modi, N., & Stevenson, J. (2005). Glucocorticoid exposure in preterm babies predicts saliva cortisol response to immunization at 4 months. *Pediatric Research, 58*, 1233–1237.

Grunau, R. E., Haley, D. W., Whitfield, M. F., Weinberg, J., Yu, W., & Thiessen, P. (2007). Altered basal cortisol levels at 3, 6, 8 and 18 months in infants born at extremely low gestational age. *Pediatrics, 150*, 151–156.

Gunnar, M. R., & Donzella, B. (2002). Social regulation of the cortisol levels in early human development. *Psychoneuroendocrinology, 27*, 199–220.

Gunnar, M. R, & Quevedo, K. (2007). The neurobiology of stress and development. *Annual Review of Psychology, 58*, 145–173.

Gunnar, M. R., & Vazquez, D. M. (2001). Low cortisol and a flattening of expected daytime rhythm: Potential indices of risk in human development. *Development and Psychopathology, 13*, 515–538.

Hack, M., Flannery, D. J., Schluchter, M., Cartar, L., Borawski, E., & Klein, N. (2002). Outcomes in young adulthood for very-low-birth-weight infants. *New England Journal of Medicine, 346,* 149–157.

Hae-Kyung, L. (2009). Cardiac vagal tone as an index of autonomic nervous function in healthy newborn and premature infants. *Journal of Korean Academy of Child Health Nursing, 15,* 299–305.

Hannesdottir, D. K., Doxie, J., Bell, M. A., Ollendick, T. H., & Wolfe, C. D. (2010). A longitudinal study of emotion regulation and anxiety in middle childhood: Associations with frontal EEG asymmetry in early childhood. *Developmental Psychobiology, 52,* 197–204.

Holsti, L., Weinberg, J., Whitfield, M. F., & Grunau, R. E. (2007). Relationships between adrenocorticotropic hormone and cortisol are altered during clustered nursing care in preterm infants born at extremely low gestational age. *Early Human Development, 83,* 341–348.

Johnson, S., Hollis, C., Kochhar, P., Hennessy, E., & Wolke, D. (2010). Psychiatric disorders in extremely preterm children: Longitudinal finding at age 11 years in the EPICure study. *Journal of the American Academy of Child & Adolescent Psychiatry, 49,* 453–463.

Kajantie, E., Phillips, D. I. W., Andersson, S., Barker, D. J. P., Dunkel, L., Forsén, T., Osmond, C., et al. (2002). Size at birth, gestational age and cortisol secretion in adult life: Foetal programming of both hyper- and hypocortisolism? *Clinical Endocrinology, 57,* 635–641.

Kliewer, W., Reid-Quinones, K., Shields, B. J., & Foutz, L. (2008). Multiple risks, emotion regulation skill, and cortisol in low-income African American youth: A prospective study. *Journal of Black Psychology, 35,* 24–43.

Lupien, S. A., McEwen, B. S., Gunnar, M. R., & Heim, C. (2009). Effects of stress throughout the lifespan on the brain, behaviour and cognition. *Nature Reviews, 10,* 434–445.

MacMillan, H. L., Georgiades, K., Duku, E. K., Shea, A., Steiner, M., Niec, A., Tanaka, M., et al. (2009). Cortisol response to stress in female youths exposed to childhood maltreatment: Results of the Youth Mood Project. *Biological Psychiatry, 66,* 62–68.

McCrory, E., De Brito, S. A., & Viding, E. (2010). Research review: The neurobiology and genetics of maltreatment and adversity. *Journal of Child Psychology and Psychiatry, and Allied Disciplines, 51,* 1079–1095.

McEwen, B. S. (2003). Mood disorders and allostatic load. *Biological Psychology, 54,* 200–207.

McLaughlin, K. A., Fox, N. A., Zeanah, C. H., & Nelson, C. A. (2011). Adverse rearing environments and neural development in children: The development of frontal electroencephalogram asymmetry. *Biological Psychiatry, 70,* 1015–1008.

Miskovic, V., Schmidt, L. A, Georgiades, K., Boyle, M., & MacMillan, H. L. (2009). Stability of resting frontal electroencephalogram (EEG) asymmetry and cardiac vagal tone in adolescent females exposed to child maltreatment. *Developmental Psychobiology, 51,* 474–487.

Monfils Gustafsson, W., Josefsson, A., Ekholm Selling, K., & Sydsjö, G. (2009). Preterm birth or foetal growth impairment and psychiatric hospitalization in adolescence and early adulthood in a Swedish population-based birth cohort. *Acta Psychiatrica Scandinavica, 119,* 54–61.

Nomura, Y., Wickramaratne, P. J., Pilowsky, D. J., Newcorn, J. H., Bruder-Costello, B., Davey, C., Fifer, W. P., et al. (2007). Low birth weight and risk of affective disorders and selected medical illness in offspring at high and low risk for depression. *Comprehensive Psychiatry, 48*, 470–478.

Oosterman, M., De Schipper, J. C., Fisher, P., Dozier, M., & Schuengel, C. (2010). Autonomic reactivity in relation to attachment and early adversity among foster children. *Development and Psychopathology, 22*, 109–118.

Phillips, D. I. W. (2007). Programming of the stress response: A fundamental mechanism underlying the long-term effects of the fetal environment? *Journal of Internal Medicine, 261*, 453–460.

Pitskel, N. B., Bolling, D. Z., Kaiser, M. D., Crowley, M. J., & Pelphrey, K. A. (2011). How grossed out are you? The neural bases of emotion regulation from childhood to adolescence. *Developmental Cognitive Neuroscience, 1*, 324–337.

Raikkonen, K., Pesonen, A., Heinonen, K., Kajantie, E., Hovi, P., Jarvenpaa, A. L., Eriksson, J. G., & Andersson, S. (2008). Depression in young adults with very low birth weight. *Archives of General Psychiatry, 65*, 290–296.

Rivkees, S. A. (2003). Developing circadian rhythmicity in infants. *Pediatrics, 112*, 373–381.

Rudolph, K. D., Troop-Gordon, W., & Granger, D. A. (2011). Individual differences in biological stress responses moderate the contribution of early peer victimization to subsequent depressive symptoms. *Psychopharmacology, 214*, 209–219.

Rutter, M., & O'Connor, T. G. (2004). Are there biological programming effects for psychological development? Findings from a study of Romanian adoptees. *Developmental Psychology, 40*, 81–94.

Salzman, C. D., & Fusi, S. (2010). Emotion, cognition, and mental state representation in amygdala and prefrontal cortex. *Annual Review of Neuroscience, 33*, 173–202.

Sanchez, M. M. (2006). The impact of early adverse care on HPA axis development: Nonhuman primate models. *Review of Psychiatry, 50*, 623–631.

Schäffer, L., Müller-Vizentini, D., Burkhardt, T., Rauh, M., Ehlert, U., & Beinder, E. (2009). Blunted stress response in small for gestational age neonates. *Pediatric Research, 65*, 231–235.

Schlotz, W., & Phillips, D. I. W. (2009). Fetal origins of mental health: Evidence and mechanisms. *Brain, Behavior, and Immunity, 23*, 905–16.916.

Schmidt, L. A., Miskovic, V., Boyle, M., & Saigal, S. (2010). Frontal electroencephalogram asymmetry, salivary cortisol, and internalizing behavior problems in young adults who were born at extremely low birth weight. *Child Development, 81*, 183–199.

Schulkin, J., Gold, P. W., & McEwen, B. S. (1998). Induction of corticotropin-releasing hormone gene expression by glucocorticoids: Implication for understanding the states of fear and anxiety and allostatic load. *Psychoneuroendocrinology, 23*, 219–243.

Seckl, J. R. (2004). Prenatal glucocorticoids and long-term programming. *European Journal of Endocrinology, 151*, 49–62.

Shonkoff, J. P., Boyce, W. T., & McEwen, B. S. (2009). Roots of health disparities: Building a new framework. *Journal of the American Medical Association, 301*, 2252–2259.

Slattery, D. A., & Neumann, I. D. (2008). No stress please! Mechanisms of stress hyporesponsiveness of the maternal brain. *Animal Research*, 2, 377–385.

Smit, D. J. A., Posthuma, D., Boomsma, D. I., & De Geus, E. J. C. (2007). The relation between frontal EEG asymmetry and the risk for anxiety and depression. *Biological Psychology*, 74, 26–33.

Tarullo, A. R., & Gunnar, M. R. (2006). Child maltreatment and the developing HPA axis. *Hormones and Behavior*, 50, 632–639.

Thayer, J. F., & Lane, R. D. (2000). A model of neurovisceral integration in emotion regulation and dysregulation. *Journal of Affective Disorders*, 61, 201–216.

(2009). Claude Bernard and the heart–brain connection: Further elaboration of a model of neurovisceral integration. *Neuroscience and Biobehavioral Reviews*, 33, 81–88.

Thibodeau, R., Jorgensen, R. S., & Kim, S. (2006). Depression, anxiety, and resting frontal EEG asymmetry: A meta-analytic review. *Journal of Abnormal Psychology*, 115, 715–29.

Verkauskiene, R., Beltrand, J., Claris, O., Chevenne, D., Deghmoun, S., Dorgeret, S., Alison, M., et al. (2007). Impact of fetal growth restriction on body composition and hormonal status at birth in infants of small and appropriate weight for gestational age. *European Journal of Endocrinology*, 157, 605–612.

Watamura, S. E., Donzella, B., Kertes, D. A., & Gunnar, M. R. (2004). Developmental changes in baseline cortisol activity in early childhood: Relations with napping and effortful control. *Developmental Psychobiology*, 45, 125–133.

10

Maternal Depression and Children's Behavioral and Emotional Outcomes: A Review of Contextual and Individual-Level Moderators and Mediators

MATILDA E. NOWAKOWSKI, LOUIS A. SCHMIDT, AND
TRACY VAILLANCOURT

Depression, characterized by flat affect, lack of energy, preoccupation with the self, rumination, inability to concentrate, and irritability (American Psychiatric Association, 2013), affects up to 17% of mothers (Horwitz, Briggs-Gowan, Storfer-Isser, & Carter, 2007; Kessler, 2003, 2006). It is well established that maternal depression is not only associated with an increased risk of childhood depression but also with other emotional and behavioral problems, including anxiety disorders, oppositional defiant disorder, conduct disorder, and attention-deficit hyperactivity disorder (Ashman, Dawson, & Panagiotides, 2008; Bagner, Pettit, Lewinsohn, & Seeley, 2010; Cummings & Davies, 1994; Field, 1998; Goodman, 2007; Goodman, Rouse, Connell, Broth, Hall, & Heyward, 2011; Zimmerman et al., 2008). Our understanding of the factors through which maternal depression influences children's outcomes, however, is less well developed. To date, four potential factors for the relation between maternal depression and children's emotional and behavioral development have been identified. These four include (1) parenting and mother–child interactions, (2) environmental stressors, (3) genetics, and (4) dysregulation in neuroendocrine and neurophysiological systems. The first two mechanisms are illustrative of contextual influences, and the latter two are examples of individual-related influences. In the present chapter, we discuss the evidence for each of the hypothesized factors as well as identify areas for future research. We conclude with a discussion of clinical implications this work has for the field.

PARENTING AND MOTHER–CHILD INTERACTIONS

Child development theories emphasize the important role of parents in supporting children's emotional and behavioral development (Vygotsky, 1978). Parents' active involvement helps children learn new skills as well as assists in the modulation of positive and negative emotions. Thus, impoverished mother–child interactions have been postulated as a possible factor that influences the relation between maternal depression and emotional and behavioral problems in children. Maternal depression has a negative effect on parent–child interactions and parenting styles. Emotionally, depressed mothers tend to show less positive affect and more negative affect toward their infants (Martins & Gaffan, 2000) and are less likely to share in their infants' affective state (Jameson, Gelfand, Kulcsar, & Teti, 1997; Stein et al., 1991). Behaviorally, depressed mothers tend to be less responsive and sensitive to their infants' needs and tend to be more hostile and critical toward their infants (Lovejoy, Graczyk, O'Hare, & Neuman, 2000; Reissland, Shepherd, & Herrera, 2005). Depressed mothers also spend less time in joint attention states with their infants (Field, Healey, Goldstein, & Guthertz, 1990; Goldsmith & Rogoff, 1997; Jameson, Gelfand, Kulcsar, & Teti, 1997; Stein et al., 1991) and engage in fewer interactive activities, such as reading, singing, and telling stories (Field et al., 1990; Goldsmith & Rogoff, 1997; Lovejoy et al., 2000; Paulson, Dauber, & Leiferman, 2009).

Using both cross-sectional and longitudinal designs, researchers have found that negative parenting practices moderate and partially mediate the relation between maternal depression and emotional and behavioral problems in toddlers, children, and adolescents (Barry, Dunlap, Lochman, & Wells, 2009; Bolton et al., 2003; Elgar, Mills, McGrath, Waschbusch, & Brownbridge, 2007; Foster, Garber, & Durlak, 2008; Gravener et al., 2012; Harold et al., 2011; Leckman-Westin, Cohen, & Stueve, 2009; Silberg, Maes, & Eaves, 2010; Tully, Iacono, & McGue, 2008). In general, mother–child interactions characterized by negative parenting behaviors (e.g., lack of responsiveness and sensitivity, low positive affect, high negative affect, high levels of criticism, low mutual interactions and play) are associated with greater emotional and behavioral problems in children, while positive parenting behaviors (e.g., responsiveness, sensitivity to the child's emotional and physical needs, modeling and teaching of emotion-regulation skills, engagement in interactive play, and positive affect) mitigate the association between maternal depression and children's emotional and behavioral problems.

In addition to using path and mediation analyses to assess the role of parenting in the relation between maternal depression and children's emotional and behavioral problems, research focusing on adopted children has also provided insight into the role of mother–child interactions in children's development. Natsuaki and colleagues (2010) found that for infants who were born to depressed mothers but who were adopted, fussiness, a risk factor for later emotional and behavioral problems (Caspi, Henry, McGee, Moffitt, & Silva, 1995; Shaw, Owen, Vondra, Keenan, & Winslow, 1996), was influenced by the responsiveness of the adoptive mothers, defined as an interactive style characterized by contingent responses to the child's needs, high levels of positive affect, and positive reinforcement (Landry, Smith, Swank, Assel, & Vellet, 2001). Infants who were born to depressed mothers and raised by adoptive mothers who were low on responsiveness had significantly higher levels of fussiness compared to infants born to depressed mothers but raised by adoptive mothers high on responsiveness. The findings of Natsuaki and colleagues (2010) illustrate the importance of considering gene-by-environment interactions in the development of childhood emotional and behavioral problems and highlight the important role of responsive mother–child interactions in children's development.

Researchers recently have begun to investigate whether there is a sensitive period during which maternal depression is most strongly associated with children's development. The few studies that have attempted to answer this question have found that the presence of maternal depression during the early years of a child's life appears to be most strongly related with toddlers' and children's emotional and behavioral outcome (Bagner et al., 2010; Goodman et al., 2011). A number of factors may explain this pattern. First, infants and younger children are more dependent on their mothers, and this lack of autonomy means that their cognitive and emotional development is intimately linked to the environment provided by the caregiver. Indeed, given the deleterious effects of maternal depression on parenting and mother–child interactions, infants and young children of depressed mothers do not receive the responsive and warm parenting that they need for optimal emotional and behavioral development. Consequently, these children may develop maladaptive emotion-regulation strategies in an attempt to modulate their affective reactions, placing them at risk for future emotional and behavioral problems. If maternal depression first develops when children are older, it may have less of an impact, as children are more developed cognitively and emotionally and also do not rely as exclusively on their mothers, given that they can reach out to other individuals, such as peers, teachers, and other family members. Consequently, maternal depression later on in the child's life is less strongly associated with the development of children's emotional and behavioral problems compared to maternal depression that occurs earlier in the child's life (Crick & Dodge, 1996).

Another area for further investigation is the relation between variations in the course of maternal depression and children's emotional and behavioral outcome. There is a large amount of individual variability in the course of depression. For instance, some individuals experience chronic levels of depression while others experience depressive episodes that are separated by periods characterized by normal functioning. Maternal depression that is more chronic appears to have a stronger relation with children's outcome, especially if it occurs during the first few years of life, compared to maternal depression that is more episodic in nature (Brennan et al., 2000; Goodman et al., 2011).

ENVIRONMENTAL STRESSORS

It is well established that environmental stressors increase the risk for emotional and behavioral problems in children (Cicchetti, Rogosch, & Toth, 1998; Cummings & Davies, 2002). Consequently, it has been postulated that exposure to environmental stressors may moderate and partially mediate the relation between maternal depression and children's emotional and behavioral problems.

Depression is associated with higher rates of environmental stressors, such as high levels of family stress, marital conflict, poverty, single parenthood, inadequate housing, and lack of social support (Cicchetti, Rogosch, & Toth, 1998; Hammen, 2002; Matheson et al., 2006). Across studies, environmental stressors, including marital conflict, marital dissatisfaction, lack of maternal social support, single parenthood, and high levels of emotional reactivity amongst family members, have been shown to both moderate and partially mediate the relation between maternal depression and children's emotional and behavioral problems (Ashman et al., 2008; Cicchetti et al., 1998; Dawson et al., 2003; Du Rocher Schudlich & Cummings, 2007; Hannington, Heron, & Ramchandini, 2011; Murray et al., 2011; Pugh & Farrell, 2012; Weinfield, Ingerski, & Coffey Moreau, 2009). Single parenthood may moderate the relation between maternal depression and children's emotional and behavioral outcomes due to the child's sole reliance on the mother and the lack of a second caretaker to assist the mother with caretaking and to possibly provide a more sensitive and warm parenting style.

Given the cross-sectional nature of the research to date, it is difficult to identify the direction of effects between maternal depression and environmental stressors. One possibility is that environmental stressors lead to the development of depression in mothers. Consistent with this view, Kiernan and Huerta (2008) found that the relation between economic deprivation, defined as living in poverty, experiencing significant financial stressors, and relying on subsidized housing, and children's emotional and behavioral problems at 3 years of age was mediated by parental depression, suggesting that low socioeconomic status increased mothers' risk of depression, which in turn increased the risk of behavioral and emotional problems in children. It is also possible, however, that the symptoms of depression lead to the onset of environmental stressors. For instance, symptoms associated with depression (e.g., lack of concentration and problem solving, irritability, fatigue, and lack of motivation) may lead to conflicts with one's partner or to difficulties at work, thus creating marital and financial stressors. Although the direction of effects is still unclear, environmental stressors, whether present before the onset of maternal depression or occurring as a response to maternal depression, appear to play a role in the relation between maternal depression and emotional and behavioral problems in children.

GENETIC INFLUENCES

Genetic factors play a role in the transmission of depression. Based on family studies, children of a depressed parent have a 50% chance of developing some type of emotional or behavioral problem, while the rate of specifically developing depression ranges between 20% and 40% (Hammen & Brennan, 2001; Pilowsky et al., 2006). Depression appears to have the greatest heritability when it is associated with an early age of onset (i.e., young adulthood), a recurrent, chronic course, and is severe and functionally impairing (Levinson, 2006; Mondimore et al., 2006; Sullivan, Neale, & Kendler, 2000; Zubenko, Hughes, Stiffler, Zubenko, & Kaplan, 2002). One of the limitations with family studies, however, is that it is difficult to separate genetic and environmental factors in the estimation of heritability, given that children who have a depressed parent are influenced not only by the genes they inherited from the parent but also by the parent's behaviors, cognitions, and interactive style. Therefore, twin studies, in which the degree of heritability of a particular disorder is compared across monozygotic and dizygotic twins, have been used to address this limitation. Across twin studies, it is well established that there is a greater degree of concordance of depression in monozygotic than dizygotic twins, thus providing evidence for the role of genetic factors in the development of depression. The estimated heritability of depression based on twin studies is between 31% and 42% (Sullivan et al., 2000).

With the advent of new genetic techniques, researchers have been able to move beyond the identification of estimates of heritability and toward identifying the specific genes that may be involved. Given the complexity of depression, it is clear that a number of different genes contribute to the manifestation of the disorder. To date, a lot of research has been focused on genes that are involved in the synthesis, breakdown, and transmission of the neurotransmitter serotonin. Specifically, the serotonin transporter gene (5-HTT), which is involved in the formation of molecules that control the reuptake of serotonin (Lesch et al., 1996), has been implicated as potentially playing a role in depression (Levinson, 2006).

It is unlikely, however, that genetics act in isolation, and a number of research groups have investigated the role of gene–environment interactions in the development of depression, leading to mixed findings. For instance, the 5-HTT gene has three variants: a short/short allele variant, a short/long allele, and a long/long allele variant. Although some researchers have found that individuals with the short/short allele variant are at an increased risk for developing depression only when they are exposed to an environmental stressor (Caspi et al., 2003; Eley et al., 2004; Jacobs et al., 2006; Wilhelm et al., 2006), a recent meta-analysis based on 14 studies with a total of 14,250 participants failed to find a significant association between variants of the 5-HTT gene and later depression or a significant interaction between environmental stressors and variants of the 5-HTT gene in the prediction of depression (Risch et al., 2009). Thus, although it is clear that genetics play a role in the development of depression, there remains debate as to the role of the specific genes involved as well as their interactions with environmental stressors.

DYSREGULATION IN NEUROENDOCRINE AND NEUROPHYSIOLOGICAL SYSTEMS

Although few studies have specifically assessed the potential role of physiological and neural activity in moderating and mediating the relation between maternal depression and children's internalizing and externalizing behaviors, it has been suggested that parenting style and environmental stressors may influence the relation between maternal depression and children's physiological and neural reactivity, which in turn may increase risk for the development of emotional and behavioral problems. Using both nonhuman animal and human studies, it is well established that the quality of the early mother–infant relationship plays a significant role in the development of the stress response in offspring, as measured by activity of the hypothalamic-pituitary-adrenocortical (HPA) system (see Lupien, McEwen, Gunnar, & Heim, 2010, for a review). Individuals with normally developed stress responses show a rapid and acute response toward a stressor in the environment. In contrast, individuals with poorly developed stress responses experience dysregulation of the stress response, resulting in stress responses that may be chronic, hypersensitive, or hyposensitive.

Much of the research investigating the effects of mother–child interactions on the development of the offspring's stress system has been conducted with rodents. While in humans, variation in mother–infant interactions centers around such behaviors as reciprocity, sensitivity, and positive affect, in rodents, variations in mother–pup interactions center around differences in the amount of maternal licking/grooming behaviors (LG) and arched-back nursing (ABN; Champagne, Francis, Mar, & Meaney, 2003). Mothers who engage in low levels of maternal LG and ABN have offspring who as adults show an exaggerated stress response, physiological difficulties in down-regulating the stress response, and increased fearfulness (Caldji et al., 1998; Liu et al., 1997). Cross-fostering experiments have shown that this dysregulation of the stress response is specific to the variability in maternal behaviors and not to other factors (Francis, Diorio, Liu, & Meaney, 1999). Specifically, offspring of mothers that were low in LG and ABN but who were cross-fostered at birth to mothers who were high in these behaviors showed a normal stress response as adults, while offspring of mothers that were high in LG and ABN but that were cross-fostered at birth to mothers that were low in these behaviors showed a dysregulated stress response as adults (Francis et al., 1999; Weaver et al., 2004).

The research on rodents illustrates the important role that the mother plays in the development of the infant's stress response. Of course, the rat brain is significantly less complex and developed than the human brain (Fitzgerald & Anand, 1993), thus limiting the generalizability of the findings from rodents to humans. However, much research on the influence of early experiences on the HPA system has also been done on monkeys, which have a number of similarities with humans, including similar developmental pathways for brain development, social structures, cognitive abilities, and shared genomic material (about 90% of the genome for humans and monkeys is identical; see Suomi, 1997, for a comprehensive review). In monkeys, unexpected separations from the mother and irregular feeding schedules result in higher rates of insecure attachment, hyperresponsiveness to stress in the offspring, and abnormal changes in cortisol levels (Andrews & Rosenblum, 1991, 1993; Coplan et al., 1996; Rosenblum et al., 1994; Sanchez, 2006; Sanchez et al., 2005).

In humans, an association has been found between sensitive parenting, characterized by responsiveness toward the child's needs, and children's increases in cortisol levels in response to daily stressors (Albers, Riksen-Walraven, Sweep, & de Weerth, 2008). Specifically, children who are exposed to sensitive parenting from their mothers evidence significantly smaller increases in cortisol levels in response to everyday stressors compared to children who are exposed to insensitive parenting. Thus, parenting style and mother–child interactions appear to play an important role in regulating the HPA system's functioning. If children are exposed to chronically insensitive parenting, as is often the case in maternal depression, then this can potentially lead to long-term dysregulation of the HPA axis, placing children at an increased risk for future emotional and behavioral difficulties.

In addition to elevated cortisol levels, infants and children who are exposed to maternal depression also exhibit frontal brain asymmetries characterized by increased right frontal activation due to left frontal hypoactivation (Ashman et al., 2008; Dawson et al., 2003; Diego et al., 2004; Diego et al., 2006; Feng et al., 2012; Jones et al., 2009; Thibodeau et al., 2006; Tomarken et al., 2004). Asymmetries in frontal lobe activity are associated with the expression of different emotions and behaviors. Greater left frontal activity is associated with positive emotions and approach behaviors, while greater right frontal activity is associated with negative emotions and withdrawal behaviors (Davidson, 2000). Greater right frontal activity due to a decrease in the left frontal activity that is seen in infants and children of depressed mothers suggests that these infants may be predisposed to experience more negative emotions and difficulties with emotion regulation (Davidson, 1998).

There has been some suggestion that the quality of mother–child interactions during the first few years of life may play a role in the development of abnormal brain activity in children. The development of the brain can be described as experience dependent. That is, through repeated exposure to various stimuli, neural networks are formed in the brain (Courchesne, Chisum, & Townsend, 1994; Merzenich et al., 1984). Consequently, the neural development of the brain is heavily determined by the infant's early environmental experiences and exposures. Given that the mother is typically the main environment for the infant during its first few years of life and that emotions are one of the key factors associated with the organization of the developing brain (Siegel, 1999), early mother–child interactions and the quality of the attachment relationship between the mother and child are associated with the development of the infant brain. Sensitive and attuned interactions result in the formation of neural networks that facilitate the ability of the infant to effectively cope with stress (Schore, 2001a, 2001b, 2005). Conversely, interactions between the mother and infant that lack sensitivity and affective attunement lead to the development of maladaptive strategies to regulate emotions (Field, 1994, 1995, 1998; Schore, 2005). Thus, early mother–child interactions appear to be critical for the development of affective self-regulation.

Although no studies to date have investigated the role of parenting in the relation between maternal depression and children's brain activity, two studies have investigated the role of frontal brain activation on the relation between maternal depression and children's development of depressive symptoms. Dawson and colleagues (2003) found that in a sample of 3-year-old children born to mothers who were depressed, greater right frontal activity partially mediated the relation between maternal depression and children's depressive symptoms. However, when this relation was investigated in the same group of children when they were 6.5 years old, frontal brain activation no longer mediated the relation between maternal depression and children's depressive symptoms when also considering environmental stressors (Ashman et al., 2008).

In summary, there is some preliminary evidence that changes in physiological and neural activity play a role in the relation between maternal depression and children's risk for emotional and behavioral problems, but there is a need for more research that considers the potential combined role of parenting and physiological and neural activity in explaining the relation between maternal depression and children's emotional and behavioral development.

LIMITATIONS AND DIRECTIONS FOR FUTURE RESEARCH

There has been a shift in recent years from looking at the relation between maternal depression and children's emotional and behavioral problems to trying to understand the factors that underlie this relation. Thus far, four potential factors have been identified, and the literature supporting each of the suggested mechanisms is growing. Although the research to date is a good start, there are a number of limitations that should be addressed in future studies.

First, many of the studies utilize a cross-sectional design and statistical methods are used to identify potential mediators and moderators for the relation between maternal depression and children's emotional and behavioral outcomes. Although this is a natural method to use as a starting point, now that we have identified a number of possible moderators and mediators, there is a need for more longitudinal studies to adequately identify the order of the factors as well as the relation between them. Second, many of the studies to date have relied solely on maternal report for both maternal symptoms of depression and children's behavioral and emotional outcome. There is some evidence that the relation between maternal depression and children's behavioral and emotional outcome as well as the role of parenting variables as mediators differs depending on the informant of the child's outcome (i.e., mothers, fathers, teachers, or children; Bennett et al., 2012; Pugh & Farrel, 2012). This suggests that part of the relation may be accounted for by informant discrepancy. Consequently, there is a need for studies to look at various informants (e.g., diagnostic interviews with clinicians, teacher reports, father reports, etc.) to further clarify the strength of the relation between maternal depression and children's behavioral and emotional outcome as well as potential mediators and moderators that may influence this relation. As well, many of the studies have focused solely on self-report measures for the assessment of parenting. Although self-report measures do add value to the research in that they provide a more global perspective on parenting, studies should also include behavioral observations of mother–child interactions. Lastly, given the complexity of human development, it is natural that more than one factor will influence the relation between maternal depression and children's behavioral and emotional outcome. Although a few studies have considered the combined effects of more than one factor (Ashman et al., 2008; Dawson et al., 2003; Kiernan & Huerta, 2008; Murray et al., 2011), there is a need for more studies that assess a number of different factors and investigate the degree to which the various factors make statistically significant, independent contributions to the explanation of the relation between maternal depression and children's outcome. By including all potential factors, we can obtain a better understanding of which factors play the greatest role in the relationship, which will also provide insights as to what factors should be most strongly targeted in prevention and treatment interventions.

CLINICAL IMPLICATIONS

Early identification and treatment of maternal depression, as well as psychoeducation about parenting and mother–child interactions, is essential. Treatment of maternal depression should include a focus on parenting and mother–child interactions, as this will increase the mother's sense of efficacy and effectiveness in her interactions with her child as well as decrease the risk of negative emotional and behavioral outcomes. Studies have shown that when mothers receive treatment for their depression, this influences the child's emotional and behavioral reactions (Pilowsky et al., 2008; Weissman et al., 2006). Furthermore, the treatment of children suffering from depression should take a holistic perspective and consider all the factors leading to the development and maintenance of depression in the child, including environmental stressors and parenting and mother–child interactions.

CONCLUSION

A number of different contextual and individual-level factors are involved in the relation between maternal depression and increased risk for emotional and behavioral problems in children, including parenting, environmental stressors, genetics, and dysregulation in neuroendocrine and neurophysiological systems. There is a growing body of literature illustrating the role that each of these factors plays in the relation between maternal depression and children's outcome. Moving forward, there is a need for more studies to investigate all of these factors together to provide more insight as to which factors are most important in the relation between maternal depression and children's outcome. The results of the studies to date illustrate the complexity of human development and the importance of early identification and treatment of maternal depression in decreasing the risk for children's emotional and behavioral problems.

ACKNOWLEDGMENTS

The writing of this chapter was supported by a predoctoral scholarship from the Social Sciences and Humanities Research Council (SSHRC) of Canada awarded to the first author under the direction of the second author and operating grants from SSHRC and the Natural Sciences and Engineering Research Council (NSERC) of Canada awarded to the second author.

REFERENCES

Albers, E. M., Riksen-Walraven, M. J., Sweep, F. C. G. J., & de Weerth, C. (2008). Maternal behavior predicts infant cortisol recovery from a mild everyday stressor. *Journal of Child Psychology and Psychiatry*, 49, 97–103.
American Psychiatric Association. (2013). *Diagnostic and statistical manual of mental disorders, 5th edition (DSM-5)*. Arlington, VA: APA.

Andrews, M. W., & Rosenblum, L. A. (1991). Security of attachment in infants raised in variable- or low-demand environments. *Child Development*, 62, 686–693.

———. (1993). Assessment of attachment in differentially reared infant monkeys (Macaca radiate): Response to separation and a novel environment. *Journal of Comparative Psychology*, 107, 84–90.

Ashman, S. B., Dawson, G., & Panagiotides, H. (2008). Trajectories of maternal depression over 7 years: Relations with child psychophysiology and behavior and role of contextual risks. *Development and Psychopathology*, 20, 55–77.

Bagner, D. M., Pettit, J. W., Lewinsohn, P. M., & Seeley, J. R. (2010). Effect of maternal depression on child behavior: A sensitive period? *Journal of the American Academy of Child and Adolescent Psychiatry*, 49, 699–707.

Barry, T. D., Dunlap, S. T., Lochman, J. E., & Wells, K. C. (2009). Inconsistent discipline as a mediator between maternal distress and aggression in boys. *Child & Family Behavior Therapy*, 31, 1–19.

Bennett, T., Boyle, M., Georgiades, K., Georgiades, S., Thompson, A., Duku, E., et al. (2012). Influence of reporting effects on the association between maternal depression and child autism spectrum disorder behaviors. *Journal of Child Psychology and Psychiatry*, 53, 89–96.

Bolton, C., Calam, R., Barrowclough, C., Peters, S., Roberts, J., Wearden, A., & Morris, J. (2003). Expressed emotion, attributions and depression in mothers of children with problem behaviour. *Journal of Child Psychology and Psychiatry*, 44, 242–254.

Brennan, P. A., Hammen, C., Andersen, M., Bor, W., Najman, J. M., & Williams, G. M. (2000). Chronicity, severity, and timing of maternal depressive symptoms: Relationships with child outcomes at age 5. *Developmental Psychology*, 36, 759–766.

Caldji, C., Tannenbaum, B., Sharma, S., Francis, D. Plotsky, P., & Meaney, M. (1998). Maternal care during infancy regulates the development of neural systems mediating the expression of fearfulness in the rat. *Proceedings of the National Academy of Sciences of the USA*, 95, 5335–5340.

Caspi, A., Henry, B., McGee, R. O., Moffitt, T. E., & Silva, P. A. (1995). Temperamental origins of child and adolescent behavior problems: From age three to age fifteen. *Child Development*, 66, 55–68.

Caspi, A., Sugden, K., Moffitt, T. E., Taylor, A., Craig, I. W., Harrington, C. H., et al. (2003). Influence of life stress on depression: Moderation by a polymorphism in the 5-HTT gene. *Science*, 301, 386–389.

Champagne, F., Francis, D., Mar, A., & Meaney, M. (2003). Variations in maternal care in the rat as a mediating influence for the effects of environment on development. *Physiology & Behavior*, 79, 359–371.

Cicchetti, D., Rogosch, F. A., & Toth, S. L. (1998). Maternal depressive disorder and contextual risk: Contributions to the development of attachment insecurity and behavior problems in toddlerhood. *Development and Psychopathology*, 10, 283–300.

Coplan, J., Andrews, M., Rosenbaum, L., Owens, M., Friedman, S., Gorman, J., & Nemeroff, C. (1996). Persistent elevations of CSF concentrations of CRF in adult non-human primates exposed to early life stressors: Implications for the pathophysiology of mood and anxiety disorders. *Proceedings of the National Academy of Sciences of the USA*, 93, 1619–1623.

Courchesne, E., Chisum, H., & Townsend, J. (1994). Neural activity-dependent brain changes in development: Implications for psychopathology. *Development and Psychopathology*, 6, 741–758.

Crick, N. R., & Dodge, K. A. (1996). Social information-processing mechanisms on reactive and proactive aggression. *Child Development*, 67, 993–1002.

Cummings, E. M., & Davies, P. T. (1994). Maternal depression and child development. *Journal of Child Psychology and Psychiatry*, 35, 73–122.

(2002). Effects of marital discord on children: Recent advances and emerging themes in process-oriented research. *Journal of Child Psychology and Psychiatry*, 43, 31–63.

Davidson, R. J. (1998). Anterior electrophysiological asymmetries, emotion, and depression: Conceptual and methodological conundrums. *Psychophysiology*, 35, 607–614.

(2000). Affective style, psychopathology, and resilience: Brain mechanisms and plasticity. *American Psychologist*, 55, 1196–1214.

Dawson, G., Ashman, S. B., Panagiotides, H., Hessl, D., Self, J., Yamada, E., & Embry, L. (2003). Preschool outcomes of children of depressed mothers: Role of maternal behavior, contextual risk, and children's brain activity. *Child Development*, 74, 1158–1175.

Diego, M. A., Field, T., Hernandez-Reif, M., Cullen, C., Schanberg, S., & Kuhn, C. (2004). Prepartum, postpartum, and chronic depression effects on newborns. *Psychiatry*, 67, 63–80.

Diego, M. A., Field, T., Jones, N. A., & Hernandez-Reif, M. (2006). Withdrawn and intrusive maternal interaction style and infant frontal EEG asymmetry shifts in infants of depressed and non-depressed mothers. *Infant Behavior & Development*, 29, 220–229.

Du Rocher Schudlich, T. D., & Cummings, E. M. (2007). Parental dysphoria and children's adjustment: Marital conflict styles, children's emotional security, and parenting as mediators of risk. *Journal of Abnormal Child Psychology*, 35, 627–639.

Eley, T. C., Sugden, K., Corsico, A., Gregory, A. M., Sham, P., McGuffin, P., et al. (2004). Gene-environment interaction analysis of serotonin system markers with adolescent depression. *Molecular Psychiatry*, 9, 908–915.

Elgar, F. J., Mills, R. S. L., McGrath, P. J., Waschbusch, D. A., & Brownbridge, D. A. (2007). Maternal and paternal depressive symptoms and child maladjustment problems: The mediating role of parental behavior. *Journal of Abnormal Child Psychology*, 35, 943–955.

Feng, X., Forbes, E. E., Kovacs, M., George, C. J., Lopez-Duran, N., Fox, N. A., & Cohn, J. F. (2012). Children's depressive symptoms in relation to EEG frontal asymmetry and maternal depression. *Journal of Abnormal Child Psychology*, 40, 265–276.

Field, T. (1994). The effects of mother's physical and emotional unavailability on emotion regulation. *Child Development*, 59, 208–227.

(1995). Infants of depressed mothers. *Infant Behavior and Development*, 18, 1–13.

(1998). Maternal depression effects on infants and early interventions. *Preventive Medicine*, 27, 200–203.

Field, T., Healey, B., Goldstein, S., & Guthertz, M. (1990). Behavior-state matching and synchrony in mother–infant interactions of nondepressed versus depressed dyads. *Developmental Psychology*, 26, 7–14.

Fitzgerald, M., & Anand, K. J. S. (1993). The development, neuroanatomy, and neurophysiology of pain. In N. Schechter, C. D. Berde, & M. Yaster (Eds.), *Pain management in infants, children, and adolescents* (pp. 11–32). Baltimore, MD: Williams & Williams.

Foster, C. E., Garber, J., & Durlak, J. A. (2008). Current and past maternal depression, maternal interaction behaviors, and children's externalizing and internalizing symptoms. *Journal of Abnormal Child Psychology*, 36, 527–537.

Francis, D., Diorio, J., Liu, D., & Meaney, M. J. (1999). Nongenomic transmission across generations of maternal behavior and stress responses in the rat. *Science*, 286, 1155–1158.

Goldsmith, D. F., & Rogoff, B. (1997). Mothers' and toddlers' coordinated joint focus of attention: Variations with maternal dysphoric symptoms. *Developmental Psychology*, 33, 113–119.

Goodman, S. H. (2007). Depression in mothers. *Annual Review of Clinical Psychology*, 3, 107–135.

Goodman, S. H., Rouse, M. H., Connell, A. M., Broth, M. R., Hall, C. M., & Heyward, D. (2011). Maternal depression and child psychopathology: A meta-analytic review. *Clinical Child and Family Psychology Review*, 14, 1–27.

Gravener, J. A., Rogosch, F. A., Oshri, A., Narayan, A. J., Cicchetti, D., & Toth, S. L. (2012). The relations among maternal depressive disorder, maternal expressed emotion, and toddler behavior problems and attachment. *Journal of Abnormal Child Psychology*, 40, 803–813.

Hammen, C. (2002). Context of stress in families of children with depressed parents. In S. H. Goodman & I. H. Gotlib (Eds.), *Children of depressed parents: Mechanisms of risk and implications for treatment* (pp. 175–199). Washington, DC: American Psychological Association.

Hammen, C., & Brennan, P. A. (2001). Depressed adolescents of depressed and nondepressed mothers: Tests of an interpersonal impairment hypothesis. *Journal of Consulting and Clinical Psychology*, 69, 284–294.

Hannington, L., Heron, J., & Ramchandini, P. (2011). Parental depression and child outcomes – is marital conflict the missing link? *Child: Care, Health and Development*, 38, 520–529.

Harold, G. T., Rice, F., Hay, D. F., Boivin, J., van den Bree, M., & Thapar, A. (2011). Familial transmission of depression and antisocial behavior symptoms: Disentangling the contribution of inherited and environmental factors and testing the mediating role of parenting. *Psychological Medicine*, 41, 1175–1185.

Horwitz, S. M., Briggs-Gowan, M. J., Storfer-Isser, A., & Carter, A. S. (2007). Prevalence, correlates, and persistence of maternal depression. *Journal of Women's Health*, 16, 678–691.

Jacobs, N., Kenis, G., Peeters, F., Derom, C., Vlietinck, R., & van Os, J. (2006). Stress-related negative affectivity and genetically altered serotonin transporter function: Evidence of synergism in shaping risk of depression. *Archives of General Psychiatry*, 63, 989–996.

Jameson, P. B., Gelfand, D. M., Kulcsar, E., & Teti, D. M. (1997). Mother–toddler interaction patterns associated with maternal depression. *Development and Psychopathology*, 9, 537–550.

Jones, N. A., Field, T., & Almeida, A. (2009). Right frontal EEG asymmetry and behavioral inhibition in infants of depressed mothers. *Infant Behavior and Development*, 32, 298–304.

Kessler, R. C. (2003). Epidemiology of women and depression. *Journal of Affective Disorders*, 74, 5–13.

Kessler R. C. (2006). The epidemiology of depression among women. In C. L. Keyes & S. H. Goodman (Eds.), *Women and depression: A handbook for the social, behavior, and biomedical sciences* (pp. 22–37). New York: Cambridge University Press.

Kiernan, K. E., & Huerta, C. (2008). Economic deprivation, maternal depression, parenting and children's cognitive and emotional development in early childhood. *British Journal of Sociology*, 59, 783–806.

Landry, S. H., Smith, K. E., Swank, P. R., Assel, M. A., & Vellet, S. (2001). Does early responsive parenting have a special importance for children's development or is consistency across early childhood necessary? *Developmental Psychology*, 37, 387–403.

Leckman-Westin, E., Cohen, P. R., & Stueve, A. (2009). Maternal depression and mother–child interaction patterns: Association with toddler problems and continuity of effects to late childhood. *Journal of Child Psychology and Psychiatry*, 50, 1176–1184.

Lesch, K. P., Bengel, D., Heils, A., Sabol, S. Z., Greenberg, B. D., Petri, S., et al. (1996). Association of anxiety-related traits with a polymorphism in the serotonin transporter gene regulatory region. *Science*, 274, 1527–1531.

Levinson, D. F. (2006). The genetics of depression: A review. *Biological Psychiatry*, 60, 84–92.

Liu, D., Dioro, J., Tannenbaum, B., Caldji, C., Francis, D., Freedman, A., et al. (1997). Maternal care, hippocampal glucocorticoid receptors, and hypothalamic-pituitary-adrenal responses to stress. *Science*, 277, 1659–1662.

Lovejoy, M. C., Graczyk, P. A., O'Hare, E., & Neuman, G. (2000). Maternal depression and parenting behavior. *Clinical Psychology Review*, 20, 561–592.

Lupien, S. J., McEwen, B. S., Gunnar, M. R., & Heim, C. (2010). Effects of stress throughout the lifespan on the brain, behaviour, and cognition. *Nature*, 10, 434–445.

Martins, C., & Gaffan, E. A. (2000). Effects of early maternal depression on patterns of infant–mother attachment: A meta-analytic investigation. *Journal of Child Psychology and Psychiatry*, 41, 737–746.

Matheson, F. I., Moineddin, R., Dunn, J. R., Creatore, M. I., Gozdyra, P., & Glazier, R. H. (2006). Urban neighborhoods, chronic stress, gender and depression. *Social Science and Medicine*, 63, 2604–2616.

Merzenich, M. M., Nelson, R. J., Stryker, M. P., Cynader, M., Schoppman, A., & Zook, J. M. (1984). Somatosensory cortical map changes following digit amputation in adult monkeys. *Journal of Comparative Neurology*, 224, 591–605.

Mondimore, F. M., Zandi, P. P., MacKinnon, D. F., McInnis, M. G., Miller, E. B., Crowe, R. P., et al. (2006). Familial aggregation of illness chronicity in recurrent, early-onset major depression pedigrees. *American Journal of Psychiatry*, 163, 1554–1560.

Murray, L., Arteche, A., Fearon, P., Halligan, S., Goodyer, I., & Cooper, P. (2011). Maternal postnatal depression and the development of depression in offspring up to 16 years of age. *Journal of the American Academy of Child and Adolescent Psychiatry, 50,* 460–470.

Natsuaki, M. N., Ge, X., Leve, L. D., Neiderhiser, J. M., Shaw, D. S., Conger, R. D., et al. (2010). Genetic liability, environment, and the development of fussiness in toddlers: The roles of maternal depression and paternal responsiveness. *Developmental Psychology, 46,* 1147–1158.

Paulson, J. F., Dauber, S. E., & Leiferman, J. A. (2006). Individual and combined effects of maternal and paternal depression on parenting behavior. *Pediatrics, 118,* 659–668.

Pilowsky, D. J., Wickramaratne, P., Rush, A. J., Hughes, C. W., Garber, J., Malloy, E., et al. (2006). Children of currently depressed mothers: A STAR*D ancillary study. *Journal of Clinical Psychiatry, 67,* 126–136.

Pilowsky, D. J., Wickramaratne, P., Talati, A., Tang, M., Hughes, C. W., Garber, J., et al. (2008). Children of depressed mothers 1 year after the initiation of maternal treatment: Findings from the STAR*D child study. *American Journal of Psychiatry, 165,* 1136–1147.

Pugh, K. L., & Farrell, A. D. (2012). The impact of maternal depressive symptoms on adolescents' aggression: Role of parenting and family mediators. *Journal of Child and Family Studies, 21,* 589–602.

Reissland, N., Shepherd, J., & Herrera, E. (2005). Teasing play in infancy: Comparing mothers with and without self-reported depressed mood during play with their babies. *European Journal of Developmental Psychology, 2,* 271–283.

Risch, N., Herrell, R., Lehner, T., Liang, K. Y., Eaves, L., Hoh, J., et al. (2009). Interaction between the serotonin transporter gene (5-HTTLPR), stressful life events, and risk of depression: A meta-analysis. *Journal of the American Medical Association, 301,* 2462–2471.

Rosenblum, L. A., Coplan, J. D., Friedman, S., Bassoff, T., Gorman, J., & Andrews, M. W. (1994). Adverse early experiences affect noradrenergic and serotonergic functioning in adult primates. *Biological Psychiatry, 35,* 221–227.

Sanchez, M. M. (2006). The impact of early adverse care on HPA axis development: Nonhuman primate models. *Hormones and Behavior, 50,* 623–631.

Sanchez, M. M., Noble, P. M., Lyon, C. K., Plotsky, P. M., Davis, M., Nemeroff, C. B., & Winslow, J. T. (2005). Alterations in diurnal cortisol rhythm and acoustic startle response in nonhuman primates with adverse rearing. *Biological Psychiatry, 57,* 373–381.

Schore, A. N. (2001a). The effects of early relational trauma on right brain development, affect regulation, and infant mental health. *Infant Mental Health Journal, 22,* 201–269.

(2001b). Effects of a secure attachment relationship on right brain development, affect regulation, and infant mental health. *Infant Mental Health Journal, 22,* 7–66.

(2005). Back to basics: Attachment, affect regulation, and the developing right brain: Linking developmental neuroscience to pediatrics. *Pediatrics in Review, 26,* 204–217.

Shaw, D. S., Owen, E. B., Vondra, J. I., Keenan, K., & Winslow, E. B. (1996). Early risk factors and pathways in the development of early disruptive behavior problems. *Development and Psychopathology, 8,* 679–699.

Siegel, D. J. (1999). *The developing mind: Towards a neurobiology of interpersonal experience.* New York: Guilford Press.

Silberg, J. L., Maes, H., & Eaves, L. J. (2010). Genetic and environmental influences on the transmission of parental depression to children's depression and conduct disturbance: An extended Children of Twins study. *Journal of Child Psychology and Psychiatry*, 51, 734–744.

Stein, A., Gath, D. H., Bucher, J., Bond, A., Day, A., & Cooper, P. J. (1991). The relationship between post-natal depression and mother–child interaction. *British Journal of Psychiatry*, 158, 46–52.

Sullivan, P. F., Neale, M. C., & Kendler, K. S. (2000). Genetic epidemiology of major depression: Review and meta-analysis. *American Journal of Psychiatry*, 157, 1552–1562.

Suomi, S. J. (1997). Early determinants of behaviour: Evidence from primate studies. *British Medical Bulletin*, 53, 170–184.

Thibodeau, R., Jorgensen, R. S., & Kim, S. (2006). Depression, anxiety, and resting frontal EEG asymmetry: A meta-analytic review. *Journal of Abnormal Psychology*, 115, 715–729.

Tomarken, A. J., Dichter, G. S., Garber, J., & Simien, C. (2004). Resting frontal brain activity: Linkages to maternal depression and socio-economic status among adolescents. *Biological Psychology*, 67, 77–102.

Tully, E. C., Iacono, W. G., & McGue, M. (2008). An adoption study of parental depression as an environmental liability for adolescent depression and childhood disruptive disorder. *American Journal of Psychiatry*, 165, 1148–1154.

Vygotsky, L. S. (1978). Prehistory of written speech. *Social Science*, 17, 1–17.

Weaver, I., Cervoni, N., Champagne, F., D'Alessio, A., Sharma, S., Seckl, J., et al. (2004). Epigenetic programming by maternal behavior. *Nature Neuroscience*, 7, 847–854.

Weinfield, N. S., Ingerski, L., & Coffey Moreau, S. (2009). Maternal and paternal depressive symptoms as predictors of toddler adjustment. *Journal of Child and Family Studies*, 18, 39–47.

Weissman, M. M., Pilowsky, D. J., Wickramaratne, P. J., Talati, A., Wisniewski, S. R., Fava, M., et al. (2006). Remissions in maternal depression and child psychopathology: A STAR*D child report. *Journal of the American Medical Association*, 295, 1389–1398.

Wilhelm, K., Mitchell, P. B., Niven, H., Finch, A., Wedgwood, L., Scimone, A., & Blair, I. P. (2006). Life events, first depression onset and the serotonin transporter gene. *British Journal of Psychiatry*, 188, 210–215.

Zimmermann, P., Bruckl, T., Lieb, R., Nocon, A., Ising, M., Beesdo, K., & Wittchen, H. U. (2008). The interplay of familial depression liability and adverse events in predicting the first onset of depression during a 10-year follow-up. *Biological Psychiatry*, 63, 406–414.

Zubenko, G. S., Hughes, H. B., Stiffler, J. S., Zubenko, W. N., & Kaplan, B. B. (2002). Genome survey for susceptibility loci for recurrent, early-onset major depression: Results at 10cM resolution. *American Journal of Medical Genetics (Neuropsychiatric Genetics)*, 114, 413–422.

11

Fragile X–Associated Disorders: How the Family Environment and Genotype Interact

MARSHA MAILICK, JAN S. GREENBERG,
LEANN E. SMITH, AUDRA STERLING, NANCY BRADY,
STEVEN F. WARREN, AND JINKUK HONG

The family system has long been recognized as a central context for human development, with family-level processes acting as sources of both risk and protection for children, parents, and other family members across the life course. Following a developmental psychopathology perspective, development is the result of dynamic transactions between individuals and their contexts over time wherein individuals simultaneously shape and are shaped by their environments (Cummings, Davies, & Campbell, 2000). Further, in order to adequately understand the interplay of personal and contextual contributions to lifespan development, research should delineate genetic and environmental risk factors as well as focus on how and why interaction processes work in specific subgroups (Rutter et al., 1997).

In this chapter, we explore the family as a context for children's development among families of children with fragile X syndrome (FXS), a unique population in which to investigate the interactive effects of genes and environment. FXS is an inherited genetic disorder, resulting in biologically compromised development of varying degrees in individuals with this mutation. In some cases, mothers of children with FXS and other extended family members are also affected with different and milder symptoms if they are "premutation" carriers. As such, within samples of families of individuals with FXS, it is possible to explore the influence of environmental factors at varying levels of genetic liability. For instance, developmental risk for children with FXS may be moderated by the presence of protective factors in the family environment. As another example, the level of genetic risk for mothers with the premutation may explain individual differences in reactivity to environmental stressors and adaptation over time. Thus, in this chapter, we specifically examine how family environmental factors (e.g., family emotional climate, responsive parenting, child-related parenting stress) contribute to child and maternal development in the context of genetic risk, using the special case of families of children with FXS.

Fragile X syndrome (FXS) is the most prevalent inherited cause of intellectual disability (Crawford, Acuna, & Sherman, 2001). Children with FXS may have any number of phenotypic characteristics such as intellectual disability, hyperactivity, gaze avoidance, unintelligible speech, perseverative and stereotypic behaviors, and passivity (Abbeduto, Brady, & Kover, 2007; Bailey, Hatton, & Skinner, 1998; Sterling & Warren, 2008), although there is great heterogeneity in the degree of affectedness, with males typically more severely affected than females in this X-linked condition. It is estimated that approximately 15% to 25% of individuals (mostly males, but some females) with FXS meet the diagnostic criteria for autism (Clifford et al., 2007; Rogers, Wehner, & Hagerman, 2001). Regardless of codiagnosis, 50% to 90% of males with FXS are reported to show some of the symptoms of autism, including self-injurious behaviors, stereotypic movements (i.e., rocking, hand flapping), perseverative speech, tactile defensiveness, and poor eye contact (Bailey et al., 1998; Clifford et al., 2007; Feinstein & Reiss, 1998). Males with both FXS and autism typically have more severe language and social impairments and lower IQ scores than children with FXS without autism (Bailey et al., 1998; Bailey, Hatton, Mesibov, & Skinner, 2000) and similarly have more severe behavior problems than children with FXS without autism (Smith et al., 2012).

FXS results from a mutation in the 5'untranslated region of the *FMR1* gene located on the X chromosome (Brown, 2002). In the healthy allele, there are approximately 40 or fewer repetitions of the CGG sequence of nucleotides comprising the *FMR1* gene. In the full mutation of FXS, there is an expansion to 200 or more repetitions. Importantly, smaller expansions of the CGG sequence are also associated with adverse phenotypic consequences. Individuals who have between 55 and 200 CGG repeats in the gene are said to carry the *premutation*. The premutation can expand to the full mutation when passed on from mother to child (Nolin et al., 1996). In addition, a sizeable proportion of individuals with the premutation display many of the same behavioral features of individuals with FXS, albeit typically in a less severe form (Bailey, Raspa, Olmstead, & Holiday, 2008). Specifically, premutation carriers are at risk for difficulties in attention, verbal memory, and executive function (Freund, Reiss, & Abrams, 1993; Sobesky, Hull, & Hagerman, 1994); additionally, women with the premutation of FXS are more prone to depression and social anxiety and may be more affectively labile than unaffected women (Hagerman & Hagerman, 2002; Mazzocco,

2000; Sobesky et al., 1994; Thompson, Rogeness, McClure, Clayton, & Johnson, 1996).

The premutation is also associated with elevated risk for two disorders that do not occur in individuals with the *FMR1* full mutation: *Fragile X-Associated Primary Ovarian Insufficiency* (FXPOI), which includes a continuum of ovarian dysfunction, including infertility, irregular menstrual cycles, and premature menopause, and *Fragile X-Associated Tremor-Ataxia Syndrome* (FXTAS), a late-onset neurodegenerative disorder (Cornish, Turk, & Hagerman, 2008). These difficulties are not uncommon, with prevalence rates for female carriers over the age of 50 reported to be 18.6% and 16.5% for FXPOI and FXTAS, respectively (Rodriquez-Revenga et al., 2009). Families that include one or more member who has FXS or even the *FMR1* premutation, therefore, are likely to experience higher levels of stress and nonnormative life experiences as a (direct or indirect) result of the characteristics and behaviors of the affected family members (Murphy & Abbeduto, 2005; Smith et al., 2012).

Fragile X-associated disorders, thus, constitute a multigenerational set of conditions affecting children, their parents and grandparents, and potentially other members of the extended family. Children with FXS inherit the problem gene from their mother, who would be a carrier of either the premutation or the full mutation (Nolin et al., 1996). (For more details about the inheritance profile of the *FMR1* gene, see Hagerman, 1999.) Some parents (and grandparents) of children with an expanded *FMR1* allele will be affected by many of the same challenges as their children, which may well make them less able to deal with life stressors, including those associated with their child's condition (Esbensen, Seltzer, & Abbeduto, 2007). Consequently, understanding the functioning of any individual in a family affected by an *FMR1* expansion will require examination both of his or her own genetic status and of experiences within the family, which is the underlying premise of our program of research.

The full mutation of FXS affects 1 in approximately 4,000 individuals. The premutation is much more prevalent, but it has only recently begun to be investigated. Prevalence studies have been conducted in Canada, Israel, Spain, Taiwan, and Japan, and prevalence rates vary widely, reflecting significant ethnic variation, likely a function of founder effects (i.e., mutations that appear in the DNA of individuals that are founders of a distinct population and that are passed down to other generations). In a review of the world literature, Song and colleagues (2003) pooled estimates across all studies and arrived at a premutation prevalence of 1 in 643 males and 1 in 149 females. However, pooling data from studies of different ethnic groups and sex distributions could be misleading because of the wide variation in prevalence across ethnicities and between men and women. In the first U.S. population-based prevalence study of premutation prevalence conducted on an unselected sample of Whites largely of Northern and Central European ancestry, Seltzer, Baker, and colleagues (2012) reported a prevalence of 1 in 468 males and 1 in 151 females. Two other recently published population-based prevalence studies (one by our group) provide converging evidence regarding the validity of these prevalence estimates (Maenner et al., 2013; Tassone et al., 2012).

The purpose of this chapter is to summarize our group's research findings on the family context of FXS and the premutation of *FMR1*. Specifically, we draw mainly on our published findings to elucidate how environmental factors (particularly the family environment) and genotype interact to affect the functioning and well-being of family members. We begin with an overview of our research program. Next, we turn to questions of how the family influences the development of children with the full mutation of FXS. With this life course perspective, we examine first how early maternal behavior (in particular, maternal responsivity) longitudinally affects the development of language in young children with FXS and subsequently how the family emotional climate is associated with behavior problems in individuals with FXS in childhood, adolescence, and adulthood. In the next section of the chapter, we consider the premutation of the *FMR1* gene in mothers of children with the full mutation and examine how carrier mothers are affected by the behavior problems of their children as well as other stresses in the larger environment. Thus, our goal is to examine the reciprocal relations between mother and child across the life course in the context of variations in *FMR1* genotypes.

STUDY OF FAMILY ADAPTATION TO FXS: VARIATIONS ACROSS THE LIFE COURSE

This chapter draws on data collected as part of a multisite, ongoing study on family adaptation to FXS and how the family context is associated with heterogeneity in life course patterns of development and functioning of individuals with FXS (Bailey, Hatton, Tassone, Skinner, & Taylor, 2001; Seltzer, Barker et al., 2012; Warren, Brady, Sterling, Fleming, & Marquis, 2010). This multisite study is part of an NICHD-funded Fragile X Research Center that includes 199 families in total: 52 children, 96 adolescents, and 51 adults with FXS. Documentation from laboratory or medical records confirming that the son/daughter has the full mutation of the gene causing

FXS was a requirement for participation. Families were recruited through service agencies, clinics, foundations across the United States, and university-based research registries of families having a child with developmental disabilities.

Mothers of young children with FXS ($n = 52$) have participated in a longitudinal study of family adaptation to FXS thus far spanning more than 8 years (Warren, Brady, Sterling, Fleming, & Marquis, 2010). Children's ages ranged from 10 to 40 months at the first data collection point (in 2004), and all lived in the parental home. In families with two or more children with FXS, the youngest child was the focal child for the study. Their median household income was between $50,000 and $80,000 in 2008, with incomes ranging from less than $15,000 to $100,000 or more. The majority of mothers are White (90%), currently married (73%), and had at least some college education (85%).

Mothers of adolescents ($n = 96$) and adults ($n = 51$) with FXS are participating in a companion longitudinal study of family adaptation to FXS (Greenberg et al., 2012; Seltzer, Barker et al., 2012; Smith et al., 2012). Median household income was between $80,000 and $89,000 at the start of the study in 2008, but a range in income was represented (< $9,999 to $160,000 or more). Most mothers are White (95%), currently married (82%), and had at least some college education (85%), similar to the sample of families of younger children described previously.

When considering the combined sample, the majority of individuals with FXS are sons (81%, 77%, and 94% of the children, adolescents, and adults, respectively) and have intellectual disability (ID; 83%, 79%, and 84%, respectively). The percentage of sons (vs. daughters) differs across the three age groups (Chi square = 6.18, $df = 2$, $p < .05$). However, the percentage of those with ID (vs. average intelligence) does not vary across the three stages of life.

Family Influences on the Development of Individuals with Fragile X Syndrome

There has been a long tradition of research aiming to identify aspects of the family environment that can enhance the well-being of children with intellectual and developmental disabilities (IDD; see review by Hatton & Emerson, 2003). For example, Mitchell and Hauser-Cram (2009) studied longitudinally families of children with developmental delays and found that a more positive family climate when the child was of age 3 predicted lower levels of both internalizing and externalizing behavior problems at age 5; in a companion study, this group of investigators linked a positive family climate at age 3 to growth in social skills at age 10 (Hauser-Cram, Warfield, Shonkoff, & Krauss, 2001). Maternal responsivity is associated with the development of children with IDD (see Warren & Brady, 2007, for a review), while high levels of maternal criticism are associated with an increase in behavior problems of individuals with autism and other types of IDDs (Baker et al., 2011; Greenberg, Seltzer, Hong, & Orsmond, 2006; Wamboldt, O'Connor, Wamboldt, Gavin, & Klinnert, 2000).

With regard to the impact of the family environment on individuals with FXS, the initial literature points to the family as an important context for development. In a study examining the effect of the quality of the family environment on children with FXS (based on a larger evaluation of 80 boys and 40 girls with FXS between the ages of 6 and 17 (mean age = 10.8 years), the quality of the home environment was found to be related to fewer autistic symptoms (Hessl et al., 2001), better cognitive outcomes (Dyer-Friedman et al., 2002), and better adaptive behavior (Glaser et al., 2003).

One overall purpose of our program of research, therefore, is to investigate how parenting style and the broader family environment affect the development of children with FXS across the life course. In this section of the chapter, we focus on two aspects of the family context that we have studied and found to be associated with the development of children with FXS: maternal responsivity, which is a specific type of parenting style, and expressed emotion, which is an indicator of the emotional climate of the family.

MATERNAL RESPONSIVITY AND LANGUAGE DEVELOPMENT IN CHILDREN WITH FXS

Maternal responsivity refers to a healthy, growth-producing parent–child relationship characterized by warmth, nurturance, and stability as well as specific behaviors such as responding contingent on child initiations. In studies of the general population, maternal responsivity has been shown to have a cumulative impact on children's cognitive, emotional, social, and language development (Landry, Smith, Miller-Loncar, & Swank, 1998; Landry, Smith, Swank, Assel, & Vellet, 2001). A highly responsive parent will often engage in a style of interaction that maintains the child's focus of attention, expands on the child's initiations, and only occasionally redirects the child's attention to a new topic. In contrast with highly responsive parent–children interactions, high rates of directiveness, which are typically defined as maternal control of children's behavior and/or attention, may negatively impact children's emotional, cognitive, and language development (Farran, 2001; Mahoney & Neville-Smith, 1996; Marfo, 1992; Warren & Brady, 2007).

Maternal responsivity represents a complex, dyadic interaction involving both child and maternal factors. Certain maternal variables, such as low educational attainment (i.e., less than a high school education), mild intellectual disability, substance abuse, and depression may substantively impact a mother's ability to maintain a highly responsive style of parenting (Hooper, Burchinal, Roberts, Zeisel, & Neebe, 1998; Miller, Heysek, Whitman, & Borkowski, 1996; Osofsky & Thompson, 2000; Rutter & Quinton, 1984). As the biological mothers of children with FXS are themselves premutation carriers of FXS (a small portion have the full mutation as well), they are at risk for a range of subtle to severe cognitive or emotional problems that could impact their interactions with their children. These risk factors have been associated with lower maternal responsivity (Goldsmith & Rogoff, 1995; Osofsky & Thompson, 2000).

Characteristics of the son or daughter with FXS also may pose risks to maternal responsivity. A mother with the best intentions may nevertheless have difficulty employing and maintaining a highly responsive style with a child with a developmental disability (Stormont, 2001). The elevated levels of behavior problems, hyperactivity, unintelligible speech, autism, and other characteristics that are often displayed by children with FXS could make a highly responsive interaction difficult. Over time, such behaviors may cause caregivers to become less responsive even to appropriate initiations (Murphy & Abbeduto, 2005). For example, Sterling and colleagues (Sterling, Warren, Brady, & Fleming, 2013) have shown that for young children with FXS, the child's developmental level and language abilities have a significant impact on how responsive their mothers are across a variety of contexts, while maternal IQ is a strong predictor of the mother's behavior toward the child even after controlling for child developmental level.

The presence of autism symptoms, in particular, may contribute to difficulties in establishing and maintaining responsive parent–child interactions. Since the severity of behavior problems is a predictor of maternal well-being, autistic symptoms are an important variable to examine in determining the impact of the child's behavior on maternal parenting style. Later in this chapter, we will return to the question of how child behavior and other sources of stress affecting the family may put mothers at risk for poor functioning, especially in the context of genetic vulnerability. However, we first turn to the examination of the effects of maternal parenting style on child development for children with FXS.

As noted earlier, in 2004, Warren, Brady, and Sterling initiated a study to investigate maternal responsivity in a cohort of 55 children with the full mutation of FXS and their biological mothers from across the United States. The children's ages ranged between 10 and 40 months when the study commenced. Fifty-two of the mothers were premutation carriers and three mothers had the full mutation of the *FMR1* gene. The study has continued through middle childhood. Fifty-two of these families have continued to participate in the longitudinal study. Each of these families has thus far been visited five to six times at approximately 18-month intervals. The original sample included 44 boys and 11 girls with full-mutation FXS.

At each visit, we completed several standardized tests and interviews and also videotaped mother–child interactions in several different contexts (reading a book, making and eating a snack, unstructured play, and a 30-minute naturalistic sample). During the naturalistic context, parents were instructed to conduct an everyday activity such as putting dishes away, folding clothes, or playing together. Five minutes from the book, snack, and play contexts and 10 minutes from the naturalistic context were digitized for coding, yielding a total of 25 minutes of interaction, an amount of coded interaction similar to that reported in other studies of maternal responsivity (Warren & Brady, 2007). These interactions were coded for child communication behaviors, maternal responsivity, and maternal behavior management.

Our first goal was to investigate the relation between early maternal responsivity and later child communication outcomes in these young children (Warren, Brady, Sterling, Fleming, & Marquis, 2010). The findings indicated that early maternal responsivity significantly predicted later receptive and expressive language scores on standardized tests, as well as the rate of the number of different words used by the child and the child's total communication (including both verbal and nonverbal communication) at 36 months. We measured autism symptoms using the Childhood Autism Rating Scale (CARS; Schopler, Reichler, & Renner, 1988) and overall child developmental level using the learning composite score of the Mullen Scales of Early Learning (MSEL; Mullen, 1995). Children of highly responsive mothers had better language outcomes than did children with less responsive mothers, but the effect was dampened for children with high degrees of autism symptoms. For example, children with less responsive mothers but no evidence of autism outperformed children with high autism symptoms and highly responsive mothers (see Figure 11.1). The presence of autism symptoms placed significant constraints on language development even in the context of highly responsive parent–child interactions.

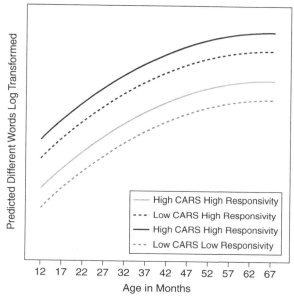

FIGURE 11.1. The impact of maternal responsivity on child expressive language: number of different words produced by child in interactional contexts.

We additionally explored maternal responsivity as the children in our study moved into middle childhood. Our data indicated stability in terms of general maternal affect: there were virtually no changes in the mothers' demonstrations of positive affect, warmth, physical control, verbal discipline, or punitive tone with their children. There was evidence of a slight increase in levels of maternal flexibility and responsiveness in their interactions with their child with FXS. Thus, one important conclusion of our research to date is that parenting style is established early in these families, and this style continues well into middle childhood.

Naturally, the types of activities in which mothers engaged their child with FXS changed by middle childhood. For example, reading as an activity had increased. Subsequent analyses indicated that the relation between early maternal responsivity and later vocabulary development actually strengthened as the children aged. However, the presence of autism symptoms continued to constrain the impact of maternal responsivity on language development during middle childhood (Brady et al., 2013).

In a second line of research with these families, we sought to determine how well the mothers adjust their parenting style to match their child's behavioral needs. In other words, would the mothers be consistent in their parenting style with all of their children (those with FXS and those not affected) regardless of the developmental level of the child, or would they instead make appropriate adjustments based on the needs of each child? To investigate this question, we selected 13 children with FXS from our original cohort of 55 families (Sterling, Barnum, Skinner, Warren, & Fleming, 2012) and compared them with a typically developing sibling. The two children within a family were tested when they were the same age. To establish a chronological age match, we first completed the assessment with whichever child in the sibling pair was older. For seven of the sibling pairs, this was the child with typical development; in five of the sibling pairs, the child with FXS was the older child, and the last pair involved dizygotic twins. Seven of the pairs were same gender (male-male), and six were male-female; all of the children with FXS were males. We waited until the younger sibling was the same chronological age to conduct the assessment with the younger sibling (within a 1-month window). The average age difference between the siblings at the time of the assessment was just 2 weeks. The chronological age matches controlled for history of interaction with the mother. The children were between 16 and 70 months of age at the time of this assessment ($M = 46$ months). We thus used a within-family design to directly compare a mother's parenting style with her child with FXS and one of her other children with typical development.

The mothers and children participated in the same interactional contexts described earlier, and the videotapes were coded for both maternal and child behaviors. In order to provide more contextual information on mothers' descriptions of interactions with their children and to provide concrete examples of maternal responsivity and behavioral management strategies, we conducted semistructured interviews before administering the quantitative assessments. These interviews elicited information on a number of domains (e.g., quality of life, impact of diagnosis), and included a section devoted to maternal responsivity.

The quantitative analysis and the interview data indicated that, in general, mothers used the same types of parenting strategies with both children (i.e., the child with FXS and the typically developing sibling) and that they made developmentally appropriate alterations in their level of interaction and expectations of the two children. The findings from this study were positive, as mothers used the same levels of praise and warmth with both children regardless of differences in developmental level. The differences in parenting focused on maternal behaviors central to either diffusing problematic child behaviors or in their use of a more conversational style of language with their children with typical development. The mothers did not exhibit high levels of differential parenting between siblings but rather employed a responsive style of parenting with both of their children that made appropriate accommodations for the developmental differences in the children. Furthermore, they were aware that they were making these accommodations and were able to describe them to the interviewer.

In summary, our findings indicated that many of the mothers in our study displayed a stable, positive affect with their child and used growth-enhancing parenting techniques well into middle childhood. However, the findings from the Warren and colleagues (2010) study indicate that for the children with high levels of autism symptomatology, the effect of maternal responsivity was more constrained than for the children with fewer autism symptoms.

FAMILY EMOTIONAL CLIMATE AND BEHAVIOR PROBLEMS ACROSS THE LIFE COURSE

Despite the clear patterns of gains in language and learning and the mothers' ability to both adapt to and support their children from early to middle childhood, the behavioral challenges posed by children with FXS remain considerable and may increase with age. Thus, we sought to understand how families and children with FXS manifest different pro-files of behavior problems at different stages of the life course and par-ticularly if the association between the family emotional climate and the child's behavioral functioning is different in childhood, adolescence, and adulthood. To do so, we compared the families described earlier with two additional groups of families of children with FXS in our multisite study, namely families of adolescents with FXS and families of adults with FXS. To obtain a common measure of the family emotional climate across these three stages of life, we turned to the concept of expressed emotion.

Expressed emotion (EE) is a measure of the emotional climate of the fam-ily. EE was originally studied in families of adults with schizophrenia, with high levels of EE found to be related to an exacerbation of symptoms and relapse (Brown, Birley, & Wing, 1972). Among persons with disabilities, high levels of EE (i.e., an emotionally charged family environment) predict symptom exacerbations across a broad range of mental health disorders and medical conditions, including mood disorders, eating disorders, Alzheimer's disease, asthma, diabetes, and Parkinson's disease (Asarnow, Thompson, Woo, & Cantwell, 2001; Bledin, Kuipers, MacCarthy, & Woods, 1990; Kim & Miklowitz, 2004, Vitaliano, Young, Russo, Romano, & Magana-Amato, 1993; Wearden, Tarrier, Barrowclough, Zastowny, & Rahill, 2000). More recently, investigators have applied this concept in research on families of children with autism and other developmental disabilities and found a similar pattern: high levels of EE in the family predicted increasing levels of behavior problems in the sons and daughters with developmental disabilities (Baker et al., 2011; Greenberg et al., 2006).

Our group is the first to examine the relation between EE and behavior problems in individuals with FXS across different stages of the child's life course (Greenberg et al., 2012). We examined two primary research questions with respect to the influence of the family emotional climate on the lives of individuals with FXS: (1) Are there differences in the family emotional climate in families of children with FXS at three stages of the family life course: childhood, adolescence, and adulthood? and (2) Are the associations between aspects of the family emotional climate and behavior problems similar across the three stages of life?

This analysis is part of our larger multisite study of family adaptation to FXS described previously. A total of 167 families of children (n = 48), adolescents (n = 85), and adults (n = 34) with FXS were included in this analysis (i.e., only mothers with the premutation and those for whom there were complete data on specific study measures). The sample of children included in this analysis ranged in age from 6 to 8 at the time when the expressed-emotion data were collected (mean = 7.2 years), while the sample of adolescents ranged in age from 12 to 21 (mean = 15.9), and the sample of adults ranged in age from 22 to 43 (mean = 27.4). Their mothers' ages were similarly diverse (means = 38.5, 46.8, 55.8 years, respectively).

The Five Minute Speech Sample (FMSS) was developed as a brief but valid measure of EE (Magaña et al., 1986). A common protocol for transcribing the speech samples was used for families in all three life stages, which were transcribed by an independent researcher. The mother was asked to speak for 5 minutes to describe her relationship with the target son or daughter with FXS and her thoughts and feelings about this child. The FMSS is coded with respect to both verbal content and vocal tone and yields ratings for multiple dimensions of the parent–child relationship, including levels of criticism, emotional overinvolvement, and parental warmth. It includes a count of the number of positive remarks made by the parent about the child as well as an overall EE rating. For criticism, emotional overinvolvement, and warmth, the codes were used to classify mothers into categories (e.g., high, borderline, moderate, low) on the particular EE dimension. Classification was performed by an independent rater with more than 30 years of experience coding the FMSS for all aspects of EE.

The mothers also completed the Child Behavior Checklist (CBCL; Achenbach & Rescorla, 2001) for their sons and daughters who were

18.5 years of age or younger and the Adult Behavior Checklist (ABCL; Achenbach & Rescorla, 2003) for their sons and daughters who were older than 18.5 years of age. The reliability and validity for the CBCL and ABCL are well established (Achenbach & Rescorla, 2001). The scores for the three summary scales, Total Problems, Internalizing Problems, Externalizing Problems, were computed.

Our first research focus concerned age-related differences in the family's emotional climate. We compared EE in families of children versus adolescents versus adults with FXS. As reported by Greenberg and his colleagues (2012), the data indicated that level of maternal criticism significantly varied across the age groups, with follow-up tests indicating that mothers of children were rated as expressing higher levels of criticism of their child than mothers of adolescents. Whereas 31% of the mothers of children with FXS and 29% of the mothers of the adults were classified as high in criticism, only 16% of the mothers of the adolescents were rated as high in this dimension. A different pattern was evident with regard to emotional overinvolvement. There was a trend for levels of emotional overinvolvement to differ among the three groups, with the mothers of adolescents showing a higher level of overinvolvement than the mothers of children. Whereas approximately 10% of the mothers of children and a similar percentage of the mothers of adults were rated as high or borderline with respect to overinvolvement, 23% of the mothers of adolescents were rated as high or borderline on overinvolvement.

However, across the three stages of life, the mothers were very similar with respect to positive dimensions of the family emotional climate. The majority of the mothers in all three life stages had high or moderate levels of warmth (73% to 88%). They averaged around three positive remarks during the FMSS, and this dimension was similar across the three life course groups. Thus, with respect to our first research question, negative measures of the family emotional climate (i.e., criticism and overinvolvement) varied across the three age groups, whereas positive dimensions of the family emotional climate (i.e., positive remarks and warmth) were more stable across the life course.

Unfortunately, we do not have access to normative data about the family emotional climate using the FMSS paradigm in families of typically developing children, adolescents, and adults. However, the pattern of findings regarding positive dimensions of the emotional climate of the family was consistent with the findings regarding maternal responsivity. The longitudinal observational data suggest stability of maternal positive affect and warmth during the child's early childhood and continuing into the school years. The cross-sectional data derived from FMSS codes similarly show rates of parental positivity that are consistent over a much longer stretch of the life course and that characterize the family emotional climate well into the son's or daughter's adult years. Our finding that mothers of adolescents and adults expressed less criticism than mothers of children was foreshadowed by the longitudinal maternal responsivity data of an increase in flexibility and responsiveness from the early childhood to the school-age period.

We next extended this life course investigation to ask whether similar associations are found between the indicators of the family emotional climate and the son's or daughter's behavior problems across the three life stages (Greenberg et al., 2012). Regarding the negative dimensions of the family emotional climate (criticism and emotional overinvolvement), we found that the associations with behavior problems were mainly similar across the three life stages. Maternal criticism was significantly related to externalizing symptoms for each of the three age groups, whereas criticism was unrelated to internalizing symptoms at any life stage. Consistent with prior research on families and individuals with developmental disabilities (Greenberg et al., 2006), emotional overinvolvement was not related to internalizing, externalizing, or total problems scores for any of the three age groups. Thus, for the population with developmental disabilities, parental behavior that has been classified in psychiatric research as reflecting overinvolvement might not have a negative effect because of the lifelong nature of the disability.

The absence of association between emotional overinvolvement and behavior problems in individuals with developmental disabilities, including FXS, suggests that for this population, descriptions of the child that in other contexts would signify unhealthy levels of overinvolvement do not result in elevated behavior problems in individuals with developmental disabilities. However, criticism is associated with higher levels of behavior problems in those developmental disabilities, consistent with other populations that have been studied. Furthermore, for individuals with FXS, the patterns reported above are the same for all age groups.

In contrast, an age-related pattern was evident in the relation between positive dimensions of the family emotional climate and behavior problems for children, adolescents, and adults. For children and adults with FXS, higher numbers of positive remarks made by mothers during the FMSS were related to significantly lower levels of behavior problems in their sons and daughters with FXS. However, for adolescents, positive remarks by the mother in the FMSS were unrelated to behavior problems. Similarly, for children and adults with FXS, a higher level of maternal warmth was significantly associated with lower levels of behavior problems, but these associations only showed a trend level effect in families of adolescents. Thus, for children and adults with FXS, higher levels of maternal warmth and positive remarks were associated with lower levels of behavior problems, but for adolescents such associations were either absent or weak.

The finding that the behavior of adolescents with FXS may be less responsive to their mothers' expressions of positivity suggests that they may be similar to adolescents in general in their struggles for autonomy. However, this interpretation warrants further exploration in longitudinal research. For children and adults, however, the significant cross-sectional associations between both positivity and negativity in the family emotional climate and the behavior problems of the sons and daughters with FXS underscores findings reported earlier from our longitudinal observations of maternal responsivity, namely that the functioning of parents and their children co-occur and that early patterns and associations are long lasting across many decades of the life course.

Challenges Facing Premutation-Carrier Mothers of Individuals with FXS

Since parenting a child with FXS has been shown to be stressful (Hartley et al., 2011) and since the mothers in these families are themselves affected by instability in the gene that causes FXS, we examine how stressful parenting and more generally how life events affecting the family may impact mothers' psychological well-being and physiological stress response. Therefore, in this section of the chapter, we describe our studies of the health and mental health of premutation-carrier mothers and then report analyses that we have conducted to examine how mothers respond to the behavior problems manifested by their son or daughter with FXS and to other life events that they or their family experienced in the previous year, and how maternal genotype may interact with their response. Understanding how mothers with the premutation respond to stress will contribute to a more complete picture of family adaptation to FXS.

OVERVIEW OF HEALTH AND MENTAL HEALTH OF PREMUTATION CARRIERS

Although premutation carriers were originally considered to be unaffected, at least some premutation carriers display signs of impairment, with high levels of premutation-containing messenger RNA (mRNA) suspected to result in "toxicity" leading to disease (Berry-Kravis & Potanos, 2004). In addition to the premutation-related conditions of FXTAS or FXPOI, risks to physical health and psychological well-being may also be a part of the premutation-carrier phenotype (Bailey et al., 2008; Chonchaiya et al., 2010; Coffey et al., 2008). Next we review the findings regarding these aspects of the premutation-carrier phenotype, including findings from our own study.

Premutation-carrier status has been linked with a variety of physical health problems. For instance, Coffey and colleagues (2008) found increased prevalence of thyroid disease, hypertension, seizures, peripheral neuropathy, and fibromyalgia in female carriers with FXTAS; carriers without FXTAS also had higher rates of muscle pain and history of tremors than women without *FMR1* expansions (Coffey et al., 2008). High rates of thyroid disease and chronic muscle pain similarly have been reported for female carriers in other studies (Rodriquez-Revenga et al., 2009). Some premutation-related problems may produce subthreshold symptomatology (i.e., a profile of problems that fails to meet clear diagnostic criteria for a particular disease) but still produce discomfort or pain. In a sample of daughters of men with FXTAS, premutation women had higher prevalence of symptoms including tremors, balance problems, memory problems, dizziness, menopausal symptoms, sleep problems, and anxiety than noncarriers (Chonchaiya et al., 2010). Chonchaiya and colleagues (2010) concluded that symptoms in premutation carriers still may be related to mRNA toxicity, although they may not be elevated consistently enough or sufficiently to meet diagnostic criteria (Chonchaiya et al., 2010).

Similar to findings regarding physical health symptoms in premutation carriers, individuals with the premutation may experience an elevated severity of neuropsychological symptoms even if the symptoms do not reach a clinical threshold (Hunter et al., 2008b). Accordingly, female carriers have been found to have heightened levels of negative affective symptoms compared to unaffected women of the same age (Bailey et al., 2008; Hunter et al., 2008a; Lachiewicz et al., 2010).

Given the potential for subthreshold symptomatology in premutation carriers, in our own work we have examined daily physical health symptoms and daily affect using a Daily Diary methodology (Almeida, Wethington, & Kessler, 2002). For our Daily Diary Study, respondents were interviewed by telephone each evening for a period of 8 days. The daily telephone interview, which lasted approximately 15 to 25 minutes, included questions about experiences in the previous 24 hours. The questions focused on time use, daily stressors, positive events, mood, and physical health symptoms.

We compared the daily health symptoms of mothers of adolescents and adults with fragile X syndrome (FXS; *n* = 112) to a nationally representative sample of mothers of similarly aged children without disabilities (n = 230) as well as to a sample of mothers of adolescents and adults with autism spectrum disorders (ASD; n = 96; Smith, Seltzer, & Greenberg, 2011). Health symptoms (e.g., headache, backache, muscle soreness, fatigue, joint pain, muscle weakness, dizziness, nausea, diarrhea, constipation, menstrual-related symptoms, and hot flashes or flushes) experienced in the previous 24 hours were recorded during telephone interviews on the 8 consecutive days of the Daily Diary Study. We found that both mothers of a son or daughter with FXS and mothers of a son or daughter with ASD had a higher proportion of days with headaches, backaches, muscle soreness, fatigue, and hot flashes than mothers of children without disabilities. The premutation-carrier mothers experienced at least one health symptom on 75% of days in the 8-day study, suggesting that the vast majority of time, premutation-carrier mothers need to cope with their own health difficulties even as they provide care for their children (Smith et al., 2011).

Using the same Daily Diary methodology as our examination of physical health symptoms, we also explored daily levels of positive and negative affect among premutation-carrier mothers (Smith et al., 2011). We found that mothers of adolescent and adult children with FXS reported higher levels of daily negative affect than mothers of similarly aged children without disabilities, although mothers of a son or daughter with FXS did not differ significantly in positive affect from mothers of children without disabilities. Further, even after controlling for child behavior problems, mothers in the FXS group had higher levels of positive affect than mothers in the ASD group (Smith et al., 2011). This finding raises questions regarding possible protective mechanisms for premutation-carrier mothers. Given that higher levels of positive affect have been repeatedly associated with better health in other populations (Cohen & Pressman, 2006; Xu & Roberts, 2010), a valuable area for future research will be to consider both what contributes to positive affect in premutation-carrier mothers and how positive affect may relate to their long-term health outcomes. Further, findings confirming the relation between positive affect and health outcomes for families with full mutation children with FXS would suggest that interventions aimed at addressing positivity may be beneficial.

In conclusion, in our work we have found evidence of significantly elevated levels of daily physical health symptoms and negative affect among premutation-carrier mothers relative to noncarrier women of the same age. However, levels of health symptoms among mothers of adolescents and adults with FXS in our sample did not differ from those of mothers of similarly aged children with ASD (Smith et al., 2011). As others have noted, the development and maintenance of health symptoms in women with the premutation may be due, at least in part, to environmental factors such as the heightened level of stress these mothers experience while caring for a child with FXS (Bourgeois et al., 2009; Hunter et al., 2009). Importantly, they also experience normative levels of positive affect, which emerge as important strengths in this group of caregiving mothers.

GENE BY ENVIRONMENT INTERACTIONS: HOW MATERNAL GENOTYPE INTERACTS WITH STRESS

The *FMR1* premutation offers a unique opportunity to examine how stressful parenting interacts with genotype to impact the well-being of carrier mothers. There are a number of genetic markers associated with the premutation, and we have examined how two of these – activation ratio and CGG repeat length – interact with stress in premutation-carrier mothers.

Activation Ratio x Child Behavior Problems

In our ongoing study, we examined how the stress of parenting an adolescent or adult with full mutation FXS might interact with maternal genotype to take a toll on premutation-carrier mothers' physiological functioning (Hartley et al., 2011). In this analysis, we employed a diathesis-stress model in which a genetic vulnerability (diathesis) interacts with environmental adversity (stress) to affect functioning. This model has not previously been tested directly in women with the *FMR1* premutation, but it has been of great value for examining psychological functioning in the general population (Caspi et al., 2002; Caspi et al., 2003; Fowles, 1992; McKeever & Huff, 2003; Monroe & Simons, 1991).

In our application of the diathesis-stress model, maternal diathesis is measured by the *activation ratio* (defined below) and the stressful challenge of parenting a child with FXS is indexed by child behavior problems. Although the activation ratio is just one of the several genetic markers of mutations in the *FMR1* gene, we focus on this indicator of genetic vulnerability to stress because it is an individual difference variable that reflects the degree of biochemical affectedness. Similarly, although child behavior problems are just one source of environmental stress experienced by mothers, they are a prominent stressor documented in past research to be of significance in FXS (Bailey et al., 2008; Cornish et al., 2008).

Mothers with the premutation of the *FMR1* gene vary widely in terms of their biochemical affectedness (e.g., Tassone et al., 2000). This variation is due in part to *X inactivation*. The process of X inactivation occurs early in embryological development in all females, and it results in the "turning off" of one X chromosome in each cell. In females with the *FMR1* premutation, the relative proportion of active and inactive *FMR1* expansion mutation-carrying alleles varies from person to person (Tassone et al., 2000). The percentage of cells with a normal X as the active X is known as the activation ratio. The activation ratio has been identified as a potentially important biological indicator of the extent to which various biochemical pathways are altered. A low activation ratio may put premutation-carrier mothers at risk for poor psychological well-being and physical health (Hessl et al., 2005; Seltzer, Abbeduto et al., 2009). Thus, a low activation ratio may serve as a diathesis, which increases the degree to which mothers with the premutation may be negatively impacted by child-related stress.

We examined the interactive effects of activation ratio and child behavior problems on maternal awakening cortisol. We selected this dependent variable because cortisol dysregulation is affected by both acute and chronic stress (McEwen, 1998) and because we have shown that the chronic stress of parenting an adolescent or adult child with autism is associated with lower or blunted maternal cortisol profiles (Seltzer et al., 2010). Our specific prediction in the present analysis was that the extent to which premutation-carrier mothers of individuals with FXS are negatively affected by their child's behavior problems will be influenced by their own genetic vulnerability. Mothers with a greater genetic vulnerability (i.e., those who have a lower activation ratio) were expected to be more negatively impacted by child-related stress, leading to a *hypo*cortisolemic response to their child's behavior problems. In contrast, mothers with less genetic vulnerability (i.e., those who have a higher activation ratio) may have a more typical response to their son or daughter's behavior problems, resulting in a pattern of a *hyper*cortisolemic activity in response to behavior problems.

For this analysis, we focus on a subsample of mothers ($n = 76$) drawn from our study of families of adolescents and adults with FXS who participated in the 8-day telephone Diary Study and who supplied saliva samples from which cortisol levels were measured. In the Daily Diary Study, the mothers reported on the behavior problems manifested by their son or daughter at the end of each day. Saliva samples were collected at four time points (awakening, 30 minutes after awakening, before lunch, and before bed) each day on Days 2 through 5 of the Diary Study and analyzed in the Kirschbaum laboratory (Dresden, Germany); results regarding the awakening time point are reported in this section of the chapter. Maternal activation ratio was measured through DNA analysis of blood samples conducted

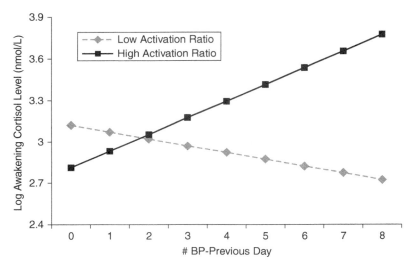

FIGURE 11.2. Number of behavior problems by the son or daughter with FXS and log of awakening cortisol on the following morning for mothers with low (1 SD below the mean) and high (1 SD above the mean) activation ratios.

by Kimball Genetics. Multilevel models were used to analyze daily variables nested within individuals across time.

We found that behavior problems were frequent in these adolescents and adults with FXS. The two most frequently occurring behavior problems during the 8-day Diary Study were unusual or repetitive behavior and uncooperative behavior, which occurred on approximately one third and one quarter of diary days, respectively. Socially offensive behavior, withdrawn or inattentive behavior, and disruptive behavior were less frequent, evident on 12% to 14% of days. Behaviors involving hurting oneself, hurting others, or destroying property occurred much less frequently, on approximately 3% to 5% of days. The large majority (85.7%) reported to have exhibited at least one episode of behavior problems during the 8-day Diary Study period.

For the present analysis, we used measures of behavior problems manifested by the child the day before to predict maternal cortisol level the next morning, and we predicted that maternal activation ratio would interact with child behavior problems. Indeed, as we hypothesized, the interaction between mothers' activation ratio and the number of previous-day behavior problems manifested by the child was a significant predictor of maternal cortisol at awakening the next morning (see Figure 11.2). Mothers with lower and higher activation ratios showed markedly different awakening cortisol values depending on the prior day's experience of child behavior problems. For mothers with low activation ratios (i.e., a smaller proportion of normal cells), the greater the number of behavior problems on the previous day, the *lower* the morning cortisol level (an abnormal response to stress). In contrast, for mothers with a high activation ratio (i.e., a larger proportion of normal cells), the greater the number of behavior problems yesterday, the *higher* the morning level of cortisol, which is a more typical neuroendocrine response to environmental stress.

Further evidence that chronic exposure to stressful parenting is associated with hypocortisolism is provided by our finding that low morning cortisol was characteristic of mothers in the present study who had more than one child with a disability. In our sample, 54% of the mothers had another child with a disability (including 36% with at least one additional child who had FXS and 18% with at least one child with another disability). Having multiple children with disabilities was predictive of low morning cortisol, consistent with our previous research on mothers with adolescent and adult children with ASD (Seltzer et al., 2010).

Our findings indicate that the activation ratio of mothers with the premutation is an important biological vulnerability factor that influences the extent to which mothers are affected at the neuroendocrine level by the behavior problems of their adolescent or adult child with FXS. Low morning cortisol level is the "biological signature" associated with feelings of fatigue and exhaustion among people who experience chronic stress (Cleare, 2003; Fries et al., 2005; Sonnenschein et al., 2007). Females with the *FMR1* premutation share this biological profile, along with increased prevalences of fibromyalgia and chronic pain (Coffey et al., 2008; Hagerman & Hagerman, 2002; Smith et al., 2011).

Thus, our own research as well as the findings of past studies suggest that the elevated level of health symptoms reported in premutation-carrier mothers may be attributed to both their genetic vulnerability and their exposure to the stress of daily behavior problems in their son or daughter with FXS. Future longitudinal research is needed to determine the magnitude and direction of the pathways between child behavior problems, maternal genetic vulnerability, maternal cortisol dysregulation, and health problems in premutation-carrier mothers.

CGG Repeat Length x Stressful Life Events

In an additional analysis, we examined whether another genetic marker of the premutation and other types of environmental stress have a similar interactive effect on mothers' functioning. To do so, we asked a related question as before, only rather than focusing on daily child behavior problems as the source of stress, we instead examined whether stressful life events experienced by the family during the previous year would interact with premutation-carrier mothers' genetic vulnerability to predict not only cortisol levels but also maternal depression and anxiety (Seltzer, Barker et al., 2012). Stressful life events included change in marital status, employment status, and caring for an aging parent among others. Events that occurred in the lives of the mother, her husband, and/or her children were considered. In this analysis, which included 82 of the mothers from our larger study of families of adolescents and adults with FXS, we measured genetic vulnerability by the number of CGG repeats. We built on past findings that revealed curvilinear associations between CGG repeat number and vulnerability to various aspects of the premutation phenotype, such as depression (Roberts et al., 2009) and age at menopause (Allen et al., 2007; Ennis, Ward, & Murray, 2006; Sullivan et al., 2005). One explanation for this nonlinear effect is that individuals with low repeat lengths are close to normal in the amount of the mRNA produced by the *FMR1* gene, but as the sequence of CGG repeats expands, there is an overproduction of mRNA, which has a toxic effect. However, as the expansion comes closer to the full mutation (i.e., closer to 200 repeats), the gene begins to shut down its production of mRNA, which results in less toxicity for those with the largest repeats. Thus, those with mid-size repeats have the highest mRNA toxicity and therefore the greatest vulnerability to stress.

Our findings were again consistent with a gene × environment interaction effect (Seltzer, Barker et al., 2012). Premutation-carrier mothers with mid-size repeats who experienced the greatest number of negative life events in the previous 12 months had the highest levels of depression (portrayed in Figure 11.3) and anxiety and the most blunted cortisol awakening response (defined as the difference between cortisol level upon awakening and 30 minutes later). These mothers with mid-size repeats (in this study, between 90 and 105 CGG repeats) were more vulnerable to stressful life events than mothers with either a smaller or larger number of repeats, consistent with past research.

This analysis of the association between genotype and environmental stress also revealed that there was a positive side to the gene × environment interaction among the mothers with a mid-sized number of repeats, but only when they were *not exposed to* stressful life events in the previous year. Following a year of relative stability, the mothers with mid-sized repeats had the best outcomes in the sample – the lowest levels of depression and anxiety and the most normative cortisol awakening response. This pattern of

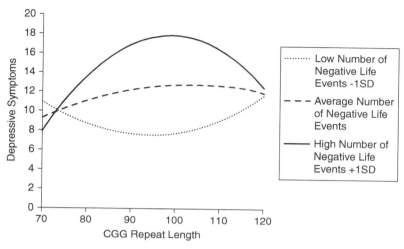

FIGURE 11.3. Curvilinear association between number of CGG repeats and depressive symptoms for premutation carrier mothers who experienced low (1 SD below the mean), average (at the mean), and high (1 SD above the mean) numbers of negative life events in the previous year.

response is consistent with the differential susceptibility hypothesis (Belsky et al., 2007; Pluess & Belsky, 2009), according to which people with certain genotypes are more likely to manifest *either* poorer or better outcomes depending on the nature of their environmental exposures. As Pluess and Belsky (2009) noted in their review, "the very same individuals who may be most adversely affected by many kinds of stressors may simultaneously reap the most benefit from environmental support and enrichment (including the absence of adversity)" (p. 886), which is exactly the pattern of results we found in the present study. More generally, these findings highlight that variations in the environment can inform genetic investigations, and this underscores the importance of examining the environment when seeking to elucidate genetic effects.

The present study has implications for counseling premutation-carrier mothers. Fully one quarter of the mothers in the present study had clinically elevated levels of depressive symptoms and more than 15% had clinically elevated levels of anxiety. As mothers become increasingly aware of their CGG repeat length, understanding the risks associated with a midsize repeat length may help them anticipate their vulnerability to stressful life events and therefore to more actively seek appropriate familial and professional support.

Summary and Agenda for Future Research

Our program of research on family adaptation to FXS brings together an interdisciplinary and multimethod approach to understanding fragile X-associated disorders in the family context. Our study's data include genetics (CGG repeat length, activation ratio), neuroendocrine measures (salivary cortisol), maternal health (daily symptoms), maternal psychological functioning (depression, anxiety, negative and positive affect), child behavioral measures (language, autism symptoms, challenging behaviors), and measures of the family context (maternal responsivity, family emotional climate, stressful events in the lives of family members). Although our studies are ongoing, new knowledge about family adaptation to FXS across the life course is already coalescing.

We have shown that the family environment, including parenting style, stabilizes early and appears to be somewhat constant across the stages of the family life course, particularly with respect to maternal warmth and responsivity. Furthermore, indicators of the family context (maternal responsivity, family emotional climate) are associated with behavioral development and functioning in sons and daughters with FXS, evident in both cross-sectional and longitudinal analyses. Thus, optimizing parenting style and supporting a nurturing family environment are important goals for family-focused services, especially for the minority of families who are struggling with a child who has co-occurring autism, more severe behavior problems, and higher levels of parental stress. For such families, psychoeducational interventions that have been shown to enhance positive family functioning in other populations could be adapted for families with FXS. Intervention studies are a necessary next step to determine whether family treatments designed to lower expressed emotion and promote positivity have a similar beneficial effect on families of children with FXS across the life course.

The family processes described in this study are bidirectional. Improved child communication both flows from responsive parenting and is likely to be associated with positive maternal outcomes because better child communication decreases frustrations and is associated with fewer behavior problems (Abbeduto & Murphy, 2004; Brady, Warren, & Sterling, 2010; Reichle & Wacker, 1993; Warren & Abbeduto, 1992). Given the health and mental health risks of mothers with the premutation, targeting early communication and behavior problems in children with FXS could alleviate some of the significant stress that parents experience. In terms of language development in young children with FXS, the impact of early language intervention coupled with parent training and support has been found to produce optimal language outcomes in children with developmental disabilities in general and would likely benefit families of children with FXS (Brady, Warren, & Sterling, 2010; Girolametto & Weitzman, 2006). This type of program would allow parents to facilitate language development while learning to diffuse problematic behaviors. Thus, interventions that improve responsive parenting are likely to have pervasive benefits for the child and family.

In addition to highlighting valuable new directions for clinical practice and services, our findings point to several areas for future research. In our sample of young children, we found that early maternal responsivity prospectively predicted language development well into middle childhood, although the presence of autism symptoms significantly constrained the benefits of positive parent–child interactions for children with FXS. Research is needed to better understand mechanisms that support developmental gains for children with FXS who have additional risk factors such as a diagnosis of autism or challenging behaviors.

Our studies also indicate that the genotype of premutation-carrier mothers interacts with environmental risk (child behavior problems, life stressors) in predicting patterns of salivary cortisol. However, we do not yet know how dysregulation of daily cortisol expression may influence long-term health outcomes in premutation-carrier mothers or how protective factors such as positive affect may moderate these associations. More work is needed in exploring the interactive effects of genotype and environmental factors in the development of cognitive, affective, and physical problems in premutation women across the life course.

To conclude, the dynamic and bidirectional influences of families and children with FXS play out in the context of the genetics of fragile X-associated disorders. As a result of a mutation in a single gene, children with the full mutation have compromised functioning, with males more seriously affected than females, on average. But such children also display strengths, gaining new language and cognitive skills as they mature and develop. Their mothers are also genetically vulnerable, but there is considerable heterogeneity in carrier women in part because of individual differences in activation ratio and CGG repeat length. Thus, the extent of genetic liability will vary considerably from family to family based on maternal genetics, child gender, and other factors discussed in this chapter. According to our data, the extent of maternal genetic vulnerability contributes to and interacts with the child's behavioral phenotype to sculpt the functioning of all family members. Further, although family patterns show continuity from one life stage to the next, there is also individual-level change accompanying maturation of all members of the family across the life course. The research summarized in this chapter emphasizes the value of the gene × environment approach and the lifespan developmental approach in elucidating the family as a context for risk and protection for children and parents, even when the children have conditions with well-defined genetic causes.

ACKNOWLEDGMENTS

This study was supported by a grant from the *Eunice Kennedy Shriver* National Institute of Child Health and Human Development to the University of North Carolina (P30 HD003100-S1) to support a Fragile X Research Center at three additional sites (Research Triangle Institute International, the University of Kansas, and the University of Wisconsin–Madison), which is led by Donald B. Bailey, Jr. The present analyses were based on data collected at the University of Kansas site (S. Warren, PI) and at the UW–Madison Waisman Center site (M. Mailick, PI). We gratefully acknowledge the contributions of our research teams (at Kansas, Kandace Fleming, PhD, and Janet Marquis, PhD; at Wisconsin, Jason Baker, PhD, Erin Barker, PhD, Sigan Hartley, PhD, and Renee Makuch). We are also extremely appreciative of the families who participated in this study, without whom our research would not have been possible. We would like to thank the National Fragile X Foundation for providing informational materials to share with families. We are also grateful for the support we received from the Kansas and Waisman Center Core Grants (P30 HD002528, J. Colombo, PI; P30 HD03352, M. Mailick, PI).

REFERENCES

Abbeduto, L., Brady, N., & Kover, S. (2007). Language development and fragile X syndrome: Profiles, syndrome-specificity, and within-syndrome differences. *Mental Retardation and Developmental Disabilities Research Reviews*, 13(1), 36–47.

Abbeduto, L., & Murphy, M. (2004). Language, social cognition, maladaptive behavior, and communication in Down syndrome and fragile X syndrome. In M. L. Rice & S. F. Warren (Eds.), *Developmental language disorders: From phenotypes to etiologies.* (pp. 77–97). Mahwah, NJ: Lawrence Erlbaum Associates.

Achenbach, T., & Rescorla, L. A. (2001). *Manual for the ASEBA School-Age Forms & Profile: An integrated system of multi-informant assessments.* Burlington: University of Vermont, Research Center for Children, Youth, & Families.

Achenbach, T. M., & Rescorla, L. A. (2003). *Manual for ASEBA Adult Forms & Profiles.* Burlington: University of Vermont, Research Center for Children, Youth, & Families.

Allen, E. G., Sullivan, A. K., Marcus, M., Small, C., Dominguez, C., Epstein, M. P., et al. (2007). Examination of reproductive aging milestones among women who carry the FMR1 premutation. *Human Reproduction*, 22(8), 2142–2152.

Almeida, D. M., Wethington, E., & Kessler, R. C. (2002). The daily inventory of stressful events: an interview-based approach for measuring daily stressors. *Assessment*, 9(1), 41–55.

Asarnow, J. R., Thompson, M., Woo, S., & Cantwell, D. P. (2001). Is expressed emotion a specific risk factor for depression or a nonspecific correlate of psychopathology? *Journal of Abnormal Child Psychology*, 29, 573–583.

Bailey, D. B., Hatton, D. D., Mesibov, G., & Skinner, M. (2000). Early development, temperament, and functional impairment in autism and fragile X syndrome. *Journal of Autism and Developmental Disorders*, 30, 49–59.

Bailey, D. B., Hatton, D. D., & Skinner, M. (1998). Early developmental trajectories of males with fragile X syndrome. *American Journal on Mental Retardation*, 103(1), 29–39.

Bailey, D. B., Hatton, D. D., Tassone, F., Skinner, M., & Taylor, A. K. (2001). Variability in FMRP and early development in males with fragile X syndrome. *American Journal on Mental Retardation*, 106, 16–27.

Bailey, Jr., D. B., Raspa, M., Olmsted, M., & Holiday, D. B. (2008). Co-occurring conditions associated with *FMR1* gene variations: Findings from a national parent survey. *American Journal of Medical Genetics*, 146a, 2060–2069.

Baker, J. K., Smith, L. E., Greenberg, J. S., Seltzer, M. M., & Taylor, J. L. (2011). Change in maternal criticism and behavior problems in adolescents and adults with autism across a 7-year period. *Journal of Abnormal Psychology*, 120, 465–475.

Belsky, J., Steinberg, L. D., Houts, R. M., Friedman, G. D., Cauffman, E., Roisman, G. I., et al. (2007). Family rearing antecedents of pubertal timing. *Child Development*, 78, 1302–1321.

Berry-Kravis, E., & Potanos, K. (2004). Psychopharmacology in fragile X syndrome – Present and future. *Mental Retardation and Developmental Disabilities Research Reviews*, 10, 42–48.

Bledin, K., Kuipers, L., MacCarthy, B., & Woods, R. (1990). Daughters of people with dementia: Expressed emotion, strain and coping. *British Journal of Psychiatry*, 157, 221–227.

Bourgeois, J. A., Coffey, S., Rivera, S. M., Hessel, D., Gane, L. W., Tassone, F., et al. (2009). Fragile X premutation disorders – expanding the psychiatric perspective. *Journal of Clinical Psychiatry*, 70, 852–862.

Brady, N., Warren, S., Fleming, K., Keller, J., & Sterling, A. (2013). The effect of sustained maternal responsivity on later vocabulary development in children with Fragile X Syndrome. *Journal of Speech Language Hearing Research*.

Brady, N., Warren, S. F., & Sterling, A. (2010). Interventions aimed at improving child language by improving maternal responsivity. In L. M. Glidden & M. M. Seltzer (Eds.), *Families: International review of research in mental retardation.* (Vol. 37, pp. 333–357). Amsterdam: Elsevier.

Brown, G. W., Birley, J. L. T., & Wing, J. K. (1972). Influence of family life on the course of schizophrenic disorders: A replication. *British Journal of Psychiatry*, 121, 241–258.

Brown, W. T. (2002). The molecular biology of the fragile X mutation. In R. J. Hagerman & P. J. Hagerman (Eds.), *Fragile X syndrome: Diagnosis, treatment, and research* (pp. 110–135). Baltimore: Johns Hopkins University Press.

Caspi, A., McClay, J., Moffitt, T. E., Mill, J., Martin, J., Craig, I. W., et al. (2002). Role of genotype in the cycle of maltreated children. *Science, 297*, 251–854.

Caspi, A., Sugden, K., Moffitt, T. E., Taylor, A., Craig, I. W., Harrington, H., et al. (2003). Influence of life stress on depression: Moderation by a polymorphism in the 5-HTT gene. *Science, 301*, 386–389.

Chonchaiya, W., Nguyen, D. V., Au, J., Campos, L., Berry-Kravis, E. M., Lohse, K., et al. (2010). Clinical involvement in daughters of men with fragile X-associated tremor ataxia syndrome. *Clinical Genetics, 78*(1), 28–46.

Cleare, A. J. (2003). The neuroendocrinology of chronic fatigue syndrome. *Endocrine Reviews, 24*(2), 236–252.

Clifford, S., Dissanayake, C., Bui, Q. M., Huggins, R., Taylor, A. K., & Loesch, D. Z. (2007). Autism spectrum phenotype in males and females with fragile X full mutation and premutation. *Journal of Autism and Developmental Disorders, 37*, 738–747.

Coffey, S. M., Cook, K., Tartaglia, N., Tassone, F., Nguyen, D. V., Pan, R., et al. (2008). Expanded clinical phenotype of women with the FMR1 premutation. *American Journal of Medical Genetics, 146a*(8), 1009–1016.

Cohen, S., & Pressman, S. D. (2006). Positive affect and health. *Current Directions in Psychological Science, 15*(3), 122–125.

Cornish, K., Turk, J., & Hagerman, R. (2008). The fragile X continuum: New advances and perspectives. *Journal of Intellectual Disability Research, 52*(6), 469–482.

Crawford, D. C., Acuna, J. M., & Sherman, S. L. (2001). FMR1 and the fragile X syndrome: Human genome epidemiology review. *Genetics in Medicine, 3*(5), 359–371.

Cummings, E. M., Davies, P. T., & Campbell, S. B. (2000). *Developmental psychopathology and family process: Theory, research, and clinical implications*. New York: Guilford Press.

Dyer-Friedman, J., Glaser, B., Hessel, D., Johnston, C., Huffman, L., Taylor A., et al. (2002). Genetic and environmental influences on the cognitive outcomes of children with fragile X syndrome. *Journal of the American Academy of Child and Adolescent Psychiatry, 41*, 237–244.

Ennis, S., Ward, D., & Murray, A. (2006). Nonlinear association between CGG repeat number and age of menopause in FMR1 premutation carriers. *European Journal of Human Genetics, 14*, 253–255.

Esbensen, A. J., Seltzer, M. M., & Abbeduto, L. (2007). Family well-being in Down syndrome and fragile X syndrome. In J. E. Roberts, R. Chapman, & S. Warren (Eds.), *Speech and language development and intervention in Down syndrome and fragile X syndrome* (pp. 275–295). Baltimore: Brookes.

Farran, D. (2001). Critical thinking and early intervention. In D. B. Bailey, J. T. Bruer, F. J. Symons, & J. W. Lichtman (Eds.), *Critical thinking about critical periods* (pp. 233–266). Baltimore: Brookes.

Feinstein, C., & Reiss, A. L. (1998). Autism: The point of view from fragile X studies. *Journal of Autism & Developmental Disorders, 28*(5), 393–405.

Fowles, D. C. (1992). Schizophrenia: Diathesis-stress revisited. *Annual Review of Psychology*, 43, 303–336.

Freund, L. S., Reiss, A. L., & Abrams, M. T. (1993). Psychiatric disorders associated with fragile X in the young female. *Pediatrics*, 91, 321–329.

Fries, E., Heese, J., Hellhammer, J., & Hellhammer, D. H. (2005). A new view on hypocortisolism. *Psychoneuroendocrinology*, 30, 1010–1016.

Girolametto, L., & Weitzman, E. (2006). It takes two to talk – the Hanen program for parents: Early language intervention through caregiver training. In R. McCauley & M. Fey (Eds.), *Treatment of language disorders in children* (pp. 77–104). Baltimore: Brookes.

Glaser, B., Hessel, D., Dyer-Friedman, J., Johnston, C., Wisbeck, J., Taylor, A., & Reiss, A. (2003). Biological and environmental contributions to adaptive behavior in fragile X syndrome. *American Journal of Medical Genetics*, 117A, 21–29.

Goldsmith, D. F., & Rogoff, B. (1995). Sensitivity and teaching by dysphoric and non-dysphoric women in structured versus unstructured situations. *Developmental Psychology*, 31, 388–394.

Greenberg, J. S., Seltzer, M. M., Baker, J. K., Smith, L. E., Hong, J., Warren, S., & Brady, N. (2012). Family environment and behavior problems in children, adolescents, and adults with fragile X syndrome. *American Journal on Intellectual and Developmental Disabilities*, 117, 331–346.

Greenberg, J. S., Seltzer, M. M., Hong, J., & Orsmond, G. I. (2006). Bidirectional effects of expressed emotion and behavior problems and symptoms in adolescents and adults with autism. *American Journal on Mental Retardation*, 111, 229–249.

Hagerman, R. J. (1999). Clinical and molecular aspects of fragile X syndrome. In H. Tager-Fluberg (Ed.), *Neurodevelopmental disorders* (pp. 27–42). Cambridge, MA: MIT Press.

Hagerman, R. J., & Hagerman, P. J. (2002). The fragile X premutation: Into the phenotypic fold. *Current Opinion in Genetics & Development*, 12(3), 278–283.

Hartley, S. L., Seltzer, M. M., Raspa, M., Olmsted, M. G., Bishop, E. E., & Bailey, D. B. (2011). Exploring the adult life of men and women with fragile X syndrome: Results from a national survey. *American Journal on Intellectual and Developmental Disabilities*, 116(1), 16–35.

Hatton, C., & Emerson, E. (2003). Families with a person with intellectual disabilities: Stress and impact. *Current Opinion in Psychiatry*, 16, 497–501.

Hauser-Cram, P., Warfield, M., Shonkoff, J., & Krauss, M. (2001). Children with disabilities: A longitudinal study of child development and parent well-being. *Monographs of the Society for Research in Child Development*, 66, 1–131.

Hessl, D., Dyer-Friedman, J., Glaser, B., Wisbeck, J., Barajas, R. G., Taylor, A., & Reiss, A. L. (2001). The influence of environmental and genetic factors on behavior problems and autistic symptoms in boys and girls with fragile X syndrome. *Pediatrics*, 108, E88.

Hessl, D., Tassone, F., Loesch, D. Z., Berry-Kravis, E., Leehey, M. A., Gane, L. W., et al. (2005). Abnormal elevation of FMR1 mRNA is associated with psychological symptoms in individuals with the fragile X premutation. *American Journal of Medical Genetics Part B (Neuropsychiatric Genetics)*, 139B, 115–121.

Hooper, S., Burchinal, M., Erwick Roberts, J., Zeisel, S., & Neebe, E. (1998). Social and family risk factors for infant development at one year: An application of the cumulative risk model. *Journal of Applied Developmental Psychology*, 19(1), 85–96.

Hunter, J. E., Abramowitz, A., Rusin, M., & Sherman, S. L. (2009). Is there evidence for neuropsychological and neurobehavioral phenotypes among adults without FXTAS who carry the FMR1 premutation? A review of current literature. *Genetics in Medicine*, 11(2), 79–89.

Hunter, J. E., Allen, E. G., Abramowitz, A., Rusin, M., Leslie, M., Novak, G., et al. (2008a). No evidence for a difference in neuropsychological profile among carriers and noncarriers of the FMR1 premutation in adults under the age of 50. *American Journal of Human Genetics*, 83(6), 692–702.

(2008b). Investigation of phenotypes associated with mood and anxiety among male and female fragile X premutation carriers. *Behavior Genetics*, 38(5), 493–502.

Kim, E. Y., & Miklowitz, D. J. (2004). Expressed emotion as a predictor of outcome among bipolar patients undergoing family therapy. *Journal of Affective Disorders*, 82, 343–352.

Lachiewicz, A., Dawson, D., Spiridigliozii, M., Cuccaro, M., Lachiewicz, M., & McConkie-Rosell, A. (2010). Indicators of anxiety and depression in women with the fragile X premutation: Assessment of a clinical sample. *Journal of Intellectual Disability Research*, 54(7), 597–610.

Landry, S. H., Smith, K. E., Miller-Loncar, C. L., & Swank, P. R. (1998). The relation of change in maternal interactive styles to the developing social competence of full-term and preterm children. *Child Development*, 69, 105–123.

Landry, S. H., Smith, K. E., Swank, P. R., Assel, M. A., & Vellet, S. (2001). Does early responsive parenting have a special importance for children's development or is consistency across early childhood necessary? *Developmental Psychology*, 37, 387–403.

Maenner, M., Baker, M. W., Broman, K., Tian, J., Barnes, J., et al. (2013). FMR1 CGG expansions: Prevalence and sex ratios. *American Journal of Medical Genetics, Part B: Neoropsychiatric Genetics*, 162B, 466–473.

Magaña, A. B., Goldstein, M. J., Karno, M., Miklowitz, D. J., Jenkins, J., & Falloon, I. R. H. (1986). A brief method for assessing expressed emotion in relatives of psychiatric patients. *Psychiatry Research*, 17, 203–212.

Mahoney, G., & Neville-Smith, A. (1996). The effects of directive communication on children's interactive engagement: Implications for language interventions. *Topics in Early Childhood Special Education*, 16, 236–250.

Marfo, K. (1992). Correlates of maternal directiveness with children who are developmentally delayed. *American Journal of Orthopsychiatry*, 62, 219–233.

Mazzocco, M. M. M. (2000). Advances in research on the fragile X syndrome. *Mental Retardation and Developmental Disabilities Research Reviews*, 6, 96–106.

McEwen, B. S. (1998). Protective and damaging effects of stress mediators. *New England Journal of Medicine*, 338, 171–179.

McKeever, V. M., & Huff, M. E. (2003). A diathesis-stress model of posttraumatic stress disorder: Ecological, biological, and residual stress pathways. *Review of General Psychology*, 7, 237–250.

Miller, C. L., Heysek, P. J., Whitman, T. L., & Borkowski, J. G. (1996). Cognitive readiness to parent and intellectual emotional development in children of adolescent mothers. *Developmental Psychology, 32,* 533–541.

Mitchell, D. B., & Hauser-Cram, P. (2009). Early predictors of behavior problems: Two years after early intervention. *Journal of Early Intervention, 32,* 3–16.

Monroe, S. M., & Simons, A. D. (1991). Diathesis-stress theories in the context of life-stress research: Implications for the depressive disorders. *Psychological Bulletin, 110,* 406–425.

Mullen, E. (1995). *Mullen scales of early learning.* Circle Pines, MN: American Guidance Services.

Murphy, M. M., & Abbeduto, L. (2005). Indirect genetic effects and the early language development of children with genetic mental retardation syndromes: The role of joint attention. *Infants and Young Children, 18,* 47–59.

Nolin, S. L., Lewis, F. A. III, Ye, L. L., Houck, G. E., Glicksman, A. E., Limprasert, P., et al. (1996). Familial transmission of the FMR1 CGG repeat. *American Journal of Human Genetics, 59*(6), 1252–1261.

Osofsky, J. D., & Thompson, M. D. (2000). Adaptive and maladaptive parenting: Perspectives on risk and protective factors. In J. P. Shonkoff & S. J. Meisels (Eds.), *Handbook of early childhood intervention* (pp. 54–75). Cambridge: Cambridge University Press.

Pluess, M., & Belsky, J. (2009). Differential susceptibility to rearing experience: The case of childcare. *Journal of Child Psychology & Psychiatry, 50,* 396.

Reichle, J., & Wacker, D. P. (Eds.). (1993). *Communicative alternatives to challenging behavior: Integrating functional assessment and intervention strategies* (Vol. 3). Baltimore: Brookes.

Roberts, J. E., Bailey, D. B. Jr., Mankowski, J., Ford, A., Sideris, J., Weisenfeld, L. A., et al. (2009). Mood and anxiety disorders in females with the FMR1 premutation. *American Journal of Medical Genetics, 150B*(1), 130–139.

Rodriguez-Revenga, L., Madrigal, I., Pagonabarraga, J., Xuncla, M., Badenas, C., Kulisevsky, J., et al. (2009). Penetrance of FMR1 premutation associated pathologies in fragile X syndrome families. *European Journal of Human Genetics, 17,* 1359–1362.

Rogers, S. J., Wehner, E. A., & Hagerman, R. (2001). The behavioral phenotype in fragile X: Symptoms of autism in very young children with fragile X syndrome, idiopathic autism, and other developmental disorders. *Journal of Developmental and Behavioral Pediatrics, 22,* 409–417.

Rutter, M., Dunn, J., Plomin, R., Simonoff, E., Pickles, A., Maughan, B., et al. (1997). Integrating nature and nurture: Implications of person-environment correlations and interactions for developmental psychopathology. *Development and Psychopathology, 9,* 335–264.

Rutter, M., & Quinton, D. (1984). Parental psychiatric disorder: Effects on children. *Psychological Medicine, 14,* 853–880.

Schopler, E., Reichler, R. J., & Renner, B. R. (1988). *The childhood autism rating scale (CARS).* Los Angeles: Western Psychological Services.

Seltzer, M. M., Abbeduto, L., Greenberg, J. S., Almeida, D., Hong, J., & Witt, W. (2009). Biomarkers in the study of families of children with developmental disabilities (pp. 213–250). In L. M. Glidden & M. M. Seltzer (Eds.), *Families:*

International review of research on mental retardation (pp. 37). New York: Academic Press.

Seltzer, M. M., Almeida, D. M., Greenberg, J. S., Savla, J., Stawski, R. S., Hong, J., & Taylor, J. L. (2009). Psychological and biological markers of daily lives of midlife parents of children with disabilities. *Journal of Health and Social Behavior*, 50, 1–15.

Seltzer, M. M., Barker, E. T., Greenberg, J. S., Hong, J., Coe, C., & Almeida, D. (2012). Differential sensitivity to life stress in FMR1 premutation carrier mothers of children with fragile X syndrome. *Health Psychology, Advance online publication.*

Seltzer, M. M., Baker, M. W., Hong, J., Maenner, M., Greenberg, J., Mandel, D. (2012). Prevalence of CGG expansions of the FMR1 gene in a US population-based sample. *American Journal of Medical Genetics, Part B.*

Seltzer, M. M., Greenberg, J. S., Hong, J., Smith, L. E., Almeida, D. M., Coe, C., & Stawski, R. S. (2010). Maternal cortisol levels and child behavior problems in families of adolescents and adults with ASD. *Journal of Autism and Developmental Disorders*, 40, 457–469.

Smith, L. E., Barker, E. T., Seltzer, M. M., Abbeduto, L., & Greenberg, J. S. (2012). Behavioral phenotype of fragile X syndrome in adolescence and adulthood. *American Journal on Intellectual and Developmental Disabilities*, 117, 1–17.

Smith, L. E., Seltzer, M. M., & Greenberg, J. S. (2011). Daily health symptoms of mothers and adolescents and adults with fragile X syndrome and mothers of adolescents and adults with autism spectrum disorder. *Journal on Autism and Developmental Disorders*, 42, 1836–1846.

Sobesky, W. E., Hull, C. E., & Hagerman, R. J. (1994). Symptoms of schizotypal personality disorder in fragile X women. *Journal of the American Academy of Child and Adolescent Psychiatry*, 33, 247–255.

Song, F. J., Barton, P., Sleightholme, V., Yao, G. L., & Fry-Smith, A. (2003). Screening for fragile X syndrome: A literature review and modeling study. *Health Technology Assessment*, 7(16), 1–118.

Sonnenschein, M., Mommersteeg, P. M., Houtveen, J. H., Sorbi, M. J., Schaufeli, W. B., & van Doornen, L. J. (2007). Exhaustion and endocrine functioning in clinical burnout: An in-depth study using the experience sampling method. *Biological Psychology*, 75(2), 175–184.

Sterling, A. M., Barnum, L., Skinners, D., Warren, S. F., Brady, N., & Fleming, K., (2012). Parenting young children with and without fragile X syndrome. *American Journal of Intellectual and Developmental Disabilities*, 117, 194–206.

Sterling, A. M., & Warren, S. F. (2008). Communication and language development in infants and toddlers with Down syndrome and fragile X syndrome. In J. Roberts, C. Chapman, & S. Warren (Eds.), *Speech and language development and intervention in Down syndrome and fragile X syndrome* (pp. 53–76). Baltimore, MD: Brookes.

Sterling, A. M., Warren, S. F., Brady, N., & Fleming, K. (2013). Influences on maternal responsivity in mothers of children with fragile X syndrome. *American Journal of Intellectual and Developmental Disabilities*, 118, 310–326.

Stormont, M. (2001). Preschool family and child characteristics associated with stable behavior problems in children. *Journal of Early Intervention*, 24(4), 241–251.

Sullivan, A. K., Marcus, M., Epstein, M. P., Allen, E. G., Anido, A. E., Paquin, J. J., et al. (2005). Association of FMR1 repeat size with ovarian dysfunction. *Human Reproduction*, 20, 402–412.

Tassone, F., Hagerman, R. J., Chamberlain, W. D., & Hagerman, P. J. (2000). Transcription of the FMR1 gene in individuals with fragile X syndrome. *American Journal of Medical Genetics*, 97, 195–203.

Tassone, F., Iong, K. P., Tong, T.-H., Lo, J., Gane, L. W., et al. (2012). *FMR1* CGG allele size and prevalence ascertained through newborn screening in the United States. *Genome Medicine*, 4, 100.

Thompson, N. M., Rogeness, G. A., McClure, E., Clayton, R., & Johnson, C. (1996). Influence of depression on cognitive functioning in fragile X females. *Psychiatry Research*, 64, 97–104.

Vitaliano, P. P., Young, H. M., Russo, J., Romano, J., & Magana-Amato, A. (1993). Does expressed emotion in spouses predict subsequent problems among care recipients with Alzheimer's disease? *Journals of Gerontology*, 48, 202–209.

Wamboldt, F. S., O'Connor, S. L., Wamboldt, M. Z., Gavin, L. A., & Klinnert, M. D. (2000). The five minute speech sample in children with asthma: Deconstructing the construct of expressed emotion. *Journal of Child Psychology and Psychiatry*, 41, 887–898.

Warren, S. F., & Abbeduto, L. (1992). Relation of communication and language development to mental retardation. *American Journal on Mental Retardation*, 97, 125–130.

Warren, S. F., & Brady, N. C. (2007). The role of maternal responsivity in the development of children with intellectual disabilities. *Mental Retardation and Developmental Disabilities Research Reviews*, 13, 330–338.

Warren, S. F., Brady, N., Sterling, A., Fleming, K., & Marquis, J. (2010). Maternal responsivity predicts language development in young children with fragile X syndrome. *American Journal on Intellectual and Developmental Disabilities*, 115, 54–75.

Wearden, A. J., Tarrier, N., Barrowclough, C., Zastowny, T. R., & Rahill, A. A. (2000). A review of expressed emotion in health care. *Clinical Psychology Review*, 20, 633–666.

Xu, J., & Roberts, R. E. (2010). The power of positive emotions: It's a matter of life or death – Subjective well-being and longevity over 28 years in a general population. *Health Psychology*, 29(1), 9–19.

12

Developmental Approaches to Understanding and Treating Autism

TONY CHARMAN

The history of autism research has had an uneasy relationship with the exploration of cultural, familial, and contextual factors that might influence the development of individuals with autism. In part, this stems from the influential but now discredited notion promulgated in the 1960s that autism was primarily a psychogenic response to frigid parenting (Bettleheim, 1967). Following the discovery that autism was a strongly genetic condition with a biological basis largely operating on the developing brain (Folstein & Rutter, 1977), the study of the environmental influences on autism fell by the wayside for several decades. More recently, a fuller understanding of the role that epigenetic and gene–environment influences play in neurodevelopmental disorders (Rutter, 2011) and an appreciation that even for predominantly biological conditions the environment plays a significant influence in development and outcome have led the field to reconsider the role of environmental influences (see Herbert, 2010, for a review). Accordingly, in this review of recent advances in our understanding of how autism emerges from infancy to the common diagnostic age of 3 to 4 years and how developmentally focused interventions may ameliorate this developmental course, I will consider several transactional aspects in which the immediate family and interpersonal context is important both for understanding how autism emerges over development and how it can exert an influence on development and outcome, including in direct ways through parent- or therapist-delivered intervention.

AUTISM EMERGES EARLY; RESEARCH WITH INFANTS AND TODDLERS ARRIVES LATE

Over the past decade, there has been remarkable progress in our understanding of the early development of children with autism. Until the 1990s, children rarely received a diagnosis of autism until 3 or 4 years of age, and in many cases considerably later (Howlin & Asgharian, 1999). Consequently, much of the historical literature on autism starts with descriptions of children aged 4 to 5 years or older. This is despite the fact that in most cases, autism has an onset in infancy (Kanner, 1943) and is the result of genetic and other organic etiological factors that affect very early brain development (Levy, Mandell, & Schultz, 2009). While both psychiatric classification systems necessitate that, at least to meet criteria for the "core" disorder of childhood autism (ICD-10; WHO, 1993) or autistic disorder (DSM-IV-TR; APA, 2000), symptoms of autism are required to be present in the first 3 years of life; until the 1990s, few studies had been conducted with samples under the age of 3 years.

During the past decade, progress has been made in the earlier identification of children with an autism spectrum disorder (ASD), and many children are now first identified in the preschool period (Charman & Baird, 2002; Mandell, Novak, & Zubritsky, 2005; Manning et al., 2011). This improvement in earlier recognition has been informed and in part driven by findings from a number of strands of research that have afforded us, for the first time, a picture of the emergence of autism – a new science of "autism in infancy" (Charman, 2010). The growth in our knowledge base regarding the presentation of autism in the early years over the past decade is demonstrated by a simple experiment. In November 2012, entering the search terms "autism" and "toddlers" into PubMed identified 236 articles: 221 of these were published *after* 2000, 205 of which were dated from 2010 onward.

Motivating these efforts to improve earlier identification is the recognition that earlier-delivered intervention may improve outcomes and prevent "secondary" neurodevelopmental disturbances (Dawson, 2008; Mundy, Sullivan, & Mastergeorge, 2009). The strands of research include studying home movies of infants who later go on to receive a diagnosis of autism (Yirmiya & Charman, 2010); the development of prospective screening instruments to identify possible cases of autism from the first few years of life (Zwaigenbaum, 2010); and the use of the genetic "high-risk" research design of prospectively studying younger siblings of children with a diagnosis of autism from the first year of life (Rogers, 2009; Yirmiya & Charman, 2010). This decade of work has uncovered important evidence regarding the developmental trajectory of autism spectrum disorder from infancy and toddlerhood, through the preschool years, into school age, and beyond.

One notable challenge emerging from this work is the substantial variability in early development trajectory in children with autism and our difficulty in disentangling the extent to which these variable trajectories for individual children are due to intrinsic versus extrinsic factors. The challenge for the next decade is to improve the evidence base for social communication and behavioral interventions that may lessen the impact of the disorder and improve outcomes for children and their families. In this latter respect, after decades in which autism researchers shied away from conducting theoretically based intervention trials, the field is at last beginning to wake up. In the last few years, a number of randomized controlled trials that build on our theoretical and empirical understanding of *development* in autism have been undertaken, promising to reveal the *mechanisms* by which autism symptoms emerge and might possibly be ameliorated (Charman, 2011). Practitioners and research have been debating issues about early intervention for young children with autism over several decades. To cut a long story short, there has been an ongoing (and not always civilized or fair-minded) debate over several decades about the effectiveness or otherwise of one particular approach – "applied behavioral analysis" (ABA), sometimes now called "early intensive behavioral intervention" (EIBI). There is not space to review this sorry saga here, but the green shoots of a rapprochement might be visible. What is clear is that both sides were debating a handful of small, mostly poor-quality studies and almost no randomized controlled trails (RCTs; Ospina et al., 2008). This contrasts with many other areas of child psychiatry and psychology in which the trial literature of psychological interventions is considerably more secure. These are not mere esoteric considerations since parents ask clinicians to be referred to treatments that "work," and service commissioners and insurance companies ask the same question, too.

In the current chapter, I will review the evidence from the strands of research on emerging autism (home movies, screening studies, high-risk sibling studies); discuss how understanding continuities and discontinuities in developmental trajectories in autism helps us understand more about the underlying processes that affect development; and then summarize the recent "new wave" of intervention trials that target social communication outcomes. Such trials are beginning to further illuminate the developmental processes that underlie autism as well as bring optimism to the clinical field in terms of an improved evidence base for early intervention.

AUTISM IN INFANCY FROM HOME MOVIES

Two decades ago, researchers began to report on infant social communication and other behaviors (e.g., motor behaviors) by analyzing early home movies taken before the child went on to receive a diagnosis of autism

TABLE 12.1 *Early signs of autism in infancy from home movie studies*

Time period	Behavior	Studies
~6 months	Dyadic and intersubjective behaviors Less attention to social stimuli Reduced affect	Maestro et al. (2002, 2005) Clifford & Dissanayake (2008)
~12 months +	Reduced response to name Less joint attention Abnormal eye contact Reduced looking at people Motor abnormalities	Adrien, Lenoir et al. (1993) Adrien, Perrot et al. (1991) Osterling & Dawson (1994); Werner & Dawson (2005) Baranek (1999) Ozonoff et al. (2008)

(e.g., Adrien et al., 1991; Lösche, 1990). Many groups have now used this method, and the data suggest that home videos of infants who later on develop autism reveal that these infants already manifest difficulties and impairments in communication, social relationships, and sensory motor development (see Table 12.1). In the very earliest time period studied (the first 6 months of life), dyadic and intersubjective abnormalities have been detected, as well as reduced amounts of time paid to social stimuli. By the end of the first year of life, a wide range of triadic early social-communicative differences are apparent (at least at a group level), including reduced orienting to name, impoverished joint attention behaviors, some early motor abnormalities, and reduced emotional expression (see Table 12.1 and also Yirmiya & Charman, 2010, for a more detailed review). These early symptoms were usually most clearly identified during the second year of life, although some researchers identified abnormalities around the child's first birthday. This methodology has some advantages in that naturally occurring behavior prior to diagnosis is evaluated. However, home movies also suffer from limitations, as the data are not standardized and parents may chose to videotape their children when the children are at their best, for example, not necessarily while manifesting some of the behaviors that may be early signs of autism.

SCREENING STUDIES

In the early 1990s, Baron-Cohen and colleagues developed the CHAT (Checklist for Autism in Toddlers) that is used to assess simple joint attention and pretend play behaviors by parental report and health practitioner observation through direct testing (Baron-Cohen, Allen, & Gillberg, 1992,

1996). In an initial study (in fact the first prospective high-risk study of younger siblings – discussed later), the CHAT showed promise as a screening instrument by identifying in a sample of 41 18-month-old siblings of children already diagnosed with autism the 4 children in the at-risk group who were subsequently diagnosed with autism (Baron-Cohen et al., 1992). Baird et al. (2000) went on to test the effectiveness of the CHAT in a population of 16,235 18-month-olds as part of routine health surveillance. Using a two-stage (screen/rescreen) procedure, the positive predictive value of the screening instrument was high (83% for all autism spectrum disorders for those who failed all five key items). However, sensitivity was poor (18%); although if a one-stage screening procedure only had been adopted, the sensitivity increased to 38%. The study demonstrated that failing a combination of joint attention and pretend play items (by both parental report and health practitioner observation and on both administrations of the screen) at 18 months indicated a significant risk for developing ASD. However, although the CHAT screen had a high positive predictive value, its sensitivity was low, and the findings cannot support a recommendation for total population screening at a single time point (Baird et al., 2000).

In the second large general-population screening study, Buitelaar and colleagues in the Netherlands developed a screening instrument (ESAT: Early Screening of Autistic Traits) to identify ASD (Swinkels et al., 2006). Dietz et al. (2006) completed screening of 31,724 children at 14 months of age. Health practitioners at a community pediatric clinic appointment administered an initial screen of four items (measuring varied play with toys, readability of emotional expression, and sensory abnormalities). If a child failed one or more of the four items, they were offered a follow-up home visit during which a longer version of the ESAT (14 items that included many social communication items such as eye contact, response to name, etc.) was administered. The ESAT correctly identified children with ASD, but it also identified children with language disorder and intellectual disability. The items that discriminated best between children with and without autism were items used to assess early social communication impairments, including "shows interest in people," "smiles directly," and "reacts when spoken to." According to this study, some aspects of the beginnings of play, emotional responsiveness, sensory behaviors, and social engagement might be present in at least some children at 14 months of age. However, at this earlier age as compared to the CHAT study (14 vs. 18 months), these early signs appear to be less specific to autism, as almost as many children who went on have other developmental disorders were identified.

A number of other research groups have also developed and begun to test screens for autism spectrum disorders. For example, Robins et al. (2001) developed the M-CHAT, a modified version of the CHAT, which is a parent report instrument that involves no direct testing by the health practitioner, that included additional items to measure other aspects of early social communication impairments that are characteristic of autism (e.g., response to name, imitation) as well as repetitive behaviors (e.g., unusual fingers mannerisms) and sensory abnormalities (e.g., oversensitivity to noise). In their initial report, Robins et al. (2001) tested 1,122 unselected children (initially at 18 months but subsequently at 24 months of age) and 171 children referred for early intervention services (considered to be at high risk of having an ASD or other developmental disability). They found that the items that best discriminated between children with ASD and children with other developmental problems were those that measured joint attention behaviors (pointing and following a point, bringing things to show), social relatedness (interest in other children, imitation), and communication (response to name). Other screens have been developed from a broader developmental framework whereby they focus on identifying not only young children with autism but also other children with language and developmental delays. Wetherby and colleagues (Wetherby, Brosnan-Maddox, Peace, & Newton, 2008; Wetherby et al., 2004) developed the Infant Toddler Checklist (ITC), an early screening tool that can be used from 6 to 24 months of age. The ITC items include early emotional responsiveness, gestures, early babble and understanding words, response to name, and social orienting. The ITC is a broader developmental screen that successfully identifies children with developmental delay as well as children with an ASD. In their most recent work, Wetherby et al. (2008) showed that the prospective identification of children who will go on to have a diagnosis of an ASD is possible toward the end of the first year of life.

Overall, these prospective screening studies (summarized in Table 12.2) indicate the possibility of prospectively identifying ASD, including children about whom parents and professionals did not have pre-existing concerns, from the age of 18 and even 14 months. The most common early signs captured by the screen are impairments or delays in early emerging social communication behaviors such as response to name, joint attention, and play behaviors, although sensory abnormalities or a restricted repertoire of play activities might also be early indicators of later ASD. However, the signs are not universal (that is, not present in all cases) in any of the studies that have employed systematic follow-up of the screened populations to identify all cases at outcome.

TABLE 12.2 *Early signs of autism in infancy from prospective screening studies*

Reference	Instrument	Age	Key items identifying autism
Baird et al. (2000)	CHAT	18 months	Joint attention; pretend play
Dietz et al. (2006)	ESAT	14 months	Initial screen: play, emotional expressions, sensory oddities Follow-up screen: above plus early social communication behaviors
Robins et al. (2001); Kleinman et al. (2008); Robins (2008)	M-CHAT	16–30 months	Most discriminating items: joint attention behaviors and social relatedness
Wetherby, Woods et al. (2004) Wetherby, Brosnan-Maddox et al. (2008)	ITC	6–24 months	Early social communication behaviors; emotional response

CHAT (Checklist for Autism in Toddlers); ESAT (Early Screening of Autistic Traits); M-CHAT (Modified Checklist for Autism in Toddlers); ITC (Infant Toddler Checklist)

High-Risk Sibling Studies

Over the past decade, a number of research groups worldwide have initiated truly prospective observational studies by exploiting the relatively high recurrence rate of autism in families (e.g., Constantino, Zhang, Frazier, Abbacchi, & Law, 2010; Ozonoff et al., 2011). This allows the possibility to recruit a cohort of younger siblings of an older child with an autism diagnosis and to follow their development over time, with the likelihood that a proportion of the cohort will go on to develop autism. This is by nature a long-term undertaking since reliable diagnosis cannot be established much before the age of 3 years. However, the design also allows one to test differences between the "high-risk" sibling group and low-risk comparison children with no family history of autism, which some groups have called a "broader autism phenotype (BAP) analysis." These researchers have found a number of differences, most of which are in the area early social communication behaviors and emerge around the younger siblings' first birthday. In addition to behavioral studies, several groups have also begun to use experimental brain imaging measures, such as evoked response potentials (ERPs), to test if there may be disrupted neural processing of both social and nonsocial stimuli in high-risk siblings (Elsabbagh et al., 2009; McCleery, Allman, Carver, & Dobkins, 2007). There is some evidence from these studies that differences in brain responses to social stimuli (e.g., eye gaze) might differentiate high-risk from low-risk groups during the first year of life (Elsabbagh et al., 2009; McCleery et al., 2007). One recent study found that ERP responses to dynamic eye gaze stimuli at 6 to 10 months of age were diminished in the infants in the high-risk group who went on to have autism at age 3 years (Elsabbagh et al., 2012). Behavioral measures taken during the same stimulus presentation (looking behavior measured using eye tracking) did not differentiate the groups.

In the past few years, several groups have incorporated the study of parent–child interactions into these at-risk sibling designs, with some surprising findings. Several studies have identified subtle disruptions in interaction in infants at risk of ASD and in infants who are subsequently diagnosed. Yirmiya et al. (2006) showed that at 4 months, infant–parent dyads showed less affectively synchronous interactions within infant-led play. Moreover, a retrospective study of parents' home videos revealed that, compared with groups who were typically developing or had intellectual disabilities, infants who went on to develop ASD showed lower orientation to the parent at 6 to 10 months (and a smaller increase thereafter) during interaction. Their parents stimulated them for longer (but were more withdrawn after the first year) and more often used touch to elicit attention (Saint-Georges et al., 2011). However, from studying 1-minute clips of mother–infant interaction, Rozga et al.'s (2011) prospective study found no 6-month differences in the amount of specific infant social and communicative behaviors observed in infants who went on to develop ASD (*n* = 8) from those who did not. Wan et al. (2012) found that at 6 to 10 months, at-risk siblings had interactions characterized by less infant liveliness and more directive and less sensitive parental behaviors compared to low-risk controls.

To date, four groups have reported on associations among early development during the first year or two of life and later diagnoses of ASDs (see Table 12.3 for a summary of findings). Zwaigenbaum et al. (2005) examined the development of high-risk and low-risk infants from 6 to 24 months and identified several behavioral markers at 12 months that predicted later diagnoses of ASD, including atypical eye contact, visual tracking, disengagement of visual attention, orienting to name, imitation, social smiling, reactivity, social interest, and sensory-oriented behaviors. From the same group, Mitchell et al. (2006) added that siblings diagnosed with ASD at 24 months in this sample had delays in gestural communication (i.e., giving, pointing, gestures) as reported by their parents at 12 months.

Landa and Garrett-Mayer (2006) found that on the Mullen Scales of Early Learning (MSEL; Mullen, 1995), the group with the ASD outcome

TABLE 12.3 *Early signs of autism in infancy from high-risk sibling studies*

Reference	N (SIBS-A)	Age (Months)	Comparison group	Findings
Zwaigenbaum et al. (2005)	65	6–24 m	TD $n = 23$	Temperament characteristics (decreased activity) at 6m and behavioral markers (orienting to name, social smiling) and language delays at 12m predicted later ASD at 24m
Mitchell et al. (2006)	97	12–24 m	TD $n = 49$	Siblings with ASD at 24m had more delays in gestural communication (giving, pointing, and nodding head) at 12m
Bryson et al. (2007)	9	6–36 m		Siblings with ASD at 36m showed early impaired social-communicative development (lack of interest in others), behavioral markers (visual fixation, repetitive behaviors), distinct temperament profile (intolerance of intrusions, dysregulated state) associated with the emergence of autism. Signs of autism emerged earlier (12m) in siblings with a decrease in IQ.
Loh et al. (2007)	17	6–36 m	TD $n = 15$	"Hands to ears" posture at 18m was more frequent in the high-risk group compared to the controls. Siblings with a later ASD diagnoses "arm waved" more frequently at 12m and 18m. The ASD and control groups had considerable overlap in their repertoires of stereotyped behaviors
Landa & Garrett-Mayer (2006)	60	6–24 m	TD $n = 27$	At 6m, no significant differences emerged among the three groups (ASD, LD, unaffected diagnosed at 24m) on the MSEL. At 14m, the ASD group performed significantly more poorly than the unaffected group on most of the MSEL scales. By 24m, the ASD group performed significantly more poorly than the unaffected group on all the MSEL scales and significantly more poorly than the LD group on the Gross and Fine Motor and Receptive Language scales. ASD group had the slowest developmental trajectory, with a significant decrease in development between 14m and 24m.

Study	n	Age	Group	Findings
Landa, Holman, & Garrett-Mayer (2007)	98	14–36m	TD n = 17	The ASD early diagnosis subgroup differed at ages of 14m and 24m from all other groups (ASD with late diagnosis, BAP, and non–BAP) in their communication and play behavior.
Nadig et al. (2007)	46	6–24m	TD n = 25	At 6m, no significant differences emerged between siblings and controls in orienting to name. However, at 12m, 75% of the siblings who failed to respond to their name being called were identified at age 24m with ASD or with other developmental delays.
Merin et al. (2007)	31	6m	TD n = 24	10 of the 11 infants with diminished gaze to the mother's eyes relative to her mouth during the Still Face were SIBS-A. No significant differences emerged between the two groups in affective displays (i.e., smiling, negative affect), in the total amount of fixation time, or in the fixation directed at the face versus other areas.
Young, Merin, Rogers, & Ozonoff (2009)	33	6–24m	TD n = 25	All three siblings with ASD at 24m (2 SIBS-A, 1 SIBS-TD) demonstrated consistent eye contact and typical affective responses at 6m during the Still Face. No associations were found between face scanning and affective responses at 6m and the continuous measures of autism symptom frequency or symptom severity at 24m.
Ozonoff et al. (2008)	35	12–36m	TD n = 31	Siblings with later ASD had increased frequency of spinning, rolling, and rotating the objects and prolonged visual inspection at 12m. Repetitive behaviors at 12m were significantly related to cognitive and symptomatic status at the 36m outcome.
Yoder et al. (2009)	43	15–34m	TD n = 24	Triadic communication (use of gestural, vocal, gaze, and/or symbolic communication that shows attention to the message recipient and the physical referent of communication), responding to joint attention, and initial language age equivalence were associated with later ASD diagnosis.

LD = language delay; TD = typically developing children; MSEL = Mullen Scales of Early Learning (Mullen, 1995); SIBS-A = siblings of children with autism; SIBS-TD = siblings of children with typical development; m = months had the slowest developmental trajectory, with a significant decrease in development between 14 and 24 months. In the same sample, Landa, Holman, and Garrett-Mayer (2007) found that siblings who received an early ASD diagnosis (at 14 months) showed diminished communication and play behavior at age 14 months, but that in those who only received a diagnosis at the later 24-month assessment, some skills continued to grow but at a slow rate between the two time points, others plateaued, while others (shared positive affect and gestures) decreased.

Ozonoff et al. (2010) were the first to report on a sample as large as 25 siblings who went on to receive an ASD diagnosis at 36 months. They compared rates of three early social communication behaviors (gaze to faces, social smiles, and directed vocalizations) captured by observers during assessment sessions when the siblings were 6, 12, 18, 24, and 36 months of age and found a *slowing* of development in terms of raw scores on the general developmental assessment (MSEL) as the high-risk siblings began to fall behind the low-risk controls. In contrast, there was an actual *decline* in the rates of the early social communication behaviors – that is, an actual reduction in frequency of social responses. This loss began around the first birthday and continued across the second year of life and, on some measures, into the third year. This pattern of loss of skills was found in over three quarters of the high-risk group. However, at age 6 months, there were no differences between the groups, indicating that the high-risk siblings who went on to meet diagnostic criteria for ASD at 36 months of age showed the same rates of early social communication behaviors as comparison children. The second notable and perhaps most surprising finding was that when interviewed their child was 36 months of age, loss of skills was reported for only a minority of those children whose social communication skills declined over the second year of life (at least when interacting in an unfamiliar setting, with an unfamiliar adult in the observations taken in the lab). This is surprising, in part, because families taking part in these "high-risk" sibling studies understand the familial nature of the design and we might expect worried parents to be hypervigilant for early signs that something is not right with their younger child.

Regression is a highly unusual and notable developmental feature in autism. We know that regression or loss of skills is present by (retrospective) parental report in some 15% to 30% of cases, depending on the definition employed and the sample (Baird et al., 2008). Ozonoff et al. (2010) suggest that regression might be the norm and not the exception in autism. Pickles et al. (2009) forwarded a similar suggestion based on retrospective parental report as they found both that regression was very specific to autism, as it was almost never found in children with language impairment without autism, and also a strong association between age of first words and likelihood of undergoing regression. Thus, frank loss of language skills was associated with switching from the most advanced early language to being amongst the slowest (in terms of eventual onset of phrase speech). We do not know what the nature and causes are of the neurodevelopmental processes that underlie regression, but this evidence of such high risk from prospective studies offers an opportunity to investigate these questions.

Another report illustrates one of the surprising findings that have emerged from the high-risk studies. In an initial study, Young, Merin, Rogers, and Ozonoff (2009) conducted the classic "still face" paradigm with 6-month-old high-risk infants. Using a combination of behavioral and eye-tracking measures, they identified variation in behaviors such as gaze aversion, negative affect, and smiling as well as an eye-mouth index from a region-of-interest analysis of the eye-tracking data. However, response to the still face was not associated with preliminary ASD outcome at 24 months of age – the infants in their sample who went on to have ASD showed the usual "distress" response to the change in their caregiver's dyadic interactive behavior. When these high-risk studies were set up, many might have predicted that disruptions in such infant–caregiver dyadic interactive communication would index those high-risk infants who will go on to show an autism presentation, but broadly, this has not yet been the case. The search for reliable early markers continues in the more than 20 sites worldwide at which such studies are conducted.

These high-risk sibling studies corroborate findings from the home movies and screening studies as showing that various behavioral indices of attention, perception, communication, temperament, social behavior, and sensory-motor development characterize children who later on develop ASD. However, perhaps against initial expectations, no clear behavioral markers have emerged as early at 6 months of age, with most evidence of predictors of an ASD outcome being identified around 12 months, including the pattern of loss of skills reported by Ozonoff et al. (2010) and Landa and Garrett-Mayer (2006). The emergence of the presentation of ASD might not be the same for each child or for each child at familial risk for ASD. No one developmental trajectory of autism emergence has been identified. Elsabbagh and Johnson (2010) outline the possible "early," "late," and "canalization" (where initial indicators of atypicality or an expression of risk emerges early on but is followed by a "recovery" so that the child does not go on to have an ASD at outcome) trajectories that might be identified in these multiple-timepoint longitudinal studies. To date, most of the researchers of high-risk siblings have examined the extent to which isolated behavioral abnormalities map onto an ASD "outcome." In future work, groups will likely begin to examine whether the following might be better predictors of developing an ASD: (i) *combinations* of abnormalities – for example, those at-risk siblings showing impairments on both social (eye gaze, orienting to name) and nonsocial (motor, attentional control) measures; (ii) *cumulative* markers over time; or (iii) *multimethod* combinations of behavioral and neural markers. The field has moved on from focusing on identifying *the* risk marker and is beginning to develop and test models of *cumulative* risk (Yirmiya & Charman, 2010).

Variability and Understanding Individual Trajectories in Development

One feature that has emerged from longitudinal studies of children with autism first identified as infants and toddlers is that the developmental trajectory of symptoms measured with a continuous or dimensional (as opposed to a categorical) metric changes over time. For example, Charman et al. (2005) described how the trajectories of the social, communication, and repetitive domain scores on the Autism Diagnostic Interview – Revised (ADI-R; Lord et al., 1994) had different developmental trajectories over time. This developmental pattern is consistent with the notion that the various aspects that make up the autism phenotype might not be tied together as closely as suggested by the current classification systems, as suggested by the notion of the "fractionation" of the autism phenotype described by Happé, Ronald, and Plomin (2006).

As is true of individuals with typical and other atypical forms of development, within cohorts of individuals with ASD, *individual variability* has been found to be relatively stable over time. That is, to take one example, early language competence predicts later language competence – including some studies in which children were followed from the toddler years into the school-age period (e.g., Charman et al., 2005; Mundy, Sigman, & Kasari, 1990). However, theoretically more interesting has been the question of whether earlier-emerging social communication abilities predict later language development. A strong psycholinguistic tradition from the study of typical language development has shown that this is the case for typically developing infants and toddlers (Bates, Thal, Fenson, Whitesell, & Oakes, 1989; Carpenter, Nagell, & Tomsello, 1998). Given that many preschoolers with autism spectrum disorders are impaired in their development of language ability *and* of early social communication abilities, the question of whether such associations also hold for toddlers and preschoolers with autism is both of clinical and theoretical interest. Demonstrating that the same association holds between early social communication abilities and later language development might suggest that similar developmental mechanisms are operating – albeit at a slower rate than in the typical case (Charman, 2003).

Mundy et al. (1990) were the first to provide evidence to support this position, finding that joint attention behaviors (alternating gaze, pointing, showing, and gaze following) measured at 45 months were associated with language outcomes 13 months later. Sigman et al. (1999) extended this finding by demonstrating associations from the preschool years to later language ability at 12 years of age. Stone, Ousley, and Littlefoot (1997) also found longitudinal associations between various aspects of imitation and play as well as joint attention abilities at 2 years of age and language abilities measured at 4 years of age. This pattern has now been replicated in several other studies (e.g., Toth, Munson, Meltzoff, & Dawson, 2006), including one in which children with autism spectrum disorders were followed from toddlerhood (20 months) into the preschool years (42 months; Charman et al., 2004). Developmental continuities between the atypical development seen in children with ASD and typically developing children are compelling, as they provide the theoretical and empirical backdrop against which clinical scientists interested in intervention have informed their approach.

Theoretically, some of the associations seen in preschoolers with autism spectrum disorders appear to be similar to that seen in typical development, suggesting that the mechanisms that operate are also similar. This is relevant to informing communication-based approaches to intervention (discussed later). Although individual stability of skills (language to language) or of one "precursor" skill to another later-emerging skill (joint attention to language) may tell us something about intrinsic characteristics of the child, they may also suggest routes to intervention. We know that the early social interactive environment has an influence on the general development of joint attention, reciprocity, and mutuality on typically developing children and, hence, effects on later socialization and communication (Murray, Fiori-Cowley, Hooper, & Cooper, 1996; Trevarthen, 1974; Watson, 1985). In the case of children with autism, evidence consistent with this was provided by Siller and Sigman (2002, 2008), who found that individual differences in maternal synchronicity (sometimes called "sensitivity") measured in joint play interactions was associated with later language outcomes even over many years. This opens the door to testing the extent to which interventions in which the social communication environment of infants and toddlers with autism are manipulated might influence social communicative outcomes.

Testing Developmental Interventions to Enhancing Social Communication Using Randomized Controlled Trials

In general, the research evidence base supports the use of behavioral, developmental, and social-communication approaches for preschool children with autism (see Howlin, Magiati, & Charman, 2009; Lord et al., 2005; Ospina et al., 2008; and Rogers & Vismara, 2008, for reviews). However, until very recently, the number of well-controlled studies that employed randomized designs, which are the best protection against bias and spurious findings, were far and few between. However, in the past few years, several promising approaches have been more rigorously tested in randomized controlled trials (RCTs) of intervention approaches that have been focused on promoting and enhancing social communication and language skills in infants and toddlers with autism. These are based on a variety of social-communication and behavioral strategies, including the promotion of joint attention, imitation, and joint social engagement skills both directly delivered by therapists and delivered by training parents in these methods. In brief, the prevailing finding across the studies is that language, developmental, and social interaction outcomes but not autism symptom severity can be improved.

Impairments in joint attention and symbolic play are among the earliest signs of developmental atypicality shown by young children with autism and thus are obvious targets for early intervention. In a randomized controlled trial, Kasari and colleagues (Kasari, Freeman, & Paparella, 2006; Kasari, Paparella, Freeman, & Jahromi, 2008) demonstrated the effectiveness of a short-term intervention to enhance joint attention or symbolic play in children who were already receiving early intensive behavioral intervention. Three groups of children (N = 58 in total; mean age 42 months) were randomized to daily 30-minute sessions for 5 to 6 weeks in which activities focused on promoting either joint attention or symbolic play skills (and a control group). After 6 weeks, there were improvements in both the intervention groups in aspects of child joint attention and play in interaction with experimenters and with their mothers (Kasari et al., 2006). One year later, both intervention groups had significantly higher scores on structural language measures than the controls (Kasari et al., 2008), in line with longitudinal evidence that there are developmental relations over time between earlier joint attention and play and later language abilities in preschool children with ASD (Charman, 2003).

In another developmentally informed intervention study, Landa, Holman, O'Neill, and Stuart (2011) compared two kindergarten programs for 29-month-olds with an ASD. The programs differed only in that one focused on "interpersonal synchrony" (IS) more than the other ($N = 50$, two groups). IS includes a range of social communication activities and constructs including joint attention, imitation, turn-taking, nonverbal social communicative exchanges, affect sharing, and engagement. The program was delivered by trained kindergarten staff and delivered for 2.5 hours per day, 4 days per week, for 6 months (overall around 200 hours of intervention). The parents also attended education classes focusing on the same strategies implemented in the kindergarten (38 hours) and a monthly home coaching visit. Landa et al. (2011) found that the IS group differed from the non–IS group on one variable only: "socially engaged imitation," defined as the proportion of imitations paired with eye contact to the examiner across a series of modeled actions (which more than doubled from baseline to endpoint). The groups did not differ in the amount of initiated joint attention or shared positive affect when interacting with an examiner, nor did their scores on a standardized language measure differ, although both groups showed some improvement.

Another intervention with a specific focus on early parent–child interaction and communication is the *Hanen More than Words (HMTW)* program (Pepper & Weitzman, 2004). In a nonrandomized case-control study, this has been shown to result in an increase in parents' observed use of facilitative strategies and in children's vocabulary size (McConachie, Randle, Hammal, & Le Couteur, 2005). However, in a recent RCT of the *HMTW* program, Carter et al. (2011) randomized 62 20-month-old toddlers with ASD in the program delivered over 3.5 months. There were no main effects of the HMTW intervention on either parental responsivity or children's communication. In contrast, there were treatment effects on child communication gains to 9-month follow-up that were moderated by the children's initial object interest. Children with lower levels of baseline object interest exhibited facilitated growth in communication, whereas children with higher levels of object interest exhibited growth attenuation. This is one of only a handful of trials in which an analysis was conducted to determine which children benefit from a particular intervention (a "moderating analysis"; discussed later).

Several other programs are based on similar principles – that is, having a focus on shared attention and parental sensitivity to the child's communicative attempts, with the goal of enhancing communicative exchanges to promote communication understanding and social engagement. Small-scale pilot RCTs (Aldred, Green, & Adams, 2004; Drew et al., 2002) have produced evidence suggestive of improvements in parental synchrony, child communicative initiations, vocabulary, and even a reduction in autism severity as measured by the Autism Diagnostic Observation Schedule (ADOS; Aldred et al., 2004; Lord et al., 2000). Similarly, the Responsivity Prelinguistic Milieu Teaching (RPMT) model (Yoder & Stone, 2006a, 2006b) is focused on helping parents to learn to follow the child's lead, on increasing motivation to communicate, and on using social games to provide natural reinforcement. RPMT has been shown to have positive effects on joint attention, turn taking, and child initiations (Yoder & Stone, 2006a, 2006b). For example, Kasari, Gulsrud, Wong, Kwon, and Locke (2010) randomized 38 30-month-old children to an 8-week (24 sessions) parent training approach focusing on joint engagement, joint attention, and interactive play. Following treatment and at 1-year follow-up, they found improvements in joint engagement (with parent), response to joint attention bids, and the number of functional play acts compared to a waitlist control group (Kasari et al., 2010).

In the largest RCT testing of a psychosocial intervention in autism to date, Green et al. (2010) reported on a multisite RCT of the PACT (Preschool Autism Communication Trial) intervention developed from that piloted by Aldred et al. (2004). One hundred fifty-two children (mean age 45 months) were randomized to receive a parent training program or community treatment as usual (Green et al., 2010). The parent program was of moderate intensity, involving twice monthly visits for 6 months and then six further monthly visits. The intervention was a video-aided program designed to increase parental sensitivity and responsiveness to child communication, as well as promoting action routines, the use of pauses, and supportive language. Green et al. (2010) found no evidence of a group difference on symptom scores measured by the ADOS but did find improvements of large effect in blinded ratings of parental synchrony and child initiations in parent–child interactive play. They also found positive effects on parent-reported measures of language and early social communication skills, which, while nonblinded, benefitted from parental knowledge of the child's communicative behavior in a range of contexts. It is unclear if these parent-reported differences are true treatment effects, a result of the treatment sensitizing parents to their child's emergent social communication effects, or a placebo effect. Green et al. (2010) interpret their findings as evidence for the PACT intervention leading to large differences in the targeted "proximal outcomes" of the parent-training approach but a progressive attenuation of treatment effect (see Figure 12.1) as measurement moves from parent behavior with the child to child behavior with the parent and then to child behavior with the ADOS administrator, and finally in more generalized settings (nursery teacher assessor).

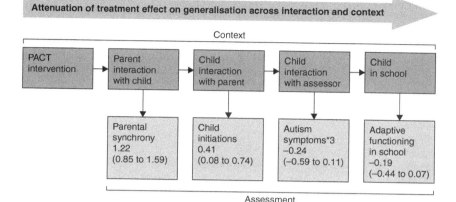

FIGURE 12.1. Context and assessment of Preschool Autism Communication Trial (PACT) intervention date are effect size (95% Cl). Negative value indicates lower abnormality in PACT group.

The described studies were all focused on promoting early social communication skills but entailed a wide range of techniques in the delivery of the therapy with variation in the balance to which developmental and behavioral approaches were combined. Employing a combination of both developmental and behavioral approaches with greater intensity, Dawson et al. (2010) randomized 48 24-month-olds to receive the Early Start Denver Model (ESDM) or local community treatments. They describe the ESDM approach as based on teaching strategies that involve interpersonal exchange, shared engagement, adult responsivity, and sensitivity. The ESDM's curriculum and teaching practices are manualized and draw extensively from previous work in two well-known, empirically supported models. First was the Denver Model, a relationship- and play-based developmental intervention relying on affective exchanges, shown to accelerate learning across a variety of developmental domains (Rogers, Dawson, Smith, Winter, & Donaldson, 2010; Rogers & DiLalla, 1991). Second was Pivotal Response Training (Koegel, O'Dell, & Koegel, 1987), the naturalistic application of applied behavior analysis aimed at optimizing child motivation to increase communication, language, and play skills under natural conditions that more closely resemble the way typically developing children acquire developmentally appropriate skills. The therapists delivered a mean of 15 hours of ESDM over a 2-year period, and parents, who were also trained in the approach, reported spending 16 hours per week using ESDM strategies (that can be incorporated into

TABLE 12.4 *Summary of recent RCTs targeting social communication for under 5s with ASD*

Study	Design	Changes in dyadic communication measures	Changes in standard communication measures	Changes in autism severity measures
Kasari, Paparella, Freeman, & Jahromi (2008)	T in nursery Daily for 6 weeks	Yes	Direct = Yes	Not reported
Dawson et al. (2010)	Intensive T and P for 24 months	Not reported	Direct = Yes P Reported = Yes	No
Kasari et al. (2010)	24 P sessions in 8 weeks; FU 12 months	Yes	Not reported	Not reported
Green et al. (2010)	Fortnightly then monthly P input 12 months	Yes	Direct = No P Reported = Yes	No
Landa et al. (2011)	Daily nursery T input and P weekly 6 months	On a single experimental measure	No	Not reported
Carter et al. (2011)	P training 3.5 months; FU 9 months	No	No	Not reported

P = parent; T = therapist; FU = follow-up

everyday activities, including mealtime, bathtime, etc.). Dawson et al. (2010) found that after 2 years, the ESDM group had increased their Early Learning Composite score on the MSEL by 18 points (compared to 7 points in the control group), with most of the change being the result of improved receptive and expressive language skills. Improvements in communication were also found on the (nonblinded) parental-reported Vineland Adaptive Behaviour Scales (VABS; Sparrow, Balla, & Cicchetti, 2005). However, Dawson et al. (2010) found no changes in symptom scores as measured with the ADOS.

The findings from this recent series of RCTs of interventions for toddlers and under 5s with autism or ASD are summarized in Table 12.4. It is too early to draw firm conclusions from this new wave of studies, but behaviors proximal to the intervention delivered may be amenable to change, in particular when measured using dyadic interaction measures of joint attention and symbolic play (Kasari et al., 2006, 2008), joint engagement (Kasari et al., 2010), parental synchrony (Green et al., 2010), and socially engaged imitation (Landa et al., 2011). There is a more equivocal pattern when one examines effects on one-step downstream variables such as formal language measures. Improvements on standardized measures of language and communication were found in some cases (Dawson et al., 2010; Kasari et al., 2008) but not others (Carter et al., 2010; Green et al., 2010; Landa et al., 2011). However, in the only studies on autism severity (at least as measured by the diagnostic instrument ADOS), this has not been amenable to change (Dawson et al., 2010; Green et al., 2010). Understanding the mechanisms that underlie this attenuation of treatment effects from directly targeted behaviors (in the child, in the parents) to more distal behaviors of language and social communication and on to autism severity and how these can be overcome is a challenge for future studies.

How are we to extract information from different studies to inform best practice, particularly when the targets, content, implementation, length, intensity, setting (e.g., home vs. clinic vs. nursery), and deliverer of therapy (e.g., parent vs. therapist) are different across the different trials? Furthermore, how does one read the different findings from the trials summarized in Table 12.4 when there is variation in the use of (and, in reporting, the emphasis given to) methodological factors such as blinding of outcome measures, prespecification of primary outcomes, and the use of intention to treat approaches to include data from all participants in the analysis? Some of these issues might one day be amenable to the powerful tools of meta-analytic methodology when sufficient randomized trials have been run; however, this will be a difficult task given that the treatments in different studies differ from one another. Comparative effectiveness of different treatment approaches can only truly be tested in equivalence trials that randomize participants to one of two treatments that differ in targeted outcomes, where possible motivated by different theoretical underpinnings (Makuch & Johnson, 1989). Following the ethical principle of "equipoise" – the notion that before a controlled trial is started, there should be "genuine uncertainty in the expert medical community about the preferred treatment" (Freedman, 1987, p. 141; van der Graaf & van Delden, 2011) – many of the RCTs conducted over the past 10 years in the autism field have entailed randomization to the "experimental" treatment versus a "treatment as usual" (TAU) or waitlist control (the latter only suitable for relatively short-term interventions). One conundrum is that as the evidence base builds for particular approaches, conducting such trials will increasingly be seen not to follow this principle. These issues cut across different intervention programs in different ways, in part particularly related to length and intensity of treatments. Specifically, the justification of the use of TAU and waitlist control designs for long and intensive treatments is more difficult once there is evidence of positive benefits for particular treatment approaches. The studies by Kasari and colleagues testing relatively short-term interventions stand out in this respect (6 weeks in Kasari et al., 2006, 2008; 8 weeks in Kasari et al., 2010). Finally, evidence about the "right" length and intensity of interventions can only securely be made *within* trials that randomize participants to the same treatment program of differing length and/or intensity. However, despite all of these limitations (at last), a positive evidence base is emerging for intervention approaches that target early social communication in young children with autism.

Using Intervention Trials to Test Developmental Theory

In a classic paper on word decoding (phonological processing) and reading, Bradley and Bryant (1983) outline the complementary strengths of demonstrating developmental associations using naturalistic longitudinal studies and randomized controlled trials. Longitudinal studies demonstrate real-life associations between precursor variables and outcome variables but do not demonstrate causality, whereas randomized trials demonstrate causality but could be arbitrary and not seen in real life. Associations between precursor and outcome variables with both methods are good evidence that a *developmental mechanism* of change has been demonstrated. The evidence reviewed earlier both from longitudinal studies and RCTs is suggestive of meaningful mechanisms between precursor skills such as joint attention, joint engagement, play, and parental sensitivity/synchrony and later language and social communication skills in young children with autism. Green and Dunn (2008) further highlight how there are heuristic links between developmental theory and intervention trials: (i) interventions should have a theoretical basis; (ii) the proximal treatment target should be a likely candidate of a mechanistic or "mediating" developmental process; and (iii) trials should measure the hypothesized mediating variable as well as the more distal (and nondirectly target) outcome variable. Despite commonly held and widely repeated assumptions of a solid body of evidence about moderating factors (which children do well?) and mediating factors (why do children make progress?) in the empirical literature on autism intervention, it is only within randomized trails that one can conduct rigorous analysis of these effects.

In the autism literature, attempts have been made to study the effects of pre-intervention child characteristics on outcome, most notably IQ and age. For IQ, this usually involves examining correlations between pre-intervention IQ and postintervention outcome (Eldevik, Eikeseth, Jahr, & Smith, 2006; Harris & Handleman, 2000; Remington et al., 2007) or the comparison of outcomes for high–IQ versus low–IQ subgroups (Ben-Itzchak & Zachor, 2007). Significant positive associations have been found between preintervention IQ and outcome. However, Yoder and Compton (2004) highlight the flaws of testing for moderators by exploring correlations or comparison of subgroups' effect sizes, as they do not account for general development influences. They emphasize the importance of using statistical methods that enable differentiation of predictors of growth or progress from predictors of intervention response. Where participants have been randomly assigned to intervention or control conditions, the appropriate method for identifying predictors of intervention response is to test for statistical interactions among child characteristics and group assignment in relation to the outcome variables. Although such statistical tests of moderator effects are well established in medical trial culture and used increasingly in the psychiatry field (Kraemer, Wilson, Fairburn, & Agras, 2002), it is only in the recent "new wave" of social communication intervention trials in the autism field that they have been used, and this vanguard of trials will be highlighted next.

Yoder and Stone (2006a, 2006b) used multiple regression analyses to demonstrate the moderating effects of baseline joint attention abilities on interventions. In their randomized trial ($N = 36$; mean age 3 years), they compared Picture Exchange Communication Training (PECS; Bondy & Frost, 1998) with Responsive Education and Prelinguistic Milieu Training (RPMT; Yoder & Warren, 1999). Children who initiated joint attention relatively more frequently at baseline benefited more from RPMT in terms of their postintervention frequency of joint attention initiations, while children who initiated joint attention less frequently at baseline benefited more from PECS (Yoder & Stone, 2006a). In a later analysis (Yoder & Stone, 2006b) using mixed-level modeling, they found object exploration also moderated intervention response. Thus, children who displayed object exploration behaviors more frequently at baseline benefited most from PECS, showing greater increases in production of nonimitative words at outcome. The children who showed lower object exploration at baseline benefited more with respect to word production if they had received RPMT. In a recent

RCT of PECS with an older sample (N = 84, mean age 7 years), Gordon et al. (2011) used multilevel Poisson regression modeling to test for moderating effects of baseline characteristics on outcome and found that less severe baseline autism symptoms (lower ADOS score) were associated with greater increase in spontaneous speech and less severe baseline expressive language impairment (lower ADOS item language A1 score), with larger increases in spontaneous use of speech and pictures together. In the Kasari et al. (2008) RCT of joint attention and symbolic play training, moderating effects were found indicating that growth in expressive language was positively predicted by a number of baseline joint attention, symbolic play, and language variables at baseline, with children with higher baseline levels of these variables showing more growth in language at outcome.

In the PACT study (Green et al., 2010), no evidence of differential intervention effect on the primary ADOS outcome was found in relation to child age, baseline autism severity, nonverbal ability, or socioeconomic status (SES), although the latter effect showed a nonsignificant trend (p = .10) in the direction of better outcome in families from lower–SES background. In a re-analysis of the data from the pilot study to the PACT trial, Aldred, Green, Emsley, and McConachie (2012) conducted a mediation analysis on the data from the Aldred et al. (2004) study and found that change in parental synchrony accounted for 34% of the reduction in ADOS social communication score. In an ongoing formal mediation analysis of the large PACT trial, Pickles and colleagues (Charman et al., 2011) have contrasted an "instrumental variable" approach to testing mediation compared to the well-known Baron and Kenny (1986) method to test changes in parental synchrony and child initiations measured at a midpoint (7 months) between baseline and the endpoint of the trial (13 months). One challenge for the autism-intervention field is to ensure that large, expensive, and time-consuming RCTs are fully exploited by using leading-edge statistical methods to help us better understand the mechanisms of treatment effects and the factors that place limits on treatment effectiveness.

CONCLUSIONS

The last decade has seen the publication of many important prospective longitudinal and intervention studies, and these have contributed to our understanding of autism as a developmental disorder. The study of high-risk siblings promises to help us understand the developmental mechanisms that underlie the emergence of autism in the first few years of life, although clearly very early indicators of an ASD outcome have not been as easy to identify as expected. The emergence of a growing body of RCTs is also to be applauded, not least because they explicitly focus on the core social communication impairments that define autism. However, in every treatment trial – even those that at a group level find significant treatment effects – variability in outcome is considerable, and while some children make great gains, others make less progress, and some children make very little progress at all. Large studies using sophisticated statistical analyses will be required to further elucidate the factors that influence this variability. Many of those involved in conducting such trials (and the families taking part in them) are beginning to discuss important overarching questions, including what constitutes an appropriate (and realizable) outcome for a young child with autism (and their family)? There is also considerable discussion and initial efforts to tackle face-on the difficulties of developing reliable, sensitive, and meaningful measures of outcomes to be used in future intervention studies. The challenge that lies ahead in the coming decade is for us to use this improved understanding of autism as a developmental disorder and the new science of autism in infancy to develop theoretically and empirically informed treatment approaches and test them in rigorous and unbiased intervention trials.

From a historical perspective, in the 1970s and 1980s it was important for mainstream science and clinical practice to repudiate the false claims of Bettleheim and others that autism resulted from impoverished parenting. However, now this argument is won, it is right and proper that more transactional models of autistic development – including the effects of parenting on a developing child and the impacts of parenting a child with a disorder such as autism – are being developed. To date, they have been limited to examining parental and family influences, but there is increasing recognition that the effects of broader cultural and societal issues will also be important to fully understand autistic development (DeWeert, 2012). These range from examining how parent–child interaction in infancy may relate to and even influence the outcome in genetically at-risk siblings (e.g., Wan et al., 2013) to the use of parent-mediated interventions that attempt to embed the therapeutic effect in the child's everyday home and family environment (reviewed above). In the 21st century, it is now clear that parents and the family environment can influence the developmental trajectory of children with autism – but this time in a positive way in terms of promoting and supporting better developmental outcomes.

REFERENCES

Adrien, J., Lenoir, P., Martineau, J., Perrot, A., Hameury, L., Larmande, C., et al. (1993). Blind ratings of early symptoms of autism based upon family home movies. *Journal of the American Academy of Child and Adolescent Psychiatry*, 32, 617–626.

Adrien, J., Perrot, A., Hameury, L., Martineau, J., Roux, S., & Sauvage, D. (1991). Family home movies: Identification of early autistic signs in infants later diagnosed as autistics. *Brain Dysfunction*, 4, 355–362.

Aldred, C., Green, J., & Adams, C. (2004). A new social communication intervention for children with autism: Pilot randomized controlled treatment study suggesting effectiveness. *Journal of Child Psychology and Psychiatry*, 45, 1420–1430.

Aldred, C., Green, J., Emsley, R., & McConachie, H. (2012). Mediation of treatment effect in a communication intervention for preschool children with autism. *Journal of Autism and Developmental Disorders*, 42, 447–454.

American Psychiatric Association. (2000). *Diagnostic and statistical manual of mental disorders, 4th edition – text revision (DSM-IV-TR)*. Washington, DC: APA.

Baird, G., Charman, T., Baron-Cohen, S., Cox, A., Swettenham, J., Wheelwright, S., & Drew, A. (2000). A screening instrument for autism at 18 month of age: A six-year follow-up study. *Journal of the American Academy of Child and Adolescent Psychiatry*, 39, 694–702.

Baird, G., Charman, T., Pickles, A., Chandler, S., Loucas, T., Meldrum, D., et al. (2008). Regression, developmental trajectory and associated problems in disorders in the autism spectrum: The SNAP study. *Journal of Autism and Developmental Disorders*, 38, 1827–1836.

Baranek, G. (1999). Autism during infancy: A retrospective video analysis of sensory-motor and social behaviors at 9–12 months of age. *Journal of Autism and Developmental Disorders*, 29, 213–224.

Baron, R. M., & Kenny, D. A. (1986). The moderator-mediator variable distinction in social psychological research: Conceptual, strategic and statistical considerations. *Journal of Personality and Social Psychology*, 51, 1173–1182.

Baron-Cohen, S., Allen, J., & Gillberg, C. (1992). Can autism be detected at 18 months? The needle, the haystack and the CHAT. *British Journal of Psychiatry*, 138, 839–843.

Baron-Cohen, S., Cox, A., Baird, G., Swettenham, J., Nightingale, N., Morgan, K., Drew, A. & Charman, T. (1996). Screening for autism in a large population at 18 months of age: An investigation of the CHAT (Checklist for Autism in Toddlers). *British Journal of Psychiatry*, 168, 158–163.

Bates, E., Thal, D., Fenson, L., Whitesell, K., & Oakes, L. (1989). Integrating language and gesture in infancy. *Developmental Psychology*, 25, 1004–1019.

Ben-Itzchak, E., & Zachor, D. A. (2007). The effects of intellectual functioning and autism severity on outcome of early behavioral intervention for children with autism. *Research in Developmental Disabilities*, 28, 287–303.

Bettleheim, B. (1967). *The empty fortress: Infantile autism and the birth of the self*. New York: Free Press.

Bondy, A., & Frost, L. A. (1998). The picture exchange communication system. *Seminars in Speech and Language*, 19, 373–389.

Bradley, L., & Bryant, P. E. (1983). Categorizing sounds and learning to read: A causal connection. *Nature*, 301, 419–421.

Bryson, S. E., Zwaigenbaum, L., Brian, J., Roberts, W., Szatmari, P., Rombough, V., & McDermott C. (2007). A prospective case series of high-risk infants who developed autism. *Journal of Autism and Developmental Disorders*, 37(1), 12–24.

Carpenter, M., Nagell, K., & Tomasello, M. (1998). Social cognition, joint attention, and communicative competence from 9 to 15 months of age. *Monographs of the Society for Research in Child Development*, 63, 1–143.

Carter, A. S., Messinger, D. S., Stone, W. L., Celimli, S., Nahmias, A. S., & Yoder, P. (2011). A randomized controlled trial of Hanen's "More Than Words" in toddlers with autism symptoms. *Journal of Child Psychology and Psychiatry*, 52, 741–752.

Charman, T. (2003). Why is joint attention a pivotal skill in autism? *Philosophical Transactions of the Royal Society: Biological Sciences*, 358, 315–324.

(2010). Autism research comes of (a young) age. *Journal of the American Academy of Child and Adolescent Psychiatry*, 49, 208–209.

(2011). Glass half full or half empty? Testing social communication interventions for young children with autism. *Journal of Child Psychology and Psychiatry*, 52, 22–23.

Charman, T., & Baird, G. (2002). Practitioner review: Diagnosis of autism spectrum disorder in 2- and 3-year-old children. *Journal of Child Psychology and Psychiatry and Allied Disciplines*, 43, 289–305.

Charman, T., Baron-Cohen, S., Swettenham, J., Baird, G., Drew, A., & Cox A. (2004). Predicting language outcome in infants with autism and pervasive developmental disorder. *International Journal of Language and Communication Disorders*, 38, 265–285.

Charman, T., Taylor, E., Drew, A., Cockerill, H., Brown, J. A., & Baird, G. (2005). Outcome at 7 years of children diagnosed with autism at age 2: Predictive validity of assessments conducted at 2 and 3 years of age and pattern of symptom change over time. *Journal of Child Psychology and Psychiatry*, 46, 500–513.

Clifford, S., & Dissanayake, C. (2008). The early development of joint attention in infants with autistic disorder using home video observations and parental interview. *Journal of Autism and Developmental Disorders*, 38, 791–805.

Constantino, J. N., Zhang, Y., Frazier, T., Abbacchi, A. M., & Law, P. (2010). Sibling recurrence and the genetic epidemiology of autism. *American Journal of Psychiatry*, 167, 1349–1356.

Dawson, G. (2008). Early behavioral intervention, brain plasticity, and the prevention of autism spectrum disorder. *Development and Psychopathology*, 20, 775–803.

Dawson, G., Rogers, S. J., Munson, J., Smith, M., Winter, J., et al. (2010). Randomized, controlled trial of an intervention for toddlers with autism: The Early Start Denver Model. *Pediatrics*, 125, e17–23.

DeWeert, S. (2012). Diverse diagnostics. *Nature*, 491, S18-S19.

Dietz, C., Willemsen-Swinkels, S. H. N., van Daalen, E., van Engeland, H., & Buitelaar, J. K. (2006). Screening for autistic spectrum disorder in children aged 14 to 15 months. II: Population screening with the Early Screening of Autistic Traits (ESAT). Design and general findings. *Journal of Autism and Developmental Disorders*, 36, 713–722.

Drew, A., Baird, G., Baron-Cohen, S., Cox, A., Slonims, V., Wheelwright, S. et al. (2002). A pilot randomized control trial of a parent training intervention study for pre-school children with autism: Preliminary findings and methodological challenges. *European Child & Adolescent Psychiatry*, 11, 266–272.

Eldevik, S., Eikeseth, S., Jahr, E., & Smith, T. (2006). Effects of low-intensity behavioral treatment for children with autism and mental retardation. *Journal of Autism and Developmental Disorders*, 36, 211–224.

Elsabbagh, M., & Johnson, M. H. (2010). Getting answers from babies about autism. *Trends in Cognitive Sciences*, 14, 81–87.

Elsabbagh, M., Mercure, E., Hudry, K, Chandler, S., Pasco, G., Charman, T., Pickles, A., Baron-Cohen, S., Bolton, P., Johnson, M., and the BASIS Team. (2012). Infant neural sensitivity to dynamic eye gaze is associated with later emerging ASD. *Current Biology* 22, 338–342.

Elsabbagh, M., Volein, A., Csibra, G., Holmboe, K., Garwood, H., Tucker, L., et al. (2009). Neural correlates of eye gaze processing in the infant broader autism phenotype. *Biological Psychiatry*, 65, 31–38.

Folstein, S., & Rutter, M. (1977). Infantile autism: A genetic study of 21 twin pairs. *Journal of Child Psychology and Psychiatry*, 18, 297–321.

Freedman, B. (1987). Equipoise and the ethics of clinical research. *New England Journal of Medicine*, 317, 141–145.

Gordon, K. R., Pasco, G., Wade, A., McElduff, F., Howlin, P., & Charman, T. (2011). A communication based intervention for non-verbal children with autism: What changes? Who benefits? *Journal of Consulting and Clinical Psychology*, 79, 447–457.

Green, J., Charman, T., McConachie, H., Aldred, C., Slonims, V., et al. (2010). Parent-mediated communication-focused treatment in children with autism (PACT): A randomized controlled trial. *The Lancet*, 375, 2152–2160.

Green, J., & Dunn, G. (2008). Using intervention trials in developmental psychiatry to illuminate basic science. *British Journal of Psychiatry*, 192, 323–325.

Happé, F., Ronald, A., & Plomin, R. (2006). Time to give up on a single explanation for autism. *Nature Neuroscience*, 9, 1218–1220.

Harris, S. L., & Handleman, J. S. (2000). Age and IQ at intake as predictors of placement for young children with autism: A four- to six-year follow-up. *Journal of Autism and Developmental Disorders*, 30, 137–142.

Herbert, M. R. (2010). Contributions of the environment and environmentally vulnerable physiology to autism spectrum disorders. *Current Opinion in Neurology*, 23, 103–110.

Howlin, P., & Asgharian, A. (1999). The diagnosis of autism and Asperger syndrome: Findings from a survey of 770 families. *Developmental Medicine and Child Neurology*, 41, 834–839.

Howlin, P., Magiati, I., & Charman T. (2009). A systematic review of early intensive behavioral interventions (EIBI) for children with autism. *American Journal of Intellectual and Developmental Disability*, 114, 23–41.

Kanner, L. (1943). Autistic disturbance of affective contact. *Nervous Child*, 2, 217–250.

Kasari, C., Freeman, S., & Paparella, T. (2006). Joint attention and symbolic play in young children with autism: A randomized controlled intervention study. *Journal of Child Psychology and Psychiatry*, 47, 611–620.

Kasari, C., Gulsrud, A. C., Wong, C., Kwon, S., & Locke, J. (2010). Randomized controlled caregiver mediated joint engagement intervention for toddlers with autism. *Journal of Autism and Developmental Disorders, 40,* 1045–1056.

Kasari, C., Paparella, T., Freeman, S., & Jahromi, L. (2008). Language outcome in autism: Randomized comparison of joint attention and play interventions. *Journal of Consulting and Clinical Psychology, 76,* 125–137.

Kleinman, J. M., Robins, D. L., Ventola, P. E., Pandey, J., Boorstein, H. C., et al. (2008). The Modified Checklist for Autism in Toddlers: A follow-up study investigating the early detection of autism spectrum disorders. *Journal of Autism and Developmental Disorders, 38,* 827–839.

Koegel, R. L., O'Dell, M. C., & Koegel, L. K. (1987). A natural language teaching paradigm for nonverbal autistic children. *Journal of Autism and Developmental Disorders, 17,* 187–199.

Kraemer, H. C., Wilson, G. T., Fairburn, C. G., & Agras, W. S. (2002). Mediators and moderators of treatment effects in randomized clinical trials. *Archives of General Psychiatry, 59,* 877–883.

Landa, R. J., Holman, K. C., O'Neill, A. H., & Stuart, E. A. (2011). Intervention targeting development of socially synchronous engagement in toddlers with autism spectrum disorders: A randomized controlled trial. *Journal of Child Psychology and Psychiatry, 52,* 13–21.

Landa, R., & Garrett-Mayer, E. (2006). Development in infants with autism spectrum disorders: A prospective study. *Journal of Child Psychology and Psychiatry, 47,* 629–638.

Landa, R., Holman, K., & Garrett-Mayer, E. (2007). Social and communication development in toddlers with early and later diagnosis of autism spectrum disorders. *Archives of General Psychiatry, 64,* 853–864.

Levy, S. E., Mandell, D. S., & Schultz, R. T. (2009). Autism. *Lancet, 374,* 1627–1638.

Loh, A., Soman, T., Brian, J., Bryson, S. E., Roberts, W., Szatmari, P., Smith, I. M., & Zwaigenbaum L. (2007). Stereotyped motor behaviors associated with autism in high-risk infants: a pilot videotape analysis of a sibling sample. *Journal of Autism and Developmental Disorders, 37*(1), 25–36.

Lord, C., Risi, S., Lambrecht, L., Cook, E. H., Jr., Leventhal, B. L., DiLavore, P. C., et al. (2000). The Autism Diagnostic Observation Schedule-Generic: A standard measure of social and communication deficits associated with the spectrum of autism. *Journal of Autism and Developmental Disorders, 30,* 205–223.

Lord, C., Rutter, M. L., & LeCouteur, A. (1994). The Autism Diagnostic Interview-Revised: A revised version of a diagnostic interview for caregivers of individuals with possible pervasive developmental disorders. *Journal of Autism and Developmental Disorders, 24,* 659–685.

Lord, C., Wagner, A., Rogers, S., Szatmari, P., Aman, M., et al. (2005). Challenges in evaluating psychosocial interventions for autistic spectrum disorders. *Journal of Autism and Developmental Disorders, 35,* 695–708.

Lösche, G. (1990). Sensorimotor and action development in autistic children from infancy to early childhood. *Journal of Child Psychology and Psychiatry, 31,* 749–761.

Maestro, S., Muratori, F., Cavallaro, M. C., Pecini, C., Cesari, A., Paziente, A., et al. (2005). How young children treat objects and people: An empirical study of the first year of life in autism. *Child Psychiatry & Human Development, 35,* 383–396.

Maestro, S., Muratori, F., Cavallaro, M., Pei, F., Stern, D., Golse, B., et al. (2002). Attentional skills during the first 6 months of age in autism spectrum disorder. *Journal of the American Academy of Child & Adolescent Psychiatry*, 41, 1239–1245.

Makuch, R., & Johnson, M. (1989) Issues in planning and interpreting active control equivalence trials. *Journal of Clinical Epidemiology*, 42, 503–511.

Mandell, D. S., Novak, M. M., & Zubritsky, C. D. (2005). Factors associated with age of diagnosis among children with autism spectrum disorders. *Pediatrics*, 116, 1480–1486.

Manning, S. E., Davin, C. A., Barfield, W. D., Kotelchuck, M., Clements, K., Diop, H., Osbahr, T., & Smith, L. A. (2011). Early diagnoses of autism spectrum disorders in Massachusetts birth cohorts, 2001–2005. *Pediatrics*, 127, 1043–1051.

McCleery, J., Allman, E., Carver, L., & Dobkins, K. (2007). Abnormal magnocellular pathway visual processing in infants at risk for autism. *Biological Psychiatry*, 62, 1007–1014.

McConachie, H., Randle, V., Hammal, D., & Le Couteur, A. (2005). A controlled trial of a training course for parents of children with suspected autism spectrum disorder. *Journal of Pediatrics*, 147, 335–340.

Merin, N., Young, G. S., Ozonoff, S., & Rogers, S. J. (2007). Visual fixation patterns during reciprocal social interaction distinguish a subgroup of 6-month-old infants tt-risk for autism from comparison infants. *Journal of Autism and Developmental Disorder*, 37(1), 108–121.

Mitchell, S., Brian, J., Zwaigenbaum, L., Roberts, W., Szatmari, P., Smith, I., et al. (2006). Early language and communication development of infants later diagnosed with autism spectrum disorder. *Journal of Developmental & Behavioral Pediatrics*, 27, S69–S78.

Mullen, E. (1995). *Mullen scales of early learning*. Circle Pines, MN: American Guidance Service.

Mundy, P., Sigman, M., & Kasari, C. (1990). A longitudinal study of joint attention and language development in autistic children. *Journal of Autism and Developmental Disorders*, 20, 115–128.

Mundy, P., Sullivan, L., & Mastergeorge, A. M. (2009). A parallel and distributed-processing model of joint attention, social cognition and autism. *Autism Research*, 2, 2–21.

Murray, L., Fiori-Cowley, A., Hooper, R., & Cooper, P. (1996). The impact of postnatal depression and associated adversity on early mother–infant interactions and later infant outcome. *Child Development*, 67, 2512–2526.

Nadig, A. S., Ozonoff, S., Young, G. S., Rozga, A., Sigman, M., & Rogers, S. J. (2007). A prospective study of response to name in infants at risk for autism. *Archives of Pediatrics and Adolescent Medicine*, 161(4), 378–383.

Ospina, M. B., Krebs Seida, J., Clark, B., Karkhaneh, M., Hartling, L., Tjosvold, L., Vandermeer, B., & Smith V. (2008). Behavioral and developmental interventions for autism spectrum disorder: A clinical systematic review. *PLoS One*, 3, e3755.

Osterling, J., & Dawson, G. (1994). Early recognition of children with autism – a study of 1st birthday home videotapes. *Journal of Autism and Developmental Disorders*, 24, 247–257.

Ozonoff, S., Iosif, A. M., Baguio, F., Cook, I. C., Hill, M. M., Hutman, T., et al. (2010). A prospective study of the emergence of early behavioral signs of autism. *Journal of the American Academy of Child and Adolescent Psychiatry*, 49, 256–266.

Ozonoff, S., Young, G., Carter, A. S., Messinger, D., Yirmiya, N., Zwaigenbaum, L., et al. (2011). Recurrence risk for autism spectrum disorder: A Baby Siblings Research Consortium study. *Pediatrics*, 128, e488–495.

Ozonoff, S., Young, G., Goldring, S., Greiss-Hess, L., Herrera, A., Steele, J., et al. (2008). Gross motor development, movement abnormalities, and early identification of autism. *Journal of Autism and Developmental Disorders*, 38, 644–656.

Pepper, J., & Weitzman, E. (2004). *It takes two to talk: A practical guide for parents of children with language delays*. Toronto: The Hanen Centre.

Pickles, A., Simonoff, E., Conti-Ramsden, G., Falcaro, M., Simkin, Z., Charman, T., et al. (2009). Loss of language in early development of autism and specific language impairment. *Journal of Child Psychology and Psychiatry*, 50, 843–852

Remington, B., Hastings, R. P., Kovshoff, H., Espinosa, F. D., Jahr, E., Brown, T., et al. (2007). Early intensive behavioral intervention: Outcomes for children with autism and their parents after two years. *American Journal on Mental Retardation*, 112, 418–438.

Robins, D. L. (2008). Screening for autism spectrum disorders in primary care settings. *Autism*, 12, 537–556.

Robins, D. L., Fein, D., Barton, M. L., & Green, J. A. (2001). The modified Checklist for Autism in Toddlers: An initial study investigating the early detection of autism and pervasive developmental disorders. *Journal of Autism and Developmental Disorders*, 31, 131–144.

Rogers, S. (2009). What are infant siblings teaching us about autism in infancy? *Autism Research*, 2, 125–137.

Rogers, S., Dawson, G., Smith, C. M., Winter, J. M., & Donaldson, A. L. (2010). *Early start Denver model intervention for young children with autism manual*. Seattle: University of Washington.

Rogers, S. J., & DiLalla, D. (1991). A comparative study of the effects of a developmentally based instructional model on young children with autism and young children with other disorders of behavior and development. *Topics in Early Childhood Special Education*, 11, 29–48.

Rogers, S. J., & Vismara, L. A. (2008). Evidence-based comprehensive treatments for early autism. *Journal of Clinical Child and Adolescent Psychology*, 37, 8–38.

Rozga, A., Hutman, T., Young, G. S., Rogers, S. J., Ozonoff, S., Dapretto, M., & Sigman, M. (2011). Behavioral profiles of affected and unaffected siblings of children with ASD: Contribution of measures of mother–infant interaction and nonverbal communication. *Journal of ASD and Developmental Disorders*, 41, 287–301.

Rutter, M. (2011). Research review: Child psychiatric diagnosis and classification: Concepts, findings, challenges and potential. *Journal of Child Psychology and Psychiatry*, 52, 647–660.

Saint-Georges, C., Mahdhaoui, A., Chetouani, M., Cassel, R. S., Laznik, M. -C., Apicella, F. et al. (2011). Do parents recognize autistic deviant behavior long before diagnosis? Taking into account interaction using computational methods. *PLOS One*, 6, 1–13.

Sigman, M., Ruskin, E., Arbeile, S., Corona, R., Dissanayake, C., et al. (1999). Continuity and change in the social competence of children with autism, Down syndrome, and developmental delays. *Monographs of the Society for Research in Child Development*, 64, 1–114.

Siller, M., & Sigman, M. (2002). The behaviors of parents of children with autism predict the subsequent development of their children's communication. *Journal of Autism and Developmental Disorders*, 32, 77–89.

(2008). Modeling longitudinal change in the language abilities of children with autism: Parent behaviors and child characteristics as predictors of change. *Developmental Psychology*, 44, 1691–1704.

Sparrow, S. S., Cicchetti, D. V., & Balla, D. A., (2005). *Vineland adaptive behavior scales: Survey form, 2nd ed.* Circle Pines, MN: American Guidance Service.

Stone, W. L., Ousley, O. Y., & Littleford, C. D. (1997). Motor imitation in young children with autism: What's the object? *Journal of Abnormal Child Psychology*, 25, 475–485.

Swinkels, S., Dietz, C., van Daalen, E., Kerkhof, I. H., van Engeland, H., & Buitelaar, J. K. (2006). Screening for autism spectrum disorders in children 14–15 months. I: The development of the Early Screening of Autistic Traits Questionnaire (ESAT). *Journal of Autism and Developmental Disorders*, 36, 723–732.

Toth, K., Munson, J., Meltzoff, A. N., & Dawson, G. (2006). Early predictors of communication development in young children with autism spectrum disorder: Joint attention, imitation, and toy play. *Journal of Autism and Developmental Disorders*, 36(8), 993–1005.

Trevarthen, C. (1974). Conversations with a two-month old. *New Scientist*, 230–235.

van der Graaf, R., & van Delden, J. J. (2011). Equipoise should be amended, not abandoned. *Clinical Trials*, 8, 408–416.

Wan, M. W., Green, J., Elsabbagh, M., Johnson, M. H., Charman, T., Plummer, F., & the BASIS Team. (2012). Parent-infant interaction in infant siblings at risk of autism: A controlled observational study. *Research in Developmental Disabilities*, 33, 924–932.

Wan, M. W., Green, J., Elsabbagh, M., Johnson, M. H., Plummer, F., Charman, T., & the BASIS Team. (2013). Quality of interaction between at-risk infants and caregiver at 12–15 months is associated with three year autism outcome. *Journal of Child Psychology and Psychiatry*, 54(7), 763–771.

Watson, J. S. (1985). Contingency perception in early social development. (1985). In T. M. Field & N. A. Fox (Eds.), *Social perception in infants* (pp. 157–175). Norwood, NJ: Ablex.

Werner, E., & Dawson, G. (2005). Validation of the phenomenon of autistic regression using home videotapes. *Archives of General Psychiatry*, 62, 889–895.

Wetherby, A. M., Brosnan-Maddox, S., Peace, V., & Newton, L. (2008). Validation of the Infant-Toddler Checklist as a broadband screener for autism spectrum disorders from 9 to 24 months of age. *Autism*, 12, 487–511.

Wetherby, A. M., Woods, J., Allen, L., Cleary, J., Dickinson, H., & Lord, C. (2004). Early indicators of autism spectrum disorders in the second year of life. *Journal of Autism and Developmental Disorders*, 34, 473–493.

World Health Organisation. (1993). *Mental disorders: A glossary and guide to their classification in accordance with the 10th revision of the international classification of diseases: Research diagnostic criteria (ICD-10).* Geneva: WHO.

Yirmiya, N., & Charman, T. (2010). The prodrome of autism: Early behavioral and biological signs, regression, peri- and post-natal development and genetics. *Journal of Child Psychology and Psychiatry,* 51, 432–458.

Yirmiya, N., Gamliel, I., Pilowsky, T., Feldman, R., Baron-Cohen, S., & Sigman, M. (2006). The development of siblings of children with ASD at 4 and 14 months: Social engagement, communication, and cognition. *Journal of Child Psychology and Psychiatry,* 47, 511–523.

Yoder, P., & Compton, D. (2004). Identifying predictors of treatment response. *Mental Retardation and Developmental Disabilities Research Reviews,* 10, 162–168.

Yoder, P., & Stone, W. L. (2006a). Randomized comparison of two communication interventions for preschoolers with autism spectrum disorders. *Journal of Consulting and Clinical Psychology,* 74, 426–435.

(2006b). A randomized comparison of the effect of two prelinguistic communication interventions on the acquisition of spoken communication in preschoolers with ASD. *Journal of Speech, Language, and Hearing Research,* 49, 698–711.

Yoder, P., Stone, W. L., Walden, T., & Malesa, E. (2009). Predicting social impairment and ASD diagnosis in younger siblings of children with autism spectrum disorder. *Journal of Autism and Developmental Disorders,* 39(10), 1381–1391.

Yoder, P., & Warren, S. F. (1999). Maternal responsivity mediates the relationship between prelinguistic intentional communication and later language. *Journal of Early Intervention,* 22, 126–136.

Young, G., Merin, N., Rogers, S., & Ozonoff, S. (2009). Gaze behavior and affect at 6-months: Predicting clinical outcomes and language development in typically developing infants and infants at-risk for autism. *Developmental Science,* 12, 798–814.

Zwaigenbaum, L. (2010). Advances in the early detection of autism. *Current Opinion in Neurology,* 23, 97–102.

Zwaigenbaum, L., Bryson, S., Rogers, T., Roberts, W., Brian, J., & Szatmari, P. (2005). Behavioral manifestations of autism in the first year of life. *International Journal of Developmental Neuroscience,* 23, 143–152.

Index

assessment strategies
  for clinicians' use, 13
  data collection as part of, 11–12
  of developmental psychopathology,
      9–20
  DSM-oriented scales in, 15–20
  informant data in, 12–15
  of parents, 33–34
assimilation, of Native American children,
      60, 70
attractiveness. *See* physical attractiveness, elite
      social status and
autism
  ABA for, 256
  ADI-R for, 266
  CARS and, 228
  CHAT for, 257–258
  contemporary approaches to, 276–277
  early child development and, 254–256
  early identification of, 255
  EIBI, 256
  environmental influences on, 254
  ESAT for, 258
  with FXS, 227
  high risk sibling studies for, 260–266
  HMTW programme for, 268–269
  individual trajectories for, 266–267
  in infancy, from home movies, 256,
      259–260
  ITC for, 259
  maternal synchronicity and, 267
  MSEL and, 228, 261–264
  RCTs for, 268–276
  regression as feature of, 264–265
  research on, 254–256
  screening studies for, 257–276
  symptom mechanisms of, 255
Autism Diagnostic Interview – Review
      (ADI-R), 266
Autism Diagnostic Observation Schedule
      (ADOS), 269–270
autonomic nervous system (ANS), 185
  brain development and, 195

bicultural youths, in Canada, 90–91,
      94–95
Blain-Arcaro, Christine, 107
boarding schools, Native American children
      in, 59–60
Bombay, Amy, 81
Brady, Nancy, 221

brain development. *See also* central-peripheral
      nervous system; developmental
      psychopathology; hypothalamic-
      pituitary-adrenal axis; prefrontal cortex
  ANS and, 195
  cultural correlates as influence on, 168–169
  CVT and, 195–196
  early adversity and, 191–196
  emotional reactivity and regulation and,
      193–195
  frontal brain asymmetry, 193–195
brain overclaim, 168–169
bullying. *See* peer victimization
Burack, Jacob, 81

Canada, shyness-inhibition expression
      in, 47–48
cardiac vagal tone (CVT), 195–196
CARS. *See* Childhood Autism Rating Scale
      (CARS)
CBCL. *See* Child Behavior Checklist
      (CBCL)
central-peripheral nervous system
  emotional reactivity and regulation,
      192–193
  prematurity and, 192–193
CGG repeat length X, 241–243
Charman, Tony, 254
CHecklist for Autism in Toddlers (CHAT),
      257–258
Chen, Xinyin, 39
Child Behavior Checklist (CBCL), 232–233
child development. *See also* age, of children;
      parent-child interactions; peer
      victimization; peers
  autism and, 254–256
  environmental stressors as factor in,
      207–208
  genetic factors for, 208–209
  HPA axis and, 210, 211
  maternal depression and, 205
  neural correlates for, 209–212
  parenting and, 205–207
  single parenthood and, 207
child psychopathology. *See also* child
      development
  in DSM-I, 8
  lack of historical research on, 8
Childhood Autism Rating Scale (CARS), 228
China, shyness-inhibition expression in,
      47–48, 49–50